F   Airle

Collect 16·1·91

£8-95

16/ 1/ 91

Glazer

THE VIKINGS

THE VIKINGS

edited by

R.T.Farrell

Phillimore

1982

Published by
PHILLIMORE & CO. LTD.
London and Chichester

Head Office: Shopwyke Hall,
Chichester, Sussex, England

ISBN 0 85033 436 5

This book has been subvented by the
Hull Fund of Cornell University

Typeset in the United Kingdom by
Fidelity Processes   Selsey   Sussex

Printed in England by
Staples Printers Rochester Limited,
Love Lane, Rochester, Kent.

CONTENTS

ACKNOWLEDGEMENTS

Many people helped in the preparation of this manuscript for publication. Ms Vicki Lacesse and Ms Valerie Eamer cheerfully retyped many pages of typescript and some complete articles for submission. A number of my students assisted in the checking of references, index, and bibliography, with Sandra McEntire and Margaret Wrenn deserving special thanks. Sarah Mary Anderson, Thomas Du Bois, Fred Jonassen, Roberta Valente and Kelly Wickham-Crowley also put some time into the book. Mr. V. Bjarnar, Curator of Cornell's Icelandic Collection, was generous with his time in the checking of references. The skill of M. Etienne Merle kept our visitors content, despite the rigours of the Ithaca weather. The generous subvention provided by the Hull Fund towards the direct publication costs of this book made it possible for contributors to have ample illustrations, both in terms of figures and plates. Noel Osborne, Editorial Director of Phillimore, was both perceptive and efficient in dealing with a *very* difficult text. I thank all of those who helped in the work of bringing so varied a collection to print, and claim such errors as still exist as my own.

R. T. F.

LIST OF ILLUSTRATIONS
(between pages 146 and 147)

LIST OF TEXT FIGURES

The Viking Settlement of Scotland: The Evidence of Place-Names
by *W. M. F. Nicolaisen*

The Gilded Vikingship Vanes: their use and techniques by *Martin Blindheim*

William Morris and Saga Translation: 'The Story of King Magnus, son of Erling' by *James L. Barribeau*

PREFACE

The publicity that surrounded the Viking exhibition (which was seen by more than a million people in England and the United States in 1980 and 1981) has obscured the fact that behind the razzmatazz was a serious purpose: namely, to bring together for the first time a totally representative exhibition of the Scandinavians in the Viking Age. Publications attended the exhibition in monstrous sequence, everything from the banal to the frivolous, from the learned to the happily popular. Television, radio and newspapers vied to get in on the act and various specialists spent most of their time revising previous books, writing and editing new ones and producing articles, lectures and broadcasts. The scholarly output was remarkable: James Graham-Campbell's *Artefacts*, Richard Bailey's *Viking Age Sculpture*, and Else Roesdahl's *Danmarks Vikingetid* are but three important books which will be used by scholars for many years. Other works swell this list.

As the Vikings became more popular and as the material was looked at more thoroughly, problems emerged and solutions were suggested. Two or three seminars in England and the United States have produced discussion papers and surveys which are yet to be published. One of the three main media of discussion was the Cornell Viking Lecture Series, much of which is published here. Robert Farrell's energy is nowhere clearer than in these papers, for without a great deal of work in often difficult circumstances such a galaxy of talent could not have been brought together. Both he and Cornell University are to be congratulated.

This book represents the whole spectrum of the Cornell Lecture Series, including within its range passion and research, individuality and brilliance, in an attempt to distil rather disparate aspects of the Viking Age. It is not a balanced series of essays; it could never be so in view of the widely differing fields and visions of the contributing scholars. Rather, it represents some of the problems which exercise contemporary scholars of the Viking Age. It is interesting, perhaps, that so many disciplines are represented here—many varied approaches to a main theme. We should consider it a happy feature of the study of this period that the various disciplines have been drawn together in this book; such is continually the case in the daily converse of scholars of the Viking Age. Literary criticism, archaeology, history, bibliography and language are all treated here.

A great exhibition often remains only in folk memory; its impact on the public and on the media is talked of for years. This book provides a more lasting memory of the work and thoughts of scholars of the Viking Age in the early 1980s. It contains many pointers to future research, demonstrating that the exhibition was not simply a publicity stunt, and that the subject lives.

DAVID M. WILSON
The British Museum

May 1981

INTRODUCTION

THE ESSAYS IN THIS VOLUME are in the main products of the series of lectures, seminars and symposia held at Cornell University in the fall of 1980. In some few instances, the papers are influenced by presentations at the Symposium on the Vikings held at the Metropolitan Museum of Art on 18 and 19 October, 1980. The Museum symposium was closely allied with the Cornell series, and the very friendly relations between the Museum and Cornell made it possible for the contributors to prepare the papers for the collection by drawing upon both their presentations at Cornell and the Metropolitan seminar. Not all of those who spoke either at the Metropolitan or at Cornell are represented in this volume. Some had prior arrangements for publication, and others presented either summaries of previous work or portions of larger works in progress.

It is our intent that all of the papers fulfil the expectations of the various sponsors of the series who are acknowledged below. We were given a brief to present our conclusions in such a way that they would be of interest not only to specialists, but also to the public at large. All the contributors have attempted to avoid the use of the terse style of writing and sometimes cryptic forms of reference suitable for communication only between experts in the field of Viking studies. When the series was originally planned, we had hoped to cover all the major areas within Viking studies, but this proved to be impossible even from the beginning. Not all those invited to take part either in the Cornell or Metropolitan observances could attend, either because of illness or prior commitment, and the untimely death of Ole Klindt-Jensen made it impossible to give adequate coverage of the Viking experience in the East.

Despite the difficulties, the essays presented here cover a range of topics in Viking studies, with contributions from historians, archaeologists, art historians, and philologists. The placing of the essays under various headings was meant as a convenience to the reader. The first group — by far the largest — opens with an historian's study of the causes of Viking activity, and ends with a survey of the field and a statement on the future of Viking studies by another historian. Within the group there are essays on Viking expansion both within and beyond Scandinavia, and on art history. Leslie Webster's contribution on the Franks Casket is included here because it is clear evidence for Scandinavian legends being popular in England from a very early date.

The second group consists of philological studies which range from the very earliest literary remains to late Scandinavian reflexes of heroic literature. The third group provides an overview of Viking Settlement on the North American continent, and a brief up-to-date bibliography of the topic. The final section deals with the interest in the Vikings in contemporary times, and the very nature of the image of these men of the North, even to the present day.

It should be clear that 'Viking' is in fact a term of convenience, for its proper referents are found in the Old Scandinavian meaning of the term, 'venturer', or 'pirate', or in the exploits of comparatively small groups of Scandinavians in the late eighth to mid-eleventh centuries. The subject of this book is the enormous impact which Scandinavia had on the rest of Europe and indeed North America. This phenomenon can be properly understood only if the full extent of Scandinavian influence, from the classical period to the present, is surveyed. It is our hope that these essays contribute in some small way to that understanding.

ROBERT T. FARRELL

3 July, 1981.   Village of Lansing, New York.

I: HISTORY, ART HISTORY, ARCHAEOLOGY

THE CAUSES OF THE VIKING AGE

P. H. Sawyer

Professor of Medieval History, Leeds

THERE HAVE been many attempts to explain why, towards the end of the eighth century, Scandinavians suddenly began to attack western Europe. To some contemporaries these raids were the judgement of God on his sinful people, but modern attempts to understand the mechanism of that divine punishment have not been entirely satisfactory. Some have sought the explanation in the Frankish conquest of Frisia and Saxony in the eighth century. This Frankish expansion clearly had a great effect on Denmark, but it can hardly explain the contemporary overseas activity of Norwegians and Swedes. Another suggestion has been that the Vikings were attracted by the internal dissensions of western Europe, but that is also unconvincing: the attacks began in the time of Charlemagne and Offa, two of the most effective of all Dark Age rulers, both of whom demonstrated their power by organizing defences against the Scandinavian pirates. Later political divisions in both Francia and England were undoubtedly exploited by Viking raiders who were quick to take advantage of such weaknesses, but the first raids cannot be explained in this way.

My own earlier discussions of the problem were in part a reaction against the views of those who, like Kendrick, considered the Viking expansion "a huge outpouring of the northern peoples" on such a scale that some special explanation was called for. I then argued that the scale of both the attacks and the later settlements had been greatly exaggerated and that the "Viking outburst" should be seen "not as an unprecedented and inexplicable cataclysm but as an extension of normal Dark Age activity made possible and profitable by special circumstances", the most important of which was, of course, the development of suitable ships.[1] This did not, however, explain why the attacks began when they did or why, if the ships were indeed the key to the Viking period, the Scandinavians did not have suitable vessels long before the age of Charlemagne.

The problem is made more difficult by the obscurity of pre-Viking Scandinavia. Our historical knowledge of the region begins with the reports of frontier disputes, Christian missions and diplomacy that followed Frankish expansion to the borders of Danish territory. Before that we are almost entirely dependent on archaeological evidence which can, of course, tell us virtually nothing about political power or social organization. One suggestion that has been canvassed on archaeological grounds is that the Viking expansion was the result of population pressure. There is, however, no good evidence for any such pressure; and in some areas, such as Rogaland, Öland and Gotland, it appears that the pressure of population was greater in the sixth than in the eighth century.[2] Recent investigations in some other areas, notably Denmark and Mälardalen, have not demonstrated any significant pressure on the available resources

1

in the period immediately before the Viking Age.[3] One important development that
did occur in that period was a dramatic increase in iron production, especially in
Norway and Sweden.[4] Iron tools and weapons were consequently more abundant
but that alone cannot explain the expansion of the Scandinavians overseas.

We may be reasonably certain that developments in Scandinavia before and during
the Viking period were as complex as they were in other, and better-documented,
parts of Europe. It would therefore be absurd to look for a simple, single explanation
of Viking activity. We should also recognize that our evidence is inadequate, and that
we can never hope to understand that activity or its causes fully. Recent studies have,
however, cast new light on the eighth and ninth centuries and suggest that the reasons
for Viking activity should not be sought only in western Europe or Scandinavia, but in
the links that joined these two areas long before the first Viking raid.

Scandinavia and the Baltic have always been important to the outside world as sources
of valued and exotic goods.[5] The earliest identifiable export, found as far away as the
Mediterranean in the Bronze Age, is amber. This fossilized resin could be obtained in
several places, but the most abundant source was the region south of the Baltic, Samland
and Jutland, and modern analyses have confirmed that many early specimens from
Greece do come from that area. Another highly-prized material was ivory, and when
elephant tusks became scarce, walrus tusks from the Arctic were used instead. Furs were
probably even more important, but they are less easily detected. Fur-bearing animals
are found in all parts of Europe, but the best furs come from the coldest regions. In the
eleventh century, Adam of Bremen emphasized the abundance of fur in various parts
of Scandinavia and commented critically on his fellow Germans' covetous desire to
possess marten skins.[6] Furs were an important part of the tribute paid in the ninth
century by Lapps to the Norwegian, Ottarr:

> Their wealth is mostly in the tribute which the Lapps pay them. That tribute is in the skins of
> beasts, in the feathers of birds, in whale-bone, and in ship ropes which are made from whale-hide
> and seal-hide. Each pays according to his rank. The highest rank has to pay fifteen marten skins, five
> reindeer skins, one bearskin and ten measures of feathers, and a jacket of bearskin or otterskin,
> and two ship-ropes.[7]

What Ottarr did with all this tribute is not explained, but he did describe the journey
from his home in the north of Norway to *Sciringes heal* and then on to Hedeby. It seems
most probable that much of the furs and other goods collected by Ottarr eventually
reached the royal and noble households, religious as well as secular, of Christian Europe.
There were other goods apart from those listed by Ottarr and we may suspect that
falcons, slaves and perhaps iron were also valued northern exports. In the Viking
period there is also evidence for the export of large quantities of soapstone vessels and
whetstones from Norway.

There had already been a lively demand in the Roman Empire for many of these
commodities. Pliny described the import to Rome of a very large quantity of amber
from the Baltic, and according to Jordanes, the Svea were famed for the beauty of their
furs which they send "through innumerable tribes . . . to trade for Roman use".[8] It has
also been suggested that leather, large quantities of which were needed by the Roman
army for boots, shields, tents, and much else, was exported from southern Scandinavia.[9]
The collapse of Roman imperial authority in western Europe in the fifth century

disrupted but did not stop this traffic with the North, but in time the barbarian kinds who inherited what remained of Roman power were able to re-establish control over long-distance trade; with their protection and encouragement, it flourished again.[10] The eighth century in particular saw a remarkable development of international coastal markets in western Europe. The most famous, and probably the largest, was Dorestad, on a branch of the Rhine,[11] but there were many others, from Quentovic, near Boulogne, to Medemblik in Westfriesland.[12] There were many similar centres in England, from *Hamwih* in the south to York in the north, including London, Ipswich, Lincoln and in Kent, Dover, Fordwich and Sarre.[13] These places appear to have been largely concerned with traffic between England and Francia, while Dorestad owed much of its importance to its good connections with the middle and upper Rhine. At least some of them also had dealings, directly or indirectly, with Scandinavia and the Baltic. Archaeological traces of contact with western Europe have been found in many parts of Scandinavia,[14] notably at Dankirke in south Jutland[15] and at Helgö in Lake Mälaren,[16] but there seems to have been a significant increase in western exports to Scandinavia in the eighth century. This is perhaps best seen in the relative abundance of glass bowls and beakers made in western Europe that were buried in eighth-century Swedish boat graves.[17] The excavations at Ribe have shown that the *portus* described in the *Vita Anskarii* began at least a century before Anskar's time.[18] In the first half of the eighth century, craftsmen were active there working with bronze, iron, antler, bone, leather, glass and amber. Ribe's contacts with the west are evidenced not only by glass, pottery and mill stones, but also by the discovery there of 32 Frisian *sceattas*. These form part of a rapidly-growing body of coin evidence for eighth-century contact between western Denmark and western Europe, especially in Frisia.[19]

The European demand for northern goods led some men to search for new supplies. Ottarr himself explained that his journey around North Cape was "mainly for the walruses, because they have very fine ivory in their tusks".[20] Eighth-century Swedish and Gotlandic activity on the eastern shore of the Baltic is best explained by their desire to gather tribute in the form of amber, furs and, doubtless, slaves.[21] The archaeological evidence from Grobin and other sites nearby agrees well with the *Vita Anskarii* which describes the *Cori*, or the inhabitants of Kurland, as having formerly been subjected to the Swedes. It should also be noted that the earliest phase of Staraja Ladoga has now been firmly dated to the second half of the eighth century.[22]

In north Russia the Scandinavians were competing in their search for supplies with others from the Volga and further south who had long exploited the riches of that region.[23] Towards the end of the eighth century, however, the situation was changed when the Khazars were forced by their Islamic neighbours to allow Muslim merchants access to the Don and Volga.[24] As a result kufic silver coins began to reach Russia, and this attracted some Scandinavians to take their slaves and furs to the Volga. The original Scandinavian interest in the lands east of the Baltic was, however, stimulated by the demands of western, not eastern markets.

By the beginning of the ninth century there were several well-attested centres for long-distance trade in Scandinavia and the Baltic: Kaupang in Vestfold, Hedeby, Birka, Truso and Staraja Ladoga. In northern Europe, as in the west, any ruler able to control such market places could hope for increased wealth. According to the Frankish Royal Annals, the Danish king Godfred deliberately removed merchants from *Reric*, an unidentified site in Slav territory, to his own lands, because the *vectigalia* were of great benefit to his kingdom. That technical term may owe more to the interpretation of a Carolingian chronicler than to the conscious adoption by a Danish king of imperial and post-imperial powers; but taken together with the evidence of the *Vita Anskarii* that some rulers were actively interested in such market places, it does suggest that some Scandinavian rulers had prerogatives that were very similar to, and perhaps derived from, those enjoyed by the kings of Christian Europe. [25]

The Frankish Annals also associate Godfred's removal of the *Reric* merchants to Schleswig with the fortification of his kingdom "with a rampart, so that a protective bulwark would stretch from the eastern bay, called *Ostarsalt*, as far as the western sea, along the entire north bank of the river Eider and broken by a single gate through which wagons and horsemen would be able to leave and enter". [26] It has, until recently, been generally accepted that the complex of fortifications in south Jutland known as the *Danevirke* originated in this way, but excavations have shown that Godfred was elaborating an earlier barrier made of timbers than can be shown by dendrochronology to have been cut down after the summer of 737. [27] This barrier may well have been made necessary by Charles Martel's campaign in 738 against the Saxons, but it also shows that whoever ruled south Jutland then had sufficiently well-organized resources to build such an elaborate structure, and that it was judged worth the effort. The *Danevirke* was a defence against a land attack from the south, but there were other threats by sea, and traders travelling in the Baltic were vulnerable to pirates. Anskar was himself attacked on his first visit to Birka.

The route from Birka to Dorestad is not certainly known. It has been claimed that it crossed south Jutland from Hedeby to the river Treene, but there is no direct evidence for such a portage. The fact that elaborate searches have so far failed to discover traces of the western end, together with the obvious disadvantage of unloading and reloading, suggests that the normal route was by boat the whole way, and that Jutland was traversed by means of Limfjord to avoid the dangerous northern coast. The early importance of Limfjord is confirmed by the presence on its banks of such important early sites as Lindholm Høje and Aggesborg. [28] The route from Dorestad to Limfjord was well sheltered by islands, or made use of inland water; from its eastern end the natural route was by either the Great or Little Belts: strong currents made Öresund a difficult stretch of water. The entrance to the Belts was controlled from the island of Samsø, which is bisected by a canal that made it possible for ships to go to either side of the island as necessary, whether the purpose was to collect tribute from passing vessels or to protect them. This canal has very recently been dated dendrochronologically to 720. In the light of the similarly early date for *Danevirke*, it seems most probable that both were constructed for the ruler of Jutland: the peninsula was certainly ruled as a unit in the early ninth century. It seems reasonable to see in both the *Danevirke* and the Samsø canal evidence for the interest of powerful men in the protection of Jutland and its coasts.

The pirates against whom protection was needed were sometimes led by members of royal families. This is best shown by an episode described in the *Vita Anskarii*:

> About the same time it happened that a certain Swedish king named *Anound* had been driven from his kingdom, and was an exile among the Danes. Desiring to regain what had once been his kingdom he sought aid of them and promised that if they would follow him they would be able

to secure much treasure. He offered them Birka . . . because it contained many rich merchants, and a large amount of goods and money. He promised to lead them to this place where, without loss to their army, they might gain much that they wanted. Enticed by the promised gifts and eager to acquire treasure, to assist him they filled twenty-one ships with men ready for battle and placed them at his disposal, moreover he had eleven of his own ships. These left Denmark and came unexpectedly to the above-mentioned town.[29]

The raiders were later persuaded to attack Slav territory instead. There are many points of interest in this passage, but particular attention should be paid here to two. First, Anound's role in leading the Danes to Birka is emphasised. The approach through the Skärgård and Lake Mälaren must have been hazardous for strangers; Adam of Bremen later[30] claimed that rocks had been placed deliberately to make the way difficult. Second, and more obvious, this is one of the earliest and fullest accounts of a Viking raid on a market place. Significantly, it was led by a former Swedish king.

The development of sailing ships in the Baltic and Scandinavia seems to have been a direct result of the trade between western and northern Europe, and the consequent piracy. The Baltic peoples had long been familiar with boats, but in the Roman period they depended on oar power: their contacts with Roman sailing ships did not lead to the adoption of sails in the north. By the end of the eighth century, Scandinavians certainly had excellent sailing ships and were accomplished sailors. It is, unfortunately, not possible to say when the change occurred. Many ships of the Viking period are known, but earlier ship finds are rare. Those that have been found in Scandinavia, as at Kvalsund in Norway or Gredstedbro in Denmark, are too poorly preserved for archaeologists to say whether they had sails.[31] We are, therefore, dependent on the Gotlandic picture stones, which depict rowing boats in the sixth century and elaborate sailing ships in the eleventh.[32] Some eighth-century stones show ships with sails, but there is no sure way of determining which are the earliest sails, or their date. It is, therefore, possible that they were already used in the seventh century. Whatever the date, the idea appears to have come from western Europe. The shape and construction of the hulls of sailing ships of the Viking period is a direct development of a long established Baltic tradition.[33] The novelty lay in the addition of mast and sail. Ole Crumlin Pedersen has pointed out[34] that, while the method of fixing the mast in Viking war ships is unique, that used in such cargo boats as Äskekärr or Skuldelev 1 and 3 is very similar to the western European method. This is consistent with the suggestion that the sail was adopted thanks to contacts with western traders. It has also been pointed out that although most ships shown on the Gotlandic stones, and on ninth-century Danish coins,[35] have the characteristic "Viking" profile, some have a sharp angle between stems and keel, much like later depictions of cogs, a type of cargo boat that was certainly widely used in northern Europe from the eleventh century onwards and that probably had antecedents in the ninth century or even earlier. The fact that ships of this type on ninth-century coins are never shown with shields displayed supports the suggestion that they represent cargo boats rather than warships, while their shape implies that they were not Scandinavian.[36]

For sea-fights, short journeys and in narrow waters, rowing was an ideal method of propulsion, but for cargo-carrying or long journeys, like the two described in the Old English translation of Orosius, Ottarr's round North Cape, and south to Hedeby, and Wulfstan's from Hedeby to Truso, sails were an obvious advantage. The Scandinavians added masts and sails to their ships in the eighth century, or perhaps earlier, not simply because they had become familiar with western sailing ships but because long voyages were needed to take the amber, furs and other goods from the far reaches of the Baltic and Scandinavia to the markets of England and Francia. In addition, the competition between traders and pirates must have been a powerful stimulus to this technological development.

Some time before the year 800, this Baltic piracy had begun to spread beyond the Baltic and affect the coasts of western Europe. In the spring of that year Charlemagne spent some time organizing defences along the coast north-east of the Seine estuary, and he built a fleet against the pirates who, according to the Royal Annals, infested the sea (s.a. 800). The fact that no attacks on that coast are recorded underlines the inadequacy of our knowledge of the first Viking raids, but it is clear that the threat was serious enough to warrant Charlemagne's personal attention. A Kentish charter of 792 shows that Offa was already arranging for defence against pagan seamen by then, and it is likely that coastal attacks had begun by 790, if not earlier. Alcuin's reaction to the attack on Lindisfarne in 793 has been taken to prove that that was the first raid, but what appears to have astonished him was that such a crossing of the sea was possible. Coastal raiding was probably no novelty and gave some chance of a warning being sent by signals or messengers: a direct crossing of the North sea was a much more alarming prospect.

The Frankish defences, which were reinforced in 810 by fleets stationed at Boulogne and Ghent, appear to have been successful for several decades. In 820 the Annals report the arrival of thirteen Scandinavian ships that were successfully repulsed from Flanders and the mouth of the Seine but finally succeeded in gathering booty from the coast of Aquitaine. It was the deposition of Louis the Pious by his sons in the autumn of 833 and the consequent preoccupation of the Franks with their internal disputes that gave the Scandinavian pirates their opportunity, and in 834 Dorestad was attacked for the first time. Once the feasibility and profitability of such a raid had been demonstrated, the number, and doubtless the size, of the raiding bands increased. Dorestad suffered every year until 837, the Thames estuary was attacked in 835, the Bristol Channel in 836—the same year that Viking raiders first penetrated the interior of Ireland. It was also the period when the religious communities of St Philibert and St Cuthbert abandoned their exposed islands and sought shelter inland. The main onslaught, however, was still to come, and began in 841 after the death of Louis the Pious and the outbreak of civil war among his sons. It was then that the Seine defences broke down and Jumièges was attacked. Four years later Charles the Bald had to buy off an attack on Paris with the huge sum of £7,000. It is hardly surprising that the coasts and rivers of western Europe were soon suffering from an even greater infestation of pirate fleets, many of which were led by exiled members of Scandinavian royal families. Some, like Anund or, later, Olaf Tryggvason, returned to power in their homelands, but others were content to establish themselves overseas in such places as the Hebrides, Dublin, York or Rouen, or east of the Baltic at Staraja Ladoga or Kiev, while some created new lordships in the new land of Iceland.

The explanation of Viking activity offered here will doubtless be modified in the light of new discoveries. We may, in particular, hope for much more information about the development of sailing ships in the north, but it does seem to provide a satisfactory framework for understanding the various elements that together made Viking activity possible.

It was the western European demand for northern products, and the parallel Scandinavian demand for western goods, that caused close contacts between the two areas, and encouraged Scandinavians to search for new supplies in the far north or east of the Baltic. This trade enhanced the power of some Scandinavian rulers, by increasing their wealth. Others who were less successful or even exiled could resort to piracy, first in the Baltic and later in the west, an extension that was facilitated by the adoption of the sail. This crucially important development was itself a result of contact between Scandinavians and western traders, and the growing need to make very long voyages. This trade also tempted pirates, and the competition between traders and merchants must have speeded up the development of the remarkable sailing ships that are indeed the key to the Viking Age.

NOTES

1. *See* Sawyer 1971, 202-3.
2. Myhre 1973; Stenberger 1979, 454-66.
3. Roesdahl 1980, 57-72; Hyenstrand 1974; Ambrosiani 1980.
4. Hyenstrand 1972; Martens 1972.
5. Sawyer 1978.
6. Adam of Bremen, trans. Tschan 1959, IV. 18.
7. Alfred's tr. of Orosius, trans. Ross 1940, 21.
8. Pliny, trans. Eichholz 1962.
9. Jordanes, trans. Mierow 1915, 56.
10. Sawyer 1977.
11. Es 1969.
12. Besteman 1974.
13. Biddle 1974.
14. Bakka 1971.
15. Thorvildsen 1972.
16. Holmqvist *et al.* 1961.
17. Arwidsson 1942.
18. Bencard 1978.
19. Kirsten Bendixen, pers. comm.
20. Alfred's tr. of Orosius, trans. Ross 1940.
21. Nerman 1958; Ozols 1976.
22. Davidan 1981, unpubl.
23. Tallgren 1934.
24. Noonan 1981.
25. Sawyer 1977.
26. Frankish Annals, trans. Scholz 1970.
27. Andersen *et al.* 1976.
28. Roesdahl 1980, 74-5 and 172.
29. *Vita Anskarii*, Chapter 19.
30. Adam of Bremen, trans. Tschan 1959, I. 60.
31. Elmers 1972.
32. Lindqvist 1941.
33. Crumlin Pedersen 1978.
34. Crumlin Pedersen 1980. Unpubl.
35. Skaare 1964.
36. Christensen 1964.

THE VIKING IMAGE

Rosemary Cramp

Professor of Archaeology, University of Durham

AN IMAGE can be either the representation of the visible or the invisible, a shadow of the visible or a materialization of the invisible. Of course these two concepts inter-penetrate just as gods walk among men unobserved, because to be remarked at all they have to take on human appearances. However, in this paper I aim to discuss the representations of the visible Viking Man as he saw himself. In this treatment iconography rather than style has proved the more fruitful field for distinction. However, the stylistic consideration of Viking figures has hardly begun, although those who have so far written on figural art such as Andersson, Arbman and Holmqvist seem to be in agreement that styles of figure drawing are remarkably conservative in the North Germanic World. This may be, however, because figural types have not been subjected to the same rigorous stylistic analysis as have animal or plant forms.

When comparing Viking figural art with that of the antique world, it is more difficult to understand the intention of the artist, since we have not contemporary writings to explain it. Was it naturalistic and representational, decorative or cryptogrammic? Is it inferior to, or different in kind from, animal ornament?

Whereas animal ornament causes us to turn away in some embarrassment from icono-graphic interpretation, the human figures force such interpretation upon us—possibly unnecessarily.

In his seminal work, *Byzantine Aesthetics*, Gervase Mathews introduces his subject by saying that any approach to the subject should take four factors into account:

> 'A recurrent taste for classical reminiscence; . . . an essentially mathematical approach to beauty, which led to an emphasis not only on exact symmetry but on *eurhythmos* and balanced move-ments; an absorbed interest in optics, . . . and finally a belief in the existence of an invisible world of which the material is the shadow — so that an image presupposes the Imaged just as a shadow presupposes the human body that casts it, and is as closely linked to it. A scene is not a mere repre-sentation of something that has once happened but a *mimesis*, a re-enactment. '[1]

Viking art as it has come down to us is like all folk art, largely applied to objects or ornaments of daily life. It spans a fairly wide social spectrum but it lacks the subtlety and indeed the articulate philosophical basis that one can adduce for the Byzantine world. It is a non-monumental art of the barbarians who lived outside the civilizing *limes* of the Roman Empire; but it would be doing less than justice to the subject to discuss it without remembering that in every generation from the fourth to the eleventh century the North Germanic people were in contact with Roman or Byzantine art and could have been aware of its aspirations. In fact one might almost say that the art of the antique and East

8

Christian world is the constant catalyst which activates and shapes the iconographies with which we are dealing.

However, although we may recognize the remnants of Classical reminiscence, the geometric if not purely mathematical approach to beauty, and certainly the understanding that the Image pre-supposes the Imaged, we have not, to my mind, in Viking Art the balanced harmony, the understanding of optics and light which give to Byzantine art a depth and subtle order. Viking figural art remains hieroglyphic and visually incoherent.

The dominance of idea and the rule of the cool and temperate mind are not applicable to the Viking world, which is in many ways childish, blundering, impulsive, and unanalytical. However, as with all primitive peoples, sometimes rituals, of which art is one manifestation, can be exacting and rigorously controlled.

There are two ever-present difficulties in considering Viking figural ornament: first, the ability to distinguish between primary and secondary models, and second, the levels of simultaneous interpretation it is reasonable to suppose. It is important to recognize, however, that Viking art is not something new — it is part of an uninterrupted development in Germanic art. In the Migration Period the North Germanic peoples lived outside the Roman *limes*, but in the course of the migrations of the fourth to the seventh centuries, which took Germanic people to the Mediterranean and Atlantic worlds, they would have come into direct contact with the three-dimensional realistic art of the Roman world, including portraiture. This contact then presented new images for acceptance alongside those established in northern and Atlantic Europe since the Bronze Age. Such scenes, all apparently religious, showed an iconography and treatment of the human figure common to the Celtic and Germanic worlds. Figures and groups are disassociated visually, but are all shown in active movement, which is capable of flowing away from the confines of the object on which it is depicted, as on the Gundestrup Cauldron and Gallerhus horns.[2] Contact with the Roman world is reflected in Vendel art, as discussed below, and in the conception of the Gotlandic stone funerary monuments covered with scenes of heroic or religious drama.

However, the second wave of migrations from the north brought the Vikings to new settlements in Atlantic and Baltic territories, where they were confronted not only with the surviving remnants of original Roman works, but also with the redefined classicizing work of Germanic and Celtic peoples who had accepted and adapted Antique art when they accepted Christianity. There are certain images which could have been brought by the Vikings to their new territories or could have been acquired there. I shall, therefore, in the iconographic study of Viking images, tend to take the larger viewpoint, while in stylistic considerations I shall focus more narrowly in time and place.

As for the levels of meaning that one can see in these images, that is something about which one cannot now be precise; however, one can be sure, from early literature, that multi-level interpretations existed!

Bullogh, in his discussion of *Imagines Regum*, says: "The full impact of the various images and effigies on the liturgies of Constantinople, Ravenna, Rome and elsewhere is effectively beyond our comprehension".[3] The barbarians in the Frankish Kingdoms and the British Isles may not have seen works of the same quality and plenitude as those in Italy, but in a more limited way comparable work did exist. On the other hand, the quality of Christian stone carvings which existed in the British Isles by the late ninth century is sufficiently high to set beside the earlier effigies, and may be seen as alternative models. Moreover, the contemporary sculptors that the Vikings would have encountered in their new homelands were the descendants of generations of craftsmen who, for two hundred years, had been accustomed to an iconography which had translated pagan imagery into Christian equivalents.

The life-size equestrian statues of the victorious Emperors would have been symbols of power to their barbarian contemporaries — victorious power, which was underlined by their magnificent armour and weapons, and often by the scantily-clad barbarian between their horses' hooves. Then there was the image of the Emperor as a victorious huntsman, as a killer of beasts, or as the controller of men and beasts presiding over the games at a circus. Another depiction of the Emperor's power showed him seated in judgement, solemnly presiding like a magistrate. For the Christian artist, rather interestingly, the mounted figure is not so much used, but Christ can be shown in military guise as *Christus-Miles*, treading down the asp and basilisk, or like David in his kingly role, bearing arms. Both David and Samson are slayers of beasts, and David and Christ can be shown in the role of a Roman magistrate enthroned and in classical dress, however misunderstood.

Arne Andersson says that the portraits of Roman Emperors "proclaimed a god by his own subjects, therefore the most important man imaginable", were a potent force in shaping Germanic art.[4] Once the Roman art of coins and medals was introduced into Scandinavia, together with the concept that the head or bust of a powerful man was sufficient to represent his whole person, then the Nordic goldsmith did not hesitate to include in his design detail totally lacking in naturalistic meaning. The mask and the bust undergo exaggerations of expression which are partly a disguise, partly an emphasis, and both continue as part of the figural repertoire into the Viking Age. Like the Viking mask from Sigtuna,[5] one can see such grotesque emphasis on the head in the Lowther hogback (Plate 1).

When the Germanic rulers first took over the Roman world, they conceived of themselves as directly replacing the accepted ruler image. Theoderic the Ostrogoth, who died in A.D. 526, conceived of himself in unambiguously late Roman terms, and this was reflected both in the nature of the portrait on his coinage and in the mausoleum in which he was buried. However, later coin/medallions of the Germanic people combine the image of the Emperor and his horse in terms of the new style of the Migration Period — Salin's Style I. In this style there is an ambiguity between the image of man and beast. The animal and human forms flow into and substitute one for another, and the mask is a particularly prominent motif. In Viking art the mask may be usually a representation of a god, as in the furnace stone from Snaptun, Denmark.[6] There is, however, a tradition, common to the Celts and the Germans from later pre-historic times, that the head symbolizes the whole being.

The Sutton Hoo whetstone, for example, is a miniature stele, on which the heads are set around a block and could in type be derived from a Celtic model. However, the type of face is one to be seen in the Germanic world over and over again: a wedge-shaped face, with staring eyes, implacable and unsmiling. This is also the image of the saint of the Viking Age, on the Aycliffe Cross (see Plate 2).

Very early in the fifth and sixth centuries the effect of Christian art may be detected interacting with the iconography of the pagan. The secular image of man and God began to be treated in the same style in the north Germanic lands. The grave stone of a barbarian but Christianized Frank from Niederdollendorf[7] pre-figures many aspects of the later Viking effigies. On one side Christ is shown in the guise of an heroic warrior in his fight against the devil. He is taken from some antique model in which the background is subdivided; he holds a spear, but has a mandorla round his head and a circle on his breast, which possibly symbolizes the Host. However, what is worthy of remark here is the style of figure drawing: the body is shown in a frontal position with feet and one leg slightly turned, shoulders absolutely square and the head shaped on a rounded oval, with dotted eyes and very simply conveyed line of mouth. It is a type that we can see later in the sculpture of the Anglo-Viking north. (Plate 3).

On the other side of the stone is a cheerful figure of a warrior combing his hair. (One remembers the symbolic combs and toilet instruments that survive from pagan cremation graves.) His dress, whether tunic or trousers, is very simply conveyed; he has a short sword in a scabbard on the right side of his body, a shield or water bottle at his feet, and he is being devoured by serpents. They could be thought of as symbols of death or as symbols of a specific Germanic god. I have stressed these early Germanic reactions to Christian symbols and Christian grave markers, because they have many of the characteristics also shown in the depictions of Viking warriors, such as that on the Middleton Cross in Yorkshire. (Plate 4).

We are accustomed in the laws of the Germanic people, as well as in some of their graves, to see their weapons and armour as symbols of status and power. On the early Roman triumphal monuments, as we have already noted, the Roman is shown as heavily weaponed and the barbarian as lightly armed — bare-headed with a spear or knife and shield. However, for the aristocratic Germans of the sixth and seventh centuries, the helmet and body armour of sword and shield, or spear and shield, were possibly borrowed signs of status. The processions or armed men round the Vendel or Valsgärde helmets[8] reflect the impact of Roman ideas of the victorious image on the northern barbarians. Moreover, the style of the figures reflects the influence of Roman art.

The mounted figures I will discuss later. The armed men, either singly or in a procession, may be examined first. The figures on the Vendel helmets are clean shaven, rather stately and thick set, betraying their stylistic origins in Roman art. But significantly emphasized details of their armour seem to be taken from their native background: the rings on their swords, their masked helmets with enormous boar or bird crests, their shields with central bosses and smaller subsidiary triple bosses. However, their stiff tunics with bound hems or edges, which leave their legs bare, are very difficult to parallel. Other figures are differently dressed: dancing figures with horned helmets, who wear trousers and, like the leading figure on the Oseberg Tapestry, could play a priestly role (Plates 5(a) and 5(b)).

We can say no more of these solemn profile processions than that they could represent the idealized contemporary aristocratic warrior. Other figures, like those dancing with spears, could be either men performing ritual dances or even the gods themselves, appearing among men. All of these figures on the helmet plates, however, follow the classical tradition in dynamic touches of naturalistic detail, for example, the beast-leader from the Torslunda die, with his delicately indicated nipples and ankle bones. They are all shown in action: dancing, walking or riding away.

It seems reasonable to suppose, partly from literary references in which men take on animal forms, partly from generalized ethnographic parallels, that beast masks could have been used in religious rituals, the man taking on the power and supremacy of the beast. It seems in some of the seventh-century forms that the masked Roman helmet and older native tradition of the beast mask fuse. One example is the helmet from Sutton Hoo,[9] on which the flying bird, flying dragon and the boar are combined to make up a human face. Another such fusion of this sort is seen in the silver head used as a pendant for Aska Aagabyhögen, Sweden, which is Vendel/Early Viking period (Plate 6). Here, the three-toed feet of the bird form the man's ears. Stylistic emphasis on the head and men with bestial heads linger in Viking art of the British Isles, as we see on a Lancaster cross.[10]

Now it remains a matter of debate as to whether the figural representatives of the Vendel/early Viking period, such as the Oseberg Tapestry[11] or early Gotlandic stones, are of gods, mythological heroes or even contemporary heroes seen in the guise of gods. Yet there seems to be a continuing tradition of representation of figures in non-classical costume among the north Germanic peoples that differentiates their art from the Christian images of northern England, which are maintained for nearly two hundred years in a form of classical, and certainly foreign, dress. It is also important to note that there are no armed figures in what I, at any rate, would consider pre-ninth century sculpture in England, save perhaps the secular figures from St Mary Bishophill, York (Plate 7).

By the ninth century in both the Midland and Northumbrian areas which the Danes conquered and settled, it is important to note that the prevailing figural images in indigenous sculpture are of two types. The first group are rather block-like, single figures, mostly three-quarter length and strictly frontal, filling their architectural frames. The second type are smaller-scale, animated figures, usually in groups, and are derived from the impressionistic art of the Carolingian world. At Halton in Lancashire (Plate 8(a)) one gets both styles, but whether one chooses the Midlands, at sites such as Bradbourne or Bakewell (where there is later distinctive Viking ornament on the monuments in the churches or churchyards), or the North at Collingham or Ilkley, the picture is the same. These hieratic figures, such as the episcopal figure with a skull cap from Halton, could be images of types, or of real people such as saints or bishops of the area. We do not know; but the solemn frontal figures are very different from the profile figures of the Viking homelands, such as those found in the Oseberg tapestry or on the Gotlandic picture stones.

I shall attempt now to show how, when the Vikings began to settle in the late eighth century in the British Isles — first in Ireland and Northern Scotland, and, from the middle of the ninth century, in England — they were affected by what they found. In addition, their own Germanic images which I have been looking at, helped to change the art of their new homelands — in particular by introducing the secular image of the armed man.

In the British Isles, the Picts in the eighth and ninth centuries depicted battle scenes and men in armed combat, or single, armed figures shown on horseback or striding out of the picture. There are 49 such examples in Pictish Scotland. As in the art of the Gotlandic stones, the figures are frozen in action. However, in style they are very different. The nearest to anything that can be seen on Gotlandic stones is at St Blaine's Bute,[12] where there is a large figure holding a spear and shield with a sword across his waist — not like Pictish art at all, and more like Viking. On the back of the stone there is a horseman. This is an area of Scandinavian settlement in Scotland, and it seems to me that this type of armed man is a Viking importation, although the style of representation is influenced by indigenous monuments. I will illustrate the interaction of Scandinavian and Northumbrian art by a selection of examples.

A very remarkable group of Sockburn-on-Tees shows single Viking warriors in two guises. Each profile figure clasps a spear in his hands: in one he wears a pointed cap (Plate 9) and in the other a bowl-like helmet (Plate 10). In one he carries a sword girded at his left side, in the other a round shield. Richard Bailey has recently pointed out that the Sockburn warrior with the bowl helmet can be cut from the same template as one from Brompton and another at Kirkleavington (Plate 11).[13] Now the Brompton centre is very important not only because it provided specifically Viking monuments such as ring-headed crosses and hogbacks, but because on the cross already mentioned there are images which directly derive from the regional Anglian tradition of detached, frontal, three-quarter figures under arches (Plate 12(a)). One holds a scroll, the distinguishing mark of a saint or priest. On the other side there is an angel whose wings are like those in late Pictish art such as at Dunfallandy (Plates 12(b) and 13). The portrait birds are also like single creatures in Pictish art (Plate 12(c)), but the horrible crossed and writhing beasts are derived from ninth-century types in the northern English area,[14] the vine scroll is also derived from the local ninth-century type (Plate 12(d)), such as those found at Hart (Durham) or at Norham (Northumberland).[15] At Sockburn the armed men, combined with distinctive plain plait-work and animals, derive from Brompton, where the figure of the saint with his cross is carved in the same style as the warrior. Has this idea of a detached image of the saint affected the method of presenting the armed man as a detached image?

Now I have digressed from iconography to style, because I wanted to make a point: namely, here was a development of the single figure in the same style of cutting used in a local school in the Tees Valley, and introducing new iconographic features but not new styles. The heavily-modelled portrait style with considerable detail of dress is reminiscent of the figure style of the Migration Period helmet plaques and can also be seen on the man with birds at Kirkleavington. There is another group of figural carvings at Sockburn, which has a different style of figure carving, not clear cut and cameo-like or stencil-like, but using animated groups and half-turned figures in what seem to be mythological scenes. These, because of their associated ornamental links with Norse styles westwards in Cumbria, may represent a less-assimilated Norwegian group.

A similar Anglo-Scandinavian inter-relationship is found on a later group of single figures from Otley in Yorkshire, West Riding, and from Weston Hall near Otley. These were derived in conception from an Anglian original, but are formally treated in a Scandinavian way. Earlier crosses from Otley depict some splendid frontal and half-turned busts of Carolingian type, set under arches with floral elements in the spandrels, and with large-scale animals above.[16] The Anglo-Scandinavian artist eschews the "unnatural" bust image. The Otley warrior is shown surrounded by an arch with floral spandrels, which somehow manage to look like spears, and above him are the remains of an animal. He is frontal with a rounded head and pointed chin, his shoulders very squarely cut and widely extended from his body; he is holding a short sword in his right hand and wearing a short tunic. This is the same style of figures that one finds in the Cumbrian West at Gosforth (Plate 14), and the same iconographic type — simply clothed with a prominent sword — is found as far south as Brailsford in Derbyshire. This is the single warrior with his attribute — a sword — which identifies him as a book or scroll does a saint.

The seated or enthroned figure has an equally long and ambiguous history in Early Medieval art. It is the position of judgement and authority, of magistrates or bishops. The famous story of how Augustine remained seated in the presence of the British bishops tells us that the seated person considers himself superior. But undoubtedly there were various seated images which are influential in Viking art— we can find the armed man, the thinker or judge, the seated 'god' and of course the enthroned evangelist or Christ himself.

The word *stol* in Old English is used alone in the sense of seat or throne, or to gloss the Latin *cathedra*, or it can be combined with various modifying prefixes to signify the thrones of earthly kings or gods. Christ possesses a *cynestol*, *ealdor-stol*, *gifstol*, or *þeoden-stol*. One remembers that the *gifstol* in *Beowulf* is something so important in the life of the hall *Heorot*, that Grendel's dispossession of the Danes from the hall and its *gifstol* is a great grief to them.[17] However, although Grendel does not allow the *gifstol* to be used for treasure giving and other ceremonies which bind together lord and retainer, he cannot participate alone in such ceremonies. Miniature chairs or thrones with rounded backs have been found at Birka[18] in graves; some of these are attached as pendants to necklaces. It could be they have nothing more than ornamental significance, but their possible symbolic function in representing thrones or high seats within the pagan context seems entirely reasonable.

Single enthroned figures from Germanic contexts could represent either gods or men. The recently-discovered potlid from a cremation cemetery at Spong Hill, Norfolk[19] (confirmed as Anglo-Saxon in date by thermo-luminescence dating) shows a thinking type of figure which is similar to the little seated figures, possibly playing pieces, from Lund. Seated or squatting figures in Viking context may be gods, and the long beard could be a god-attribute. They span a range of dates, but two from Iceland are of tenth and eleventh-century date.

The type of figure with a long beard does seem to bear a different significance from the armed man in Viking contexts. Per Gjaerder says in relation to depictions of gods, "partly for biological reasons it (the beard), has been considered a sex symbol, and the long beard is a distinguishing mark of maturity and old age. It was not only a sign of virility and strength but also of wisdom, holiness, dignity, and other venerable qualities".[20] All this is sufficient to show that there can be no single received explanation for the seated figure. It could be secular or religious. The armed man might conceivably be thought of more easily as a secular representative – the idealized warrior – but the bearded seated figure could be the god himself or his devotee.

On Irish and Scottish monuments, ecclesiastics are often seated on chairs; on Irish and English crosses, King David can be shown on his throne playing his harp, or Christ stands before Pilate, who is seated to give his judgement. Christ himself can be shown enthroned to give his blessing or judgement. Such depictions of seated figures are common in the late eighth/early ninth century; as at Masham and Aldborough in Yorkshire,[21] the figures are never armed.

A possible exception to the armed standing figure and the unarmed seated one in Germanic art occurs on the extensively-discussed crosses from Middleton in Yorkshire (Plate 4). These show frontal figures in long trousers and pointed helmets, with daggers girdled to the waist and in one case surrounded by spear, sword, axe and tiny shield. In two cases Lang has suggested that these depict armed and seated figures (although he expresses some doubts as to whether their headgear is a cap or helmet). However, he stresses the significance of the *gifstol*, "not only as a contemporary concept of authority but a continuing heroic tradition in which the chair is an indication of power".[22] It is perhaps also significant, if the Middleton figure is meant to be seen as seated, that the figure is so clearly secular and is shown so unequivocally as associated with his secular and social "attributes". The Middleton warriors are quite large-scale figures, as are the Sockburn single warriors, or the famous seated profile figure on the cross from Nunburnholme in Yorkshire (Plate 15). We have seen how the sculptured images of saints or ecclesiastics from nearby crosses could have set the scale and affected the iconography of the Scandinavian images, but at Nunburnholme the seated secular figure is directly imposed on the same cross as that which bears saints and Christian scenes, in the ninth-century tradition. This figure has been considered by some as a portrait of the Viking for whom it was raised, and it has also been assigned to widely different dates.[23] It is best seen as early among Anglo–Scandinavian sculptures and in the direct line of tradition from ninth-century work in the Midlands and South Yorkshire.

After a very detailed and convincing analysis of this cross, Lang demonstrated the work of three sculptors; he would assign this figure, the work of his second sculptor, to the early tenth century.

Although the work of the second sculptor is flatter and more crudely linear than the deeper relief and finer detail achieved by the first sculptor, it is nevertheless a remarkable depiction. The man is shown seated on a stool with rather crazily-tilted legs, holding a sword in his left hand. He is wearing a rounded cap or helmet, and a long, full garment that falls in heavy folds to cover his feet. Over this is a short, sleeveless jacket. The detail in rendering this clothing is unique in northern English sculpture, and if this figure is a Viking, his dress is not easily comparable with figures in the Viking homelands, where women are depicted with long dresses and men with short tunics over tight or baggy trousers.

Alan Binns first made the suggestion that this is a portrait figure of the deceased Jarl, a new landowner in the region; this view is supported by Pattison, who compares the style of the profile figure with the Irish cross from Banagher. Now the Banagher Cross (Plate 16) with its many interlaced panels is closely similar to much Northumbrian work, and Pattison's comparison, albeit of a seated with a mounted figure, raises the interesting problem of how much the Scandinavian settlers in northern England may already have been influenced by Christian art in Scotland and Ireland. This question is most pertinently related to the images of mounted men.

The horse seems to have been a status symbol in the Early Medieval world: Bede (HE. III 14) tell us how Oswin was enraged when the horse he had given to Bishop Aidan was almost immediately given away to a beggar. Mounted figures could signify aristocrats on, for example, Pictish symbol stones. The horse and rider are combined in bracteates derived from coins with emperor portraits. However, when the rider is accompanied by a snake or ravens and when the horse has eight legs, as on some of the Gotlandic picture stones, the rider could signify the god Ódinn. Other mounted gods are depicted on the Gosforth Cross from Cumbria (Plate 17).

The figure of the rider, whether in procession or alone, obviously has not a single iconographic referent. Roman art could have supplied equestrian statues, as previously mentioned, and these could have survived a long time. The famous East Geatish inscription from Rök (ninth century) refers to a Theodric who landed on the shore among the Hreithgoths nine generations before, but who now sits on his horse ready (or equipped) with his shield hung about him. The statue referred to has been presumed to be that of either Theodric the Frank or Theodric the Ostrogoth, whose statue was at Aachen in the ninth century. However, whichever Theodric this is, the Rök inscription recalls a statue of an antique equestrian figure that had survived for over three hundred years.[24]

Single horsemen are also depicted on Germanic brooches of the Migration Period, usually mounted and carrying a spear, and single riders with spears are also found on Anglo-Saxon sculpture, such as the Breedon friezes or on crosses in Mercia.[25]

The distinctive baggy trousers on profile figures, as on the Gotlandic stones or in the Oseberg tapestry, never occur on English carvings. The only trousers in English contexts are short breeches, such as those worn by the children in their fiery furnace on the Bilton Cross, Yorkshire, or by the figures in the procession of armed men from Lindisfarne.[26]

However, there does seem a distinctive dress for mythological figures on some crosses, for example, at Sockburn there are possibly Valkyries, with pigtails and cut-away cloaks and long, trailing undergarments.[27] At Leeds, there is on the same cross a figure in a cut-away cloak with a bird on his shoulder, and a frontal figure with a halo, who is draped in a garment of late Anglian type, with looped folds (Plate 18). What might be considered as a typically Scandinavian type of cut-away outer garment — whether for men or women — certainly occurs in Scandinavia from the eighth century onwards. However, Holmqvist put forward the idea that the origin of the figures with wing-shaped cloaks, full-length outer garments with decorated borders and divided outer clothing is to be found in late Celtic art, where it appears frequently in manuscripts.[28]

Stylistically one cannot fail to see that images of men on Anglo–Scandinavian stone carvings are considerably influenced by those existing in their new territories. I have already pointed out the relationships in Northumbria with the late Anglian tradition in the heavy, block-like figures at Brompton, which are closely linked to the single warriors at Sockburn. However, one must remember that the Vikings came into contact with Christianity and Christian manuscripts and stone monuments before they came to England, in particular the Norwegians who had earlier settled in Ireland. Some of the earlier Irish crosses, such as Castledermot, Kildare, share stylistic features with Viking monuments in north Britain.

At Castledermot (Plate 19), Christ's wedge-shaped face, curled halo and the two birds on his shoulders can all be paralleled in English sculpture. Interestingly, the two figures of the Roman soldiers below the Crucified are shown with the same type of hair dressing as the spear-bearing rider at Gainford or Hart in Durham, England. Is this an Irish trick of showing that Roman soldiers were like Vikings? It is also of interest to note that on the magnificent west cross at Monasterboice,[29] the figures of the Roman soldiers are bearded and have pointed helmets very like the Viking originals of carved men at Sockburn.

It is widely accepted that the Norse Vikings introduced the ring-headed cross as an innovatory monument into England, but very little has been said as to whether they also introduced distinctive figural styles with these monuments. The single standing figure we have seen is most plausibly derived from single figures on English crosses, but the rider figure, like the hart and hound, could have derived from hunting scenes from Ireland — they are totally unlike the rider figures from the Gotlandic stones.

Therefore, although Holmqvist's idea of Irish influence on Viking dress may seem at first sight rather improbable, it could be that there is an important relationship between Irish or Scottic and Viking figural art, but that the influences are reciprocal and each translated some elements into the other's idiom.

The figure types already established in Scandinavia could be used for minor, non-divine figures, in Christian contexts, while the images of saints and divine figures in Christian art could provide dignified images for the newly-converted Vikings. Sometimes, of course, the Scandinavian settlers preferred to use their own images and styles, but I think one can see changes of fashion, at least in sculpture.

In the Sockburn Brompton Kirkleavington group the figures are clean-cut, block-like, deeply-modelled and can be both frontal and profile. One may note that most of the figures on Gotlandic stones and/or slabs in the Isle of Man are shown in profile. Also, a part of an early (possibly Danish) tradition are frontal figures, which tend to form chains rather like beast or bird chains, and which fit into one another like pieces of a jigsaw puzzle. Such figures occur at Folkton (Yorkshire).[30]

The Norse Vikings in the mid-tenth century produced smaller-scale dramatic carvings that could have been influenced by the two styles of the local Anglian tradition. These occur, for example, at Halton, Gosforth, Weston (Plate 20(a)), Ilkley or Gainford. Norse carvings in Cumbria and Yorkshire can appear almost naked above their short kirtles and can have humped or widely-extended shoulders, such as Otley, Ilkley (Plate 20(b) and (c)), or Kirby Stephen. Sometimes such figures are shown enmeshed in interlace.

By the eleventh century, figures seem to become shorter and almost angular and all types of persons whether secular or divine seem to be treated in the same styles.

Now it may be true, as has been said, that Viking art never attempts to prolong life in an idealized form, as does classical art. Nevertheless the figures are charged with an odd vitality, and are perpetually engaged in opaque dramatic events, all of which may have been in some sense "religious". The protagonists in such events may have become as distanced from the behaviour and appearances of contemporary life as the Early Christian saints were when depicted on ninth-century English crosses. Ironically, however, it is possible that these hieratic frontal frozen figures as well as the figures in non-classical dress on Anglian carvings, could have presented an emancipation from the established tradition for the Vikings. Their impact could have been heightened not only because they were new images of a powerful religion, but because they could be translated into a contemporary idiom.

It is difficult to imagine how one could be sure whether one were supposed to be seeing a portrait or not in this early art. The "portraits" of kings on coinage at this date are not the life-like if idealized representations we expect today. Nor are they images similar to those of the emperors on Roman coins. They are in some manner, however, representatives of the ruler, and seem to be quite distinct from religious representations.

The armed figures from Sockburn or Nunburnholme could be representations of the warriors commemorated, but they need be no more like them than are some of the effigies of armed men that lie on medieval tombs. In fact, the process whereby the idea of representing in some way real people — the revival of portraiture — returns to the medieval world is difficult to chart.

Christian art developed a short-hand reference that assigned certain attributes for saints, such as a key for St Peter or a forked beard for St Paul. This distinguished them, but this is really the same principle as assigning a bird or a horse and spear to individualize Óðinn. No one living had seen these in reality, but did one "recognize" Dunstan in the figure kneeling at Christ's feet on the frontispiece to Ælfric's *Grammar*?[31]

Were some of the depictions of bishops with their skull caps, on ninth-century crosses such as Halton or Crofton, meant to call to mind specific episcopal figures, for example St Wilfrid, St Cuthbert or St Columba? It is impossible to say, but as we know from the surviving lives of such figures, they could have been presented as heroic and powerful figures to converted Vikings. St Cuthbert indeed was presented to the Vikings as an almost living menace. However, there also seems no doubt that the Vikings introduced a secularization of taste in art, as they also secularized landholdings.

The tendency to depict figures in non-classical costume had already begun before the Viking invasion, as we see in the two figures with hunting horns, their dress voluminous but short, on the cross from St Mary Bishophill Senior (Plate 7). It could be that, before the Vikings took over, it had become the custom to portray people in an appropriate, contemporary costume, and to portray events in a contemporary guise as well. We know from the funerary stele in Gotland and from the Oseberg tapestry that death and burial had developed their own dramatic iconography by the end of the eighth/beginning of the ninth century. Moreover, we have seen how Irish and Picto-Scottic art could have contributed to models and motifs. The indigenous art of the Isle of Man would seem to have had little to contribute, and the expressions of Viking figural art from the area are best considered in context of pagan religious iconography.

Werkmeister, in his discussion of Pre-Carolingian figure-styles,[32] has queried the assumption that the Christian artists of the British Isles in the seventh and eighth centuries directly confronted realistic models of high-quality Mediterranean art, which they understood as deprived of its representational qualities. I have tried to show throughout that the Vikings in their new homelands could sometimes have been confronted by representations of men in the best classical idioms. More often, however, they would have been confronted by images which had already been partly transformed into ornamental patterns. Moreover, work of high quality that had modernized classical tradition could exist in regional or even local schools.

NOTES

1. Mathews G. 1963, 1.
2. Andersson A. 1970, Fig. 47.
3. Bullough D. 1975, 223–225.
4. Andersson A. 1970, 180.
5. Graham-Campbell J. and Kydd D. 1980, Fig. 98.
6. Graham-Campbell J. and Kydd D. 1980, Fig. 46.
7. Hubert J., Porcher J., Volbach W. F. 1969, 266–7. Fig. 295.
8. Anker P. 1970, Plates 26, 27 and 86–9.
9. Bruce-Mitford R. L. S. 1978, 138–195 Figs. 136–147.
10. Collingwood W. G. 1927, Fig. 128.
11. Klindt-Jensen O. and Wilson D. M. 1966, Plate 19a.
12. Allen Romilly J. 1903, 410 Fig. 429.
13. Bailey R. N. 1980, 242–252 Fig. 78.

NOTES—*continued.*

14. Such writhing animals can be paralleled at Rothbury, Northumberland (Collingwood, 1927), Fig. 94, or Melsonby (Collingwood, 1927), Fig. 20.

15. Cramp R. J. 1978. Throughout England in the ninth century, plant-scrolls, whether trails or bushes, became more wildly entangled and lost their leaves and fruit. It is this type of scroll that the Brompton carver copies, but the plain plait panel, which is also a distinctive feature of a small Anglo-Viking school in this region, is a new device perhaps introduced with Scandinavian art.

16. Cramp 1971, 53–63.

17. The semantic development of such compounds has been explored by Jacqueline Simpson (1956). It might be significant that the so-called frith-stools — bishop's seats — in sites which have a right of sanctuary at Hexham, Beverley and Durham (although here no seat has survived) are all in the Northern Danelaw. The Scandinavian heathens may have had a special respect for such seats, and the right of sanctuary which surrounded them.

18. James Graham-Campbell *Viking Artefacts: A Select Catalogue* (London, 1980) places them in his "religious" section (*see* Nos. 520 and 521). *See also* Birgitte Arrhenius 1961, "Vikingatida miniatyren" *Tor* 7. 139-64.

19. Hills C. 1980, 52–54 and Plate VIII.

20. Per Gjaerder 1964, 35. 95–114.

21. Collingwood 1927, Fig. 55 and Fig. 32.

22. Lang J. T. 1973, 16–25, Figs. 19–20.

23. This cross has been most fully discussed by Binns (1956) "Tenth Century Carvings from Yorkshire and the Jellinge Style". Also by Pattison I. R. 1973, 226 and Lang J. T. 1977, 75–94.

24. Kemp Malone 1949.

25. For Breedon and Bakewell, *see* Cramp R. J. 1977, Plates 201c, and 223c. The Gokstad strap-mounts could be derived from English prototypes (*see* Graham-Campbell 1980, Fig. 489 and pp. 144-145), but they may be independently derived from Eastern European sources.

26. Graham-Campbell 1980, Plate 1a/b.

27. The possible Valkyrie figures, wearing cut-away cloaks and holding horns, occur on Gotlandic picture stones, and as small metal figurines (*see* Graham-Campbell 1980, Figs. 154-5). There are similar female figures on opposing faces of the Gosforth Cross, or where one represents Signy ministering to the bound god Loki, and the other either Mary the Mother of God or Mary Magdalen, standing below the crucified cross. *See* Bailey R. 1980, Fig. 23 and pp. 125–131.

28. W. Holmqvist's supposition of Celtic influence for this type of dress (Holmqvist 1960, 101-27) is difficult to reconcile with the long tradition of this dress in Scandinavia. However, it is not a dress type found in Vendel art, and it could have been derived from insular sources at the time of the early raids.

29. Henry F. 1967, Plates 86 and 87.

30. Collingwood W. G. 1927, Fig. 140.

31. Bodleian MS. Auct. Fig. IV 32. Kendrick T. D. 1949, Plate I.

32. Werkmeister 1949, 189.

STYLISTIC ASPECTS OF THE FRANKS CASKET

Leslie Webster

Assistant Keeper, Medieval and Later Antiquities, British Museum

THE FRANKS CASKET holds a unique place in the field of Anglo-Saxon studies. Its enigmatic character has exercised a fascination upon generations of runologists, linguists, iconographers, mythologists and students of Old English literature since its discovery in the nineteenth century. Much that is of value, and a sizeable amount that is not, has been written on the nature and content of the inscriptions, and on the iconography of the complex scenes which decorate the lid and four sides of the box. That scholarly attention should be concentrated on these particular aspects is scarcely surprising in view of the wide field for speculation and debate offered by the linguistic and iconographic aspects of the Casket. However, it is remarkable that in more than a hundred years of research on it, only a handful of studies have paid more than a passing glance to the Casket's quite distinctive stylistic attributes. Indeed, this is all the more surprising in view of the diagnostic qualities of the style, which so clearly offer scope in determining the date and provenance of the Casket. The important discussions of Dalton and Baldwin Brown, though still valuable, are now 50 years out of date;[1] while only few of the many studies published since the Second World War have devoted any attention to these stylistic aspects. None has provided a definitive analysis of the evidence. Beckwith's discussion is disappointingly general, conventional and short; and Amy L. Vandersall's recent bold attempt to date the Casket to *c.* A.D. 1000 on art-historical grounds is achieved only at the expense of ignoring the facts.[2]

It seems appropriate, therefore, to begin to set the record straight with a close examination of the stylistic character of the Casket, and on the basis of this, to attempt a general statement about the Casket's chronological and cultural content. Though the discussion below at times strays into the field of iconography, I have deliberately excluded any detailed discussion of the narrative content and programme of the box, which I hope to discuss more fully in a future study. Nor do I intend to give more than a summary physical description of the Casket and the history here. The reader will find full and accurate descriptions in the work of A. S. Napier, O. M. Dalton and G. Baldwin Brown; a full bibliography up to 1959 is given by H. Marquand, while R. I. Page and A. Vandersall's publications give references to the work that has appeared since.[3]

The Franks Casket is a rectangular box of cetacean bone, measuring 23 x 13 x 19 cm (Plate 21). It is constructed of four side panels pegged by dowels into four corner pieces. The base plates, of which one survives, were slotted into grooves at the bottom of the walls, and the Casket seems to have stood upon four low feet. From the lid, only one decorative panel now survives; probably, since it carried the handle, it was the principal element in the lid. The remaining plain panels are almost certainly replacements. On the outside of the box, other scars left by such fittings as the lock, the hasps, and hinges are evident; internally, there are signs of a number of crude repairs. It was discovered in private hands at Auzon in France in the early nineteenth century, but had most probably reached France at some point in the medieval period — perhaps, indeed, not long after its manufacture. The church of St Julien at Brioude, about ten miles south of Auzon, was a well-known church of pilgrimage from the early Middle Ages, and lay directly on the route from England to Rome. With the exception of the right-hand end, which seems to have become separated from the Casket at a fairly early stage after its discovery, and is now in the Bargello Museum in Florence, the Casket was purchased in Paris by Sir Augustus Franks in 1860, and subsequently presented by him to the British Museum in 1867.[4]

The five decorated panels, with the exception of that on the lid, are all surrounded by accompanying Old English texts in runes and (in one section) a Latin text in insular script and runes (Plates 22–26). Several of the panels also carry brief labels as a further aid to identification. Three of these panels can be identified with certainty. The front shows, on the left, a composite scene from the tale of Weland the Smith, and on the right, the Adoration of the Magi (Plate 22). The left hand end depicts the discovery of Romulus and Remus nurtured by the wolf (Plate 23); and the back, the only panel with a double register, shows scenes from the sack of Jerusalem by Titus in A.D. 70 (Plate 25). Various identifications have been proposed for the lid panel (Plate 26) and the right-hand end (Plate 24). Though none has found general acceptance, most scholars concur in thinking the subjects of these panels are Germanic in origin. The lid may depict an otherwise unknown scene from a lost Egil legend, since it contains an archer labelled *ÆGILI*, an Old English name possibly related to the Old Norse *Egill*.[5] The entire right-hand end, however, which has a partly encoded inscription and a particularly strange iconography, presents problems of interpretation which have so far proved intractable.[6]

All the panels, text and narrative scenes alike, are carved in low relief, with a vigorous density of incident. The treatment is simplified, no doubt in part because of the coarseness of the medium, but it is by no means lacking in artistic skill. It has all the vivacity and excitement, as well as the lapses of understanding, of a craftsman adapting himself to a new and stimulating theme — in this case, the adaptation of late Antique subjects and models to a native Anglo-Saxon taste and, even more important, the transposition of Germanic themes into an ultimately classical framework.

The Adoration of the Magi, Romulus and Remus and the Sack of Jerusalem panels all, of course, derive from late Antique and early Christian sources. It has long been recognized that a likely general source for this particular combination could have been an illustrated world-chronicle, such as the *Scaliger Barbarus*, an eighth-century Latin translation of an Alexandrian original;[7] such manuscripts are known to have reached England as early as the seventh century. The indirect influence of late Antique sarcophagus art, which played an important part in the development of narrative manuscript illumination in the west can also be traced in the busy sculptural techniques and strong narrative emphasis; for instance, in the apparent separation of individual episodes or stages of narrative in one panel by specific visual devices, as in the use of foliage in the Weland scene.[8] Late Antique influence is particularly marked in the back panel, where the use of a double register is strikingly reminiscent of the conventions of late Roman sarcophagi. The indirect influence of late Roman triumphal art may also, not surprisingly, be discerned in this scene.[9]

However, in some ways, the most classical — and most surprising — thing about the Casket is not its iconography, or its style, but its very *form*. There can be little doubt that the construction and decorative plan of the Franks Casket derive from a splendid late Antique carved ivory box of the sort now represented by the two well-known reliquary caskets from Brescia in Italy and Pola in Jugoslavia.[10]

The Brescia Casket, which dates to *c.* A.D. 400, is indeed strikingly similar in form, proportion and method of construction.[11] (Plate 26(a)). Its ivory panels are also fitted by means of tenons into four corner posts, and it carries evidence of a very similar arrangement of metal fittings. But most striking of all is the common use of a central subject or subjects on each side, surrounded by a border which forms a kind of commentary on the central scene. On the Brescia Casket this is expressed pictorially, not in written form. The Franks Casket, like the Brescia Casket, also possibly had only two panels in the lid. The narrative style of the Brescia Casket, with its many protagonists and episodic divisions, is also close in temper to the Franks Casket, forming a bridge between the art of the sarcophagi and the northern craftsmen. Just how different the Franks Casket is from native Anglo-Saxon work can be seen when it is compared to the surviving seventh-century Germanic boxes and bone carving in general. On boxes such as those from Caistor-by-Norwich urn XII, Weilbach, grave 129, Nusplingen grave 121 and Köln–Junkersdorf grave 125, the technique consists of fixing the simply-tooled bone strips and plaques to a wooden base.[12] Proportions, form and layout are also quite different. There can be little doubt that the Franks Casket is modelled on another pattern altogether. It is indeed hard to avoid the conclusion that, whatever manuscript sources were available to the carver of the Franks Casket, he also had direct knowledge of some fine late Antique ivory box. Such a box, a reliquary perhaps, could very well have been brought back to England as a gift from Rome, like the textiles, manuscripts and paintings we know were imported into Northumbria by Wilfrid, Benedict Biscop and Ceolfrith.

Yet despite these many clear intimations of a classical ideal underlying the very concept of the Casket, the decoration itself is by no means devoid of explicitly insular elements. But it is as discreetly blended into a classical framework as the insular ornament in the Canon Table decoration of the *Codex Amiatinus*, copied at Wearmouth/Jarrow in the 690s from a sixth-century Cassiodoran manuscript, is incorporated into an otherwise very faithful copy of its Italian model.[13]

It is this insular decoration that I now propose to examine in detail; and for convenience, I have grouped it into six separate categories: quadrupeds, birds, human figures, plants, architecture and lettering.

First of all, the various forms of quadruped on the Casket present certain distinctive features (Figure 1). The small crouched beasts from the four corners of the front, left- and right-hand panels both typify some of the main characteristics of the carver's insular stylistic vocabulary and invite specific comparisons with well-dated Northumbrian manuscripts. Two varieties of this creature exist: a forward-crouching animal, from the right-hand end only, and its backward-turned counterpart, whose long jaws, terminating in a lobe, are clamped across his body. Both have well-arched trunks, roundish foreheads, sharp ears, and strongly delineated muzzle- and jaw-lines. In all this, as Kendrick stressed, they strongly recall in attitude the denizens of the crouching animal friezes from the Book of Durrow (made *c.* A.D. 670) and some of its successors (Figure 2, a).[14] Indeed, the beasts look back even beyond the Book of Durrow to the back-biting, long-jawed formula of

Figure 1 (a–g)   Quadrupeds from the Franks Casket.

the Style II animals, where the figure-of-eight curve of the back-biting Franks Casket beast has its ultimate origin.[15] Particularly close parallels exist in a gospel book written and illuminated at Lindisfarne in the late seventh or early eighth centuries and now at Corpus Christi College, Cambridge, MS 197B[16] (Figure 2, b). Here the same pose and flattened, pointed ears can be seen; while in another Lindisfarne manuscript of the same date, Durham Cathedral MS A.11.17,[17] (Figure 2, c) a back-biter gnaws at its trunk with the same long, lobed snout. All the other quadrupeds on the Casket, though very different from the small beasts just described, share the same pointed ears —

Figure 2 (a–c)   Comparative quadrupeds.

either pricked forward or, more usually, flattened back — and the same trick of delineating the muzzle and jaws. Though none of the other Franks Casket quadrupeds are so closely paralleled in manuscripts, the outlined jaw and muzzle is a distinctive characteristic of seventh- and eighth-century Northumbrian manuscripts. The pose of the horse on the enigmatic right-hand end (Fig. 1, a) also has certain mannerisms which seem related to the Northumbrian conventions of depicting large-scale quadrupeds, as, for instance, in the Luke symbols in the Book of Durrow and in the Echternach Gospels (Plate 27).[18] The relatively naturalistic stance of these creatures, the flattened-back ears, and the emphasis of musculature at haunch and foreleg are surely related to the horse on the Casket.

Many of the distinctive features of the quadrupeds are also to be observed in the birds on the Franks Casket (Figure 3, a–f). In the same way that the muzzles of the quadrupeds

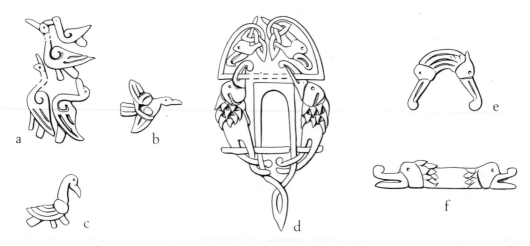

Figure 3 (a–f) Bird motifs from the Franks Casket.

are delineated, the face and beak-junction in the birds are, again, sharply defined, and the heads themselves all have the same round outline. Some of the birds, like those surrounding the Ark in the Temple scene on the back, or the enigmatic two-headed creatures on the lid, also have long knobbed raptorial beaks very similar to the lobed snout of the corner beasts (Figure 3, d, e). Again such beaks are widespread in Northumbrian manuscripts of the seventh and eighth centuries. The Corpus Christi MS 197B, for instance, contains birds with these beaks, and scaly feathers just like those flanking the Ark on the back panel[19] (Figure 4, c). This type, with scaly feathers and long beaks, is

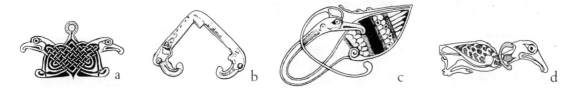

Figure 4 (a–d) Comparative bird motifs

especially common in the Lindisfarne Gospels themselves, where disembodied, interlacing birds' heads with short curved beaks like those *above* the Ark, can also be found (Figure 4, d, a). A distant echo of this can be seen on the late seventh-century Northumbrian metalwork mounts on the binding of the St Victor Codex at Fulda which once belonged to St Boniface, the Anglo-Saxon early eighth-century missionary[20] (Figure 4, b). The way on which these twin heads, again with those distinctive knobbed beaks, are yoked together also recalls the double-headed bird symbol over the woman on the lid of the Casket (Figure 3, e). This curving, two-headed device is strongly reminiscent of similar sixth- and seventh-century motifs used in Germanic jewellery and which may have held some protective function.[21] Beneath her feet lies another equally obscure symbol which I have somewhat arbitrarily chosen to classify as bird rather than beast on the absence of ears, its ruffs of scaly feathers and possibly its beaks (Figure 3, f). However, a very close parallel to this exists in the manuscript known as the Durham Cassiodorus, which was written perhaps at Jarrow around A.D. 750[22] (Plate 28). Here the composite David/Christ Triumphant is depicted treading on a very similar creature, presumably intended as a version of the treading of the beasts in Psalm 90, Verse 13, as Dr. Bailey has recently argued.[23] This parallel might suggest that the Franks Casket twin-headed creature is also a symbol of evil, in some sort of opposition to the apparently protective symbol over the woman's head.

Turning to the other birds on the Casket, the links with Northumbrian sources continue to multiply. The ducks and swans on the front panel and the bird in flight on the right-hand end form a close group (Figure 3, a–c). All have round heads, short beaks, and wings with straight, stubby feathers, scrolled at the junction of wing and body. Close cousins in stone occur on the well-known early eighth-century cross-shaft at Aberlady, East Lothian, an area under Northumbrian control in the seventh or early eighth centuries[24] (Plate 29). A similar bird head from a stone frieze dating to the same period was found in Professor Cramp's excavations at Jarrow.[25] The scroll at the head of the wings may, again, be traced in Northumbrian late seventh- and early eighth-century manuscripts, such as the Corpus Christi Gospel book, MS 197B (f. 2), the Salaberga Psalter (f. 2) and the Cologne *Collectio Canonum* (f. 1)[26] (Figure 4, c, d).

The stylistic treatment of the human figure on the Casket needs to be considered against wider questions of its iconography, which lie beyond the scope of the present study. And since nothing with such an ambitious narrative programme survives again in Anglo-Saxon art until the tenth century, it is difficult to find adequate parallels for the kind of active groups of figures we see here. However, certain general observations, and one or two specific suggestions, are worth making here. First of all, whatever the very divergent sources of the scenes on the Casket, with consequent effect upon details of clothing and gestures, the overall treatment of human form is fairly homogeneous. In particular the schematic, strongly-corrugated drapery, and bonnet-like hairstyles are common to "antique" and "Germanic" themes, as they appear on the Casket. A very similar linear schematization of draperies into parallel ridges is, again, a characteristic of early Northumbrian manuscripts, for instance, the *Codex Amiatinus* (f. 796v)[27] and the Durham Cassiodorus (f. 81v and f. 172v) (Plate 28), as well as those of the Lindisfarne group.[28] It is also a marked feature of St Cuthbert's coffin (buried on Lindisfarne, A.D. 698), where the angels and apostles also exhibit the same distinctive bonnet-like coiffure.[29] If this is a local, or at least an insular, feature, and not merely the carver's response to the difficulties of the medium, it is also appropriate to note here one or two other possible local or at least non-Mediterranean aspects of the figural treatment.

The third figure in the Weland scene, usually seen as a separate manifestation of Beadohild *en route* to her fate, carries a round-bellied traveller's flask on a cord, which has good parallels from seventh-century Frankish and Alamannic contexts and which was doubtless a type widespread in Germanic Europe.[30] Another example is carried by one of the refugees from Jerusalem on the back panel. Next to him stands another figure with a rectangular purse-like object hanging from his neck. Is this meant for a priest's breastplate, or could the carver have reinterpreted it as an insular type of book-satchel or portable reliquary?[31] The most tempting suggestion of this kind concerns the helmets, which appear on the lid, the right-hand end and the back panel. All three are very similar and appear to show a fairly elaborate parade helmet with a nasal, a crest and cheek and neck guards. On the lid, there seems to be some attempt to distinguish neck and cheek flaps by means of a scored line. Now it is perfectly possible that these helmets may represent late Roman parade helmets, as depicted in late antique sources.[32] This would be entirely appropriate in the Jerusalem scene, where the figure wearing the helmet is presumably the Roman general (later emperor) Titus, named in the caption above as fighting with the Jews. However, if the common assumption is correct, namely, that the scenes on the lid and on the right-hand end derive from Germanic legend, then we may consider an alternative: that these helmets are based on a type current in the late sixth- and seventh-century Anglo-Saxon England, Sweden and Norway, and best exemplified by the well-known example from Sutton Hoo.[33] Based ultimately on the late Roman parade helmets, they are quite different from the continental Germanic *spangenhelm*.[34] This is presumably the kind of helmet an Anglo-Saxon would have had in mind, whether he was describing Beowulf's armour,[35] or carving warriors on the

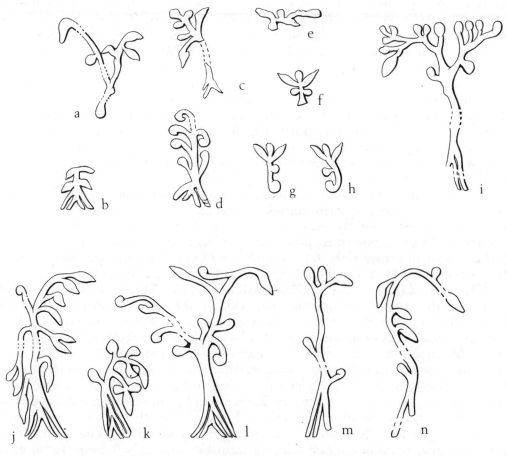

Figure 5 (a–n) Plant motifs from the Franks Casket.

Franks Casket. The Swedish helmets survived well into the second half of the seventh century, and could equally well have done so in England.

Two further aspects deserve brief consideration. The foliage appears in abundance on the Romulus panel, to a lesser extent on the ambiguous right-hand panel, and as sprigs on the front (Figure 5, a–n). Simplified as it is, the combination of round buds or berries and oval or pointed leaves, and particularly of triple clusters of bud and leaf combination, is a characteristic of Northumbrian stone sculpture, though of course more elaborate in design and execution.[36] The same sinuous stems with simple pointed leaves can be seen in the surviving canon tables of a fragmentary gospel book now in the Cathedral Treasury at Maeseyck in Belgium (e.g. ff. 5, 5v and 4v).[37] The gospels date to the early eighth century and may have emanated from Wilfrid's scriptorium at York. Very similar trees with undulating stems, knobbed tendrils and drooping triple leaf clusters, can also be seen in some of the initials in a psalter now at Stuttgart, a mid-eighth century manuscript written by an Anglo-Saxon at a continental centre.[38] (Figure 6, b). Two other manuscripts of similar date also contain related foliage elements: the Vespasian Psalter, a Canterbury product dated to the second quarter of the eighth century, and the Leningrad Bede, a copy of Bede's *Historia Ecclesiastica* written in the Wearmouth/Jarrow scriptorium of 746, ten years after Bede's death (e.g. f. 3v) (Figure 6, a).[39] Again, the ultimate source of this foliage must be Mediterranean, but the conventional treatment is wholly insular, with a strong Northumbrian bias.

a   b

Figure 6 (a–b) Comparative plant motifs.

The impression offered by the ornament of the Casket examined so far is also confirmed by the architectural elements, where they can be paralleled. Whilst the elaborate columnar arches on front, back and lid obviously have their ultimate source in late antique models, and in the case of the Adoration and Jerusalem scenes were perhaps even copied directly from Mediterranean examplars, their closest counterparts in Anglo-Saxon art are again to be found in the canon tables of the *Codex Amiatinus* (f. IV,v and f. 799), and in the canon tables of the Lindisfarne Gospels themselves. There, like the arch on the lid of the Franks Casket, columns embellished with interlace can also be seen (e.g., f. 13v, f. 15v). A plain two-strand interlace, identical to those on the lid's arch column, also appears on the arches themselves in the *Codex Amiatinus* (f. IV,v).[40] (This is perhaps also the place to mention the similar two-strand interlace which originally formed a continuous border round each panel. The best Anglo-Saxon parallel to such a frame may be found in the interlaced border on the cover of the Stonyhurst Gospel of St John, which was found in St Cuthbert's coffin at his translation in 1104, and was presumably buried with him in 698.[41]) The correspondences with the architectural elements here are of a collateral rather than direct nature, however; in particular, the Casket's arches have more substance, more architectonic quality than the two-dimensional images of the manuscripts.

It seems probable that the common architectural style reflects two separate developments from various late Antique models. The fluted columns of the arch that frames the Good Shepherd on the front of the Brescia Casket, for instance, have the same stepped bases, but more important, the same trick of placing a horizontal moulding half-way up, that appears on the framing of the Virgin and Child on the Franks Casket and, in a more elaborate version, on the Jerusalem panel.[42] The strong vertical ribbing on the Franks Casket's front and back panel columns is also presumably intended to represent the fluting of columns such as are seen on the Brescia Casket. It seems indeed very likely that these tricks were taken over from a plastic model such as a carved ivory, and not from the flattened images of a manuscript. More elaborate versions of these arches with stepped columns also occur in a later eighth-century Canterbury manuscript (British Library MS Royal 1. E.VI),[43] but this formula is evidently Northumbrian in origin.

Finally, whatever the models for the scene in the back panels of the Franks Casket — direct Mediterranean sources or local copy — there is certainly no doubt that the accompanying inscription was copied directly from a local Northumbrian exemplar. This is self-evidently true of the Old English runes, of course, but it is equally striking when the one brief excursion into Latin and non-runic script is considered (Plate 30). Most of the forms of these letters are insular majuscule, except for C, G and T, which are capitals. The carver has, moreover, sought very carefully to distinguish at various points the actual *ductus*, for example, in *u, a, n* and *m*. Manuscript, as opposed to epigraphic, influence is therefore strong, and it is not surprising to find that this mixture of majuscule and capitals, as well as the forms of the letters, seems closest to the kind of display script of the monogram pages of the Lindisfarne group of manuscripts.[44] Dr. Elisabeth Okasha would also localize this part of the inscription in the early eighth century, on epigraphic grounds.[45]

It now remains to examine briefly some of the broader reasons why this extraordinary box should have been made at such a time and place. Clearly the Casket, with its heterogeneous content, its ambitious programme and its acquaintance both direct and indirect with late antique and early medieval Mediterranean as well as native sources, must be the product of a major Northumbrian intellectual centre.

Northumbria was, around 700, not only still politically strong after a century of expansion, but an intellectual and artistic powerhouse. This was the age of Bede himself, of St Wilfrid, and of the great Abbots of Jarrow and Monkwearmouth, Benedict Biscop and Ceolfrith, who founded and enriched these libraries of outstanding scope and quality. Amongst many other gifts, Ceolfrith brought the great Cassiodoran bible known as *Codex Grandior* from Italy for his libraries at Jarrow and Monkwearmouth. There its format and illustrations were used as a model when three pandects of the newer Vulgate translation were commissioned by Ceolfrith for the monasteries. One of these three pandects, the *Codex Amiatinus* already referred to, still survives complete; its decoration in the first gathering of the manuscript is so close in spirit to its Italian model that it was thought until recently by many scholars to have been the work of an Italian or Byzantine artist.[46] Ceolfrith is also recorded as having given a cosmographical codex which had been brought from Rome by Benedict Biscop to King Aldfrith of Northumbria in exchange for eight hides of land.[47] Mention has already been made of the widely-accepted theory that a cosmographical source underlies in part the narrative programme of the Casket. Indeed, the unfinished *Scaliger Barbarus* was to have contained illustrations for the capture of Jerusalem and the story of Romulus, as its captioned empty spaces for the pictures show. Interestingly enough, it contains some vestiges of insular style in its ornament, and was written at Corbie, an area of considerable insular influence.[48] The king's role here is not insignificant, since it makes clear that secular patrons also existed for works of this kind. In view of the mixed content, it is just as likely that the Casket was produced for a secular owner as for an ecclesiastical purpose; the themes could indeed as well refer to the life of the person who commissioned it.

Before Ceolfrith, Benedict Biscop made six journeys to Rome, bringing back not only a host of treasures for his church at Jarrow but foreign workmen, glaziers and jewellers to beautify and civilize the desolate spot. At Hexham, Ripon and York, St Wilfrid had built and furnished churches of Roman magnificence. Eddius, Wilfrid's biographer, compared Ripon at its consecration to Solomon's temple, and described the great church at Hexham as without parallel north of the Alps.[49] Even allowing for a certain natural hyperbole in the descriptions, it is evident that the new stone churches of the region were extraordinary innovations in a society accustomed to build only in wood. Such buildings, with all their imported fittings, were also accessible to a wide audience. This was equally true of other forms of Mediterranean culture. Bede tells how Adamnan's account of the Holy Places was presented by the author to King Aldfrith and circulated by the king for lesser folk to read.[50] Benedict Biscop's famous painted panels, such as those with parallel scenes from Old and New Testaments, which he brought back to Jarrow after his last visit to Rome in 686, were displayed and used as a preaching vehicle in the church itself for all to see.[51] Such imports must have been, for many, their first contact with the graphic art of the classical tradition. The heady impact on native tradition of all these new ideas and forms — perhaps among them a reliquary casket like that surviving at Brescia — is readily exemplified not only by the Franks Casket's style and form but in the development of narrative art itself into new directions.

For finally, it is the intellectual temper of the Casket which confirms its placing in time and space. It is a true original, a remarkable attempt at transposing Germanic themes into a classical framework and in adapting late antique subjects to a native style. There is even some possibility that the two sets of narratives may have been intended to counterbalance each other: that the Germanic motifs form a commentary upon the other subjects in a way similar to that in which Old Testament events were interpreted as forerunners of New Testament subjects. On the front panel, for instance, the theme of redemption through a heroic birth is latent in both the scenes, a deliberate parallel is implied between the birth of Christ and the birth of Beadohild's son by Weland, the hero Widia.[52]

Much later, Anglo-Saxon and Viking sculptors were to explore these parallel themes on some of the great stone crosses of the area, as at Gosforth, Cumbria, where the Crucifixion and Ragnarök stand side by side.[53] Even though this sort of thing later becomes more common, one should not underestimate the importance of the Franks Casket's particular brand of synthesis.

The Casket is also the first surviving Anglo-Saxon attempt at extended narrative art. Whatever of wood or bone or textile in the native tradition may have vanished, thereby distorting the record, the Casket yet remains a remarkable fusion of cultures. And, so far from being a crude aping of Mediterranean sophistication, as has occasionally been suggested,[54] the confidence and exuberance of its design and execution indicate both intellectual vigour and great technical skill. The particular combination of scholarship and artistic vitality which existed in Northumbria in the years around 700 was the ideal seed bed for such a creation.

To sum up: only in such a milieu does it seem likely that the Franks Casket could have received the specific combination of influences seen in it. The Casket exhibits a dependence on late antique sources, transmitted through Mediterranean manuscripts and other portable media to Northumbria; it is indeed quite possible that a late antique casket may have served as a direct model at least for form and layout. Yet, as the elements of decoration reviewed in this paper show, the Casket's Northumbrian background is clearly revealed in its stylistic treatment. With date and provenance thus securely fixed on art-historical as well as linguistic grounds, the many remaining problems of the Casket may be more confidently confronted.

NOTES

1. Dalton 1909, cat. no. 30, 27-32. Baldwin Brown 1930, 18-51.
2. Beckwith 1972, cat. no. 1, 117 and 13-18. Vandersall 1972, 9-26. The conventional dating of the Casket has also recently been questioned by Professor Frank in her penetrating review of Becker, 1973 (*Speculum* 52, no. 1, pp. 120-122). Vandersall 1975, a fresh attempt at identifying a scene from an *Achilleid* in the lid has not been available to me.
3. Napier 1900, 362-381. Marquardt 1961, 10-16. Page 1973, 174-182, 188-9. Vandersall 1975, 24.
4. British Museum, Department of Medieval and Later Antiquities, reg. no. M&LA 1867, 1-20, 1.
5. Page 1973, 180.
6. Page 1973, 180-2.
7. Paris, Bibl. Nat. lat. 4884: see Lowe 1950, cat. no. 560.
8. Sprigs of foliage are used to separate what appear to be three distinct episodes in this composite scene: Weland presenting a skull-cup to Beadohild or her mother; a second woman, perhaps Beadohild again; and a bird-catcher, possibly Egill, Weland's brother.
9. *See*, for instance, Dinkler 1979, figs. 53 and 56; and Weitzmann 1979, cat. nos. 372, 373 and 58, Gaehde 1974, 380, pls. 92 and 100, and Gaehde 1975, 384-6 and pls. 100-102.
10. Volbach 1976, cat. no. 107, pp. 77-78 and pl. 57, and cat. no. 120, 85, pl. 64. Kollwitz 1033.
11. Kollwitz 1933, texttafel I (b).
12. Caistor: Myres and Green 1973, pls. XX, XXI. Weilbach: Schoppa 1953, 44-50. pls. 8 and 9. Nüsplingen: *Fundber aus Schwäben* 1938-51, 125. Köln-Junkersdorf: La Baume 1967, 78-9, p. 7.
13. Florence, Biblioteca Medicea Laurenziana MS Amiatinus 1: Alexander 1978, cat. no. 7, 34. Bruce-Mitford 1969, fig. 2.
14. Kendrick 1938, 125.
15. E.g. Speake 1980. fig. 8a, c, d, f, g and h; fig. 9a, b, c, g and h; fig. 10a.
16. f2: Alexander 1978, cat. no. 12, 44.
17. f2: Alexander 1978, cat. no. 10, 40-42.
18. Paris, Bibl. Nat. lat. 9389, f. 115v: Alexander 1978, cat. no. 11, pl. 55, Dublin, Trinity College MS A 4, 5 (57), f. 124v: Alexander 1978, cat. no. 6, pl. 15.
19. Alexander 1973, pl. 49.
20. Wilson 1961, 199 ff.
21. E.g. Speake 1970, 11: Vierck 1967, 116.

NOTES—*continued*

22. Durham Cathedral Library MS B.11.30: Alexander 1978, cat. no. 17, 46, pl. 75.
23. Bailey 1978, 11.
24. Bruce-Mitford 1960, 255, pl. 52 (c).
25. Bruce-Mitford 1969, pl. XIX (1).
26. Alexander 1978, cat. nos. 12, 14 and 13, pls. 69, 64 and 60.
27. Bruce-Mitford 1969, pls. XIII and XIV.
28. Bailey 1978, pls. 1 and 2.
29. Kitzinger 1956, 280, pls. VII–X.
30. E.g. Paulsen and Schach-Dörges 1972, 80–86, figs. 54, 56 and 59: Doppelfeld and Pirling 1966, 102.
31. E.g. Waterer 1968, 70–82, pls. IV–VII.
32. E.g. Klumbach 1973, *passim*.
33. Bruce-Mitford 1978, figs. 104, 105, 158 and 159. Note also contemporary depictions of such helmets in figs. 157 and 164 (e).
34. E.g. Doppelfeld and Pirling 1966, plates on 47, 49 and 69.
35. *See* Cramp 1957, 60–63.
36. E.g. Kendrick 1938, pls. XLVII (1) and L.
37. Maeseyck, Church of St Catherine, Trésor, s.n.: Alexander 1978, cat. no. 22, pls. 91, 90 and 95.
38. Stuttgart, Württembergisches Landesbibliothek, Cod. Bibl. 2°12, f. 1, f. 32, f. 63: Alexander 1978, cat. no. 28, pls. 140–142.
39. Alexander 1978, cat. no. 19, pl. 83; for British Library Cotton Vespasian A.1., f. 30v, *see* Alexander 1978, cat. no. 29, pl. 146.
40. Bruce-Mitford 1969, pls. XVII, VI.
41. Powell 1956, 362–374, pl. XXIII.
42. Kollwitz 1933, Tafelmappe, pl. 2.
43. Alexander 1978, cat. no. 32, pl. 163.
44. E.g. The Lindisfarne Gospels, f. 3, f. 45. Alexander 1978, pls. 137, 45.
45. Okasha 1971, 50–55.
46. E.g. Nordhagen 1976, 138–145, figs. 1–6.
47. Bede, *Hist. Abb.*, cap. 15.
48. Lowe 1950, cat. no. 560.
49. Eddius Stephanus; *Vita Wilfridi*, cap. 17 and cap. 22.
50. Bede, *Hist. Eccles.*, Book 5, cap. 15.
51. Bede, *Hist. Abb.*, cap. 9. *See also* the account of paintings brought back to Wearmouth after Benedict's fifth visit to Rome (*ibid.*, cap. 5).
52. The same theme is given prominence in *Deor*, where Widia's birth is also presented as the triumph of good over evil: Meyvaert 1979, 63–77.
52. Bailey 1980, 101–142.
54. Kendrick 1938, 124; "The work is both arid and incompetent".

VIKING SILVER HOARDS: AN INTRODUCTION

James Graham-Campbell

Lecturer in Medieval Archaeology, Dept. of History, University College, London

SNORRI'S *Heimskringla* records a tenth-century episode, entitled "Of the Icelanders and Eyvind Skaldaspiller", that makes a particularly apposite introduction to a general survey of the use of silver in the Viking Age. He writes that:

> Eyvind composed a poem about the people of Iceland, for which they rewarded him by each bonde giving him three silver pennies, of full weight and white in the fracture. And when the silver was brought together at the General Thing, the people resolved to have it purified, and made into a shoulder-pin, and after the workmanship of the silver was paid, the shoulder-pin weighed some fifty marks. This they sent to Eyvind: but Eyvind had the shoulder-pin broken into pieces, and with the silver he bought a farmstead for himself.

Professor Peter Foote, as editor of this translation, adds by way of a final comment to this passage that "the shoulder-pin was used to secure a cloak. One weighing fifty marks (twenty-five pounds) was obviously better spent on a farm".[1] This rather dry observation apart, the story of Eyvind's reward can be probed somewhat further, for whether or not it is true in detail (and it must be remembered that it exists for us only in a version recorded some 250 years after the events are supposed to have taken place), it can be shown to summarize conveniently many of the Vikings' attitudes to silver.

First, it might be noted that the silver is said to have been collected together in the form of coins, although no coins were minted in Iceland during the Viking Age. This was, however, the normal form in which the Vikings obtained the greater part of their silver supply, whether from western Europe or from the Near East. The coins are specified as having been "of full weight and white in the fracture", demonstrating a concern for the quality of the silver, which is reflected archaeologically in the nicking, slicing, and pecking that is to be observed on many silver coins, ingots and ornaments in Viking-Age hoards.

Second, the Icelanders thought it more appropriate that Eyvind's reward, as a great poet, should take the form of a large brooch rather than a bag of coins — a brooch that he would be able to wear as a visible symbol of his fame. The weight given by Snorri for the silver of the brooch (after an unspecified amount had been deducted to pay the craftsman) is undoubtedly an exaggeration, perhaps by a factor of ten. The heaviest examples of the largest type of Scandinavian brooch known from the Viking Age cannot have weighed more than about two pounds of silver — the so-called "thistle-brooches" of tenth-century date (Plate 31).[2] If there was silver left over from the manufacture of the brooch, doubtless Eyvind received it in the form of the coins themselves, or cast into ingots.

Finally, it can be seen how Eyvind, his reputation in any case secure from his poetry, dispensed with his prestigious gift, by cutting it up and using as many of the silver pieces as was necessary to make up the price of the farm that he wished to buy. The evidence for the use of silver in Iceland in this manner during the Viking Age is contained in a number of mixed hoards.[3] In brief, therefore, to make a silver ornament, coins were collected together, melted down in crucibles, and then cast and fashioned by a jeweller. But, however costly the result, the ornament was ultimately no more than a large lump of silver bullion, to be cut into pieces and weighed out when required in a balance, such as those known from Scandinavian Viking-Age burials and towns.[4]

A description by the Arab traveller, Ibn Fadlan, who met a party of northern merchants on the River Volga in the early tenth century, provides a contemporary witness to substantiate this picture of Viking attitudes to silver. His eye-witness report states that:

> Each woman carries on her bosom a container made of iron, silver, copper, or gold — its size and substance depending on her man's wealth . . . Round her neck she wears gold or silver rings; when a man amasses 10,000 dirhams he makes his wife one gold ring; when he has 20,000 he makes two; and so the woman gets a new ring for every 10,000 dirhams her husband acquires, and often a woman has many of these rings.[4a]

The wearing of rings and ornaments of silver and gold was not in fact confined to women, as indicated by the story of Eyvind's brooch. It is hard to imagine how the massive silver "thistle-brooches", found in the areas of Norse settlement in the British Isles (whence the fashion spread to Scandinavia),[5] could have served other than to fasten men's heavy cloaks of fleece or fur, given their size and weight, but they do show clear evidence of wear. Even so, one must suppose that they would have been worn only to impress on special occasions, given the spectacular, but unwieldy, length of their pins (up to 22 inches), as can be seen from Plate 31.

In addition, it must be remembered that the giving of rings was a traditional method in Germanic society by which a king might reward his retainers. Some surviving rings are, again, of such size and weight as to suggest that they were made to be worn by men, such as the largest known gold neck-ring, found in 1977 at Tissø, Sjælland, Denmark, with a diameter of 14 inches and an original weight of over four pounds.[6]

Thus, silver coins, obtained by loot, ransom or trade, were regularly melted down to make ornaments both for men and for women, although some coins were themselves occasionally turned into pieces of jewellery.[7] Ostentatious display was the norm, and silver ornaments served as the visible sign of a successful Viking and his lady; but as necessity arose or dictated, ornaments might be cut up to serve his mercantile interests, for coins as such were of limited use in a native economy that only gradually learned to use counted money during the Viking Age.

Despite the many silver ornaments that survive from this period, it is important to note that it is unusual to find much in the way of plain silver and gold in pagan Viking graves. Reasons for this could have included a wish to avoid grave robbing (a well-documented practice, as at Oseberg), but there must exist also the possibility that silver was considered too valuable an asset to be abandoned to the dead, regarded perhaps as farm or family wealth to be inherited like land. The result is that most Viking-Age silver objects have been found either singly or in hoards of varying size. For present purposes a hoard may simply be defined as two or more silver objects found together, but they range in size from this absolute minimum through small hoards of personal jewellery[8] or a merchant's coins[9] to the great mixed hoards which, in Scandinavia and the British Isles, achieve a maximum weight of about 18 pounds (with the notable exception of the Cuerdale hoard from north-west England, discussed below, that appears to have weighed between 80 and 90 pounds).

Such single-finds and small hoards may sometimes be the result of the accidental loss of an ornament or purse. Occasionally, it is clear that a hoard was buried as an offering, such as the treasure of 110 coins placed in the foundation trench of a stone church at Roskilde in Denmark, about the year 1040.[10] In the majority of cases, however, we must be dealing with precious metal that has been deliberately hidden in the ground and never recovered by its owners. This aspect of deliberate concealment, mostly, it appears, away from the settlement, means archaeological research projects cannot be mounted to locate and excavate new examples of Viking silver hoards to test hypotheses arising from their study, except to investigate further the find-spots of chance discoveries, for only by chance can they be found. But the fact is that they have been found in large numbers over the centuries and still continue to be found. This suggests that we are, after all, in a reasonable position to attempt to interpret the nature and significance for the Scandinavians of the Viking Age of this attractive and easily portable form of wealth.

The Viking Age was *the* silver age of the northern world — well over a thousand hoards of gold and silver have been found from this period in Scandinavia alone, and their distribution is far wider, from Iceland in the west to the Urals in the east. Despite this enormous wealth of silver that can be seen to have passed through Viking hands into Scandinavian soil, it must be emphasized that there are *no* known native sources of silver that were being worked in Scandinavia during the Viking Age. Their silver was all imported — but from where?

It is those coins that were not melted down that help to answer this question. For coins of the period generally bear the name of the authority that issued them, and many also carry the name of the mint at which they were struck. Their study demonstrates that the great majority of surviving coins that reached Scandinavia during the ninth and tenth centuries were from the Islamic world. Several hundred thousand dirhams (Arabic silver coins) have been found singly or in hoards from Russia to Ireland, of which some 62,000 have so far been discovered in Scandinavia. But this source seems to have dried up in the 970s. The cessation of imports may have been due to an interruption in the trade routes between the Volga and the Baltic. But ultimately of greater significance was a developing silver crisis in the Islamic world, particularly in the eastern Caliphate, where the mines were being worked out so that smaller dirhams were struck than before and their silver content reduced. A trickle of dirhams did continue, for they are found in Viking hoards of the late eleventh century, continuing even into the twelfth.[11]

From coin inscriptions and Arabic literature we know of silver mines in Spain, Africa, Armenia and particularly Persia, but the most detailed evidence available is that for the most easterly parts of the Caliphate, Khurâsân and Transoxania. Professor Sture Bolin[12] believed that the mine of Shâsh (Tashkent), in Transoxania, was likely to have been producing about thirty tons of silver annually in the early part of the ninth century. He also noted that the Viceroy of Khurâsân was levying between forty and fifty million dirhams annually in the ninth century — that is between 120 and 150 tons of silver, whereas official documents show that the Caliph's total income in silver around the year

800 was some 400 million dirhams "or twenty-five times the world production in 1500".[12a] It is well to remember in studying the Viking silver hoards of Scandinavia (and indeed of the rest of the Viking world) from the ninth and tenth centuries that we are, for the most part, only dealing with the overspill from this fantastic output, obtained in the main by northern merchants who travelled through Russia in search of Arab merchants with whom to barter their furs and slaves in exchange for dirhams — for Arab sources state that they refused to accept payment in anything other than silver coins, although other souvenirs of these ventures also found their way back to Scandinavia.[13]

With the drying up of the Islamic source, the Scandinavians turned to England and Germany during the second half of the tenth century to supplement, and then to replace, their silver supplies. The most important source of silver for Europe at that time lay in the Harz mountains where German silver mines were increasingly exploited from the mid-tenth century onwards. So from the tenth and eleventh centuries, some 70,000 German coins are known from Scandinavia, together with well over 40,000 Anglo-Saxon ones. The latter figure represents a larger total than that of the number of Anglo-Saxon coins to have survived in England from that period, but even this figure fades into insignificance when it is appreciated that the *Anglo-Saxon Chronicle* records that England paid gelds between 991 and 1014 of at least £150,000, a sum equivalent to 36 million coins.[14]

This was not, of course, the first west European treasure to reach Scandinavia. Vikings raiding in the west had taken loot and extorted tribute in vast sums during the ninth century. Professor Peter Sawyer[15] states that the total references in the Frankish sources to such payments amount to 685 pounds of gold and 43,042 pounds of silver, and if some sums were exaggerated, then there were no doubt others that went unrecorded. At the same time, similar raids for loot, and occasionally for tribute, were taking place on Britain and Ireland. Remarkably little of this treasure has been found in Scandinavia, or in the areas of Scandinavian settlement in the British Isles, in the form of the coins in which such tributes would have been paid. Most of it must have been melted down to make ornaments, although some of it will have been recycled in the west in the purchase of supplies and even land. But in the early Viking period there appears to have been only one area of Scandinavia that had any familiarity with the proper significance of coin, and that was southern Denmark.

Already in the eighth century, Frisian merchants from the southern coastlands of the North Sea were reaching centres such as Dankirke and Ribe on the south-west coast of Jutland, where their distinctive coins have been found. The Danish king Godfred established a trading-centre at Hedeby at the beginning of the ninth century, and soon after the earliest Scandinavian coinage was probably minted there.[16] The designs of these coins copy and modify those of the Frisians, including one type with a dragon on one side and a face encircled by rays on the other.[17] Other designs include ships, some perhaps based on Frisian trading-vessels, but others clearly represent Viking longships, with displayed shields.[18] But this coinage represented no more than the faint beginnings of a coin-using economy in Denmark, for it appears to have been a short-lived phase of about 30 years. The striking of coins was revived in Denmark during the first half of the tenth century, although there was no large output until about 975, during the reign of Harald Bluetooth.[19]

National coinages were not really established in Scandinavia until the eleventh century, by which time the designs of Anglo-Saxon coins formed the predominant influence and there were Anglo-Saxon moneyers working for the Scandinavian kings.[20] On the other hand, Byzantine influences can be seen in the coins of Svein Estridsson of Denmark (1047–75), whose moneyers drew on the Christian types of Byzantine coins for inspiration.[21]

In England, in the Viking royal capital of York, there was a somewhat similar pattern of development. The designs of its earliest coins, struck just before 900, were mainly Carolingian in inspiration; later, Anglo-Saxon imitations dominated. There is, however, a number of original and vigorous designs amongst the York issues, including a standard, a bow and arrow, a sword with a Thor's hammer, and a raven.[22] The Viking kings of Dublin minted coins from about 997, and these, too, followed closely the designs of Anglo-Saxon coins.[23]

As Marion Archibald has commented: "Coins are the commonest individual class of artefact surviving from the Viking Period, but they have much more than mere statistics to assure them a place among the most important of the extant material".[24] Yet only one further aspect of their presence in Viking silver hoards can be considered here, and that is their value for dating. For the many other aspects of their importance for Viking-Age studies, and for the new approaches being developed for their study, the reader must refer to the sources listed in the notes, with their extensive bibliographies.

The simplest form of coin-hoard dating is to establish the date at which the latest coin in the hoard was struck, which therefore establishes a date after which the hoard must have been buried. With the larger hoards, however, numismatists are able to estimate the deposition date more closely by also considering which coins are absent that should reasonably have been present had the hoard in question been of later date. Professor Michael Dolley believes that such estimates are generally accurate to within a quinquennium for the Viking-Age coin-hoards of the British Isles.[25] When it is possible to establish a deposition date for a mixed hoard, then it is certain that the ornaments that it contains must have been made before that date. By taking into account the contents of other such coin-dated hoards, archaeologists can gradually build up a framework of dates for when different types of objects were in fashion, as also for the changing art-styles used to decorate them.[26]

The study of the deposition dates of hoards also gives rise to the possibility of establishing how the number of hoards being concealed changed from period to period. When the deposition pattern of the Viking-Age silver hoards found in Ireland is plotted (Figure 1), it reveals a significant peak about the year 980, when the Vikings in Ireland suffered a major defeat at the hands of the Irish at the battle of Tara, after which the Norse kings of Dublin had to pay tribute to them.[27] In other words, a period of unrest seems to have led to an increase in the burial of hoards and the failure to recover them later.[28] This is not in itself a very remarkable conclusion, but the equation cannot always be so readily made, for the one can be shown not necessarily to have led to the other.[29] It can equally well be argued that in the days before banks and safe-deposits, many hoards were buried as a matter of course and dug up only when needed (as was the practice in some areas until relatively recent times). In the latter case, a deposition peak of the kind noted above must also be a direct reflection of the period during which an area country was at its richest.[30]

Before considering more closely the actual contents of some of the Viking silver hoards, a few comments need to be made about gold, for although most Viking treasure was

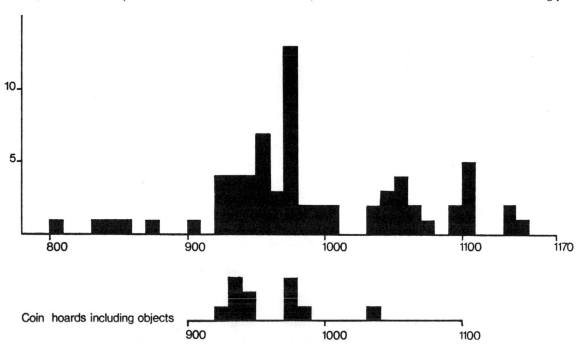

*Figure 1. Deposition of Viking-Age coin hoards of Ireland (780–1170),
from Graham-Campbell 1976.*

in the form of silver, there was also a certain amount of gold in circulation (compare
the figures in the Frankish sources, given above, for the relative payments in gold and in
silver made to the Vikings). The largest gold hoard from Scandinavia is that found in the
nineteenth century in Norway, at Hon near Oslo (Plate 32); it weighs about 5½ pounds
and the coins that it contains, converted into pendants, show that it cannot have been
buried any earlier than about 860.[31] It contains a wide range of other pendants and
rings, including a ninth-century Anglo-Saxon gold finger-ring; the finest object is a trefoil-
shaped gold ornament of superb quality of Carolingian workmanship. This hoard is,
however, only half the weight of another nineteenth-century discovery, from Hare
Island in the River Shannon in Ireland; this has since been melted down for its gold, but
it is known to have consisted of ten massive arm-rings.[32] But such finds are exceptional,
and the majority of gold finds tend to be of smaller objects such as finger-rings, like the
hoard of four from Stenness, Orkney, Scotland,[33] representing miniature versions of
standard types of arm-ring and neck-ring. Many objects of bronze were, however, gilt
to give them at least the appearance of gold.

   The numerous single-finds of gold and silver ornaments, whatever their individual
beauty or rarity, can never provide useful information for the archaeologist in the
manner that can be obtained from the study of groups of associated material such as
grave-goods and hoards. It has already been noted that little in the way of pure gold and
silver is found in graves, although of course the higher the status of the deceased, the
greater is the likelihood that the grave will contain something of precious metal. For
instance, a small silver cup was amongst the objects left behind in the Danish royal

burial-mound at Jellinge when the body, presumed to be that of King Gorm, was removed for Christian burial.[34] The result is that hoards constitute the primary source material for the study of Viking silver.[35]

The hoard material can be divided into four categories of objects: coins, ingots, complete ornaments, and hack-silver (Plate 33). Hack-silver consists of the cut-up fragments of ingots and ornaments, used as small change. Following the remarks about the importance of the coin material, the other three categories will now be considered.

Ingots are simply a convenient way in which to store bullion, for it is obviously easier to handle and store a few ingots rather than large numbers of loose coins. Most Viking-Age ingots are sausage-shaped and were cast in open moulds that were quick and easy to make; no more was needed than a groove in a convenient stone.[36] A building stone found at Whitby Abbey on the Yorkshire coast has been used for just such a purpose; it is often claimed that it was made by the Viking raiders who plundered Whitby in 867 to melt down and share their loot.[37]

Ingots are also a convenient form of silver storage in that whatever fraction of silver is required may be readily cut from the end, so that many are incomplete when found. Their surfaces are often deliberately cut or nicked with a knife to test the quality of the silver and, no doubt, to establish the genuineness of the ingot in question, for some counterfeit objects are known.[38] An important area of research yet to be followed up in detail is into the weights of complete ingots and fragments to determine what they can reveal of the different and changing weight standards used in the Viking Age – for there is evidence that ingots were made and cut to specific weights for some purposes. A group of unusually shaped, sub-rectangular ingots in the Cuerdale hoard appear to have been made to the weight standard of the Carolingian Empire, approximating to a third of its pound, whereas the other ingots in the hoard, of normal Scandinavian types, are not.[39]

Objects other than ingots found in hoards were also sometimes made with a specific weight of silver in mind. This seems to have been the case with various types of ring,[40] including the so-called "ring-money" that forms such a prominent feature of the tenth- and eleventh-century hoards found in Scotland (Plate 34).[41] Again, this is an area that requires further research, although one type of ring is better known: the so-called "Permian" ring, or spiral ring. These rings, probably made in the form of neck-rings, were imported into Scandinavia in the ninth century from Central Russia and Bulgar in the bend of the River Volga, but when found in Viking hoards they are twisted into spirals (only fragments are known from hoards in the British Isles). The weights of those in the Sandby, Öland, hoard are approximately 300, 200 and 100 grams, a unit of 100 grams represents a quarter of the Persian pound.[42] It is thought likely that the Persian pound and its divisions may have influenced the decrease in weight of the Scandinavian ounce, which came down from an equivalent of 27.3 to 24.5 grams during the Viking Age.

Aside from the subject of weights, the ornaments found in Viking hoards open up numerous other interesting areas of research. Through them one can detect not only the great distances travelled to obtain the silver, but also its subsequent spread (as from the coins). They reveal something of the basic uniformity of the material culture that the Scandinavians spread throughout the Viking world. The neck-rings and arm-rings of twisted or plaited rods are essentially the same whether they are found in Russia, Scandinavia, Britain, Ireland or Iceland. At the same time, one can observe the develop-

ment of regional preferences and differences, such as on Gotland[43] or amongst the
Norse and Danish settlers in Ireland (Plate 35).[44]

There is space only to touch on two or three other areas of interest. First, as was
mentioned above, the study of the hoard material is of the greatest importance for
the student of Viking art in building up a chronology for the different styles —
particularly those of the late Viking period when silver hoards form our main source of
ornate metalwork, following the decline and abandonment of the practice of burying
grave-goods. For this reason great emphasis tends to be put on these often beautiful
or spectacular pieces and their ornament in the study of Viking art, rather than on the
duller, often mass-produced, objects worn by the majority of Scandinavians during the
Viking Age, such as the women's standard oval brooches.[45] It was, however, in the
majority of cases, the objects of gold and silver that are found in the hoards, and their
decoration, that set the fashions that were imitated in cheaper metals for the less wealthy.
It has often been commented on, for instance, that the decoration of cast-bronze metalwork in the Borre style has nicked contours in apparent imitation of filigree. Imitations
of the great silver "thistle brooches" are represented by a series of small bronze brooches,
originally tinned and with crudely cross-hatched ornament, found in tenth-century
Norwegian farmers' graves (Plate 36).

Included in the hoard material is a variety of silver pendants of interest to the student
of Viking beliefs, and these represent the last complete objects selected for brief consideration here. In some cases it is clear that such amulets were carefully buried as
precious possessions because they are found in excellent condition; but there are others
that appear to have lost their special significance and to have been treated by their owners
as any other lump of bullion. For instance, the fine pendant crucifix from the eleventh-
century Lilla Klintegårda, Gotland, hoard is nicked more than 40 times to test the quality
of its silver.[46]

Some pagan amulets are easier to interpret than others, such as the stylised hammer
of Thor (Plate 37), which is of wide distribution, although there is a remarkable concentration on Öland where Professor Mårten Stenberger noted 18 from 16 hoards.[47] Others
take the form of miniature weapons and chairs, believed to be associated with the cult of
Odin;[48] male and female figures are also known.[49] Some amulets appear ambiguous, to
modern eyes at any rate, such as that from the Goldsborough, Yorkshire, hoard that
was buried about 920 (Plate 38).[50] An Icelandic pendant found at Foss (a single find) has
an animal head suspension loop and a three-armed terminal suggestive of a Thor's
hammer, but its form is not far from being that of an equal-armed cross.[51] An ambiguous
pendant might well have served the purpose of one of mixed beliefs, such as the Icelander,
Helgi the Lean, who is said to have "believed in Christ and yet made vows to Thor for sea
voyages or in tight corners, and for everything which struck him as of real importance".
From the eleventh-century hoards come a number of superb crucifix pendants,
characteristically displaying the figure of Christ as bound to the cross and stylised
according to the conventions of late Viking art; some draw their inspiration from western
Christendom, others from the traditions of the Byzantine Church.[52]

The remaining component of the hoards consists of hack-silver, or cut-up fragments,
small though these often are, they cannot be neglected. Even though the study of
fragments is like working on a series of jig-saw puzzles with most of the parts missing,
complete objects can often supply the missing pictures. Fragments of ornaments assist

us in tracking the movement of silver around the Viking world, observing also for how long fragments of once-fashionable objects might stay in circulation as simple bullion. The main reason, however, that hack-silver cannot be ignored is the straightforward fact that there is so much of it, particularly from the tenth century, with the economic consequences that this entails. During that century there was plenty of silver in circulation and trade appears to have been continually increasing; more and more hack-silver was needed for use for small payments in internal trade (as substitute coinage), until its use declined in favour of actual coins and their use as counted money.[53] The use of hack-silver in the Viking-Age economy was not, however, entirely a tenth-century development, as is demonstrated by the contents of the Cuerdale hoard that was buried about 903 (Plate 39).[54]

The Cuerdale hoard was concealed in a lead chest in the south bank of the River Ribble, near Preston in Lancashire. As stated above, it is the largest known Viking silver hoard from Scandinavia or the west and must have weighed nearly 90 pounds. The silver takes the form of about 7,000 coins and some 1,300 other pieces, consisting of ingots and hack-silver from west and east, but with only a handful of complete ornaments. Whether this represents an army leader's share or a well-to-do merchant's hoard is impossible to establish today. But it may stand as a final witness in support of Professor Peter Sawyer's observation on the Viking Age that "the efforts of Scandinavians to satisfy their appetites for silver . . . however it was regarded, were remarkably successful".[55]

NOTES AND REFERENCES

Note: For the most part references are given to Graham-Campbell 1980 (cited as *Viking Artefacts*) in which catalogue illustrations and detailed bibliographies may be found.

1. Sturlvson, Snorri (Everyman edition, pp. 125–6).
2. *Viking Artefacts*, no. 195.
3. Eldjárn 1956, *passim*.
4. *Viking Artefacts*, 85 and no. 306.
4a. Translation from J. Brøndsted, *The Vikings*, London, 1965, 265).
5. *Viking Artefacts*, nos. 195–8 and 427; Graham-Campbell (forthcoming).
6. *Viking Artefacts*, no. 215.
7. *Viking Artefacts*, nos. 155–6, 159–62 and 354.
8. E.g. the Hatteberg, Hordaland, Norway, hoard that consists of a silver penannular brooch (*Viking Artefacts*, no. 194), a silver neck-ring and a gold arm-ring (Bøe 1934).
9. E.g. the many tenth-century coin-hoards found in Ireland consisting mainly of Anglo-Saxon coins for trade with England (Dolley 1966; Graham-Campbell 1976). Randsborg (1980) has recently advanced the controversial claim that variation in size of hoards in a region reflects the equality or otherwise of the structure of its society,
10. *Danefæ*, no. 38.
11. N. M. Lowick in *Viking Artefacts*, 98–99, nos. 344–8; T. S. Noonan in Blackburn and Metcalf, 1981.
12. Bolin 1953.
12a. *Ibid.*
13. *Viking Artefacts*, nos. 349–53.
14. For a general introduction on the flow of silver into Viking-Age Scandinavia, *see* Sawyer 1971, but more particularly the important group of papers collected in Blackburn and Metcalf, 1981.
15. Sawyer 1971, 99.
16. M. M. Archibald in *Viking Artefacts*, 104 and no. 391.
17. *Danefæ*, no. 59.   18. Skaare 1964.

19. M. M. Archibald in *Viking Artefacts*, no. 393.

20. *Ibid.*, 104. The most important general introductions and surveys are those by Bendixen 1967; Dolley, 1966, 1978; Lagerqvist 1970; Malmer 1968; and Skaare 1976.

21. *Ibid.*, 104 and no. 411.

22. *Ibid.*, 104 and nos. 365-7 and 371-5.

23. *Ibid.*, nos. 381-2.

24. *Ibid.*, 103.

25. Dolley 1966, 48.

26. Wilson 1978 lists the relevant coin-hoards for the student of Viking art; *see also* Jansson 1969.

27. Graham-Campbell 1976, 47 and fig. 2.

28. Cp. Wilson 1968, fig. 2, plotting the deposition of coin-hoards in England between 830 and 940, peaking 869-78.

29. Malmer 1973.

30. For a recent novel interpretation of factors relating to hoard deposition, *see* Randsborg 1980.

31. *Viking Artefacts*, no. 486.

32. Graham-Campbell 1974.

33. *Viking Artefacts*, no. 238.

34. *Medieval Scandinavia*, vii (1974); *Danefæ*, no. 85; Roesdahl 1982.

35. Fór general introductions to the hoard material, *see* Rasmussen 1961, Sawyer 1971, and the relevant entries in *Kulturhistorisk leksikon for nordisk middelalder*. The major Scandinavian surveys and inventories include Grieg 1929; Hårdh 1976; Skaare 1976; Skovmand 1942; and Stenberger 1947-58.

36. *Viking Artefacts*, 123 and nos. 2, 414, 426, 428-9.

37. *Viking Artefacts*, no. 2.

38. *Viking Artefacts*, no. 304.

39. I am grateful to Mrs. Jennifer Lewis for this information.

40. Hardh 1973-4.

41. *Viking Artefacts*, no. 235; listed and discussed in Graham-Campbell 1975-6 and Warner 1975-6.

42. *Viking Artefacts*, no. 331; the weights have been studied by Lundström (1973, 74-8).

43. *Viking Artefacts*, no. 237.

44. *Viking Artefacts*, no. 234.

45. *Viking Artefacts*, 27-8, nos. 112-24; I. Jansson in Wilson and Caygill 1981, 1-19.

46. *Viking Artefacts*, no. 531.

47. *Viking Artefacts*, nos. 22-3; Paulsen 1956, 205f; Stenberger 1958, 169.

48. *Viking Artefacts*, nos. 519-21.

49. *Viking Artefacts*, nos. 516-18.

50. *Viking Artefacts*, no. 524.

51. *Viking Artefacts*, no. 526.

52. *Viking Artefacts*, nos. 530-3; S. H. Fuglesang in Bekker-Nielsen *et al.* 1981, 73-94.

53. Lundström 1973; Hårdh 1977-8.

54. *Viking Artefacts*, no. 301.

55. Sawyer 1971, 86.

THE EMERGENCE OF URBAN COMMUNITIES IN VIKING-AGE SCANDINAVIA

The Problem of Continuity

Charlotte Blindheim

Keeper, Viking Department, University Museum, Oslo

IN SCANDINAVIA, as in a great many other European countries, the expansion of the old town centres (the Altstädte) and the resultant accumulation of information on town life in earlier days has provided a tremendous challenge to urban archaeologists. On the other hand, the relationship with the town planning authorities has become tricky and difficult, so that there are great problems concerning the publication of new material. To simplify matters very much, one might say that one of the major problems is that of continuity. I will confine myself to this problem here.

Professor Edith Ennen, one of the most distinguished town historians in western Europe, has dealt with this more thoroughly than has any other scholar in her field. Her point of departure is whether the "old Roman municipal organization disappeared completely with the fall of the ancient civilization by the invasion of the Germanic tribes" or whether there was a shift of the centres only. In discussing the continuity of town life in Europe from the Roman period onwards, Ennen distinguished three zones or regions: (1) the north German area, to the east of the Rhine and in Scandinavia, which was not directly influenced by the urban culture of the Mediterranean, (2) the zone which corresponds to northern France and the valleys of the Rhine and the Danube. Here the remains of the towns of antiquity have largely disappeared, but not without leaving some traces (pre-Norman England is closely attached to the north German area); and (3) the southern regions, where Roman urban traditions continued with respect to the possession of the land, housing, and manner of life.[1] It is, of course, zones 1 and, to a certain degree, 2 which interest us here. For Scandinavian town archaeology the continuity problem involves questions as to whether our medieval towns had a pre-urban stage, and from where did the Scandinavians get the idea of creating urban centres and marketplaces now revealed all over Scandinavia? Obviously, at least the latter question is to a great degree dependent on different geographical positions, so let me introduce my discussion with a few words on the physical features of Scandinavia (Figure 1). For this sketch of the different physical background I follow the Norwegian professor Fridtjov Isachsen.[2]

Sweden and Norway together are often referred to as the Scandinavian peninsula, but in present-day usage the name Scandinavia denotes three countries — Denmark, Sweden and Norway — taken together. The two other Nordic sovereign countries, i.e. Iceland and Finland, should not be included unconditionally in the term "Scandinavia". Indeed,

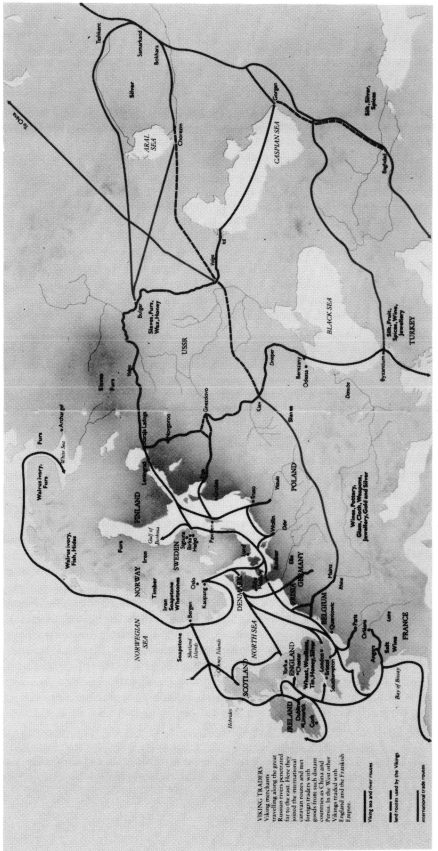

VIKING TRADERS
Viking merchants
travelling along the great
Russian rivers penetrated
far to the east. Here they
joined the international
caravan routes and met
foreign traders with
goods from such distant
countries as China and
Persia. In the West other
Vikings traded with
England and the Frankish
Empire.

▬▬▬ Viking sea and river routes

━━━ land routes used by the Vikings

▬▬▬ international trade routes

Figure 1.   Viking Trade Routes: after Graham-Campbell.

many Finns would object as strongly to being called Scandinavians as would some Irish object to being included in the English ethnic group! I have, therefore, excluded Iceland as well as Finland from my paper. To a certain degree, however, Gotlandic material will be included in my discussion, in spite of the fact that Gotland has a different physical background from the Swedish mainland — with which it has been united since 1645. For 300 years prior to that, it had been part of Denmark.

It should be remembered that the area inhabited by these three linguistically closely connected peoples (Norwegians, Swedes and Danes) provides a wide range of possibilities for settlement. Obviously, people could not live the same kind of life or in the same kind of houses on the bleak coast of Finnmark as by the Skagerak, the Baltic or in the high mountains of southern Norway. In most of the peninsula, economic growth has had to contend with the limitations set by an inhospitable environment, whilst southern Sweden — Scania — which formed a part of Denmark until 1660, is a low-lying land — much more fertile than the rest of Scandinavia. Even today's population density is a striking illustration of this: in Norway there are 11 and in Sweden 18 inhabitants per square kilometre, whilst in Denmark there are 103. But one important feature is common to us all: *we are coastal countries, dependent on navigation for our intercourse with the rest of Europe.*

I think we are entitled to say that this is even more true for Norway than for the rest of Scandinavia, a feature which can be illustrated, *inter alia*, by the fact that all the medieval Norwegian towns are situated along the coast — with one exception only: the city of Hamar. This town is, however, situated on the largest inland "fjord" in our country — Lake Mjøsa (Figure 2). In Sweden and even in Denmark the picture is somewhat different (Figures 3 and 6). It should also be noted that Denmark is the only one of the Nordic countries which is linked by land to the Continent.

Before the postwar, large-scale excavations of old town sites all over Scandinavia, by which archaeology attained the first-rate position it now holds regarding the urbanization process in Scandinavia, our historians had put up two major theories regarding the impetus to the growth of the Scandinavian towns. Old town sites were regarded either as royal foundations or as having their origins as episcopal seats. This implied that urban life had not been established throughout Scandinavia before the eleventh century. There was *one* obstacle to these theories. In his *Vita Anskarii*, Rimbert, Ansgar's successor to the archepiscopal see of Hamburg–Bremen, makes reference to three *ports* or *vici* which Ansgar must have visited already in the ninth century: Danish *Hedeby* on the river Schlei, with access to the Baltic as well as to the North Sea; *Ribe* on the North Sea side of the Jutland peninsula; and last but not least Swedish *Birka* on an island in Lake Mälaren, facing the Baltic and the eastern European trading routes rather than the western routes (Figure 1). But there is also some evidence at Birka of trading relations with western Europe. For nearly a century it has been a bone of contention between archaeology and history whether these three ports should be regarded as towns or not. This also goes for the Norwegian port, which under the name *Sciringesheal* in King Alfred's translation of Orosius' *Historia adversum paganos* is said to have been situated on the western coast of the Oslo fjord (Figure 2).

Personally, I must confess that I find much of the controversy hair-splitting. My opinion is that the question of town origins is so complex that it is hardly worthwhile trying to reach a complete definition. Each occurrence should be studied separately

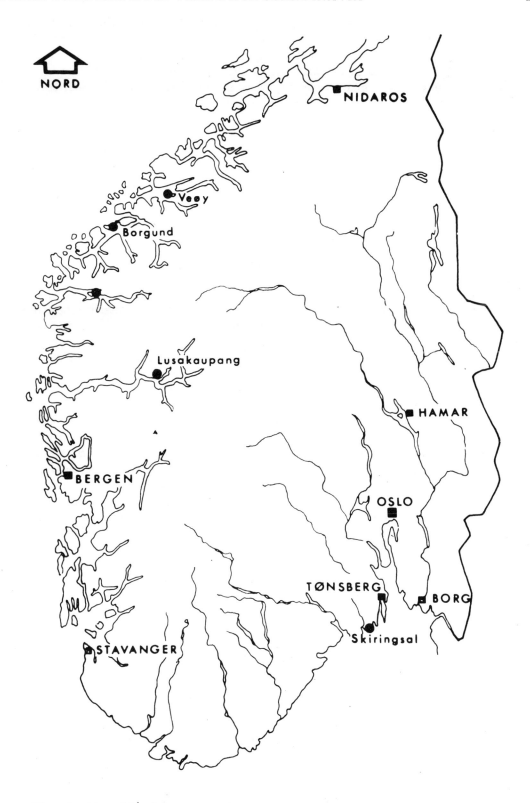

Figure 2.   Map of Southern Norway showing the most important old urban communities.

and be seen in connection with the physical geography of the region in which it occurs However, since this problem of definition is now very much linked to the problem of continuity, I shall have to return to it in my concluding remarks. Let me first give a presentation of our material in the different Scandinavian regions. I have had to choose to deal with a few sites, which are in my view the most significant in each country. I start with DENMARK (Figure 3). Town-archaeology in the 1960's was concentrated on the city of Århus Jutland, well-known from literary sources from 948 onwards. Here for the first time was established a firm chronology giving unquestionable proof of continuity from an open marketplace of the Viking Age, dating from around A.D. 900, into a real, ramparted, medieval city with centralized administration, a cathedral and a mint. The Århus excavations thus hold something of a key position in Scandinavia's urban archaeology.

What then about Ribe, mentioned very early by Rimbert? Because of this early appearance in literary sources, it has always been maintained that Ribe might boast of being the "oldest town of Denmark", very conveniently situated as it is on the sailing route westwards to Flanders, France and England, while Århus would seem to look towards the Danish waters and the north. But for a very long time the oldest finds from Ribe could certainly not be linked to Ansgar's visit to the place. It seemed as if Ribe flourished in the thirteenth century, when it had a name well-known in the whole of Europe, and had special connections to the Netherlands.

In the 1950s an intensive campaign was started in the very substantial layers underneath Ribe's "Alt-Stadt", but these excavations brought the archaeologists no further back than the 1100s. Rather desperately, Danish archaeologists started to look for Ansgar's Ribe outside the medieval Ribe proper. For long they searched in vain but eventually one found it, around the corner, so to speak, or rather on the opposite side of the river — close to the well-known Nørre Port (the northern gate) of the later city, for medieval Ribe was walled — like Århus. The area was called *suburbium* in the later literary sources — rather significant insofar as a *suburbium* is the *terminus technicus* for the settlement outside the walls of a medieval city. In the Ribe case, however, the *suburbium* could be demonstrated to be earlier than the *urbs* itself![3]

Excavations carried out from 1973 and onwards by Mogens Bencard have shown us that when Ansgar visited Ribe in the 860s there already must have been a settlement, which may well be called "urban". In the layers of this settlement were found, *inter alia*, coins of an early type, *sceattas*, bringing us back to about 725. Bencard thinks he can show the development of the earlier and later Ribe, as illustrated in Figures 5 and 6. He also found highly significant remnants of the occupation of early Ribe: bead-making and metal working, especially bronze-casting. Certain types of bronze brooches, i.e. so-called *equal-armed brooches*, hitherto regarded as native products, at least by Norwegian archaeologists, now seem to be Ribe products or products of metal workers trained in Ribe. This again would point to itinerant artisans. A completely new aspect of Viking-Age economy has thus been opened by the Ribe excavations. Let it also be mentioned that recently Kristina Ambrosiani (1981) has published the substantial antler, horn and bone waste from the Ribe excavations and convincingly showed that there must have been comb-makers at work already in Ribe's earliest phases. Does Ribe, like Århus give unquestionable proof of continuity from the pre-medieval into the medieval city? The answer so far is "no". We are faced with the following problem: we have rich and

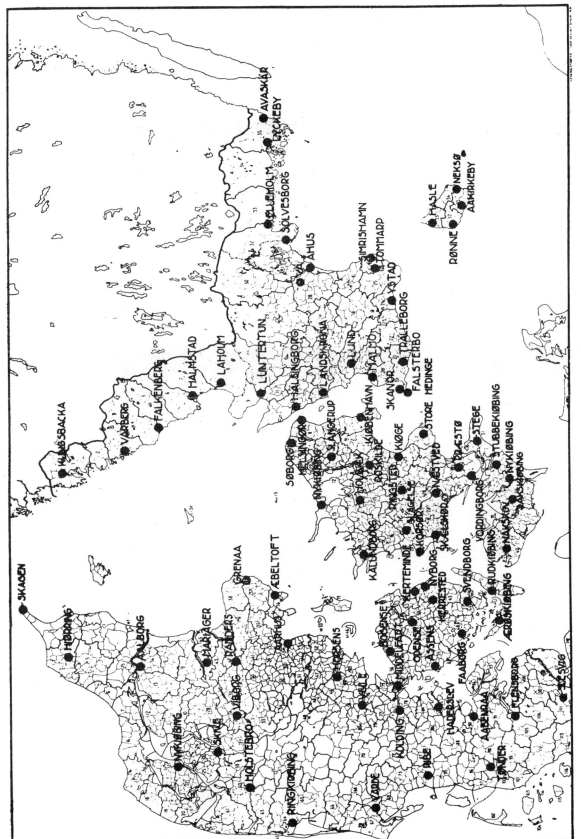

Figure 3.   Denmark's Medieval towns: after Nordisk Kultur

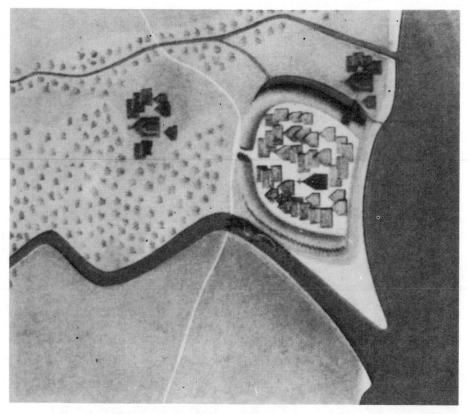

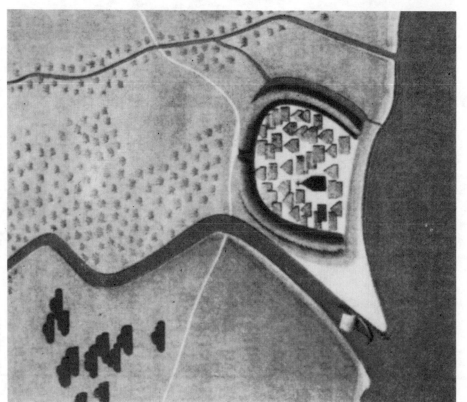

Figure 4.   Århus, circa 950 and circa 1100: after Andersen, Crab and Madsen

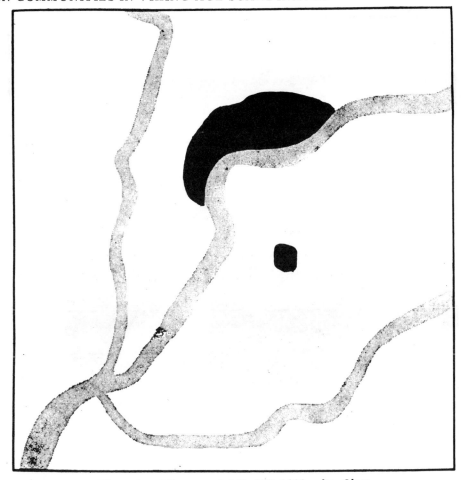

Figure 5.   Ribe around A.D. 700–1100: after Olsen.

significant eighth-century material, a reliable ninth-century written source and again rich archaeological material from about 1100 onwards. Was there a break in the habitation of Ribe during the Viking Age proper? Surely not. Ribe would have held a key position in the early traffic, with rich possibilities of expanded commerce with western Europe.

The only other town or marketplace in Denmark which until now was said to be as old as Ribe is Hedeby on the Jutlandic coast, doubtless the most important and best known of all the Viking-Age market centres in Scandinavia (Figures 7 and 8). For a very long time it was thought that Hedeby could not be dated earlier than A.D. 800. Recent excavations have, however, demonstrated an eighth-century stage outside the big rampart, which seems to be a tenth-century structure, erected when Hedeby had reached its maximum size of 24 ha (60 acres) — by far the largest of the Scandinavian import/export centres. It has an even more commanding position than its "sister town" Ribe, situated as it is on the Baltic side at the base of Jutland, but with easy access mainly by the river Schlei to the North Sea side of the peninsula where the small

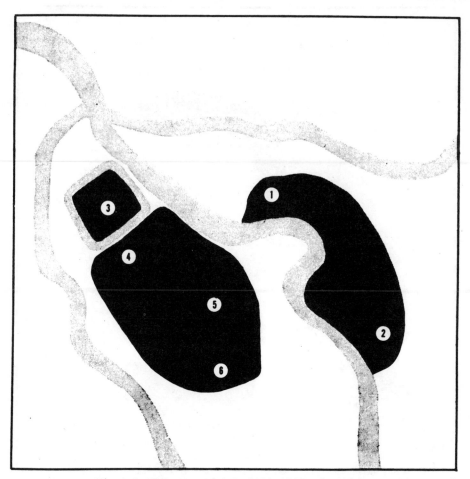

Figure 6.   Ribe around A.D. 1100–1230: after Olsen.

settlement of Hollingstedt must have served as a harbour towards the west though we lack convincing archaeological material to substantiate this. The famous north/south passage through Jutland, the "Oxenpassage" or "Army Road", runs close by. It ends in the big earthwork, Danevirke, which protected what was then Denmark's southern border. It was originally dated to the early ninth century, when King Gotfred of Denmark is said to have transferred merchants from Reric to Hedeby. Recent excavations in the Danevirke have given a dendrochronological dating of 737–38 for the earliest phase of the earthworks.

The Danevirke provides us with good correspondence with the eighth-century stage of the habitation site of Hedeby itself. Surely one discerns a strong royal power behind these ambitious features. The gravegoods and especially the material from the habitation site itself reflect Hedeby's wide-ranging contacts: Frankish pottery, Oriental textiles, Rhenish glassware, Norwegian hones and soapstone vessels being some of the more conspicuous items. Among the best sources of information regarding daily life are cemeteries, but because the Christian influence is so strong in Hedeby, its cemeteries

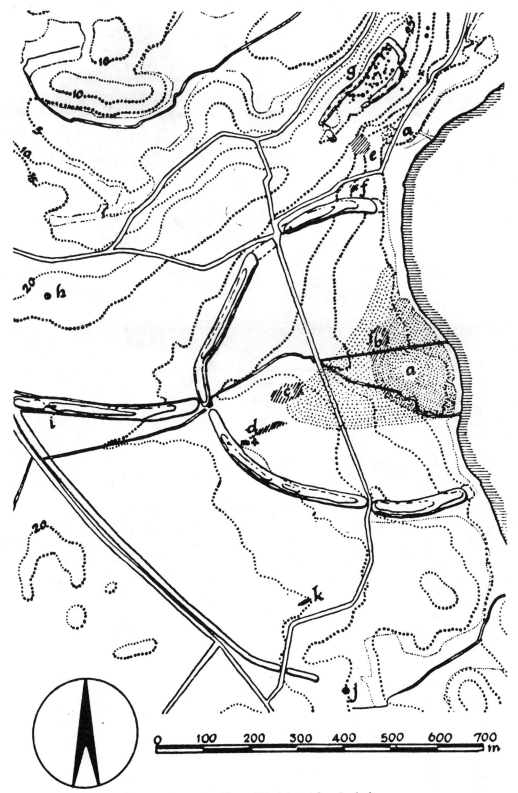

Figure 7. Plan of Hedeby. After Jankuhn.

Figure 8.   Reconstruction sketch of Hedeby: after Graham-Campbell.

provide rather scanty information. The part of the habitation site which has been under more or less constant archaeological excavation and observation since the 1930s has yielded convincing evidence of a series of different handicrafts having been carried out within the rampart. Even more important is the fact that the old house-grounds have proved to be the same throughout the generations (Figure 8). This makes a very strong case for the advocates of the theory that Hedeby had a permanent resident population, which again is one of the criteria one would demand for calling a market centre a town. I will come back to this later, when we discuss the problems of the definition of a town.

Before we turn to Sweden, let me only mention that in spite of intensive partial excavation campaigns, only in Denmark has a pre-urban stage been proved to exist on the same spot as the later medieval cities. The continuity problems remain unsolved, but I do think that Ribe has given us some very useful information with regard to future work: one should not automatically take it for granted that a town has been situated on the same spot since its very beginning.

Lund (Figure 1), the centre of Scania and thus a Danish town until 1660, provides an example of another type: here Blomqvist maintains that the town of Lund emerged from a "Three-hills" — market — a few kilometres east of the cross-roads where King Canute founded the town in 1019-1020. This is supposedly modelled after an English town and indeed fits well with the fact that Canute was king of England as well as of Denmark.

In SWEDEN where the towns and cities which had origins in the Middle Ages are very numerous, that time was indeed short for extensive excavation (Figure 9). In 1974 a project for the study of the urbanization process in Sweden was initiated under the heading: "Urban archaeology in central Sweden: present position, problems and possibilities". To a large extent the work has been based on the assumption that it is essential to start from data elucidating chronology, topography and structure. The data thus collected is not regarded as a goal in itself, but certain very important facts concerning the urbanization process have come out of the project, with only a minimum of archaeological excavation. Until quite recently the project was confined to the Lake Mälaren valley, where physical conditions are comparatively uniform. The Middle Sweden district is also by far the richest in prehistoric remains in the whole of Sweden (Figure 10). It contains examples of Viking Age as well as Early, High and Late Medieval urbanization.

These excavations — we all know — may be long and indeed expensive. As the leaders of the project state: "The central aim was that the material should be of equal importance to the antiquarian and the town planning authorities and that it should be presented in such a form that it could be the point of departure for further research into the urbanization process".[4] The idea for such an approach was taken from England, where London's earliest history has been elucidated in the same way. The method has also, as we shall see, been applied to Norway's most important city, Trondheim.

The most important Viking-Age phenomenon is of course Birka, mentioned in *Vita Anskarii* as a centre on a level with Ribe and Hedeby (Figure 11). It has always played an important role in Scandinavian discussions on town origin. Some scholars maintain that it was a real town, since Rimbert's account so clearly shows that the Crown was closely associated with Birka, the royal castle being situated on a neighbouring island. Rimbert also tells us that Birka had its own jurisdiction, with a *praefectus* as a representative for the king himself on the *thing*-meetings. It is a curious fact that the oldest urban law codified in Scandinavia is called the *Bjarkøyar rettr*, possibly going back to Birka or Bjørkø (where Birka is situated). According to Rimbert one distinguished between the *negotiatores* (the foreign tradesmen) and the *populi* (the permanent inhabitants). At its largest, Birka must have been half the size of Hedeby, but was nevertheless important enough to Ansgar to visit it twice in the ninth century. Its rampart was, like Hedeby's, built in the tenth century — indicating an expansion at that time. It was long thought that Birka had had its own mint, but Brita Malmer has now convincingly shown that so-called "Birka-coins" were manufactured in Hedeby in the ninth century.

To put it briefly: it would seem that Birka fulfilled the criteria proposed by the distinguished Swedish town historian, Adolf Schück, who in 1926 formed this definition of a town prior to *circa* 1300: "A relatively densely built-up area the inhabitants of which, due to their common trading interests, form a social unit either economically or legally, or both". The main obstacle is that we know far too little about the habitation

Figure 9. Sweden's Medieval towns: after Nordisk Kultur

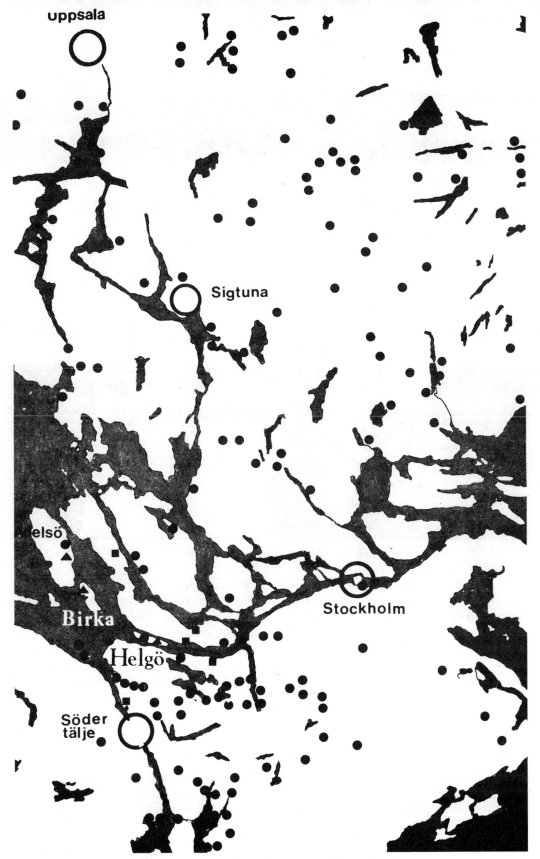

Figure 10.   *The Mälardalen Valley: after Holmqvist.*

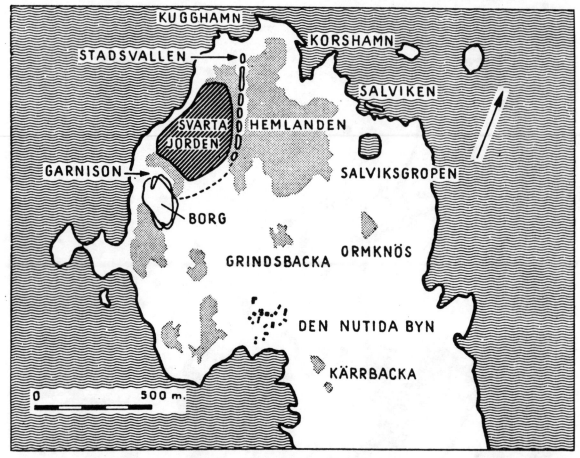

Fig. 11.   Plan of Birka. After Arbman.

pattern at Birka, compared to that of Hedeby. We have, however, a very rich assemblage of grave-goods at our disposal. This certainly reflects Birka's character as an international trading centre. The habitation site, called *Svarta Jorden* ("the black earth") has yielded convincing material for different kinds of handicrafts such as metalworking. It should be remembered that the better part of the goods transported to or through Birka would never be preserved in an archaeological context — articles like salt, furs, slaves, spices, textiles, and similar perishables. In Ribe, local handicrafts have been proven, as I stated earlier, but so far there is just *one* specialized product which can convincingly be attributed to Birka's Workshops: certain types of knives. As in Ribe, comb-making has been identified by Ambrosiani. Finally, a small group of graves takes us back to the eighth century for the earliest proven habitation on Bjørkö, identified by Birgit Arrhenius.[5]

Have settlement traces been found for a habitation earlier than 800 at Birka? No, but a centre which must be considerably older has in recent years been excavated on an island not far from Birka, on Helgø (Figure 12). The Helgø excavations, conducted by Wilhelm

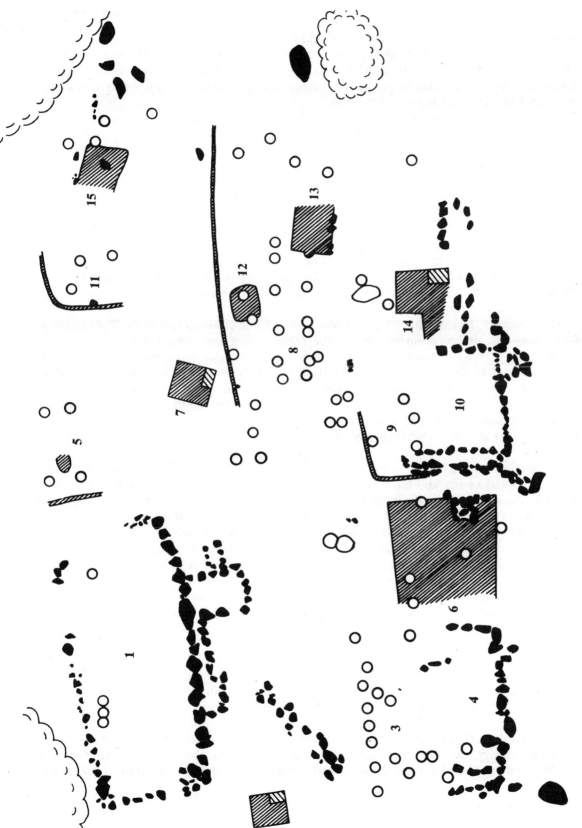

Figure 12. Part of habitation site of Helgö: after Holmqvist.

Holmqvist since the years after the last World War, have yielded house grounds and work-shops which reflect trade activities on a very large scale but no settlement area; no "black earth" similar to that at Birka has been found. Helgø is a "collection of single farms and workshops clearly planned to serve a large market".[6] One of its specialities must have been certain types of brooches.

The power behind Helgø may well have been the rich chieftains of central Sweden who engaged in a sort of "private enterprise" long before the Viking Age. Helgø experienced its greatest prosperity during the fifth, sixth and seventh centuries, and Birka must have grown out of it.

We can see from the finds that Birka had played out its role as *the* important centre for trade in the Mälar region towards the end of the tenth century, but as early as 1016 the Swedish king, Olof Skoot-konung, had a mint in Sigtuna (Figure 10) not far from Birka. Of all the cities on Sweden's mainland Sigtuna has kept most of its original appearance. At least five of its medieval churches can be dated to 1050–1170. Moreover, it became a bishopric as early as 1060. There can hardly be any doubt that Sigtuna is a direct descendant of Birka. The shift of centre may have resulted from the newly-founded church's desire to maintain the profitable trade while abandoning the old place where Ansgar's mission ultimately had failed.

The sequence Helgø/Birka/Sigtuna has a somewhat classic position in all discussions concerning the urbanization process in the Mälar region and indeed also for the rest of Scandinavia. It has been asked whether this was a typical pan-Scandinavian phenomenon — indicating that the real urban communities, the medieval city proper, had independent roots, growing out of more of less centralized trade and specialized handicrafts. There are traces of a similar development at Hedeby, where the medieval town Schlesvig is regarded by some scholars as a descendant of Hedeby. The situation was, however, some-what different at Århus. What then about NORWAY?

For reasons which I need not go into here, post-war excavations of the medieval town grounds started earlier and have been more extensive in my own country than in any of our neighbouring countries. With Bergen as the starting point, excavations of the old town centres have been carried out or are still under way in all of Norway's medieval towns, with the exception of Stavanger. (*Kongehelle*, which belonged to Norway until the mid-seventeenth century, has not been excavated either.) By way of our Fornminne-lov (The Ancient Monument Act), we can force town authorities to let us excavate before any demolition for expansion can take place in any old town area. This is, however, not as much of a shortcut to an archaeological paradise as it sounds, since the Act has no provision whatsoever for the publishing of the material. Unpublished, important material from the excavations had been accumulating in the museum stores over the years and something had to be done.

Oslo is a good example of the new ways one has gone beyond the provisions of the Fornminnelov (Figure 13). The Oslo material is now being published quickly, efficiently and comparatively cheaply in interim reports with English summaries, with emphasis put on stratigraphy and topography. Those find groups which would seem to give the most reliable dating evidence have been given priority. Footwear and pottery take us back to about A.D. 1100, but there are traces of the oldest buildings going back to the eleventh century. A very important observation has been noted: "The boundaries of the lots can be traced on the same spot throughout the archaeological layers from the

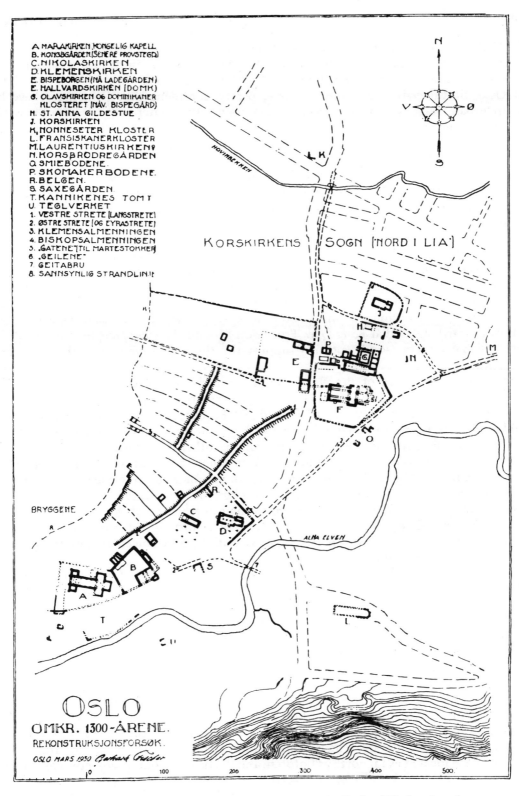

KORSKIRKENS SOGN [NORD I LIA]

BRYGGENE

ALNA ELVEN

OSLO
OMKR. 1300-ÅRENE.
REKONSTRUKSJONSFORSØK.
OSLO MARS 1950 Gerhard Fischer

0   100   200   300   400   500

Figure 13. Oslo around 1300. Conjectural map drawn by Gerhard Fischer, *based on archaeological material and written evidence*

Late Middle Ages down to the lowest layers with only slight fluctuations".[7] The same observations have been made at Hedeby. Archaeological finds in the surroundings, place-name studies, and observations made when excavating the oldest stone church of Oslo, St Clemens, make me, for one, pretty confident that Oslo must have had a pre-urban stage as marketplace, now completely obliterated by the Norwegian Railway Company, which, characteristically enough, has its base here. The strategic/ topographic situation is of such importance that there *must* have emerged a centre here at a very early stage.

As already mentioned, in Trondheim — which became the archepiscopal see of Norway in 1153 and was thus the ecclesiastical centre of Norway (as well as the North Atlantic Isles, including Greenland) — pre-war excavations of the town area had been casual. The magnificent cathedral was given priority over all other research work. In the 1970s large-scale excavations were started, but gave such confusing results that it was decided to apply the above-mentioned London method here (Figure 14); emphasizing the urbanization process, archaeologists presented the material to both antiquaries and town planners. Øyvind Lunde focused his research on collecting all available information on earlier finds in the town ground itself.[8] A very interesting picture of the urbanization process there has emerged, but nothing definite about its earliest stage can be said. One historical source (Snorri) states that King Olav Trygvason "founded" *a kaupang* here in *circa* 995. Two reliable sources (scaldic poems) support the thesis that *circa* 1070 there certainly was a town there.

In Bergen, the centre of the North German merchants association, "The Hansa", in the High and Late Middle Ages, large-scale excavations of parts of the Old Wharves (*Bryggen*) took place between 1955 and 1968, but comparatively little has been published. With regard to topography, one striking feature has been stressed by the leader of the excavation, Asbjørn Herteig: whilst all the other Norwegian medieval towns are found at the natural centres for traffic, "often where traffic from a distant hinterland meets seagoing traffic and where there was room for natural expansion outside the original built-up core",[9] the topographical background for Bergen is indeed a different case (Figure 2). Therefore, the theories concerning the origins of the town of Bergen are more controversial than those for any of the other Norwegian towns which originated in the middle ages. It seems as if Herteig's excavations have solved at least the problem concerning the core of the town.

Herteig maintains that the potential building area along the foot of the mountain cannot have been more than 6 ha (15 acres). A very ingenious means of expansion was then employed, demonstrated convincingly by his excavations (Figures 15 and 16). Herteig's model indicates a much better harbour than previously assumed and thus provides us with a better understanding of *why* the town of Bergen was founded here. For founded it must have been: Herteig's plans clearly show that already at the earliest stage covered by his excavations — the 1130s and 1140s — one can discern a plan which remained unaltered by later generations. Who was the founder — the Crown or the merchants? Very close to Bergen we have the royal farm of Ålrekstad, well-known from the sagas. It would seem as if there is a connection between this and the growth of a town on this rather unlikely place. In the later Middle Ages the trade in dried cod-fish (*skrei*), known from literary evidence from about 1100, was of utmost importance. The fisheries were located as far north as Lofoten, and the fish was sold *via* go-betweens who had

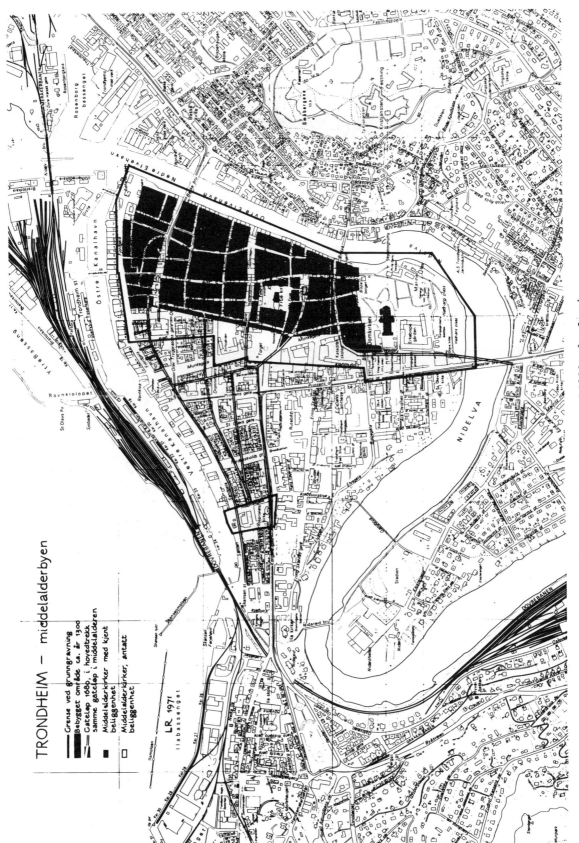

Figure 14. *Trondheim around 1300: after Lunde.*

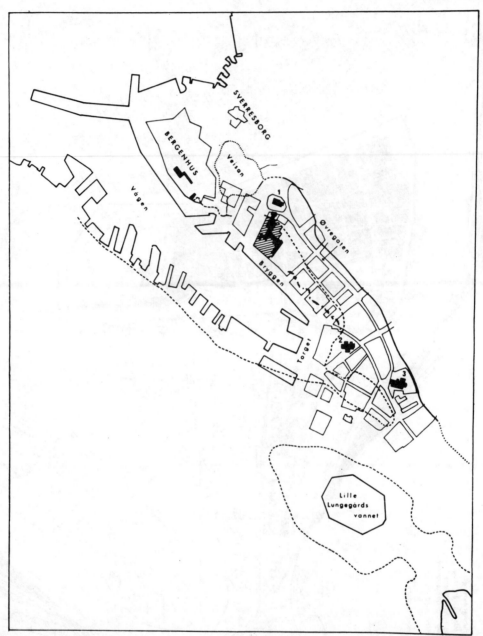

Figure 15. Bergen, sketch map of the town centre, the burial area on Bryggen hatched: after Herteig.

to meet at a certain place. It is as such that Bergen gets its importance, and it would seem that this trade must have interested the king very much — or so Herteig would hold.

In summary, the picture in Norway would seem to be this: on the basis of the latest excavations, Oslo may have had a pre-urban stage, a marketplace serving the rich farming

*Figure 16. Plan of Bryggen with the excavated area contoured and the exclusions in front of
the jetties dotted: after Herteig.*

districts around the city. This view is partly based on place-name studies, partly on one
striking topographic feature which emphasized Oslo's importance to its hinterland: in
our other medieval towns "the main streets and buildings were oriented exclusively in
relation to the sea and the shore", whereas in Oslo we find that the overland traffic
routes provide the guiding lines for the earliest topography of the city.[10] This points
strongly, I think, to some sort of centralized activity taking part already at an early
stage. But so far this has not been convincingly demonstrated by archaeological material.
By contrast, Bergen has no hinterland at all, its "hinterland" being the fjord and the coast
in front of it. Here there are no traces of a pre-urban, marketplace stage. Specialized
trade and the Crown would seem to be the forces which controlled its development.

In Trondheim the situation is not so clear but if one is to judge from the archaeological material only, it would be my opinion that Viking-Age trade had its centre farther
up the Trondheimsfjord, where we find the richest farming districts, very rich
archaeological material and the renowned pagan centre at *Mære*, near *Steinkjær*, which
again is mentioned as "Kaupang" by Snorri. Trondheim would then seem to have taken

over as centre when the Crown and the Church had established themselves in the eleventh century and the pilgrimages to St Olav's grave had become numerous. Thus, these three important medieval cities would seem to have emerged from different backgrounds, each dependent on local conditions and different political situations. We discern in two of them tendencies to the centralization of trade in an earlier period.

That such earlier centres have in fact existed in Norway in the Viking Age has been demonstrated by my own excavations at Kaupang in Vestfold. Here we have uncovered a concentration of rich, pagan graves, dating from the late eighth to the tenth century, and parts of the contemporary habitation site (Figures 17 and 18). It *must* be the site of the port of *Sciringesheal* we have located here. Comparing our plan to that of Hedeby is almost like comparing a changeling to a human child. And yet the same term — "port" — is employed about these two settlements as well as the contemporary Birka in reliable written sources. We may well ask: how can such apparently dissimilar phenomena really be described by the same term?

The answer, in my opinion, would seem to be that there cannot have been a very sharply drawn definition of a marketplace or "kaupang" while they existed. If we adduce material for comparison from outside Scandinavia itself but from Ennen's first zone — like Frisian Dorestad near the mouth of the Rhine or the trading centre Paviken on Gotland (Figure 19), just to mention a few among many) — we will see that the group includes settlements of many different types, with only one feature common to them all: *their situation near to the coast.* The majority of these places are also favourably situated for *local* trade. There is one very important exception: *Hedeby*, whose importance appears to be primarily due to its extremely favourable position for *foreign* trade. It also seems reasonably clear that at its Viking-Age stage Hedeby was established by a kind of "royal charter". Birka, on the other hand, like Kaupang and Paviken, served a densely-populated hinterland. Dorestad, according to the latest investigations, seems to have had a semi-agrarian form of settlement.

To restate the issue another way, the terms "port" or "kaupang" apparently could refer to settlements very different in structure, but similar in the important role they played in the extensive North Sea and Baltic trade of the Viking Age. The difference and/or functional specializations of these various settlements exemplify, I think, the different stages in the process of urbanization. Even before the Viking Age, places appear where the existence of trade and specialized craft can be observed — places like Helgø, Paviken, Kaupang, and early Ribe. They are important to our understanding of the emergence of urbanization, but they will remain "blind eyes" on the face of Scandinavian urban society, as the Danish scholar Johs. Brønsted once put it. With Hedeby and Birka, it is somewhat different. At the beginning of the tenth century, they were walled. But they both disappeared by the end of the century, and no medieval town grew up in their place. Do they fulfil Schück's conception of a town? Only partly. They certainly were "relatively densely built up" but we do not know whether the inhabitants formed a social unit either economically or legally, even if we can see from the archaeological material that there were "common trading interests" within the area. And here we are up against our greatest difficulty. We are almost entirely dependent on archaeology, which can give us a lot of information with regard to the material culture. But archaeology itself certainly has its limitations, for we cannot derive from it anything with regard to the legal status either of these centres or of their inhabitants from artefacts.

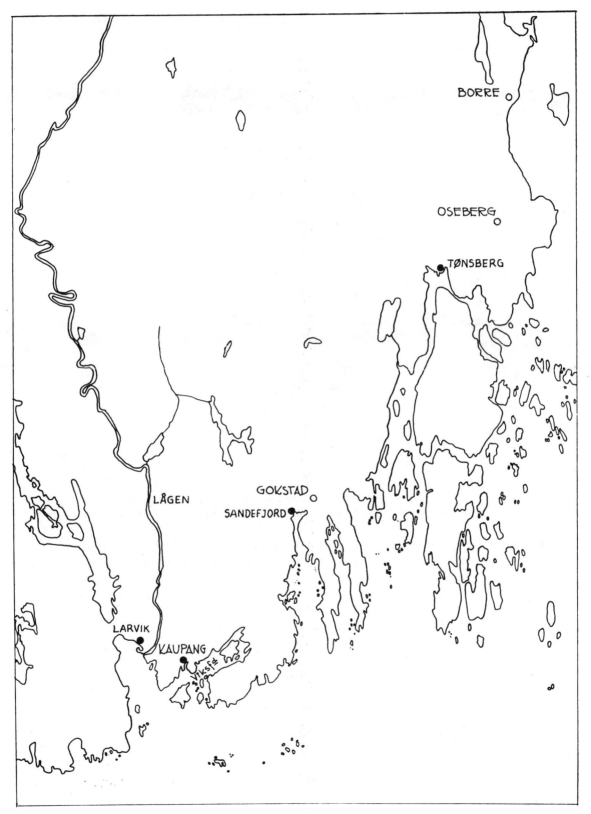

Figure 17. Sketch-map of county of Vestfold, showing the situation of Kaupang.

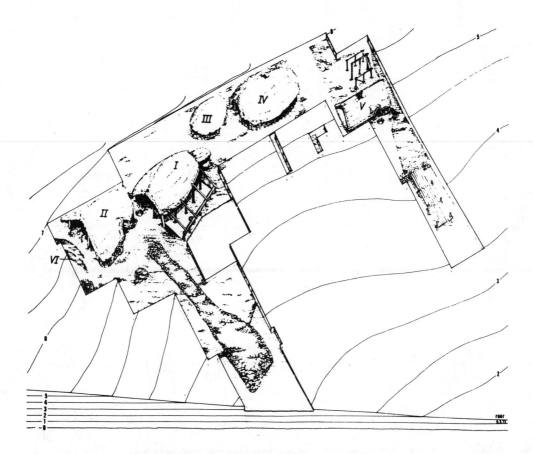

Figure 18. Reconstruction of the house-groups uncovered in the settlement site at Kaupang.
Two jetties down in the beach. From these cobbled "streets" lead up to the houses: after Blindheim.

Still less can we speak about the dominance of royal, mercantile, or ecclesiastical power in the administration of these places. Here we must content ourselves with speculation. But it is of course of great interest that the majority of the earlier medieval towns in Sweden and Norway at least seem to be connected with older social structures: market-places, *thing*-assemblies and cult-places. In Norway this is especially evident at Kaupang, which must have been closely connected with a *thing*-place and a *hof*. In Norway the only town which must be regarded as having been founded by the Crown and probably inspired by English models is Bergen (Herteig). In Sweden one stresses very strongly that the earliest Middle Swedish towns, were "in one way or another closely tied to administrative structures, either secular or ecclesiastical. Some of them were episcopal seats and/or deaneries: others were royal citadels or mints. It can thus be shown that in these early towns there was a close connection among economic, ecclesiastical and secular administrative functions. In many instances the structure of provincial centres can be traced far back to *things* and cult places".[11]

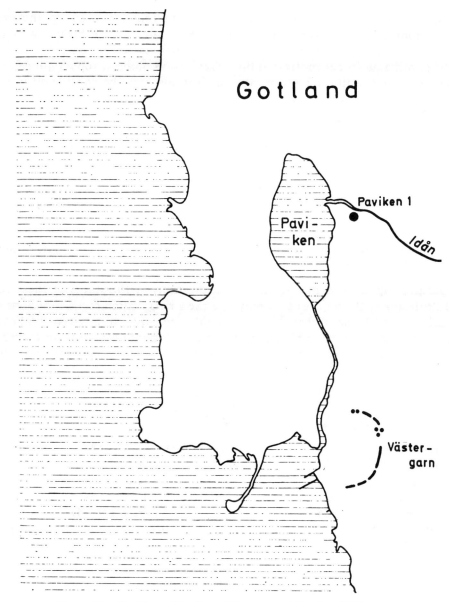

Figure 19. Position of Paviken-Västergarn. After Lundström.

In Denmark, on the other hand, one is inclined to regard all marketplaces and medieval towns as connected in some way or another with the King. This corresponds well with the fact that the royal power obviously established itself earlier and more manifestly in Denmark than on the Peninsula. For cultural, geographical and administrative reasons, it is infinitely easier for a strong person (king) to maintain full control over an area like southern Scandinavia than over the heavily forested and mountainous countries of Sweden and (even more so) Norway.

We thus return to our point of departure, Edith Ennen's stress on the diversity of urban development in Europe. She did not specifically include Scandinavia in her discussion. But it would seem that here in the North as well as in her zones 2 and 3, different conflicting forces motivated the urbanization process: topographical, economic, religious, legal and political features and institutions must be considered in each single case. No special feature can be singled out as more "town-making" than others.

We have a different perspective on this question in the theories of Professor Knut Helle of the University of Bergen. When discussing what meanings should be assigned to the concept of a trading centre and what is the relationship between trading centres and towns, he pointed out three possible aspects:

— the relation between trading centres and towns can be studied as a development through time (the continuity problem);
— the relation can be studied synchronically as a functional division between different types of contemporary centres, and
— the relation can be studied as the interaction between the trading functions and other urbanizing functions.[12]

These perspectives do not include the legal questions of the status of these towns, but instead Professor Helle chooses to emphasize the strictly commercial functions of a town or a marketplace. As an archaeologist I would agree with him, given the Scandinavian material as it appears today. Our main source of information about the earlier stages of urbanization in Scandinavia is *archaeological* and will remain *archaeological* in the future.

NOTES

1. Ennen 1968, 12–13.
2. Isachsen 1961.
3. Olsen 1975.
4. *Medeltidstaden* 1 (1976).
5. Arrhenius 1976, 178–184.
6. Anderson 1978, 41.

7. Lidén 1973, 104.
8. Lunde, 1977, 10.
9. Herteig, 1973, 50–61.
10. Lidén 1973, 124.
11. Anderson 1978, 41.
12. Helle, *Medeltidstaden* No. 18 (1980) 16–23.

REFERENCES

Most of the material I have used in this paper is drawn from various, more recent articles in journals and publications on town archaeology. I am indebted to all authors listed here. I have also found it important to draw the reader's attention to a few major works which I have listed on top of this select bibliography.

Adolf Schück, 1926: Studier rørande det svenska stadsväsendets uppkomst och äldsta utveckling. Stockholm.
Edith Ennen: The variety of urban development, pp. 11–18, in J. Benton, 1968.
Edith Ennen, 1972: *Die europäische Stadt des Mittelalters.* Gøttingen.
Grete Authén Blom, 1977, "Middelaldersteder", *Urbaniseringprosessen I Norden*, Det. XVII nordiske historikermøte Trondheim.

Margaretha Biørnstad and Hans Andersson 1979: *Handelsplats-Stad-Omland.* Symposium om det medeltida stadsväsendet i Mellan—Sverige. Sigtuna 7–8 februari. Medeltidsstaden 18. Stockholm.
Vor-Frühformen der europäischenstadt und Symposion in Reinhausen bei Gøtingen vom 18. bis 24. April 1972. Teil I und II. Herausgegeben von Herbert Jankuhn, Walter Schlesinger. Heiko Steuer. Die Zeit der Stadtgründungen im Ostseeraum. 1963. *Acta Visbyensia* I. Gotlands Fornsal, Visby.
Hauser und Höfe im Ostseeraum und im Norden bevor 1500, 1972.*Acta Visbyensia* V. Gotlands Fornsal, Visby.
Herbert Jankuhn: 1972 New Beginnings in Northern Europe and Scandinavia, in Barley, 1979: *European towns.* London–New York–San Francisco.
Byer og bybebyggelse. Nordisk Kultur. Oslo–Stockholm–København.

DENMARK

Ribe: Mogens Bencard, 1974: *Ribe zur Zeit der Wikinger. Acta Visbyensia* V, Visby.
Ribe: Olaf Olsen, 1975: Nogle tanker i anledning af Ribes uventet høje alder. Fra Ribe Amt. Festskrift til H. K. Kristensen.
Hedeby: Herbert Jankuhn, 1963: *Haithabu. Ein Handelsplatz der Wikingerzeit.* Neumünster.
Århus: Hellmuth Andersen, P. J. Crab and H. J. Madsen, 1971: Arhus Søndervold, en byarkeologisk undersøgelse. Jysk arkeologist selskabs skrifter. Vol. IX.
Danevirke: Hellmuth Andersen *et al.*, 1976: Jyllands vold. Århus.

NORWAY

Halvdan Koht, 1921: Upphave til dei gamle norske byane. Norsk Historisk tidsskrift. Oslo.
Oslo: Hans Emil Lidén, 1973. Oslo I. *Development of urban structure in the 12th and 13th centuries.* II. *The beginnings.*
Archaeological contributions to the early history of urban communities in Norway. The Institute for Comparative Research in Human Culture. Oslo/Bergen/Tromsø.
Bergen: Asbjørn E. Herteig: Bryggen, the mediaeval wharves of Bergen. *Ibid.* 1973.
Kaupang: Charlotte Blindheim: Kaupang by the Viks Fjord. I and II. *Ibid.* 1973.
Trondheim: Øyvind Lunde, 1977: *Trondheims fortid, i bygrunnen.* Riksantikvarens Skrifter II. Oslo.

For the physical background:

Fridtjov Isachsen, 1961: Norden. *A Geography of Norden.* Ed. Axel Strømme. Oslo.

SWEDEN

The series *Medeltidstaden*, No. 1, 1976. No. 6 Sigtuna, 1978. No. 7, Hans Andersson: Urbaniserings-processen i det medeltida Sverige (with an English summary), 1978; No. 19: *Stadssarkeologien i Mellan-Sverige, Läge, problem, møjlighet*, 1980, No. 26: Lund, 1980.
Helgø: *See* Holmqvist in *Vor- und Frühformen der europäischen Stadt.*
Paviken: *See* Lundstrøm in *Vor- und Frühformen der europäischen Stadt.*
Birka: *See* Ambrosiani, in *Vor- und Frühformen der europäischen Stadt.*
Birgit Arrhenius, 1976: "Die ältesten Funde von Birka". *Praehistorische Zeitschrift.* 51 Band, Heft 2, Berlin.
Kristina Ambrosiani, 1981: *Viking Age Combs, comb-making and comb-makers in the light of finds from Birka and Ribe.* Stockholm.
Brita Malmer, 1966: Nordiska Mynt føre at 1,000. *Acta Archaeologica Lundensia* Ser. In 8vo. No. 4.
Ragnar Blomqvist, "Die anfange der Stadt Lund", *Acta Visbyensia* I.

THE VIKINGS IN THE BRITISH ISLES:

Some aspects of their settlement and economy

Christopher D. Morris*

Lecturer in Archaeology, University of Durham

IN THIS PAPER, I intend to examine some aspects of the settlement and economy of the Viking peoples in the British Isles, indicating especially the contribution of some recent excavations towards a re-assessment of the period, and particularly the impact upon, and relationship with, the native peoples. There can be no attempt to be comprehensive, for, on the one hand it would become a summary and catalogue of work mostly by other people, and on the other, it is a theme whose compass should be that of a book, rather than a short paper. I am actively preparing such a book, which of necessity will be more wide-ranging both in scope and in material considered. Whilst it is my credo that work in a protohistoric period must be multidisciplinary, in this paper I shall largely, though not exclusively, deal with the material remains of archaeology. In doing so, however, we have to be aware that it is in the differences between categories of evidence, as well as between different areas or ethnic and cultural groups, that some of the major problems and paradoxes arise. Recent re-examination of historical material relating to the Vikings in Ireland has, for instance, very wide-ranging implications for the interpretation of archaeological and other material — and it is interesting that the most recent re-examination of the art–historical material has drawn similar implications for the interpretation of the Viking impact on Ireland.[1]

Even in examining one category of evidence, it is quite clear that broad-sweeping generalizations are inappropriate. English and French annalistic accounts could be utilised to assert that the Vikings in the British Isles had an overriding concern with politics, and a desire to control power. But such an interpretation of Viking activity in England would be over-simplified. The *Anglo-Saxon Chronicle* entries for 876, 877 and 880[2] indicate that other motives could also be present among the leaders and men of the *micel here* of the late 860s and 870s:

---

* This paper represents the revision of a paper presented at the Symposium held under the auspices of the Metropolitan Museum, New York in October 1980. Some parts of it were also presented, with other material, in lectures given at Cornell University, Ithaca, New York; Dartmouth College, Hanover, New Hampshire; and Plymouth State College, University System of New Hampshire. The author is grateful to these institutions for their invitations and hospitality, and in particular Professor Robert T. Farrell, of Cornell University, who master-minded the arrangements.

876 . . . And that year Healfdene shared out the lands of the Northumbrians, and they proceeded to plough and to support themselves.

877 . . . Then in the harvest season the army went away into Mercia and shared out some of it, and gave some to Ceolwulf.

880 . . . In this year the army went from Cirencester into East Anglia, and settled there and shared out the land. . . .

In a similar fashion, Mr. Graham-Campbell has distinguished between the nature of the Viking-Age silver hoards of Ireland and Scotland.[3] On the one hand, the greater amount of the Irish material and its distribution is explained in terms of the flourishing trading towns of Ireland and their hinterlands. On the other, Scottish material is taken to be far less concerned with the activities of traders, and the point is made that, as far as current knowledge goes, there were no urban communities there comparable with Dublin or other Irish towns. Indeed, the further point made — that no distinctive Scottish-Viking coinage is to be seen — emphasizes the contrast with Ireland where, towards the end of the tenth century, a Hiberno–Norse coinage emerged.[4]. Thus, immediately, it would appear that there is a contrast to be seen in the surviving evidence from the two regions of the British Isles, pointing to a considerable distinction in the nature of Viking settlement in, and impact upon, the two areas. In Ireland, being based upon towns, the Irish Vikings were much concerned with overseas trade; in Scotland, being based upon dispersed rural settlement, the Scottish Vikings were farmers with no great contacts in overseas trade. However, even this level of generalization may hide a complex situation, only partially understood. The wealth of the hoards from the Orkney Islands, particularly from Burray and Skaill, to my mind requires particular explanation, as Graham-Campbell suggests for the enormous Cuerdale hoard from northwest England.[5] The situation in parts of Ireland where hoards have been found, but where no coinage was current, also suggests that the contrast with rural Scotland should not be over-drawn.

Recent detailed historical analysis by Dr. Alfred P. Smyth has, in addition, demonstrated quite clearly that the distinction made in secondary works between Danish and Norwegian Vikings in Britain and Ireland was far more blurred at the time.[6] Indeed, the rulers of Dublin in the tenth century, normally considered to be Norwegian, and like their followers described as "White Foreigners", have been shown to be of Danish stock. Further, Dr. Smyth has argued that the traditional explanation of the distinction made by Irish writers between the Norwegians of Dublin and their rivals, the Danes (probably of York), as one between the *Finn Gaill* or "White Foreigners" and the *Dubh Gaill* or "Black Foreigners", may well have been a mistranslation, the contrast being, instead, between "old" and "new" foreigners in Ireland.[7] Professor Peter Sawyer has added the observation that there was co-operation between both groups in the attack on Dumbarton in 870,[8] and it has long been observed that the Danes of Normandy were led by Rollo or Hrólf, a Norwegian who was a son of Rognvald, Earl of Mòre, the traditional founder of the Orkney earls' dynasty.[9]

It is thus clear that variety was the order of the day, and, while considering general themes, it is the purpose of this paper to point out differences among the various areas and peoples. I see the quality of adaptation to circumstances as the overriding factor in the range of activities engaged in by the Vikings and in the variety of the nature of their settlements.

Figure 1. Places mentioned in the text.

SETTLEMENT

It is in Ireland that we are immediately faced with a crux, for the evidence, as it stands at present, appears to point to an almost exclusive concern by the Norsemen for urban settlement. There were five or more major urban centres in Ireland in the Viking period — Cork, Waterford, Wexford, Limerick and Dublin — which are all attested to in the literary sources. As is well-known, Dublin has produced abundant evidence of buildings, craft-activities and commercial contacts in the archaeological record.[10] The origins of Dublin probably lie in the establishment by the Norse of a *longphort* towards the middle of the ninth century.[10a] It was, therefore, a *de novo* settlement-cum-stronghold, which developed into a major commercial centre. Despite the Vikings' political and economic position in these centres, it does not appear as if they were able to generate any extensive and dependent rural settlements. Despite, also, the very considerable wealth distributed in Ireland, as reflected by the hoards,[11] there is no indication (from concentration of distinctive artefacts) of Viking settlement even on pre-existing Irish sites. Occasionally, artefacts, apparently of Viking origin, have been found in rural locations: for instance at Beginish, County Kerry, where Professor O'Kelly found a steatite bowl of Viking type and a runestone which reads "Liv erected this stone; M . . . carved (the runes)".[12] However, there is no evidence that the settlement implied by the earthworks and field boundaries was founded by Vikings. Indeed, its proximity to Church Island, an Early Christian (i.e. pre-Norse) eremitical or monastic establishment, may well point to an earlier beginning, with the continuance of an extant farming settlement in the Viking period. The excavator's interpretation of the runestone is that "though it gives concrete proof of a Viking visitation of Beginish, there was no evidence that the visit resulted in pillage, destruction and slaughter. In fact, all the evidence available to us goes to show that the islanders lived at peace".[13] Such evidence is, however, relatively rare, and there is no clear evidence of a rural settlement founded by Scandinavians in Ireland.

However, one or two sites can change dramatically a received picture. This is certainly true of what are now called "the Western Isles", but which to the Norse formed, with the Isle of Man, "the Kingdom of the southern isles" or *sudreyar*. Here only two unequivocally Viking sites have been excavated and published.[14] A site on Drimore Machair, South Uist, excavated in two weeks in 1956, produced the plan of a building 14 m x 5 m internally, which may have had, to judge from the published plan of the east end, at least one rebuilding phase.[15] Within the limited time and resources available, it was not possible to excavate any more extensively either around the building or below. Finds such as a hog-backed comb and nail-headed pins were used to place the site in the second half of the ninth century or early tenth century, by analogy with Jarlshof in Shetland. The second site, excavated by Dr. Iain Crawford at Coileagan an Udail ("The Udal") in North Uist, by contrast has been excavated for many years, and represents almost an optimal archaeological opportunity. This was an undisturbed, multi-period group of sites, with the ultimate possibility of presenting a picture in microcosm of settlement in this area of Scotland.[16] Within the late Iron Age/Early Medieval period it has already revolutionized our picture of pre-Viking settlement;[17] although the evidence is not yet published, the excavator is quite adamant that there was a sudden, violent disruption of this existing pattern of ovoid, almost anthropomorphic, buildings, by the superimposition

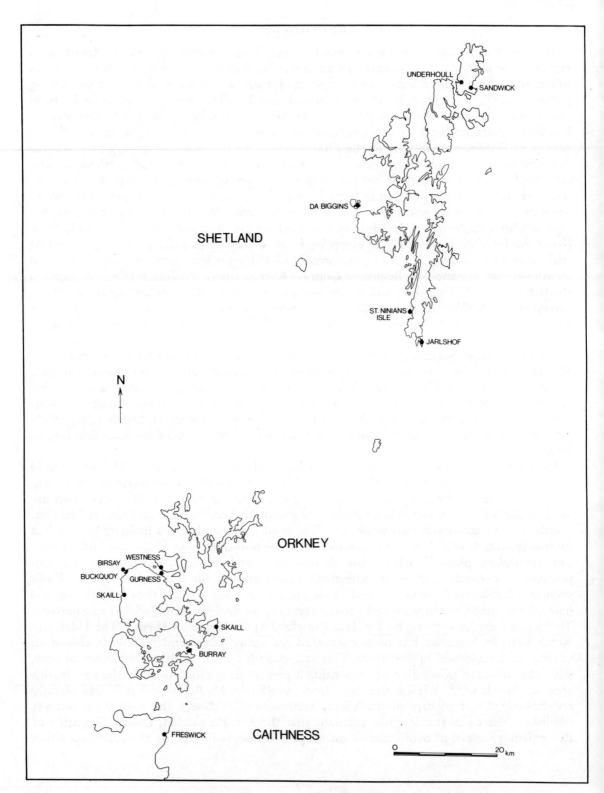

Figure 2. Places mentioned in the text.

by Scandinavians of buildings on top with a completely different alignment.[18] A "fortlet" was established in the mid-ninth century, early-Viking phase, emphasizing the aggressive nature of this takeover.[18] Carbon-dates, coins and other material provide an interlocking dating scheme spanning the Viking period, and documentary material comes into play for the transition to the late Norse/Medieval phases of the site's history.[19] In addition to the vitally important evidence provided by this site for the question of the relationship of native to incomer at the beginning of the Viking period, it is also of great importance in relation to this later transition period, for the archaeological evidence, as interpreted at present, indicates a relatively sharp break. The implications of this for the debate over an origin for the Hebridean blackhouse in the Viking longhouse are considerable.[20]

Another site which spans the later transition period is that of Freswick in Caithness (Figure 3). In the 1930s, Dr. A. O. Curle excavated part of this site,[21] and in 1942 Professor V. G. Childe excavated another part because sand was being quarried for Wick aerodrome.[22] Some of the finds from these excavations were published (but many were not), and they seemed to indicate that a date into the eleventh or twelfth century would be in order — although there was residual earlier material. The buildings found were complex (Figure 4), and tantalising hints were given by Curle of earlier structures below, such as one of post and wattle below the so-called "boat naust".[23] However, Curle's rather disparaging remark that "the Freswick settlement discloses by its relics a class of occupants in poorer circumstances"[24] seems to be at variance with the calibre of stray finds collected on the Freswick Links by a number of persons since Curle's day.[25] Much grass-tempered pottery, some steatite and other objects have since been collected in the more recent surveys of 1979 and 1980, under the direction of Ms. Colleen Batey and myself, and it is clear that material erodes in quantity each year. Furthermore, a survey of the cliff edges shows that, in addition to inland sites being disturbed by rabbit action, the coast has been cut back in places (in the main by actions of wind and wave) up to 40 or 50 metres since 1942. Some of this is due to quarrying for sand, but much is disturbed each year by winter storms. (Plate 40). Structures as well as artefacts are tumbling out of the cliff edges, and a programme of rescue excavation was begun in 1980 on this, the only proven mainland Scottish Viking settlement site.

Apart from the post-and-wattle structures at Freswick, whose dating and archaeological relationships are unclear, there is yet little hint of a pre-Viking settlement, for the sites of the broch — relocated in the 1980 excavations — and the possible souterrains[26] have not yielded any material that might be classed as "Pictish". So, as yet, Freswick has little to offer to the debate about the nature of the initial Viking impact in northern Britain, and there is no published excavation evidence for other Norse settlement sites in Caithness and Sutherland.[27] Whether the situation was similar to that in the Western Isles is unknown, and more intensive survey work and selective excavation is needed in this region to provide basic data.[28] But the picture of disruption, and their submergence in terms of material culture, of the pre-Norse at the Udal demonstrates the differences that can appear between different areas of the British Viking world, for, on the basis of excavated evidence from the Orkney site of Buckquoy in the Bay of Birsay, Dr. Anna Ritchie has postulated considerable integration between the Norse and pre-Norse Pictish people.[29] Her ovoid "Pictish" buildings — large-scale versions perhaps of Crawford's buildings at the Udal — are themselves built and rebuilt within the Pictish period, and

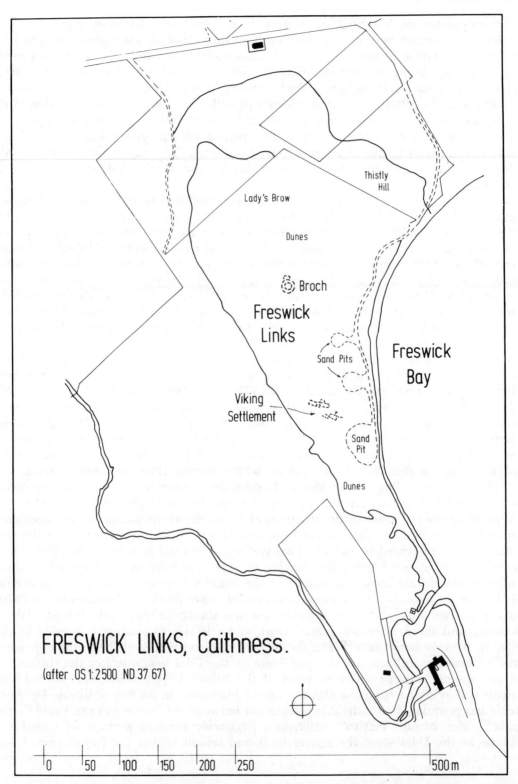

Figure 3.   Freswick: general plan showing remains of buildings discovered.

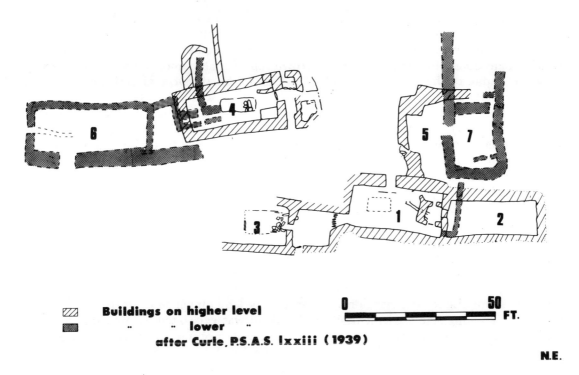

Figure 4. Freswick Links: general plan showing remains of buildings discovered.

the latest building (House 4) is partially superimposed by the northeastern part of the early Norse farmstead (Building 3). However, the cultural assemblage associated with the Norse building and its two successors, Houses 2 and 1, are notable for the occurrence of native types, especially bone pins and composite bone combs. For instance, the three high-backed comb fragments illustrated by Ritchie (Numbers 47, 48, 49) came from the latest Norse building phase, but were of a distinctive type which "would appear to have been a local Orcadian fashion, most probably among the Pictish population, and does not appear to have been found outside Orkney".[30] The composite double-sided combs, from middle and late Norse phases (IV and V), were also "of native rather than Norse form, while perhaps reflecting Norse influence in the incised decoration".[31] There are other objects apparently clearly Norse in character, such as three gaming boards, probably of the game *hnefatafl* (although even here it has been pointed out that similar games were known in the Celtic areas).[32] The site went out of use and was eventually utilized for a burial, much more clearly in the Norse tradition.

As Dr. Ritchie has pointed out, of the amazingly small number of excavated Norse settlements found in Scotland, all but three were built literally on top of earlier settlements.[33] A single building from Gurness, Orkney, overlay small trefoil-shaped buildings set around a broch, akin to the early Pictish phase at Buckquoy,[34] and at Jarlshof in Shetland most of the stone utilized for building the Norse houses must have come from the walls of the broch and wheelhouse.[35] Jarlshof is well known and often used as a type-site for the Norse settlement in the north of Britain.[36] The dwelling-houses are

long, slightly bow-shaped buildings and there are also subsidiary buildings more
rectangular in form. The site has provided us with a detailed picture of the growth of a
settlement over several centuries from one "parent" dwelling to a complex settlement,
which Alan Small has described as a "township".[37] The impression of complexity,
however, is due to the successive building at this site on the prime farming land in Shetland, from the early prehistoric until the post-Medieval period, and to the nature of the
consolidation of the remains, rather than to the original nature of the Viking settlement.
The plan is indeed complex, but even in the Viking period it represents several phases
superimposed on top of one another. It is quite clear from J. R. C. Hamilton's brilliant
analysis of the stratigraphy and phasing that at any one time there were probably no
more than three families living at this site.[38] Thus, although it is a nucleated settlement,
it is certainly not a "town" in the conventional sense of the term, and only in the strict
Northern Isles sense can it be called a "township", with a derivation from an agrarian
origin in Old Norse *tun*.[39] Certainly, the material found here has been interpreted in
agricultural terms, and, perhaps surprisingly for a site so near to good fishing, exploitation of the sea's resources appears to have been secondary.[40] There is very little exotic
imported material such as might have been expected from a "town" or trading post.
That a settlement on such an important site is dominated by agriculture suggests that
the original impulse for immigration was a search for land on which to settle.

A second Viking Age settlement site in Shetland was excavated by Mr. Alan Small at
Underhoull on Unst, which was a smaller single-building unit, possibly with a second
unit nearby.[41] On the basis of these two sites, Alan Small has constructed a model of the
ideal, basic environmental factors for a settlement of the Viking Age.[42] It envisages an
economy based on mixed agriculture, with fishing also playing an important role. To
provide utensils and tools, access to sources of bog-iron and steatite (soapstone) is
desirable, and peat would be necessary for fuel. This model is valuable in focusing our
attention on the essential features of Viking settlement units, but one needs to remember
that essentially it applies to Shetland and Faroe — very different landscapes from
Orkney.[43] Small himself has drawn out the available land for such settlement in Shetland,
and environmental factors make a very small percentage of the land mass suitable (the
picture is the same for Faroe).[44] Orkney, on the other hand, is very fertile,[45] and it need
not surprise us if the resulting pattern may turn out to be somewhat different from
Small's model for Shetland — but that is a matter for future work. Even in Shetland the
picture is likely to be modified somewhat, as work is also in progress at "Da Biggins",
Papa Stour and Sandwick, Unst, which, although from the Late Norse/Medieval period,
have a bearing upon earlier settlement patterns, and upon the exploitation of the
environment.[46]

One aspect of Viking settlement that has been much debated concerns the nature
of the initial impact of the incomers on pre-existing settlement and settlers. Part of the
debate has centred on whether there were any occupied sites when the earliest Vikings
came. As regards Jarlshof, Hamilton quite clearly stated that "When the Viking colonists
arrived about A.D. 800 the site was still occupied by a few scattered families living in
the small huts on the landward side of the mound and still making use of the older
wheel-and-passage houses".[47] If he is correct that "the boundary wall enclosing this
settlement influenced the siting of the new farmstead . . . (which) was situated to the
east of this enclosure",[48] then this is of considerable significance for the relationship

of native to Norse on this site. Earlier contributions have tended to generalize the debate as to whether the pre-Norse inhabitants of the Northern Isles were dealt with violently, were subdued and enslaved, or simply fled at the advent of the Vikings.[49] For the latter suggestion, there is, for instance, the association by Dr. Radford and Mr. Cruden of the deposition of a finely-decorated work box in a bog in Orkney with the advent of the Vikings. They were discussing another Viking site, that of the Brough of Birsay, Orkney:

"This early site at Birsay is of a small ecclesiastical settlement which must have been in occupation in the eighth and early ninth century, and probably earlier. It is reasonable to associate with it a wooden box and tools of c. 800 which have been found in a bog about 2 kilometres away. This was probably dropped by one of the inmates flying before the Norse pirates from Dicuil, writing c. 820, reports as having recently caused the flight of Irish monks from the Faroes . . ."[50]

Apart from the fact that it was probably found at a considerably greater distance away[51] than two kilometres, it seems essentially unlikely that such an object could be dated with such precision that one could associate it in this way with a general comment about a quite separate group of islands in the North Atlantic.[52] I am afraid that I remain unconvinced that such disparate historical and archaeological material can be associated.

At present, the problem of the relationship of native peoples to incoming Scandinavians is unlikely to be resolved on the basis of individual site reports. Dr. Ritchie's suggestion of cultural integration, mentioned above, is a reasonable interpretation of some aspects of the material from Buckquoy, Birsay, and Orkney,[53] just as the evidence of the buried hoard at St Ninian's Isle, Shetland, can reasonably be interpreted in terms of panic on the part of the native peoples at the advent of the Vikings, whether the material is interpreted as ecclesiastical or secular.[54] The most recent brief discussion simply juxtaposes the one interpretation against the other, and attempts to assert the greater significance of the St Ninian's Isle evidence.[55] Methodologically, this is hardly convincing and certainly not conclusive. On the general level, as opposed to the specific interpretation of individual sites, it seems to me that such questions can be meaningfully posed and answers attempted only when there is a greater range of sites to discuss.

Recent years have seen a considerable increase in the number of sites and areas being examined in Orkney, which may have a bearing upon these matters. Mr. Peter Gelling of Birmingham University has been engaged for a number of years on a multi-period examination of sites around the Bay of Skaill, Deerness. His own summary of the work will shortly be available, and therefore will not be discussed here.[56] Another important series of excavations, under the direction of Dr. Sigrid Kaland of Bergen University, is taking place around the Bay of Westness, Rousay. Despite a recent statement that a ninth-century farmstead has been found here with its family cemetery,[57] it will be some time before definitive interpretations of what are, at present, discrete archaeological sites can be made. The interim report on the earlier phase of excavations by Dr. Kaland[58] has indicated the high quality of both buildings and graves, but the precise relationship between the cemetery, the boat naust, the dwellings, the earlier grave from the Knowe of Swandro,[59] the place-name Skaill (to the west of the site and now associated with a deserted settlement),[60] and the probable castle-site of "The Wirk",[61] indicates that the evolution of settlement in this area was a complex process.

The Brough of Birsay, mentioned above, is a tidal island at the north-west of a bay in Orkney that includes the area of Buckquoy where Dr. Ritchie excavated. There can be no doubt that this site was important in both the pre-Viking and Viking periods. It has, for

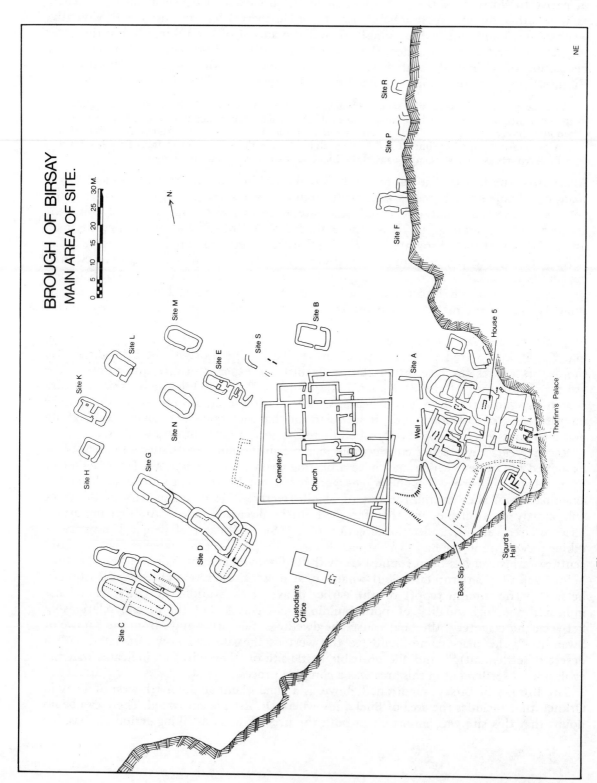

Figure 5. Brough of Birsay, Orkney. Main area of site.

instance, a small church with graveyard around that has been seen to go back to the Early Christian period, if it was not in fact a monastic establishment (Figure 5).[62] There is an abundance of artefactual material from a number of excavations,[63] including ones carried out over the past seven years by myself and my colleague, Dr. John Hunter of Bradford University.[64] Examples of pre-Norse material include a Pictish ogam stone (Plate 41) and moulds for pre-Norse penannular brooches of the St Ninian's Isle type.[65] Bone pins of native type, with a "hip" or swelling, and high-backed composite combs similar to those from Buckquoy have also been found.[66] A superficially unpretentious piece of metalwork has emerged under X-ray as a very fine example of a mount with interlace and a cross design (Plate 42). Radio-carbon dates have also been received, which clearly cluster in the pre-Norse period; some of the dates came from deposits below the walls of Norse buildings. These Norse buildings are to the west and north of the churchyard — significantly, in my opinion, respecting the line of the enclosure — and vary in size from large buildings, 15 or 20 metres long, to small ones, whose walls demonstrate clearly that there has been constant rebuilding on this site. Clearly, much assimilation of evidence has to be done before final judgements can be made about the relationship of Norse and pre-Norse here, but sufficient evidence has perhaps been mentioned to indicate its potential importance on a more general level.[67]

Indeed it is now clear that Buckquoy and the known site of the Brough of Birsay are but two settlement sites among many in this area.[68] Recent monitoring of the coast, which suffers greatly from storm-damage and erosion, has demonstrated that this area was an attractive one for settlement in the past, from the Bronze Age onwards. Excavations on a number of sites have revealed structures or artefacts of the pre-Viking and Viking periods (Figure 6). About one hundred metres away from the Buckquoy site excavated by Dr. Ritchie was a complete building with an internal figure-of-eight shape, now set on the edge of a cliff, next to the circular end of a building akin to the "Late Pictish" building at Buckquoy, that had mostly fallen over the cliff (Plate 43). Two graves below carefully constructed cairns nearby (Plate 44), are stratigraphically earlier than a Viking period cist-grave, and are arguably pre-Norse.[69] Other buildings probably from the Viking period have been found at sites both in the village of Birsay and on a completely separate part of the Brough of Birsay (Plate 45), also as a result of rescue or salvage archaeology. It is thus clear that there is ample material for the study of settlement evolution in one small area of the Viking world. Hopefully this will go some way towards answering questions not only about the relationship of native and Norse in northern Scotland, but also about the nature of the Viking settlement itself in that area of Orkney which was chosen by the Earls for their seat.

With the multiplication of sites at Birsay, it is evident that projects of rescue archaeology, within a research framework that emphasizes area survey and the relationship of sites both spatially and temporally, are likely to be academically more satisfying than projects emphasizing single sites. In northern England, two such intensive survey projects in upland areas have revealed settlement sites that are probably from the Viking period, related to extensive field systems.[70] Both are situated high up in the Pennines on what now is regarded as marginal land, for sheep and/or grouse, but clearly both have in the past seen extensive and intensive exploitation of the land. The sites are of similar form, with buildings added to the boundaries, and set around a courtyard. Coin dating at Ribblehead places it in the mid-ninth century, and provisional carbon-dating on one of

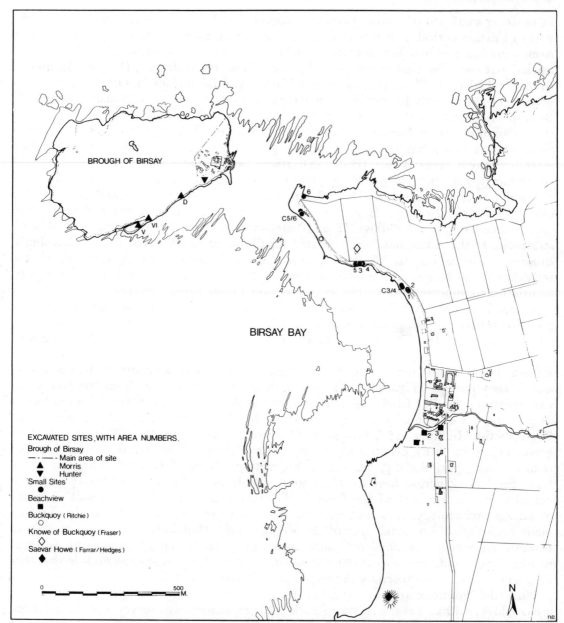

EXCAVATED SITES, WITH AREA NUMBERS.
Brough of Birsay
— ·—·— - Main area of site
▲   Morris
▼   Hunter
Small Sites
●
Beachview
■
Buckquoy (Ritchie)
○
Knowe of Buckquoy (Fraser)
◇
Saevar Howe (Farrar/Hedges)
◆

Figure 6.   Birsay Bay, Orkney. Excavated sites, with area numbers.

the Simy Folds sites might place it a little earlier. The problem here for the excavators, Mr. Alan King at Ribblehead and Mr. Dennis Coggins at Simy Folds, is that of archaeological identification, for there is little in the cultural assemblage at either site that is distinctive. In an article referred to above, Dr. Ritchie noted that "It is clear that the absence of imported artefacts is a common situation on Norse colonial sites", and quoted the example of L'Anse aux Meadows in Newfoundland "where the only foreign artefacts were an Icelandic stone lamp and a Hiberno–Scottish ring-pin".[71] In these two northern English cases the problem is that there are no distinctive artefacts: has integration taken place to such an extent that Scandinavians are no longer culturally identifiable, or are these non-Scandinavian upland settlements of the Viking period?

The question is even more acute for lowland areas of England, where in the past the only criterion used for establishing a link with the Vikings has been a "bow" or "boat" shape for buildings, based upon evidence from sites such as Jarlshof, with distinctive Scandinavian artefacts. Scandinavian connections have been suggested for one or two English sites without such artefacts.[72] It is difficult to use satisfactorily negative evidence – in this case the absence of Viking artefacts – for we are unaware as archaeologists of the precise circumstances for their absence. It is obvious that exotica are more likely to be found at either commercial centres or sites belonging to the upper echelons of society, but there is also the factor of the nature of the soil matrix, which can either preserve or destroy many artefacts (such as leather goods) which when found are often quite distinctive. Also, recent work has indicated that a simple association of this building form with the Vikings or Viking period is no longer justifiable, for not only is it found earlier than this in Scandinavia,[73] but also, according to the excavators of sites in Germany, Frisia and southern England, in non-Scandinavian contexts.[74] It may be that some of the "classic" examples cited, such as Jarlshof, could well now be seen more as variants on a basic rectangular form than as distinctive forms. It would follow then that the typological development implied from a bow-shape to rectangular would be open to doubt.[75] The situation in England will only be resolved by the intensive area study of the kind presently being carried out in North Uist, Orkney and Caithness. The dramatic results that can be obtained from large area work in lowland locations is demonstrated by the recent Danish excavations at Vorbasse and other sites in Jutland which have revolutionized concepts of the nature of settlement in this period in Jutland.[76]

Similar problems have already arisen in the Isle of Man. Here a number of excavations, mostly by Mr. Peter Gelling, have taken place on settlement sites apparently of the Viking Age.[77] Cronk ny Merriu, for instance, has produced a building of sub-rectangular form with benches along the inside of the walls of turf and stone, but no clear dating evidence from artefacts was recovered here in the confines of a small Iron Age promontory form. Inland, a large farm appears to be represented at the site of the Braaid where circular, rectangular and sub-rectangular or bow-shaped buildings have been excavated.[78] It is not known whether the circular building, of pre-Norse form, survived into the Viking period or, if it did, whether it was used as a dwelling or an animal-pen.[79] In the absence of clear, stratigraphical evidence (the site was first excavated in 1935–37) and of finds in association with the buildings, this is unlikely to be resolved without further excavation, and quite possibly not then. Attribution of the bow-shaped building to the Viking period is on the basis of house-type[80] – as indeed it is at the much smaller farm of Doarlish Cashen, where the excavator said that "the sole evidence for date in the Norse period consists of the oblong plan and the tripartite division of the main part of the building into a central floor with two raised benches".[81] Some of the few finds made at these Manx sites emphasize the continuance of such settlements (or even their foundation?) in the late Norse or Viking/Medieval period.

The problem faced in England, therefore, is here also: how can such sites be demonstrated to be Viking? An answer may be given, as it is in northern England for

Ribblehead, on the basis of political probability and the existence of other evidence of a more circumstantial nature, such as stray finds, place-names, or stone sculpture in particular styles found in the vicinity. The Isle of Man was under Norse rule for a considerable length of time, and other evidence such as that from graves, place-names and sculpture provides background evidence for the settlements.[82] Dr. Gerhard Bersu also emphasized the role of promontory forts in the Viking period,[83] but they are difficult to date to this period because of a general lack of artefacts.[84] Indeed, Cronk Ny Merriu, mentioned above, was re-occupied at a time when the defences were ruinous,[85] while the site of Vowlan, Ramsey, excavated by Bersu, was considered to be Viking on the basis of the form of rectangular wooden buildings, and the probability that Viking raiders would first establish themselves in temporary structures in defensible positions.[86] Bersu's interpretation could be correct, of course, for there is no doubt that there was a period of disruption when Vikings raided many locations in the British Isles. Such sites might be taken to indicate that settlement proceeded first on one basis and then on another, but in the absence of dated artefacts this cannot be conclusive.

Changing circumstances are perhaps more clearly demonstrated in York, the political heart of Northumbria, which was taken twice by Scandinavians, first in 867, and then in 919.[87] This centre became in 867 a power-base not only for establishing control of the immediately adjacent area, but also for forays farther afield, both north and south. But then in 876, as quoted above, land settlement took place. Similarly, in the second decade of the tenth century, land was taken over after the initial military and political action. Political history is somewhat confusing in the period after 919, but behind the apparent confusion seem to be two factors: a dynastic squabble in Dublin, with whom the York rulers were linked;[88] and the apparent determination of the Archbishop Wulfstan (with the backing of a group of nobles in Northumbria) to act as "king-maker".[89] However, it is notable that, although the Viking rulers of York were numerous and rapidly-changing, there was no great revolt against Scandinavian rulers as such and considerable opposition to the West Saxon kings' pretensions. A truly Anglo-Scandinavian community grew up not only in York itself, but also in its hinterland, which manifests itself now in the survival of large groups of Scandinavianized settlement names and of a distinctive approach to ornamentation on stone sculpture.[90]

Unlike Dublin,[90a] York was a town already in existence in the mid-ninth century. However, it is clear from the archaeological evidence that its character changed fundamentally in the Anglo-Scandinavian period.[91] In the first place, the focus of the town shifted from the erstwhile Roman fort to an area between the rivers Ouse and Foss, with a new bridge leading into this area. Second, it is clear that a pattern of streets and property divisions, which have lasted in many cases to the present day, go back to the Anglo-Scandinavian period. The "gates" of York (from ON *gata* = "street")[92] were clearly named then, and on a number of sites, including the recent extensive and spectacular excavations by the York Archaeological Trust at Coppergate, it has been evident that the property boundaries and buildings were built and rebuilt on top of each other. Recent excavations have shown the existence of shops set along the street fronts, with workshops behind. Woodworking was a major activity on the site,[93] and, if Radley's interpretation of features discovered in 1902 is correct, other working-areas were nearby, including that of a tanner.[94] The earlier buildings appear to have been of wicker or wattle, subsequently replaced in the later period by buildings of plank-built construction, which themselves are reminiscent of the wooden buildings of Hedeby, the Danish trading-town, and display a considerable sophistication in timber technique. Dating evidence has been provided by coins, and the preservation of thousands of objects, many organic, in the hundreds of contexts should ensure a comprehensive picture of settlement here.

ECONOMIC ASPECTS

Mention of the workshops of York serves to lead into a consideration of some economic aspects of the Viking settlement in the British Isles. The fundamental work that has taken place over the last two decades on the origin, nature and development of towns has demonstrated clearly that, while some towns began as defensive places or *burhs* in the time of Alfred or Edward the Elder, some had a commercial function well before the Viking period. Literary sources mention Frisian traders at York and London, and archaeological investigation at Southampton has begun to indicate the position of this centre in the European trading network of the eighth century.[95] However, while the exotica and external trade connections are easiest to discern in the archaeological record, basic to our understanding of the functioning of such centres must be the less spectacular material and goods brought into the towns from their hinterlands. It is not easy to identify internal trade, archaeologically,[96] but it is essential to grasp the hierarchy of activity, land organization and sites that contribute to the functioning of the economic system as a whole, of which the towns form the apex. Within the system at one level, two elements must have been of considerable importance: royal involvement and/or control, and ecclesiastical or monastic patronage. The more obvious of these is the royal involvement, with the exaction of taxes and tolls by kings, their granting of land to individuals or the Church, and their control of markets.

One of the major beneficiaries of land grants from the kings was the Church.[97] In many cases, grants were of land to support monastic establishments: St Wilfrid was, for instance, given considerable land holdings in the Pennines area for his monastery at Ripon. Similarly, Benedict Biscop, his contemporary, was given land in two grants for the new monastery of Jarrow–Wearmouth, which was described as fit to support 70 and 40 families. We know that St Cuthbert's monastery of Lindisfarne gathered together very extensive estates in the pre-Viking and Viking periods, and the description of one grant – that of Cartmel – as *omnes Britannos cum eo* does draw attention to the likelihood that many grants were operating economic units or estates, with people on the land. There are occasional references also to individuals who appear to be estate managers, holding the land in return for "rendering full (or faithful) service" to the community. Thus, the lands granted to the monasteries are likely to have been developed so that they produced not just the immediate means of living, but also surplus that would then go back to the monasteries. It is this surplus, presumably, which enabled monasteries like Jarrow to produce great manuscripts such as the *Codex Amiatinus*, the vellum for which required 500 sheep- or calf-hides, and men such as Benedict Biscop to go on journeys to the Mediterranean world to procure other books for their own monasteries. It need not surprise us, therefore, to find clear evidence in the Viking period in northern and midland England of Scandinavians taking over such estates. Sometimes, as Professor Sawyer has pointed out, these estates may have been bought,[98] but, not surprisingly, we also know of estates being seized — as for instance *circa* 919 when Ragnald, a new King of York, gave some of the Lindisfarne estates in north-east England to his followers, Scula and Onlafbal.[99] Certain place-names such as Copeland in Cumbria (ON *Kaupa-land*) or Holderness in Yorkshire (ON *hold*) also seem to reflect this process,[100] and Amounderness (Lancs.) was bought back by the church at York from Asmundr in the tenth century.[101] I would suggest that it is such a process of taking over estates that is implied in the *Chronicle* entries for 876, 877 and 880 quoted above, and that, on both occasions in 876 and 919 when a Scandinavian ruler seized York, the political control was followed by economic takeover of estates.

It is the relationship of these estates, and the settlement units within them, to York that is so important for our understanding of the nature of the Scandinavian settlement in this northern English area. In archaeological terms, this is perhaps one of the most difficult things to establish. Without particularly distinctive material from an individual site or estate, it is well-nigh impossible to trace the links. It is not known, for instance, how much of the iron-working discovered at one of the two Simy Folds sites referred to above might have been surplus to the needs of the farming communities in Teesdale.[102] From analysis of faunal data, it has been established that the community at Ribblehead, rather surprisingly, was consuming (and presumably farming) cattle as much as sheep.[103] This indicates that the micro-economy (and presumably micro-environment and climate) there was different from the present situation, and this is backed up by the presence of parts of a quern-stone for corn grinding.[104] But, again, how much was surplus we do not (and probably cannot) know. The finding of objects at Ribblehead that were not merely related to self-sufficient, subsistence, agricultural activity (such as the spearhead, the coins and, conceivably, the bell) might well indicate exchange, and therefore an agricultural surplus, but beyond that inference we cannot go at present.

However, there is a way forward at the other end of the network, at York, which demonstrates its role as a centre for agriculture and the exploitation of the Northumbrian hinterland. It is now generally accepted that conventional methods of excavation miss much of the vital information, which is unspectacular and more likely to arise from analysis in the laboratory of samples from refuse layers and pits. Systematic on-site sampling can enable recovery of material that is more comprehensive, so that the zoologist, for instance, is given a full faunal spectrum to analyse, which includes the small mammals, fish and bird bones, as well as bones of the larger mammals.[105] One of the great achievements of the York Archaeological Trust has been the advances in environmental archaeology that have resulted. Not only has work been carried out on the implications of the faunal and other material recovered, but new methods have been developed, for instance in the study of insect remains[106] and in the relationship of each category of evidence to the other within the particular archaeological context of Anglo-Scandinavian York. At the Lloyds Bank site, for instance, the working of leather was demonstrated not only from the recovery of artefacts such as shoes and knife sheaths, but also from the debris of animals hairs from cleaning the skins, and the decomposers that feed on such waste. In addition, the presence of oak bark chips, sometimes used in the preparation of the hides, and a particular type of beetle, *Trox scaber*, also suggested tanning activities.[107] Even if more recent work might question some of the more wide-ranging implications drawn from analysis of the debris from a particular site, nevertheless, this example from York emphasizes the importance of trying to glimpse the *association* of the town with its hinterland around, and of the *association* of the artefacts and structures with environmental material.

Distinguishing subsistence activity and consumption from commercial activity and production is obviously important to the archaeologist. In relation to faunal material, it would be necessary to find differential deposits of animal bone, with certain types of bone present or absent according to the situation (e.g. a dump of sheep heads at a butcher's yard), and this sort of material is emerging from York. The achievement of the York Trust, and its environmental research fellows, is adequately indicated by their contribution to the CBA research report on *Viking Age York and the North*;[108] and their detailed reports in relation to particular sites are eagerly awaited.

Some of the activities that must have been dependent on the hinterland of York are already well known from the work so far.[109] Working of leather has already been mentioned, and there is abundant material to demonstrate the working of deer antler in every stage from shed antler to finished combs. Similarly, the working of bone presumably must have had an intimate connection with the activity of the meat traders at York. It has become clear from the work on the site of Coppergate that here one of the main craft activities was the working of wood by coopers. The excavated material has provided evidence from the various stages of manufacture up to the finished product — in this case wooden bowls. Sometimes the raw material will have come from York's own hinterland: this is probably the case with jet from the Whitby area, and it is conceivably the case with the amber — although here it may be debatable how much could be collected from the beaches and how much might have been imported as raw material. Other objects found in the recent excavations which are witness to York's role as a centre of craft activity and manufacture include the stone slab decorated in Jellinge style[110] and the series of slabs found below York Minster.[111] As my colleague James Lang has recently observed,[112] one of the main problems in York is knowing whether material found that necessarily reflects activity in that city. It is now clear from the finding of a mould at Blake Street, that production of brooches, arguably of a mainstream Scandinavian form, was undertaken here.[113] On the other hand, it is by no means certain whether the Coppergate scabbard-chape, so like ones from Iceland and Finland, was made at York, or was imported as a finished product. James Lang has pointed out the possibility that some objects found at York — particularly pewter disc brooches imitating higher-grade silver work, with filigree at the edges — may have been copies of higher-class goods made for general consumption.[114]

Thus, York's importance as a centre of craft activity and, to a lesser extent, as a centre for distribution to northern England, is evident. Extant material from York testifies also to its role as an *entrepôt*: steatite moulds for ingots, and honestones both illustrate these wider connections with Scandinavia, while the recent find of a silk pouch from the Mediterranean exemplifies the exotic material to be found in the international centres of the Viking world.[115] Material occasionally found at other sites in Britain shows the link in the other direction: recently a finely-decorated bone knife-handle was found in Canterbury; its decoration is best compared to northern English, if not York material, as James Lang and James Graham-Campbell have observed.[116] Finally, one may reflect upon the implications of the finds of valuable silver in hoards such as those from Goldsborough and Bossall/Flaxton in the hinterland or York.[117] While they may be connected with Hiberno–Norse incursions into the north of England in the tenth century, it is also possible that they reflect the introduction of wealth to York as a commercial centre, and the redistribution of such wealth to the hinterland of the city – just as Mr. Graham-Campbell has suggested that the hoards in Ireland reflect the distribution of wealth from Dublin and the other Irish urban commercial centres of the Viking Age to their hinterlands.[118] The renewed development of coinage at York in the late ninth and tenth centuries also reflects the role of York within the economy of Anglo-Scandinavian and Anglo-Saxon England.[119] The local production of this coinage has been demonstrated by the recent discoveries in the Coppergate excavations of lead strips for testing coin-dyes[120] as well as an iron coin die.[121]

York may be taken as an example here of the range of material to be found in the Insular Viking-Age towns. Dublin is clearly demonstrating a similar rich array of survivals from the Viking period, both in structures and in artefacts, and, when fuller publication has taken place of the recent work in both centres, it will be fascinating to compare them. In particular, Dublin's relationship with its hinterland is a matter that will need consideration, for, despite the lack of evidence for a coin-using economy in Ireland until the end of the tenth century,[122] the hoards found on Irish soil demonstrate that wealth was distributed here.[123] Mr. Graham-Campbell's analysis of the material in Ireland and of that from Scotland has already been referred to, and he has emphasized the lack of urban and commercial centres and a native coinage in Scotland as compared to Ireland. However, Dolley's work on the Hiberno–Norse coinage has shown that these native coins were of little value outside their origin centres,[124] and it is far more likely that units of measure of silver would have been in terms of weight, as represented by ingots or the arm-rings to which both Graham-Campbell and Warner have drawn attention.[125] These are found in both Ireland and Scotland, and there can be little doubt that the western areas of Britain would have been affected by, if not linked to, the growing commercial centres in Ireland.[126] Since Graham-Campbell's articles were written, it has in fact been demonstrated by Professor Dolley that a Hiberno–Manx coinage existed,[127] and this provides a link on the one hand with Ireland, and on the other with the Kingdom of the Isles (the *sudreyar*), of which Man was a part. It is not really possible to speak at this time of "Scotland" as a whole, for the political realities of the day were rather of the Kingdom of the Picts and Scots (united *circa* 947 by Kenneth MacAlpin) in the central and eastern mainland, and two Scandinavian-dominated areas in the Orkney Earldom and the Kindom of the Isles. Merchant graves of the Viking period in the western isles,[128] and large hoards from both the Isle of Man and Orkney,[129] both appear to me to demonstrate the economic interconnection of the different political units within the British Viking world.

As has been implied above, there is a danger in being over-impressed by the spectacular, and to underestimate the significance of more mundane material. In the eleventh century, legal clauses referring to Billingsgate in London mention goods such as fish and timber as imports; and there are other references to dairy products, wine, down, fur and salt, which are all equally fugitive in the archaeological record.[130] Perhaps we underestimate the extent to which wealth could be acquired and accumulated on the basis of the exploitation of basic commodities and raw materials. Reference has been made above to the estates of northern Britain, and it is inconceivable that considerable profit was not to be had out of land holding. While there are no such records for northern Scotland as those from northern England, occasional references to "estates" in the *Orkneyinga Saga* do hint at the exploitation and management of land here.[131]

One such "estate" is that of Freswick in Caithness. Mention of previous excavations and the continuing destruction of the site has been made, but perhaps even more significant than the artefacts recovered from the site are the middens. Along much of the coastline of the bay, for several hundreds of metres, are midden deposits. One of the environmental consultants for the Viking and Early Settlement Archaeological Research Project has stated that the potential here is vast, and probably one of the best chances to examine archaeological and environmental material from the Norse period in detailed relationship to each other outside York. For instance, here the sheer size of the fishbone recovered from surface collection and sampling indicates that cod were caught of a size up to two metres long — a size apparently seldom caught nowadays! At one point on the eroding coast there is an almost solid layer of fishbone, and excavation of a small area in 1980 uncovered several articulated partial fish skeletons. Both column samples and the first test excavation area have yielded, after fine sieving and flotation, massive amounts of fishbone. Work in the last two years on a small scale has, therefore, raised the possibility for a similar study here of the detailed relationship of a settlement, its economy, and its own environment to that at York. However, the likelihood is that Freswick represents a different kind of site, possibly a centre for food production in contrast to York's role as a centre for consumption. It is potentially one of the links in the economic chain or network that at present we imperfectly understand. That more than the domestic consumption of a rural settlement is involved is evident not only from the vast amount of material, but also, for instance, from the recovery in the test excavation area of a preponderance of bones of the head and upper vertebrae of fishes. The area excavated is too small to permit generalizations, but it must suggest that nearby was an area where a quantity of fish were gutted and prepared. The scale of the material — both in quantity and size — indicates that larger area excavation would be likely to indicate that a fundamental aspect of the settlement of the "estate" established here was its ability to exploit the fishing grounds. This is as yet speculative, but the potential is considerable for an understanding, through biological analysis and excavation, of the Norse economy and exploitation of the environment in the north of Scotland.[132] Previous work at Buckquoy, and current projects at Birsay and at Sandwick, Unst, Shetland,[133] raise the possibility that comparison may be made with the two island groups to the north at this time.

Conclusion

This, then, brings us back to our understanding of the system as a whole. For rural areas in Viking Britain, the way forward is to undertake intensive economic and environmental projects linked to settlement studies in the area, just as such intensive study has been undertaken in towns such as York. Once these are undertaken in different areas, it will be possible to see how these areas differed from each other in economic terms, and how these settlements related to the political realities of the time. What is certain is that the nature of Viking settlement in the British Isles was exceedingly complex. The complexity within an urban commercial centre of the Viking period is being revealed at York and Dublin, as well as some indication of the relationships to the immediate hinterlands as well as the wider world. But, as has been argued above, since town and country were intimately connected in an economic continuum, it is necessary to have detailed studies of these rural settlements and their economic bases to understand the connection. Work has begun, but much more is needed.

Acknowledgements

Without the stimulus of the invitations from Cornell University and the Metropolitan Museum, it would have been difficult to bring this paper to fruition. Without the help of friends and colleagues, it might have proved impossible. The foot-notes indicate my indebtedness to specific people for particular information, but in particular Peter Addyman and Richard Hall have always been free with information about the excavations at York. James Lang has had the dubious privilege of sharing the teaching with me of a course on "Norway, Britain and Ireland in the Viking Period" in Durham: his contributions in discussions both formal and informal over the years have ranged far more widely than his own researches on Viking art and artefacts in north Britain, and helped me greatly. Colleen Batey has read each illegible draft of the text from beginning to end, and made valuable comments over and above those concerned with Caithness. I am particularly grateful for her immense help with the bibliography. Norman Emery has, again, managed to translate vague ideas into the substance of the accompanying figure drawings, for which I give him my thanks. Finally, I must acknowledge the technical assistance of the Archaeology Department at Durham, and in particular Vera Sudworth, who has cheerfully typed from an appalling manuscript.

NOTES

1.   *See* Lucas 1966 and 1967; Morris 1979a; Graham-Campbell 1978-9.

1a.   Summaries for particular areas have been published in Wilson 1968-1976; Wilson 1971; Wilson 1974; Wilson 1976.

2.   The translation used is that of Professor Dorothy Whitelock in Whitelock, Douglas and Tucker 1965.

3.   Graham-Campbell 1975-76 and 1976.

4.   Dolley 1966.

5.   Graham-Campbell 1976, 53-4.

6.   Smyth 1975 and 1977.

7.   Smyth 1975-76.

8.   Sawyer 1978b, 118.

9.   Anderson 1873, cxxxii.

10.   O'Riordain 1971 and 1976; Barry 1979; National Museum of Ireland 1973; Curriculum Development Unit 1978.

10a.   Recent historical and topographical analysis by Howard B. Clark (1977) has led to his suggestion that Viking Dublin was preceded by two eighth-century settlements. If future archaeological support can be adduced for this suggestion of pre-Viking origins for Dublin, then many assumptions about the Viking impact here will need close re-examination.

11.   Dolley & Ingold 1961; Dolley 1966, ch. II: Graham-Campbell 1974a; Graham-Campbell 1976.

12.   O'Kelly 1955-6 and 1961.

13.   O'Kelly 1955-6, 191.

14.   I leave out of consideration here the site of Little Dunagoil, Bute (Marshall 1964). Despite the fact that it has been cited in the past as a Viking settlement, there is no positive evidence for such an identification. Cf. also Wilson 1971.

15.   Maclaren 1974.

16.   Crawford 1974 and 1977. Also *see* Crawford 1965, 43-7 and 55.

17.   *See* for example the reports in Crawford 1971, 1972, 1973.

18.   Crawford 1974, 9-11; 1977, 131.

19.   Crawford 1965 Table 1 and 36-41, 1975 11-13, 1977, Fig. 2 and 131-2; Graham-Campbell 1973; Graham-Campbell 1974b; Dolley & Skaare 1973.

20.   Crawford 1965, 56; Crawford 1974, 1; Crawford 1977, 132-3; Roussell 1934; Curwen 1938; Kissling 1943; Fenton 1978. But *N.B.* Crawford 1975 reports a continuity in corn-kiln here.

21.   Curle 1938-9.

22.   Childe 1942-3.

23.   Curle 1938-9, 94.

24.   Curle 1938-9, 107; Laing 1975, 198.

25.   Much of this material is unpublished. Ms. C. E. Batey is undertaking to catalogue all the Freswick finds for a higher degree at Durham University. I am grateful to her for the information in this paragraph. For a re-assessment of all previous work *see* Batey (forthcoming).

26.   *See* Batey (forthcoming) with references therein to Anderson 1900-1, Edwards 1925 and Edwards 1927.

27.   Information from Ms. C. E. Batey.

28.   Some survey work has already taken place and been published: Fairhurst 1967-68; Reid, David and Aitken 1966-67; Mercer 1980. Coastal survey of the area is being undertaken by Mr. R. J. Mercer of Edinburgh University and Ms. C. E. Batey of Durham University. There are hopes that some new settlement sites of the Viking/Late Norse period have been located (information from Ms. C. E. Batey), but identification in this area remains a problem: *see* Mercer 1980, 79-83.

29.   Ritchie 1974; Ritchie 1976-77, 192.

30.   Ritchie 1976-77, 188.

31.   Ritchie 1976-77, 186.

32.   Ritchie 1974, 29-30; Ritchie 1976-77, 187; Sterckx 1970; Sterckx 1973a and b.

33.   Ritchie 1976-77, 189.

34.   RCAMS 1946, No. 263, 75–9; Ritchie 1975, 25–6; Ritchie & Ritchie 1981, 177.
35.   Hamilton 1956a.
36.   E.g. Hamilton 1951; Wainwright 1962, 150–2.
37.   Small 1968, 9; Small 1971, 79.
38.   *See* phase diagrams in Hamilton 1956a, and re-drawn figure in Small 1968, 9.
39.   Clouston 1919–20; Marwick 1951, 199–200; Marwick 1952, 216–23.
40.   Hamilton 1956a, 114, 134, 137, 141, 154, 157 and Fig. 85 (line Sinkers); Hamilton 1956b, 215 and 219; Hamilton 1953, 7–8.
41.   Small 1966.
42.   Small 1968, 6–9; Small 1971, 75–9.
43.   *See*, for instance, Brøgger 1929, 35.
44.   Small 1967–68.
45.   *See*, for example, the maps in Hedges 1974–5, 65 (after O'Dell).
46.   *See* Crawford 1978, 1979 and 1980: Bigelow 1978; Bigelow & McGovern 1980a and b. The unpublished undergraduate dissertation of Shimmin 1978 compares the "site territories" and "marine environments" of all three sites.
47.   Hamilton 1956, 106.
48.   *Ibid*.
49.   Brøgger 1929, Lecture II; Wainwright 1962, 152–4; Clouston 1932, 5–7; Marwick 1951, 34–7.
50.   Cruden 1965, 25.
51.   The description of the locality in Cursiter 1886 (repeated in RCAMS 1946, No. 126, 36) is clear: it was "on the borderland between the parishes of Birsay and Evie". This is perhaps 11 kilometres as the crow flies from the Brough.
52.   A less specific, and more acceptable, dating of the box to "between the eighth and tenth centuries" is given by Henderson 1967, 212.
53.   Ritchie 1974, 34; Ritchie 1976–77, 192.
54.   McRoberts 1965; Wilson 1970; Small, Thomas & Wilson 1973.
55.   Graham-Campbell 1980a, 68–9.
56.   Gelling (forthcoming). For preliminary notices *see* Wilson & Hurst 1961, 311; Wilson & Hurst 1965, 207; Wilson & Hurst 1966, 176; Webster & Cherry 1972, 169–70; Cruden 1960a.
57.   Graham-Campbell 1980a, 69.
58.   Kaland 1973. *See also* Wilson & Hurst 1964, 240, and Stevenson 1968. A brief summary of the recent work is in Kaland 1980.
59.   Barry 1805, 62; Anderson 1872–74, 563–6; Brøgger 1929, 131–2; Brøgger 1930, 178–9; Greig 1940, 88–90; RCAMS 1946, 220; Stevenson 1968, 25; Kaland 1973, 81.
60.   Marwick 1947, 28–9, 87; Marwick 1952, 65.
61.   Clouston 1925–26, 295; Clouston 1931, 27–33; RCAMS 1946, No. 550, 191–2; Cruden 1960b 21; Marwick 1947, 30, 95.
62.   Radford 1959; RCAMS 1946, No. 1, 1–5; Cruden 1958; Cruden 1965.
63.   Curle 1972–74; Curle (forthcoming). I am grateful to Mrs. Curle for discussing her material with me.
64.   For a summary of the work up to 1977, *see* Hunter & Morris 1981. Later reports are Morris 1980, Morris 1981, Morris 1982 and Hunter 1980.
65.   Curle 1972–74.
66.   Curle (forthcoming).
67.   For some further details *see* Morris 1981a.
68.   *See* Morris 1979b; Morris 1980; Morris 1981a; Morris (forthcoming), Donaldson, Morris and Rackham 1981.
69.   For the general context of such graves, *see* Ritchie 1974, 31–2; Ritchie & Ritchie 1981, 174–5; Ashmore 1978–80
70.   King 1970; King 1978; Coggins & Fairless 1978; Batey, Coggins & Fairless 1980; Morris 1981b; I am grateful to both Messrs. King and Coggins for their generous provision of information about these sites.
71.   Ritchie 1976–77, 192.

72. *See* Tebbutt 1962 and Hope-Taylor 1962; Wade-Martins 1970, 230-1; Wade-Martins 1980, vol. I, 202-5 and 243-4. A similar attribution for a rectangular building has been claimed for a site at Waltham Abbey: *see* Huggins 1976.

73. *See*, for example, Hope-Taylor 1962, 20-1 and Schmidt 1973, 59-60. For recent work at Hodde, *see* Hvass 1973. This has been discussed also in the context of the "bowshaped" buildings from Fyrkat, Olsen & Schmidt 1977, 139-48 (summary in English pp. 237-8).

74. Winkelmann 1954, *passim*, Van Es 1969, 194-6; Holdsworth 1975, 199-202; Holdsworth 1976, 35-40.

75. Cf. Hamilton 1956a, 102-3; Small 1966, 237; Couden 1958, 162.

76. Cf. Hvass 1976, 1977, 1979; Stoumann 1977; Jørganson & Skov 1978; Nielsen 1977-78.

77. Gelling 1952; Gelling 1958.

78. Fleure & Dunlop 1942; Gelling 1964; Wilson 1974, 12; Gelling 1977, 79.

79. Gelling 1958, 54-5; Gelling 1964, 204; Bersu 1968, 88 suggests the circular structure is a *Thing*-place.

80. Gelling 1964, 200-1.

81. Gelling 1970.

82. For general surveys of the other evidence from the Isle of Man in the Viking period, *see* Kinvig 1975, chs. 4 and 5; Megaw & Megaw 1951; Wilson 1974; Bersu 1968.

83. Bersu 1948, 77-9; Bersu 1968, 88.

84. Gelling 1958; Wilson 1974, 14-16.

85. Gelling 1953, 313; Gelling 1958, 55.

86. Bersu 1948, 74-6.

87. The history of Viking Northumbria has often been considered. For recent accounts, *see* Morris 1977; Hall 1976; Smyth 1978.

88. *See* Dolley 1965; Smyth 1975, ch. VI.

89. Whitelock 1959.

90. Some of the more recent work can be seen in Fellows Jensen 1969 and 1972; Lang 1978a and b; Bailey 1980.

90a. *See* footnote 10a on page 73.

91. General surveys are by Waterman 1959; Dickins 1960; Cramp 1967; Hall 1976; Hall 1978; Addyman 1980a and b; Hall, Daniells 8 York 1978; Hall 1980a.

92. Smith 1937, 280-300. For a recent survey of street names *see* Palliser 1978.

93. *See* Addyman 1976, 6 and 11; Addyman 1977, 4-13; Addyman 1978, 31, 33-4; Addyman 1979, 32, 34-46 *passim*; Addyman 1980a, 82-3; Addyman 1980b, 16-18; Addyman 1980c, 27-30, 33-41 *passim*; Hall 1980a, 4-6; Hall, Daniels & York 1978. I am very grateful to both Mr. Addyman and Mr. Hall for their discussions of the site on several occasions, and their assistance in providing references and slides for use in the lectures upon which this paper is based.

94. Radley 1971, 43 and Fig. 10.

95. There are too many references to list here individually: Biddle 1976 is a recent survey of the subject.

96. The historical background and discussion of this topic can be seen in Whitelock 1952, 115-25 and Loyn 1962, 98-116.

97. A number of works have appeared on this topic: Craster 1954; Morris 1977, Morris 1981; Roper 1974.

98. Sawyer 1978c, 4-5.

99. I have discussed the implications in Morris 1977 and Morris 1981b.

100. Armstrong *et al.* 1950, I, 2; Smith 1937, 14-15; Fellows Jensen 1972, 96; Binns 1963, 25-6.

101. Whitelock 1955, No. 104, 505-8; Sawyer 1978c, 4.

102. Batey, Coggins & Fairless 1980, 21.

103. King 1978, 25. I am grateful for further information on this from Messrs. King and Rackham.

104. King 1978, 22.

105. Although much has been done in terms of methodology and interpretation since the publication of Higgs (ed.) 1972, the papers in that volume were of fundamental significance in this respect for British archaeology.

106. *See* Addyman *et al.* 1976, 225–7; Buckland 1976; Buckland 1974; Kenward 1976; Kenward *et al.* 1978, 65–7. These give further references to papers by Kenward and Buckland.

107. Addyman 1972, 22; Buckland 1974, 9–11; Addyman 1974, 218–24; Buckland, Greig & Kenward 1974; Selkirk 1973; Addyman 1980b, 14–16.

108. Kenward *et al.* 1978.

109. Waterman 1959; Radley 1971; MacGregor 1978.

110. *See* Addyman 1977, 5 and 11; Addyman 1980b, 21–2 and Plate; Bailey 1980, 50–6 and Plate 12.

111. Hope-Taylor 1971, 24–7; Pattison 1973; Lang 1978a and b, *passim.*

112. In a lecture to the CBA Group 3 Conference on "Aspects of Viking Archaeology in North Britain". I hope to edit and publish some of these lectures, and other relevant papers, on the Anglo-Scandinavian North of England in the near future.

113. Addyman 1975, 36 and 37; Hall 1976, 25; MacGregor 1978, 42: Hall 1980, 20–1. Jansson has, however, recently questioned the Scandinavian attribution: Jansson 1980, 275.

114. Waterman 1959, 72; Hall 1980, 20; Hall 1976, 25–7; Graham-Campbell 1980b, 75. Lang unpublished lecture (*see* note 112 above). *See also* Addyman 1980c, 41 and Plate 22.

115. MacGregor 1978, 37–9; Ellis 1969, 148–55, 180–2; Hall 1980, 13–15. *See also* Addyman 1980c, 41 and Plate 21.

116. Graham-Campbell 1978.

117. Shetelig 1940, 30–1 (Bossall/Flaxton listed as "York"). Thompson 1956, 64; Dolley 1954, 88–9; Wilson 1957; Dolley 1955–7; Hall 1976, 18. However, Mr. Graham-Campbell is to write about the Goldsborough Hoard in the publication referred to in note 112 above.

118. Graham-Campbell 1976.

119. Dolley 1965; Dolley 1978.

120. Addyman 1980a, 83–85; Addyman 1980b 16–19; Hall 1980a, 19; Hall 1980b; Addyman 1979, 39 and Plate 30; Addyman 1980c, 40 and Plate 18.

121. Anon. 1980; Hall 1980b; Addyman 1980c, 40–1 and Plate.

122. Dolley 1965; Dolley 1966.

123. Dolley & Ingold 1961; Graham-Campbell 1976; Graham-Campbell 1974a.

124. Dolley 1966, 121.

125. Graham-Campbell 1975–76, 125–6; Warner 1975–76.

126. *See* Smyth 1977, chs. X and XI, for the link in terms of a "slave-trade". Also *see* Greig 1940, 29–30 and 48–61 for examples of merchants graves, and Loyn 1976 and Dykes 1976, 17–20 for Welsh evidence.

127. Dolley 1976b. *See* Dolley 1976a, Plate 61 opp. p. 240.

128. *See* examples quoted in note 126 above.

129. Graham-Campbell 1975–76; Megaw 1938; Dolley 1969; Wilson 1974, 36–40.

130. Quoted and discussed in Loyn 1962, 92–5; *see also* Whitelock 1952, 115–20.

131. E.g. Orphir (ch. 550, Freswick (ch. 92), Frakokk's estates in Sutherland (ch. 55), Duncansby (ch. 56) etc. *See* translation by Taylor 1938 and Palsson & Edwards 1978.

132. Brief Reports on the first two seasons' work are published in *Discovery and Excavation in Scotland* 1979 and 1980 (Morris, Batey & Rackham 1979, 16; Morris, Batey & Pearson 1980, 18). *See* more detailed information in recently published Summary Report of 1978–80 (Batey, Jones, Morris and Rackham 1981) and Progress Report on 1981 (Batey, Jones and Morris, 1982).

133. Ritchie 1976–77 (with specialist reports on biological material by Noddle, Bramwell, Wheeler, Evans & Spencer); Donaldson, Morris & Rackham 1981; Bigelow 1978; Bigelow & McGovern 1980a and b.

THE VIKING SETTLEMENT OF SCOTLAND:

Evidence of Place-Names

W. F. H. Nicolaisen

Professor of English, State University of New York at Binghamton

THE CORNELL VIKING LECTURE SERIES 1980 and this volume which has grown out of it are, because of their close contact with the Viking Exhibition at the Metropolitan Museum, almost by definition largely concerned, perhaps even preoccupied, with the artistic, religious, archaeological and historical aspects of the Viking period, and within that context especially with Viking art and material culture. Although by no means totally excluded, language plays, on the whole, a minor and supportive or explanatory role in these deliberations. This discussion of the toponymic facet of Viking verbal culture and its implications for the settlement history of one of the countries severely and lastingly affected by Viking activities departs notably from the ways in which other contributing scholars view and assess the world of the Vikings, their existence in that world and their impact on it.

Since, quite apart from their linguistic embeddedness, names in general, and place-names in particular, are such strange verbal phenomena, it is perhaps necessary to say a little about their nature and significance before exploiting them as evidence for the extent and history of Scandinavian settlement in Scotland.[1]

The primary — one might almost say the exclusive — function of names, no matter whether of places, persons, cows, or race horses, is to individualize, to make distinctions, to separate, to create or to define discrete entities; and names are *used* as convenient devices in the recognition of those individual, distinct, separate, discrete identities. Indeed, without the act of recognition, the act of naming would be pointless. A name is not a name until somebody apart from the namer recognizes it as such; otherwise a name would be a useless functionless label, a bizarre and slippery linguistic item with little chance of survival. Through the recognition of a name as a name, however, identity is created — this hill, that river, this person, that ship. Anything that does not have a name is only with difficulty, if at all, perceived to exist. Identity is made staunchly possible through the acts of naming and recognition.

Naming and recognizing *one* identity is, however, not enough: it is, in fact, impossible. An identity is recognizable only in contrast to, in relationship to, other recognizable identities. Similarly, a name cannot exist without other names; it *is* only through those other names. Therefore, names exist in clusters, in networks, in onomastic webs, in fields of one kind or another, delineating, honing, and clarifying each other. They *are*, in one sense, because of what they *are not*. Through naming — and only human beings name — we master the world around us, turn a threatening wilderness into a habitable landscape, convert a seething, heaving, surging mass of humanity into a manageable, structured society. Naming is survival; namelessness spells oblivion.

The curious, perhaps even unexpected, thing about all this is that it ultimately does not really matter what the names that we give and employ mean as words. They may have accessible word meaning or they may not, but neither semantic transparency nor semantic opacity turns them into better names. Initially, and perhaps even for a considerable period of time after the act of naming, they may indeed have a lexical meaning available to all speakers of the language with the help of which they have been coined, but this fact does not imply that they will function less effectively as names when that initial meaning becomes obscure, fuzzy or forgotten. In fact, word meaning does not normally interfere with name function at any time. What really matters is that a name, in order to function, should have content which is known to those who want to use that name appropriately. It is this content which is the real name meaning, permitting a name to function well in its intended denotative fashion.

These basic considerations, perhaps stated too densely and too abstractly, have some important consequences if we want to understand fully the significance of place-names in the elucidation of our main concern — the settlement of Scandinavians in Scotland during the Viking period. In the first place, we are reminded of the unavoidable need for new settlers to name geographical features, both natural and man-made, in order to survive, especially when existing names used by an earlier population are not readily available and adoptable; that certainly seems to have been the case when Scandinavian settlers reached the islands in the Scottish north and west from about A.D. 800 onwards. There is no implied suggestion that these islands had been uninhabited before the arrival of the Scandinavians, but rather that the incomers' contacts with the earlier inhabitants, presumably non-Celtic-speaking Picts, were minimal and of such a nature that already-existing names were not easily passed on, and that toponymic items which have survived from pre-Scandinavian times are therefore limited almost solely to the names of some of the more prominent islands — *Unst, Yell, Lewis, Uist*, etc. It is not overly dramatic to state that the Scandinavians who reached Shetland, Orkney and the Hebrides in the early ninth century were confronted with what turned out to be, under the circumstances, a virtually nameless landscape, in fact a wilderness rather than a landscape. In order to remove its threat and its bewildering aspect, it was essential to throw over it a net of identifying place-names, thus taming it, almost domesticating it, certainly bringing it under control. This structuring, through naming, was undoubtedly as essential for the survival of the mind as the availability of food, drinking water and shelter was for the survival of the body.

Those ninth-century settlers, therefore, had to name extensively and effectively and had to do so quickly. While this is a formidable task even in ideal circumstances, it is more than daunting when the potential namers are inexperienced and untutored in the skill of naming. The people whom we call Vikings are not likely to have been the sort of folk who risked their lives and faced unknown dangers because they were well known as namers of places at home or had risen to the challenge of creating a whole new place-nomenclature in colonial territory wrested from an earlier, presumably hostile, population. Practically none of them, including their leaders, had probably ever named a place in their lives because they had grown up in landscapes with a long cultural heritage and, for that reason, saturated with names. The need or the opportunity to name a place had simply never arisen before.

What resources do people have available to them in this unusual kind of predicament? As I see it, they can fall back on three different types of suitable linguistic material. First of all, there is a sector of the vocabulary that contains words with topographical connotations: words for hills, streams, stagnant bodies of water, islands, peninsulas, and the like. Whether used alone or as generics in compound names, these words obviously form the most immediate and most appropriate reservoir in the coining of new names and, when combined with specifics from other, more wide-ranging but equally suitable sections of the lexicon, their value and service in the process of naming cannot be overrated. They are the natural major resources for would-be namers, even when the nature of the new terrain demands modifications in their connotation and creative semantic shifts. In this process of primary naming, words become names; their lexical meaning takes on name content, while their connotative, inclusive function becomes denotative and exclusive.

While it is unlikely that the names resulting from this process of converting words into names will look very different from the names which the colonial namers left behind in their homeland, there is, nevertheless, a certain amount of flexibility in the endeavors of the namers. It is theoretically possible, although improbable, that this procedure will produce names completely unknown at home, especially with regard to particular combinations of generics and specifics. The opportunity to be truly creative in a new land, by cutting the umbilical cord in an onomastic sense, is always there.

There is, however, a second source at hand for the hard-pressed namer which does not permit any degree of flexibility at all: the nostalgic and commemorative naming of a place in the new country or colonial territory after a place in the old country or homeland. Of course, this form of naming sounds both familiar and plausible in a country with names like Plymouth, Massachusetts, Hamburg, New York and Warsaw, Indiana. However, it cannot be assumed to have been as common in ninth-century *Scotia Scandinavica* as in seventeenth- or eighteenth-century America. Nevertheless, names in this category, forging an onomastic link between the new and the old, the courageously faced and the nostalgically remembered, were without a doubt included in the place-nomenclature of the Scandinavian colonists on Scottish soil, although their proportion seems to be relatively small. It is not always easy to isolate them, and they are most easily detected when their overt word meaning apparently does not fit the place to which they apply, as, for instance, a typical shore name found in the middle of an island, or when they are one of a kind on both sides of the North Sea. These names must have been transported from Scandinavia to Scotland intact and unanalysed, as whole names.

These two ways of creating new place names by settlers in a strange land have always been assumed to be the only methods. It has, however, occurred to me recently that there is a third possibility which must be taken into serious consideration. This possibility is the transfer not of whole names with identifiable counterparts in Norway but of name types, including particular name models. There are very large numbers of Scottish names of Scandinavian origin, which have identical equivalents in Norway. After examining in particular the common occurrence, in Scotland, of such names as *Lerwick* (ON * *leir-vik* "mud-bay"), *Laxay* (ON *laxá* "salmon river"), *Sandwick* (ON *sandvik* "sand bay"). *Sowerby* (ON *saur-býr* "mud village"), *Tingwall* (ON þing vǫllr "parliament field"), and *Oronsay* (ON *Ørfiris-ey* "tidal island"), I have come to the conclusion that the Scandinavians in the ninth century and in the two or three centuries which followed must have brought with them, as part of their mental baggage, so to speak, a seemingly contradictory category of connotative names — a name stock, as it were, in addition to their word stock, on the one hand, and to specific individual names on the other. They possessed an onomasticon as well as a lexicon, a name vocabulary as well as a word vocabulary, and quite naturally drew on the former as well as on the latter. In fact, it would probably be more precise to say that they possessed an onomastic dialect as well as a lexical or linguistic one and applied it whenever called upon. Once a certain association has been made with regard to a certain place requiring a name, then only one specific name and none other could be given. If, for example, the major association for a particular island was that it was linked with the mainland or another island at low tide but separated from it at high tide, then it had, of necessity and not from choice, to be called *Ørfiris-ey*, "tidal island", because this was the name given to such islands in the homeland. The same principle appears to have applied also to human settlements — farms, villages, and the like — that were built near such natural features, although in many instances there must have been a later transfer or extension of names from one feature to the other, from the natural to the artificial, so that there might then be a farm called *Sandwick*, "sand bay", or a village called *Tingwall*, "parliament field".

As these last two examples demonstrate, such a transfer of names can be accomplished only if the word meaning no longer matters, if a name can function effectively as a name without being transparent semantically. It is this special property of names which, more than any other quality, distinguishes them from words and which allows names to survive in situations in which words die. We have to remember, after all, that all the Scottish names of Scandinavian origin which provide the substance for this discussion have not come down to us directly through the mouths of speakers of a Scandinavian language. The Scandinavian names in Orkney and Shetland, for instance, are now embedded in English, whereas the Scandinavian names of the Hebrides are now part of a third language, having passed through Gaelic before reaching English. It is axiomatic that names instantly lose their word meaning when they pass from one language into another, if indeed they still had such meaning in their language of origin. Since their proper function does not depend on such word meaning, however, and is quite divorced from it, place-names, especially if they structure the landscape satisfactorily, have a knack of surviving such passages. It is for this reason that it is possible for us to use them as evidence for the chronological sequence and spatial distribution of Scandinavian settlement in Scotland, in a kind of investigation that might best be described as linguistic archaeology. In this approach, names or parts of names serve the same purpose as artefacts in the study of prehistoric material cultures. That they must first be properly etymologized goes without saying. Each dot on any of the accompanying distribution maps is, therefore, to be regarded as the visual result of both intensive and extensive linguistic research and not simply as the haphazard plotting of a modern name in its English form. Only such time-consuming preliminary work permits us to use these names confidently, as raw material that goes beyond their etymological reconstructions as words.

Ideally, whole names would undoubtedly be the best evidence for this kind of enquiry, but it has been customary, because easier, to concentrate on certain parts of names — the so-called generics. These are the basic elements of names — like the *-ton* in

Binghampton, the *-ville* in Harpursville, or the *Lake* in Saranac Lake—which define for us the type of topographical feature to which a name was primarily applied. In any given linguistic stratum, there are lexical items which were not or have not been used as place-name generics throughout the period during which that language was, or has been, spoken in a given geographical area. There tend to be times when certain generics are more fashionable than others. At the end of such a period of preferred usage, such "favorite" generics often become obsolete, never or seldom to be used again. The reasons for this phenomenon are complex and need not worry us here. What is of special interest to us, however, is the fact that, as a result of such changing and chronologically limited application, it is possible to work out a relative stratification for such elements. When they are plotted on maps, their distribution patterns can be related to the discrete periods of time in question. Consequently, name elements for which relative chronological limits have been demonstrated and for which distinct spatial scatters can be made visual are excellent points to periods of settlement history; the Scandinavian names in Scotland are no exception in this respect.

Indeed, we are in a much more favorable position regarding Scandinavian names than we are with most other languages which have left toponymic traces on the palimpsest of the Scottish map. From extra-onomastic sources, mostly historical and archaeological, we have fairly firm absolute dates for the beginning and the end of the Norse period in various parts of Scotland. The turn of the eighth to the ninth century is its initial date, and 1263, the year of the Battle of Largs, is an important date in the concluding phases of Scandinavian domination in the Western Isles and the Scottish west in general. 1469, the year of the marriage of the young James III of Scotland to the daughter of the King of Norway, who brought Orkney and Shetland as her dowry to Scotland, is an equally significant date in the final phases of Scandinavian predominance in the Northern Isles. With the aid of appropriate place-name generics, we are also able to trace the settlers to their Norwegian homelands. Although it would be fascinating to establish the basic features of the onomastic dialects of these homelands, it cannot be part of this discourse. What interests us here is the use the settlers made of that dialect in their new surroundings and what the traces it has left behind can tell us about their settlements. Not where they came from, but where they went and when, is our theme.

One further word of caution: the method which underlies our investigation — the interpretation of distribution patterns of certain generics[2] for the purpose of the reconstruction of a relative settlement stratification — is much better suited to allow conclusions concerning the end of substrata than the beginning. It is always possible, indeed more than likely, that a place-name generic has already been productive for a considerable length of time before it replaces another generic. Putting it in its most extreme form, one might even say that a place-name generic may have been used simultaneously with the replaced generic not only for a while, but during the whole period of that generic's productivity. It would be simplistic to think that the newly-arrived settlers from Norway would use only one or two generics first, then another couple, then some more, when the onomastic dialect which they brought with them contained several dozen of these, all of which would have been familiar to them, and, therefore, potentially productive. Some of these may have proved unusable because of the nature of the terrain in the new country, and others may have turned out to be somewhat inappropriate in the early phases of settlement and may have come into play only later. But from the very beginning, there must have been the potential for diversity, although not easily detected or detectable 1,200 years later. Survival, on the other hand, is much more accessible to the researchers.

Of the several generics available to us for our purposes, I have chosen four whose distribution appears to be significant enough for them to yield relevant information for our quest. The first of these is *staðir*, "dwelling-place, farm", formally the nominative plural of Norse *staðr*. This is a generic which is found from the second half of the seventh century onwards in Norway, where it most often occurs in the names of farms resulting from division, although in certain parts independent farms with primary *staðir*- names also exist. It is in the latter sense that it must have been used in the Scottish colonial territory. Concerning its popularity there is no doubt, since there are over 2,500 *staðir*- names in Norway, a number so overwhelming that the new settlers could not help using it in the formation of new names, both from lexical and onomastic stock (Figure 1). Consequently, there are 37 examples in Shetland, 25 in Orkney, and 25 in the Hebrides. Examples from Shetland would be Gunnista, Wethersta, Colsta, Grista, and Hunsta. In Orkney there are Grimeston, Hourston, Berston and Tormiston, as well as Costa, Gangsta, and Yinstay. In the Hebrides we find Skegirsta, Tolsta, Mangersta, Scarasta, Connista, Shulista, Hosta, and the like. In its distribution the *staðir*-name is limited to Shetland, Orkney, Lewis and the north end of the Isle of Skye; in its Hebridean context, it is found especially in coastal areas. In view of the Norwegian evidence, it is likely to have been productive from the very beginning of Scandinavian settlement in the islands of the Scottish north and west; its very limited distribution and preponderance on good soil and favorable sites appear to indicate an early settlement stratum, perhaps to be dated largely to the first two or three generations of settlers. What the map (facing page) makes visual therefore, may well be the extent of Scandinavian settlement in these parts of Scotland around the middle of the ninth century. Not every name represented may have been coined by that time, but may have been added somewhat later, simply consolidating the pattern. It would, however, be erroneous to regard this circumscribed distribution merely as a matter of regional dialect, without chronological significance, as the following maps will show.

The distribution of the generic *setr*, for example, mirrors both consolidation and greater density of population in the areas already settled in the stadir-period and further expansion in the northernmost part of the Scottish mainland, especially the eastern half of Caithness where *staðir* is absent (Figure 2). It would be misleading to think of *setr*-names as a later introduction in the wake of later emigration from certain parts of Norway, although some examples of setr in place-names may have reached Scotland in this fashion. On the whole, however, *setr*-names apparently remained productive longer than *staðir*-names and are, therefore, also found in areas settled later by Scandinavians. Perhaps one can attach a date like 900 to their scatter, although the place names themselves do not, of course, provide any clues as to their absolute dating. Their greater number also argues for a later date than *staðir*. It has been claimed that there are 170 examples in Shetland, 34 in Orkney, at least 56 in Caithness, and 60 in the Outer and Inner Hebrides. When adding up the evidence, however, it must be borne in mind that, as far as our modern anglicized place-name spellings and pronunciations go, it is impossible to distinguish between Old Norse *setr* and *sætr*. These two words are cognate, and both originally referred to pastoral dwellings and herding activities. But whereas

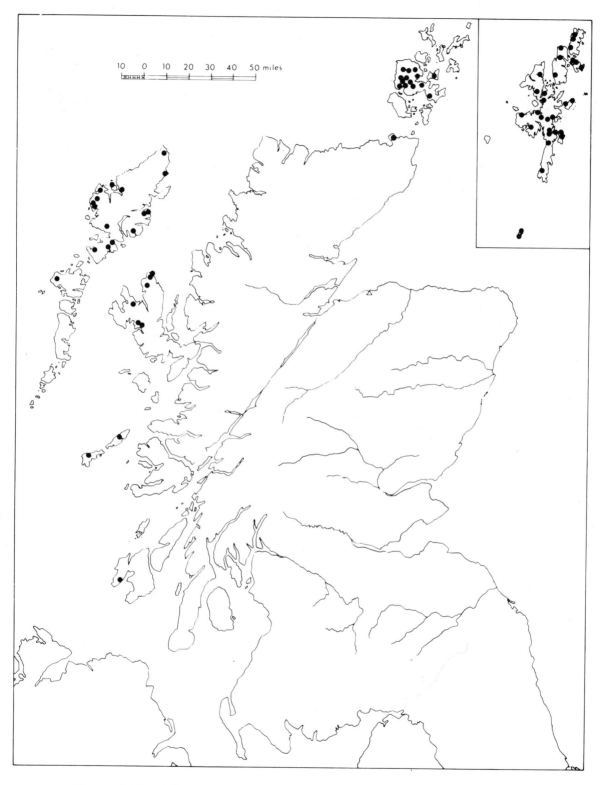

● Name containing *staðr*

Figure 1.

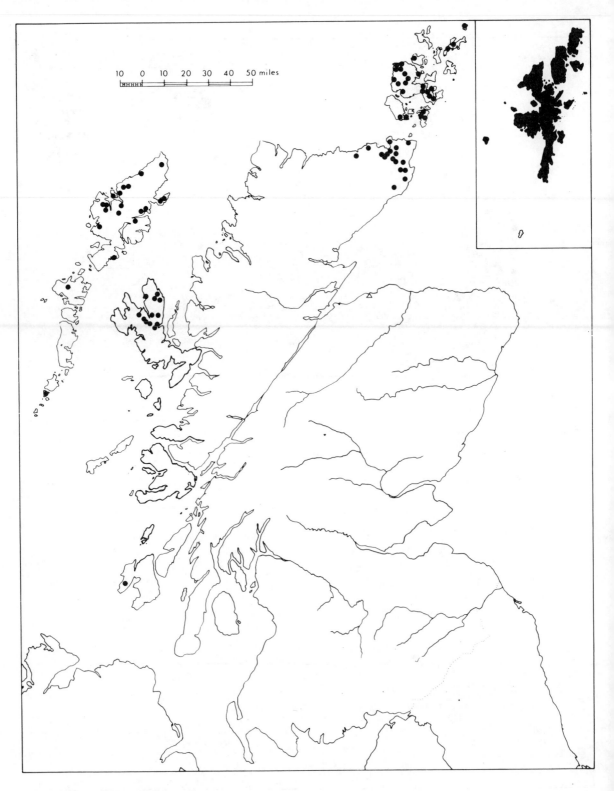

10 0 10 20 30 40 50 miles

●   Name containing *setr*

■   Shetland, with **124** *setr* names

Figure 2.

setr (our word) developed the general meaning of "dwelling", *sætr* came ro refer to a "sheiling", a temporary structure used for seasonal housing on summer pastures. It is sometimes possible to make a distinction between the two elements through scrutiny of the specifics of the compound names in question or on the basis of their geographical location, but this has not been attempted for the construction of this map, which accordingly shows *setr* and *sætr* side by side. Chronologically, they must belong to more or less the same period of settlement. Representative of the many Shetland examples are Setter, Voxter, Swinister, Dalsetter, Vatsetter, and Stanesetter. In Orkney we find Setter, Mossetter, Inkster and Melsetter. Caithness supplies names such as Seater, Tister, Reaster, Wester, Thurster: and Hebridean reflexes of *setr* or *sætr* are Shader, Grimshader, Linshader, (Loch) Uiseader, Uigshader, (Loch) Eashader, and Ellister. *Shader* in all these cases is evidence that the names in question passed through Gaelic before being used by English speakers. Not represented on this map, but possibly belonging to this category, are northern Sutherland names ending in -*side*, Gaelic -*said*, like Linside (Gaelic *Lionasaid*), Fallside (Gaelic *Fealasaid*), Sandside, and so on. If they are to be included, and the evidence is not yet conclusive, they would, not surprisingly, extend the Caithness evidence westwards along the coast.

Orkney farm names containing Old Norse *bolstaðr* occupy relatively central positions in their various parishes (Figure 3); they are situated on good fertile ground and their size shows many of them to have been relatively early settlements, probably going back to before the tenth century. Some of them may be as old as the Norse settlements themselves, although it would be difficult to isolate individual names for which such claims can be substantiated. What is, however, even more important is the observation that *bolstaðr* seems to have remained a creative name-forming generic for longer than both *staðir* and *setr/sætr*, and that it was used wherever permanent settlements were formed by the Norsemen. It certainly has a much wider distribution than either of the other two elements, and I wish to suggest that a distribution may of names containing *bolstaðr* makes visual the total area of Norse settlement in the Northern and Western Isles of Scotland and on the adjacent mainland. If this assumption is correct, such a map reflects the period when Norse power was at its height, probably in the tenth and eleventh centuries. All other place-name generics referring to permanent settlements — farms, hamlets, villages, and the like — are found within this *bolstaðr* area. Some of these become productive later, others cease to be used earlier, but none adds anything to what the *bolstaðr*- names teach us — that there was a Scandinavian settlement area in the islands from the northernmost point of Shetland to the southernmost tip of Islay, with large parts of the coastal areas of Sutherland and the north-eastern half of Caithness added. This is the most significant portion of *Scotia Scandinavica*; in fact, I would be quite prepared to call it *Scotia Scandinavica* proper.

For reasons inherent in the process of sound substitution and general phonological adaptation when names pass from one language into another and later perhaps into a third, the interpretation of the distribution of *bolstaðr*- names is much less difficult than their detection, for they appear on modern maps and in local usage in a number of disguises. The most common form in the Northern Isles is -*bister*, as in Kirkabister, Norbister, Isbister, and Symbister in Shetland, and Mirbister, Sandbister, Kirbister and Swanbister in Orkney. Names ending in -*bist* are also quite frequent in Orkney (Kirbist, Grimbist, Geldibist, for example) and -bust, as in Grobust; and -*buster*, as in Wasbuster,

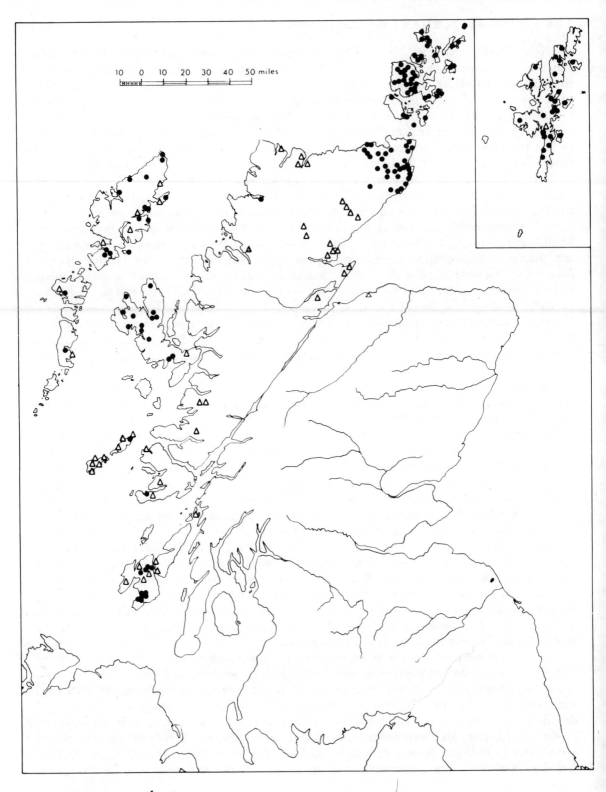

Name containing *bólstaðr*

● in form *bister, bster, bost, bus*

△ in form *boll, pol etc.*

Figure 3.

occurs there, too. In Caithness, the process of vowel reduction has produced such endings as *-bster* and *-pster*, as in Lybster, Brubster and Scrabster, on the one hand, and Strompster, Achilipster, and Achkeepster, on the other. Sometimes the only indirect evidence of the original presence of the first element *ból* is the bilabial nasal *-m-* in a name like Stemster from ON *steinn – bolstaðr* "stone farm", or "farm near a standingstone". Here the *-b-* has changed the preceding *-n-* to an *-m-* through assimilation between *staðir* and *bolstaðr* is, therefore, not always easy to make and even greater caution than usual is called for.

In the Hebrides, the islands of Lewis and Skye display *-bost* as the modern reflex of *bolstaðr*, as in Habost, Shawbost, and Leurbost in Lewis, and Carbost, Culbost and Breabost in Skye. Further south, Islay has developed the form *-bus*, as in Coullabus, Cornabus, Kinnabus, and the like. This can be shown to be comparatively recent, for as late as the seventeenth century name forms in *-bolls, -bols,* and *-bollis* are on record in profusion. In other areas again, the second part of *bolstaðr — staðr —* has completely disappeared in the modern names. In Sutherland, for example, we have Unapool, Eriboll, and Learable; in Western and Eastern Ross we find Ullapool and Arboll, respectively; and in the island of Tiree, we encounter Crossapool, Heylipoll, and Kirkapoll. The most drastic shortening has occurred in such south-east Sutherland names as Embo, Skelbo, and Skibo. One possible explanation of this seemingly confusing variety of modern echoes of *bolstaðr* may be a difference in stress. The names which passed through Gaelic into English favor a fairly strong emphasis on the first element so that the *-er* from *-aðir* disappears altogether. In the thoroughly Scandinavian areas of Shetland, Orkney and north-eastern Caithness, where there was a direct contact between Norse and English, the stress may have been stronger on the second part, preserving it fairly well, while allowing the first part to deteriorate or vanish. Although this may be the basic reason, the corresponding division is not as easy as it looks because it does not accommodate the *-bist* and *-bust* forms of Orkney. Whatever the cause or causes of this great variety of sound developments may have been, there is no doubt that ultimately all the modern reflexes, however reduced, go back to *bolstaðr* and are genuine representatives of this important Norse generic.

This is perhaps the point to ask why the Scandinavian settlement area in the north and west of Scotland remained restricted to these parts of the country in which names in *bolstaðr* are found. The answer to this question is probably two-fold — choice and opportunity. Shetland and Orkney were clearly the first two groups of islands reached because of their comparative proximity to Norway. Even today it is said of Shetland that its closest railroad station is in Norway and not in Scotland, and that statement takes into account the stations at Thurso and Wick in the north-easternmost corners of the Scottish mainland. The Northern Isles were, therefore, convenient areas for prospective settlers, especially if these were interested in a mixed economy consisting of farming and fishing. The Hebrides, according to our place-name evidence, form a natural extension off the Scottish west coast. Both sets of islands must have been known and were probably reconnoitred by the Vikings in their preceding raiding days. *Scotia Scandinavica* was, consequently, mainly an island dominion with a few bridgeheads on the adjacent mainland, particularly in the north-eastern half of Caithness.

Why were the Scandinavians satisfied with this limited extent of their rule? Why did they not penetrate the mainland any farther? The answer seems to lie in another distribution map, this time of Gaelic *baile*, "a homestead, a farm, a village" (Figure 4). As this map

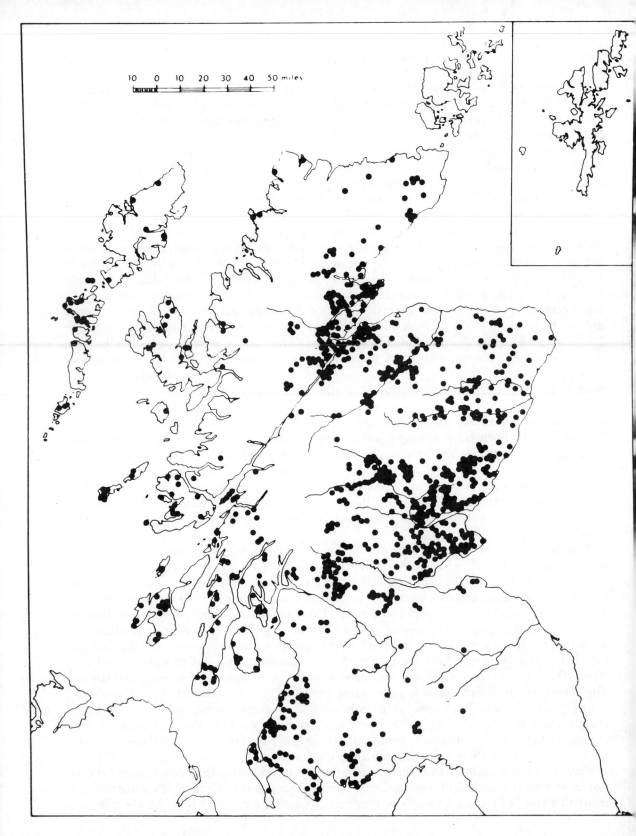

● Name containing *baile*

Figure 4.

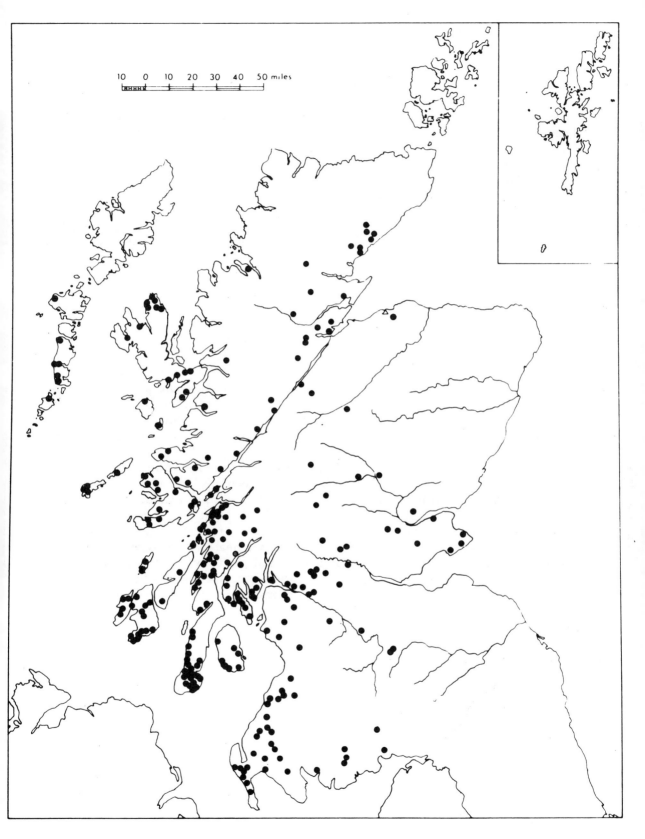

Figure 5.

● Name containing *cill*

shows, and it could be supplemented by others, there was a time when Scottish Gaelic, the Celtic language which had reached Scotland from Ireland from the fourth or fifth century onwards, was spoken practically everywhere in Scotland, apart from the area dominated by English speakers in the south-east and the very parts in which we have been able to detect Scandinavian presence in the north and west. This is particularly true of the Northern Isles and of Caithness where names in *bolstaðr* and names in *baile* hardly overlap at all, so that one can speak of a Gaelic and of a Scandinavian half of the country. While *baile* does, of course, not permit any dating, another Gaelic element does: the generic *cill*, "church, church-yard", whose distribution stops short not only of the Anglian and Scandinavian areas mentioned but also of much of the Pictish area (Figure 5 – page 107). Since we know that Gaelic did not invade that part of Pictland until the middle of the ninth century, we can be reasonably certain that the distribution of names in *cill*, like Kilbride, Kilmarnock, or Kilmacolm, represent a date somewhere in the first half of that century, i.e. at the very time when Scandinavians were first beginning to settle on the fringe of Scotland. Any *baile*-names found in the Outer Hebrides or in Skye must go back to a post-Norse Gaelic stratum there. With regard to our original question, we must conclude that the Scandinavians were prevented from extending their settlement area to much of the mainland by the Gaelic-speaking Celts.

This does not mean, however, that they were completely confined to the islands in all their activities; the next map makes visible the distribution of names containing the Scandinavian generic *dalr*, "a valley, a glen" (Figure 6). These are primarily names of natural features, although many of them are nowadays names of villages or farms as well. What I have in mind are names like Arisdale and Wormadale in Shetland, Knugdale and Durrisdale in Orkney, Tresdale and Berriedale in Caithness, Helmsdale and Mudale in Sutherland, Udale and Ulladale in Ross-shire, Borodale and Scamadale in Inverness-shire, Easkadale and Carradale in Argyll, Dibadale and Grundale in Lewis, Laxadale and Rodel in Harris, Udal and Gramsdale in North Uist, Lochboisdale and Hellisdale in South Uist, Bracadale and Bernisdale in Skye, Scallastle in Mull, Brosdale in Jura, Tormisdale in Islay, Ardroscadale in Bute, Glenasdale in Arran, and not only dozens but hundreds of others. As becomes clear, this map (facing page) includes those mainland and island areas adjacent to permanent settlements in which seasonal exploits such as hunting and fishing and summer grazing were carried out, and probably the odd military raid or friendly visit. A distribution map of *dalr* is, therefore, not a map of permanent Norse settlement but rather a visual reminder of the Norse sphere of influence. This distinction is crucial to our understanding of the extent and power of *Scotia Scandinavica* between, let us say, A.D. 800 and the middle of the thirteenth century.

Summing up our place-name evidence for these parts of Scotland, we can say that the names in *staðir* provide a picture of what the Norse settlement area was like before and up to the middle of the ninth century, whereas *setr*-names speak of consolidation and expansion well into the second half of that century. The map of *bolstaðr* in its various disguises supplies an overall visual impression of Scandinavian settlement in the north and west at a time when it was at its most extensive. Finally, the distribution of *dalr* seems as a reminder that "settlement area" and "sphere of influence" are not the same, and that the Scandinavians must have known the western coastal districts of the mainland from Cape Wrath to the Mull of Kintyre extremely well, even if they hardly ever had any permanent farms or other settlements there.

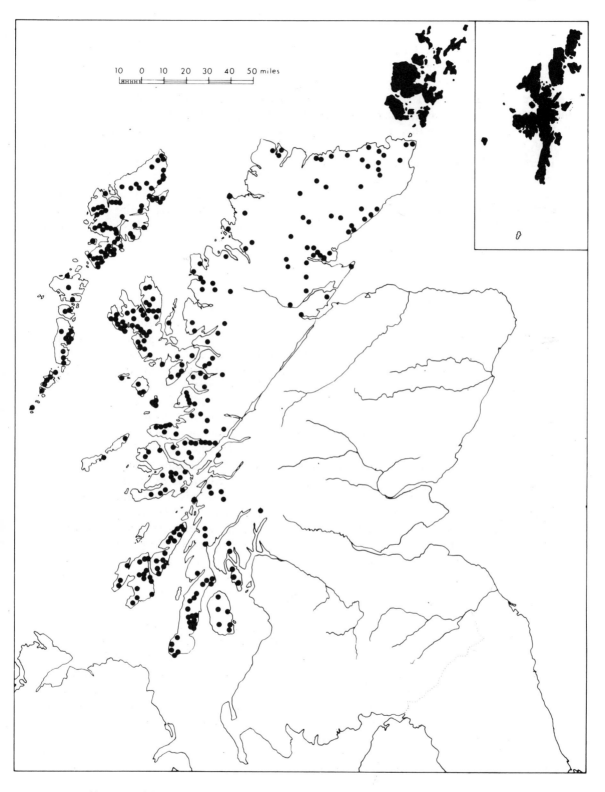

10   0   10   20   30   40   50 miles

●   Name containing *dalr*

⬛   Area of frequent occurrence

Figure 6.

Shetland, Orkney, the Outer and Inner Hebrides and the accessible and available parts of the mainland nearby are the natural settlement areas of land-hungry people whose homelands are in Scandinavia, especially in various western parts of Norway. The presence of Scandinavian settlers in Scotland is, however, not limited to this extensive region, but can also be documented elsewhere, particularly in the Scottish south-west. The major evidence for this presence consists, again, of place-names and their elements, although not all of them have equal significance or allow the same conclusions.

There are, first of all, names containing ON *bekkr*, "a stream", primarily stream-names, of course, but in secondary usage often transferred to settlements (Figure 7). These have their major concentration in the county of Dumfries, although a few examples are found just across that county's borders in adjacent Roxburghshire, Lanarkshire and Kirkcudbrightshire. Names in question would be Allerbeck, Fishbeck or Greenbeck, which might well go back to Scandinavian settlers themselves; while the Norman personal name in Butcherbeck, the Gaelic personal name in *Gillemartinbech*, the Scots *craig* or Gaelic *creag* in Craigbeck, the English specifics in Mere Beck, Muckle Hind Becks or Kings Beck point to post-Norse, or at least non-Norse, origin, perhaps justifying the assumption that *beck* was adopted as a loanword in the regional dialect of English. The same types of *beck*-names also occur south of the present Scottish–English border, especially in Cumberland and Westmorland, but also in the North Riding of Yorkshire and in Lancashire, many times producing identical equivalents to the Scottish names. The conclusion that has to be reached on the basis of this evidence must surely be that the Scottish *beck*-names are part and parcel of that northern English distribution pattern, although the Scottish may, on the whole, be a little later than their English counterparts.

This tentative conclusion is confirmed by names ending in ON *býr* "a farmstead, a village" (Figure 8). From their inception, these have obviously been names of human settlements and have survived as such. Sorbie, Corsby, Newby, Aldby, Mumbie, Bombie, Canonbie, Denbie and Esbie come to mind as typical examples. Their stronghold is again Dumfries-shire, and their connection with the plethora of *by*-names south of the English border is again obvious; there are 150 instances in the North Riding or Yorkshire alone, 70 in Cumberland, 15 in Westmorland and 18 in Lancashire, many of them identical with names in Scotland. In contrast to *beck*, however, there are a few scattered outliers of *by* in other parts of Scotland, probably due to small groups of Norse settlers in what were otherwise non-Scandinavian communities. *By*-names also occur sporadically in the Scottish north and west, but the evidence does not permit us to connect them with the Scandinavian settlers who coined the names in Dumfries-shire and in the north of England.

The picture provided by names in -*beck* and -*by* is reinforced by names containing ON *þveit* (Figure 7), "a clearing, a meadow, a paddock", such as Thorniethwaite, Murraythwaite, Cowthat, Howthat, Slethat, Butterwhat or Harperswhat, or even Branteth and Moorfoot. Again, the majority of specifics which feature as first elements in the Scottish names appear in the same combinations in England, just as the greatest frequency of names in *þveit* is in the four counties in which names on -*beck* and -*by* are found so often: Cumberland, Westmorland, Lancashire and the North Riding of Yorkshire. In Scotland they are almost completely confined to Dumfries-shire.

Even when taking into account the fact that all three elements clearly remained productive in the post-Norse period, the cumulative evidence is strong, indeed overwhelming.

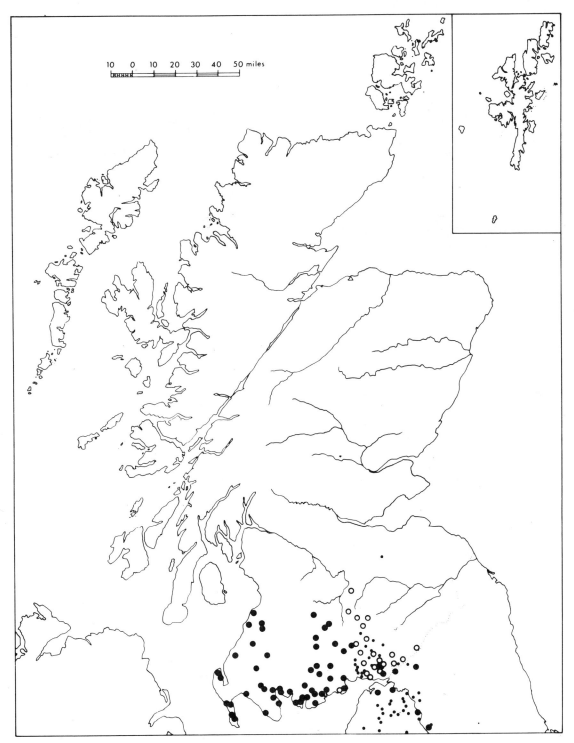

Name containing

- þveit
- ○ bekkr
- ● kirk

Note : This map demonstrates the distribution of these place-names in
the area south of the river Forth only. The distribution of bekkr
in Northern England is Cumberland, 67 names; Westmorland, 4;
Lancashire, 7; Yorkshire, North Riding, 39; Durham, 3 late names;
Northumberland, none.

Figure 7.

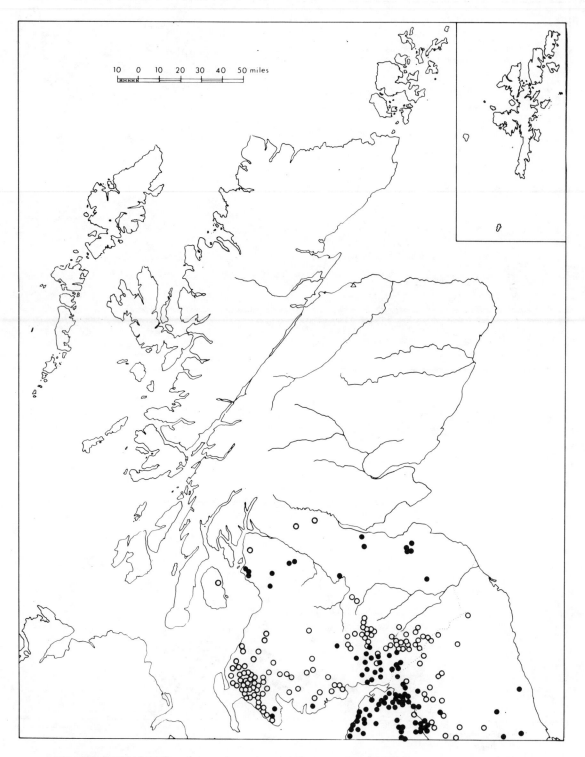

●   Name containing *býr*

○   Name containing *fell*

Note :   This map demonstrates the distribution of these place-names in the area south of the river Forth only.

Figure 8.

It loquaciously links the Scottish names found north of the Solway Firth with their English counterparts south of it, and the circumscribed area of Scotland in which they occur is, to all intents and purposes, the northernmost appendix of a Scandinavian settlement area reaching as far south as Derbyshire. The people who coined the *beck-*, *by-*, and *thwaite*-names in southern Scotland were the same who coined the *beck-*, *by-* and *thwaite*-names in northern England; they were not — and this is crucial — direct descendants of the Vikings who first raided and then settled in the Scottish north and west. The separate ways in which place-name studies in Scotland and England were conducted until fairly recently prevented us from seeing this closely. The present border between England and Scotland is obviously irrelevant in this context.

Unfortunately, the picture in the Scottish south-west is a little more complicated, but helps to avoid the kind of over-simplifications sometimes voiced in the past. We have already seen that all the Scandinavian generics presented so far seem to have survived, as creative elements, the Scandinavian period itself. This is especially true of *beck*, which must have been used productively by speakers of English as well as of Norse in the formation of new place-names. Hill names containing the Old Norse word *fell* or *fjall* are even more extreme in this respect. Compared with *by*, but also with *þveit* and *beck*, *fell*-names are much more widely distributed (Figure 8). Particularly striking is the large number of instances west of Dumfries-shire, in Wigtownshire, as well as in Kirkcudbrightshire. There are no *becks* and no *þveits* in these two counties, and three *bys* in coastal districts meagrely represent an element so common in other areas once occupied by Scandinavians. In England, their distribution is densest in the north-western-most counties, forming an impressive block with the Scottish south-west. If, apart from the different distribution, we scrutinize the corpus of Scottish *fell*-names more closely — Balmurrie Fell, Glenkitten Fell, Ewenshope Fell — we must come to the conclusion that only very few of them, if any, were given by the Scandinavian settlers themselves. Even Borgue Fell, another instance in which the specific of the name is the name of another geographical feature in the vicinity, is likely to have been named by speakers of English, and we have to view *fell* as a place-name generic which had passed into the local English dialect as a loanword before becoming one of the distinctive features of the place-nomenclature of south and south-west Scotland, as well as of north-west England. Only when Lowland Scots began to supersede Gaelic in the south-west did this element enter the Wigtownshire toponymy. In the place-names of this area it has to be regarded as an English dialect word borrowed from Scandinavia, rather than as a Norse element. This is in contradistinction to the Northern and Western Isles, where it is a well-known feature of the hill-nomenclature and undoubtedly part of a genuine Scandinavian heritage.

Our final element causes problems of a different kind and reflects a different linguistic situation which further highlights the complexity of some of the cultural relationships for which place-names have survived as witnesses, sometimes as sole witnesses. The generic in question in Norse *kirkja*, "a church" (Figure 7). This is a word which has had extensive linguistic repercussions in Scotland, for, in addition to its genuine Scandinavian usage in place-names such as Kirkwall, the capital of Orkney, it has, by adoption, become *kirk*, the Scottish equivalent of English *church*. As such it has entered many place-names, both as a generic, as in Whitekirk, Muirkirk, Falkirk, or Selkirk, and as a specific, as in Kirk Burn, Kirkcleuch, or Kirkhill. As a shorthand for *Kirktown of* — it also appears in such names as Kirkliston, Kirknewton, and Kirk Yetholm. All these usages are to be seen as part of the English onomastic dialect. There is, however, one further application which is of considerable interest to us: the type of name formation for which Kirkbride may serve as a model, i.e. the generic *kirk* followed by a saint's name, in this case *Brigit*. Kirkcolm, Kirkcowan, Kirkcormack, and Kirkpatrick would be other examples. The normal Germanic word order in such names would have been specific plus generic, as in Brydekirk, "St Brigit's church", which also occurs in Dumfries-shire, or in Oswaldkirk in the North Riding of Yorkshire, and the type Kirkbride or Kirkoswald has therefore become known as an "inversion compound" because the two elements are inverted — inverted, that is, from a Germanic, both English and Scandinavian, point of view. The word order generic plus specific is, however, the norm in Celtic compound words and names, as in Kilbride, Kilpatrick, Kilmorie, or Kildonan. The initial *Kil-* here is again the locative *cill* of Gaelic *ceall*, "cell, church, churchyard", the distribution of which we discussed earlier. Brydekirk and Kilbride are, therefore, the kinds of formation which we would expect in Germanic and Celtic languages, respectively; Kirkbride stands in the middle, in so far as it contains the Scandinavian generic *kirkja*, but shows Gaelic word order. Such a formation, and the distribution of the names in which it occurs confirms this, can have come about only in a bicultural, at least a bilingual, situation in which a Germanic and a Celtic language, in this instance Norse and Gaelic, were in contact. This must have been the case in Galloway, the area in which our names are found, and in the circumstances, it is difficult, but fortunately unnecessary, to say whether Kirkbride is a Scandinavian name with Gaelic word order, or a Gaelic name utilizing the Norse generic *kirkja*. The way in which some of the recorded instances fluctuate between *Kil-* and *Kirk-* as first elements makes me inclined to think that it is probably the latter rather than the former. Names like Kirkoswald and Kirkcudbright do, on the other hand, extend this morphological principle beyond the expected combination of a Norse generic with a Gaelic saint's name. St Oswald, the Northumbrian king who was slain in 642, and St Cuthbert, the influential seventh-century missionary and Bishop of Lindisfarne, were, after all, neither Scandinavians nor Gaels, but Angles, and names like Kirkoswald and Kirkcudbright, therefore, point to a tricultural mix in this area: Gaelic word order, a Norse generic, and an Anglian specific.

It has sometimes been claimed that *Kirk-* names and other so-called "inversion compounds" prove that Norse settlers imported this type from the Viking colonies in Ireland or from the Isle of Man or the Hebrides. In the first place, such names have no Irish counterparts worth mentioning, and as far as the Isle of Man and the Hebrides are concerned, exactly the same conditions obtained there as in Galloway: Norsemen and Gaels living together over a considerable period of time. Since we know, again from place-name evidence, that there must have been Gaelic-speaking settlers in the Scottish south-west contemporary with the fifth-century settlements in Argyll, it is not difficult to imagine that the linguistic contact happened right here, and there is no need to postulate an immigration of bilingual Norse–Irish settlers from Ireland. Elements like *bekkr*, *býr*, and *þveit* have, after all, unmistakably established the presence of Scandinavians north of the Solway as part of a settlement area and movement that included much of the north of England. That they should come in touch with Gaelic speakers further west is not only surprising but inevitable; the dividing line runs right through Dumfries-shire in the same way in which it runs through Caithness. Once the pattern of *Kirk* plus saint's name had been established in the toponymic usage of the region, neither the Gaelic nor the Norse stimulus was necessary any longer.

It should be mentioned, at least in passing, that there is also some slight evidence for the presence of Scandinavians in the Scottish south-east, where a number of place-names containing Norse personal names are to be found, but since these do not occur in any discernible pattern and since they are usually part of names with English generics like *-tūn*, they at best speak of individual Scandinavian owners of farms in an otherwise English environment. Anyhow, it is reasonable to assume that most of the bearers of these names were not Scandinavians but Englishmen who had been given fashionable Scandinavian names by their English parents.

This establishes the Scottish north and west, on the one hand, and the Scottish south-west, on the other, as the principal areas of *Scotia Scandinavica*. It is my reading of the place-name evidence that, despite some occasional contact which may have existed, these two areas have to be regarded and interpreted quite separately, one as the natural colonial territory of seafaring people approaching Scotland, in the first place, from parts of Norway, the other as the northernmost appendix of the Scandinavian settlements in the north of England. Whether the term "Viking" can be applied to either or both of them is another question. Whatever terminology we may prefer to use, it has been possible to delineate both these areas on the basis of place-names which fortunately happen to have come down to us from the periods in which they were coined. Their study utilizes the fact that names do not need to be meaningful on a lexical level in order to survive. Their study also pays due attention to the need for structural naming, for turning a threatening wilderness into a habitable landscape, as a device not only for orientation, but also for mental survival. There is no other linguistic evidence available which could have done the same for us and done it so elegantly. We should be grateful to the Viking variety of *homo nominans*.

NOTES

1. Naturally, this description owes much to Chapter 6, "Scandinavian Names" in my book, *Scottish Place-Names: Their Study and Significance*. It also makes use of various other writings on the subject, both by myself and by other scholars, both Scandinavian and British; these are not identified in every instance, and those interested in extending their reading on this topic should turn to the relevant entries on names in the bibliography.

2. The maps in question were first prepared by myself for *An Historical Atlas of Scotland c. 400– c. 1600,* edited by Peter McNeill and Ranald Nicholson; they are here reproduced with the kind permis- some of the Trustees of the Conference of Scottish Medievalists.

THE GILDED VIKINGSHIP VANES

Their Use and Technique

Martin Blindheim

Keeper, University Museum, Oslo

THE PURPOSE of this paper is to discuss the ship vanes which have come down to us from the end of the Viking period, that is around the eleventh century. In Old Norse they were called either *veðrviti,* which according to Hjalmar Falk were vanes usually positioned in the prow, or *flaug* which were intended for the top of the mast.[1] Two of these objects are now in Sweden (Söderala and Källunge, Plates 46 and 47), and two in Norway (Heggen and Tingelstad, Plates 48 and 49).[2] Discussion of the objects, which have come down to us as weathervanes on the top of church towers, has been almost exclusively devoted to their importance as art objects.[3] I will try to explain how they were made, why they are *veðrviti,* for the stem and not *flaug* for the mast, and how in later time they were changed into *flaug.*

As far as form is concerned the four vanes even today retain almost the same appearance — a triangle in which a long bending line combines the two straight lines, one long and one short. On the outer pointed end is placed an animal. The objects are not only close in basic form — all the motifs show an element of magic in the conflict.

On both sides of the Söderala vane a big serpent-like animal with one front leg and one back leg, perhaps a lion, is being attacked by a much smaller similar creature and by a small snake. One side of the Källunge vane has got two big serpents intertwined in each other and surrounded by four small snakes. The other side is adorned with the well-known Mammen-Ringerike-style motif — the big lion in deadly struggle with a serpent. A closely similar lion is seen to better advantage on one side of the golden Heggen vane, but this time walking majestically with a smaller identical lion in front of it which turns its head back, as if to observe the bigger brother who follows. At the other side another royal creature — the eagle — is seen in deadly fight with a serpent. The youngest of the vanes — Tingelstad — marks the beginning of a new period as to motif and style, but the fight continues. David is rescuing the lamb from the lion's mouth.

The four vanes were noticed by archaeologists and art historians during this century, the Söderala vane being the first in 1916, the Källunge vane the last in 1930, and the Heggen and the Tingelstad vanes in between. An account of the Söderala vane was first published by Henrick Cornell and thereafter discussed by Bernhard Salin in 1921, the Heggen vane by Anton Wilhelm Brøgger in 1923, the Tingelstad vane by Anders Bugge in the same paper as the Heggen vane, and the Källunge vane was briefly mentioned by Johnny Roosval in 1930. A good many art historians and archaeologists have subsequently dealt with the vanes in books and articles from a stylistic point of view and

Figure 1. Graffiti on inner wall of Urnes Stave Church,   Figure 2. Graffito on inner
Sogn, Norway.   wall of Borgund Stave Church,
                                                                 Sogn, Norway.

have dated the three oldest ones, the Ringerike-style vanes, to roughly the first half of
the eleventh century, which was the same date given to them by the first authors. It is
debatable on what side of the year 1100 the Tingelstad vane should be placed, in the
latter half of the twelfth century according to Anders Bugge, or in the latter half of the
11th century according to Hanns Swarzenski. But because it is a very interesting object
which was made in the Viking tradition, like the three oldest vanes, it is tempting to stick
to Swarzenski's interpretation by way of changing his dating to about the beginning of
the twelfth century.[4]

Salin could hardly escape noticing the 110 degree angle in the Söderala vane. On the
background of all the places in the Sagas where gilded vanes are mentioned in connection

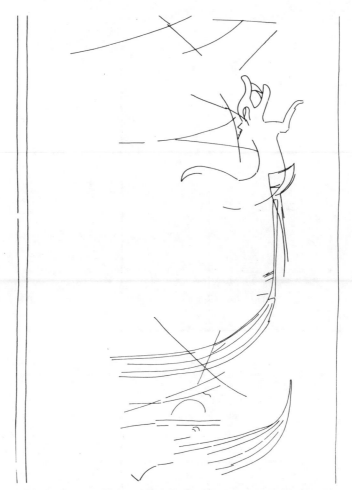

*Figure 3.   Graffiti on inner wall of Kaupanger Stave Church,
Sogn, Norway.*

with ships, he drew the only obvious conclusion that the Söderala vane was originally a ship vane, and he reinforced his argument by seeing it appropriately placed on the top of a ship's mast, thus paralleling the placement of a triangular object depicted on a Gotlandic picture stone to which he referred.

Brøgger proposed that the Heggen vane had been used as a *merki* (standard) and that it was intended to be placed on top of a staff and carried about; a practice such as this is depicted on the Bayeux Tapestry. However, the standards that appear on Bayeux do not have the same form as the vanes.

Anders Bugge cited the sagas, as did Salin, for there are many allusions to golden vanes in that body of literature. It appears that such vanes were easily taken down and put up again, and that they were used on warships as signs of importance. They could be seen shining in the sun at some considerable distance, and people would infer from the shining that warships were approaching. Basing his argument in part on the advice of Einar Lexow, Bugge inferred that the vanes ought to be placed on the ships in such

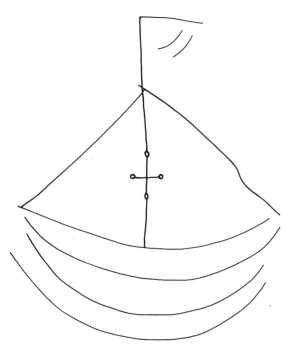

Figure 4. Graffito on outer wall of Reinli Stave
Church, Oppland, Norway.

a position that the upper line became horizontal. This would not happen on top of a vertical mast but only on a slightly sloping stem. Bugge cited certain late medieval Scottish gravestones and a thirteenth-century candelabrum in the shape of a ship as parallels (Plate 50).[5]

It should be clear that Lexow and Bugge are correct. Today we can point out many more parallels which support their opinion. Only with the help of additions or drastic reductions was it possible to make these early vanes stand horizontal on church spires or gables as do ordinary weathervanes.

The ship graffiti found on a stick during the Bergen excavation (Plate 51) and dated to the first half of the thirteenth century[6] prove how these vanes were originally placed. They were raised on the very top of the ship stems. This can only have been possible by fastening an iron or bronze pole to the uppermost part of the stem. In order to swing slightly and to avoid the wood of the stem, the pointed bottom of the vanes had to be shaped in a circular or broken way, similar to that of the two Swedish vanes. In the Sagas again and again we hear about gilded vanes which were erected or taken down over a short time. In one case in *Haakon Haakonsson*'s *Saga* two men from Hardangerfjord collided with archbishop Einar's ship. The stem of the archbishop's ship was damaged. The *veðrviti* got stuck in their sail and the men set off with it.

That their place was not at the mast top is also shown by the story in *Haakon Haakonsson*'s *Saga* about his stratagem in a hard fight against the Ribbungs, when he allowed the small ships to go first and the galleys afterwards with masts raised, in order that the enemy should be deceived into thinking that they were cargo ships, which

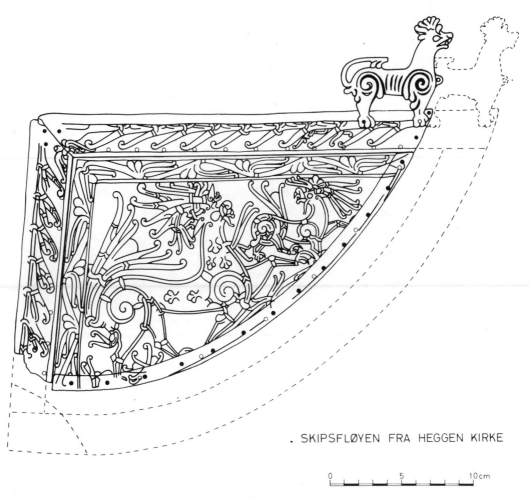

. SKIPSFLØYEN FRA HEGGEN KIRKE

Figure 5.   Reconstruction drawing of Heggen vane by Tone Strenger.

usually did not use oars. Only when the Ribbungs rowed out and got near to the small boats did they catch sight of the vanes of the galleys and discovered who it was that was coming (*Fornamanna sögur* XI, 437). Had the vanes been at the mast tops they would have been noticed at once. This description shows that the vanes apparently marked the vessels as galleys, warships to be feared. This interpretation is further confirmed in the narrative of Haarek of Tjötta's passage through the Sound, when he took his sail in, draped the ship in grey cloth and rowed softly with few oars, in order to deceive Knut the Mighty's sentry into thinking that it was a herring barge. But as soon as it had slipped past, he raised the mast, set sail and put up the wind vane (Flatey Book II, 286) (39). From this we also see that the vanes could be taken down and set up at will.

Almost always when vanes are mentioned they are spoken of as being gilded. Clearly, saga writers saw this as a distinctive feature. Thus the vane that Haarek set up was gilded (*gylta veðrvita*), like the one Haakon Haasson placed on his ship when equipping for his voyage back to Norway, while Svein Ulfsson was King of Denmark. On the

SKIPSFLØYEN FRA TINGELSTAD KIRKE

Figure 6.   Reconstruction drawing of Tingelstad vane by Tone Strenger.

magnificent ship which brought Harald Hardrada home the vanes looked like red gold (*veðrvitar varu svá at sjá sem rautt gull væri*). The glitter of gold is also referred to in a lay in Sigurd Slembe's saga: "skok veðrvita í vátum byr gulli glæstan of gramskipi" (*Fornamanna sögur* VII, 340). And it was that which caught the eyes of the unsuspecting Ribbungs when they saw the vanes glitter on the galleys when the sun shone on them as Haakon Haakonsson's fleet glided forward (*veðrvitar glitudu ved á storskipunum er sólen skein á*) (*Forn. sög.* XI, 437).[7]

It is interesting to note that the animals at the outer end of the Bergen vanes, despite their unclear shape, do not look like the animals of our four vanes. They give the impression of being heads where the vanes are the bodies. Their parallel could possibly be the thirteenth-century Höyjord vane (Plate 52) or the vanes on the ship candelabrum and not any of the eleventh-century vanes. Among the many graffiti of ships of the Viking type, the Bergen stick is not the only one to depict ships with vanes. The stavechurch graffiti from about 1150 to about 1250 in the Urnes, Borgund, Kaupanger and Reinli stavechurches reveal that those engaged in building crafts were familiar both with ships and with vanes (Figures 1-4). Most of the vanes are fastened to the stems as *veðrviti*, and some to the masts as *flaug*. Other ships have stemheads and *flaug* on the masts — but never stemheads and *veðrviti* at the same time. There are never animals on these vanes, nor do the vanes end in heads.

The two Swedish vanes are almost complete. The Söderala lion on the top of the vane was missing but was found at the side of the church (Plate 53).[8] It had fallen down. The tail and a head-decoration of unknown shape are now missing. The bottom of the tube is very worn (Plate 54). Salin is certainly correct in concluding that the uppermost strap at the bottom was originally placed at the top instead of the secondary strap which is there now. He noticed as well that the decoration and the gilding on the vane itself continued under the bottom strap and that the decoration on the straps is cruder than on the vane. The straps may be secondary but are not therefore necessarily much younger. Källunge (Plate 47) has only lost its tube for the pole at the shorter side, or the original ferrules. The height of the Söderala vane is 25 cm and the length 34.5 cm, with the modern ferrule included. The diagonal is 45.9 cm. The opening of the tube is only 1.5 by 1.2 cm. The weight is 1.5 kilos. The dimensions of the Källunge vane are 23.3 by 35.5 cm. The diagonal is 39 cm, taken without tube or ferrule and with the bottoms and vertical lines drawn right out till they meet. The Swedish vanes are almost the same size, whereas the two Norwegian ones are smaller and not so well preserved. I shall return to these later. The Swedish vanes have kept their original main lines with an angle of about 110 degrees at the upper inner corner. Both vanes have got a series of drilled holes in the bottom rim. On Källunge two of them are open. Others are extended downwards into oblongs and thus on their way to becoming open. On Söderala a fair number are open in the same way. Certain authors have noted this phenomenon and have concluded that some material or fabric was fastened through the holes. There exists an abundant number of drawings and paintings of ships from the Late Middle Ages where material flutters from rectangular vanes in the mast tops or on poles carried by hand. I doubt that material alone could destroy the holes, though material fastened to rings probably could. Metal objects fastened to rings in the holes would certainly do this. These are to be seen on the Bergen stick and are without doubt gilded like the vanes.

Let us now turn to the two Norwegian vanes. In 1880 the Heggen vane (Plate 48) came into a private collection in Drammen and in 1923 into the Universitetets Oldsaksamling in Oslo. It is now deprived both of its original and of its secondary mounting. The three holes neatly drilled in a triangle in the upper inner corner give an indication of strap ends or of the fastening of a loose tube to the vane.

It is clear that at one time (in the Middle Ages) the vane had been reduced in size. The narrow bending rim could never have been the original, for the two others are rich in ornamentation. Besides, the rim runs over the lines of the ornamentation on the vane, a feature which can best be seen with the help of X-rays.[9] On the lion side of the vane the bottom rim now covers most of a bending line which at the beginning is double (Figure 5). This line must be one which is drawn between the inner acanthus tendril strip to the left and above the lions. Clearly a bordering acanthus strip ran along the curving side as well, about 1.2 cm broad. To this would be fastened the outer rim of about two cm, just as on the other two sides and in the same way as on the Söderala and

Källunge vanes. The reconstruction gives an impression both of the present vane and possibly of how it originally looked.

All this means that the Heggen vane was originally considerably bigger and heavier than it is today. The lion of course would be placed at the end of the lost tip and not where it is now. It is possible that the inner bottom end of the vane was shaped in the same way as on the Söderala vane or perhaps as on the Källunge vane. Not a trace of this original feature has been preserved. We can only guess as to how it was fastened to the metal pole – a loose tube fastened to the vane partly with the help of ferrules, or solely by ferrules? Nobody knows. The dimensions of the present shape are 19 by 28 cm. Reconstructed without the tube it would measure about 23.5 by 33 cm and the diagonal to a reconstructed bottom corner would be about 42 cm. With a tube added, the size would be about the same as for the Söderala vane. Only an angle of about 110 degrees of the upper corner ensures a place on the prow for a *veðrviti*.

Both the Heggen and the Söderala vanes were hit by several arrow shots which left deep marks. This may have happened in glorious sea battles, but the cause may also be less glorious – greedy farmer boys who in the sixteenth to eighteenth centuries tried to shoot down the golden weathervanes so highly prized by everybody.

For centuries the Tingelstad vane (Figure 4) on the top of the medieval Tingelstad church was believed to be made of gold and to be a present from the mightiest woman the people of the parish had ever heard of – the queen Margareth of Norway, who, as a widow, became a chosen ruler of her homeland Denmark and also of Sweden. She died in 1412.

According to the legend two Swedes tried to steal it. One of them made a vow to God if he managed to climb up to it. He succeeded, and when he touched it he cried: "Now I have it. Now I will take it. And now I can manage by myself", whereupon he slipped and killed himself. The vane fell down at least once and was repaired and put up again. It was taken down several times between 1589 which is the oldest year marked on it, and 1820, which is the most recent. It was repaired for the last time in 1809. Several inscribed names have been identified.[10] The oldest graffito on it, a ship stem (Plate 49) is gilded at the bottom and may have been made by the artist himself.

The motif of the vane is of European origin – David rescuing the lamb out of the lion's mouth. The leaves are early Romanesque, which in some places can be dated back to as early as the latter half of the eleventh century. The hunched back of David was a popular Ottonian feature of the eleventh century. On the top of the vane is placed a menacing European dragon, not the royal lion as on the three Ringerike-style vanes. On the vane there is not even a suggestion of the Urnes style which was in vogue in Scandinavia at that time. If it is to be dated to the last half of the eleventh century, or even to the beginning of the next, it can hardly have been manufactured by a Scandinavian but possibly by an Englishman or a Norman in Norway, in England or in Normandy.

It can be easily seen that the metal has been cut vertically, and that it has lost more at the bottom than at the top. We can actually follow a straight sloping line from the top about 5-6 cm down. At one side of the line there is gilding, but at the other there is no gilding, because that part was covered by a gilded rim which was later removed. If we draw the line down to meet the horizontal line from the bottom rim, we discover that the angle in the upper corner will be about 110 degrees. It means that the Tingelstad vane was made as a *veðrviti* for the stem of a longship on the open seas and not as a *flaug* for a mast or a church spire. In a drawing (Figure 6) it is possible to reconstruct the main outlines of the original vane but we do not know how the bottom corner was made, nor do we know the details of the lost tendrils and leaves or by what means the vane was fastened to the pole of the ship. The present dimensions without rim and pole are 22.5 by 28.9 cm and the diagonal 36.6 cm. Reconstructed it would not be higher, but the length would be about 33–34 cm and the diagonal more than 40 cm.

All four vanes are now established as *veðrviti* — the only ones from the Early Middle Ages extant in Scandinavia. There are three younger vanes in Norway which were constructed as *flaug* with an angle of 90 degrees in the upper corner: Høyjord, Norderhov and Tovdal.[11] Their date is thirteenth to fourteenth century. It must be confessed that I am uncertain as to where on the ship they were placed — in the mast or on the stem of the ship. A vertical pole could easily have been raised in the stems as well. Theoretically it is even possible that they were made for the church spires.

A few words should be said about the craftsman's work. These observations are based on studies of the Søderala, Heggen and Tingelstad vanes conducted by Oscar Sørensen, Goldsmith, and former teacher at the Oslo Applied Art School, and myself. The samples plus a sample from a horse from a lost 11th-century vane found in Lolland, Denmark, were analysed by the Oslo University laboratories. I am much indebted to all of them. Though the vanes are usually described as brass in the literature, they are actually made of copper: Søderala *c.* 95 per cent, Heggen *c.* 90 per cent, Källunge 90–95 per cent and Tingelstad *c.* 97 per cent, and the same for the Tingelstad dragon. The Søderala and Heggen lions were made of brass. The Søderala lion consists of about 80 per cent copper and about 20 per cent zinc and the Heggen lion of about 70 per cent copper, about 20 per cent zinc and about 5 per cent lead plus 5 per cent other metals. I became curious as to the composition of the Källunge lion and the Lolland horse in the Nationalmuseet in Copenhagen. The Källunge and the Lolland horse were analysed later than the other samples. I hoped these two top animals would be of brass as well because that would make a sort of logic in the production of 11th-century vanes and their top animals. Both turned out to be made of copper. The Källunge lion is made of 90–95 per cent copper and half a dozen other metals, all of them not present in the plate. The Lolland horse is made of *c.* 90 per cent copper plus from 1 to 5 per cent iron, zinc, tin, silver, etc. It is curious and perhaps significant that the smiths made some of the top animals in brass, but when they made them of copper (the primary material of the plates) the copper in the animals came from a different smelt.

The material in all the vanes is gilt copper. The way the metal was treated, the goldsmith's technique, is the same, at least in the three vanes I have studied, and that is the techniques described in the III Book of Theophilus the Monk's famous early twelfth-century work: *De diuersis artibus.*[11]

The Söderala vane weighs 1.5 kilos (Plate 46). The copperplate which the goldsmith worked ended up by being about 1 mm thick. He cut it up in a sort of triangle with two straight lines, one long and one short, meeting in about 110 degrees in the upper corner, and a long bending line combining the two in a pointed end. A sheet of copper not more than .50 mm thick and about 6 cm broad was bent over the upper edge, covering about 1.5 cm of the plate. In the bottom was laid down an iron wire to give the upper edge a rounded form. Thereafter the whole strip was fastened with 11 copper nails. The same procedure was practised on the under side but without the iron wire in the bottom. In this case about 2 cm of the plate was covered and fastened with 15 nails. The strip must have been forged both to achieve the bending form and to avoid wrinkling. The back mounting was possibly made last of all. Here the copper was hammered out into a tube for the upright pole. Possibly 10 nails were used to fasten it. Only at this point could the goldsmith start to draw the ornamentation and to work it out with a burin. Often the wriggling line has been planed at the bottom with a chisel. The lines often cross the nail-heads. An iron to make small circles, a punch iron, is used between them. On the plate itself the open parts were cut away with different chisels from one side and the edges smoothed with files. The lion at the top is cast and fastened with two nails. It has been reworked with a chipping-iron. At the end the whole vane was flamegilded the way Theophilus describes it.

The Tingelstad vane weighs now 2.15 kilos. The plate is considerably thicker than the Söderala vane, 2-3 mm compared with 1 mm. In his book Theophilus says that when you are going to make an *opus interrasile*, that is an open work, the copperplate should be thicker than usual; Söderala must be seen as an exception. It is not thicker than the Heggen and Källunge vanes, which are not open works. This plate was worked out with chisels from the right hand side (the dragon to the right). The copper bars were profiled before they were fastened to the sides of the vane with the bending side first and brazed together. This was done with silver. The missing bars at the back end must have been thicker, or broader than the others, which measure about 1.2 cm. Each half is only about 2 mm thick.

The dragon is made out of 5 pieces. The body consists of two halves which are driven up, not cast, and brazed. The wings and feet are also driven up but the two pieces of the tail are forged. A chipping-iron was used on the body. All lines on the dragon and on the vane itself are made with an engraver. The wriggling is very visible (Plate 55). All nails applied to the dragon are secondary and without gilding.

Gilded objects also hung from the bending side of this vane and even from the mouth and the neck of the dragon. Of the twelve original holes, only four are now open, others having been filled in for some reason still undetermined.

Why were the *veðrviti* placed on church spires or on church gables all over Scandinavia? The few which have survived may only be remnants of the original part, just as all kinds of objects left over from the Middle Ages are only remnants of the original stock. I believe we can rule out the legend of presents. We cannot do that for the *flaugs* because some of them could have been made as weathervanes for churches.

In Norway the laws for the "leidang", the fleet of warships, said that the leidang-obligations went as far inland as the salmon was able to swim up river.[12] In some places that was quite a long way. The leidang system meant that in case of war a district had to muster a fixed number of ships with equipment and with men. In times of peace the ships had to be put away in common boat-sheds and sails and other objects had to be kept in special central places. In the Middle Ages these places were the churches. Because there were some protests in the thirteenth century, a royal instruction of 1281 said that sails and other objects should be kept in the churches in the same way as in old days.[13] In the fifteenth century the old Viking ship types could not do very much against the much higher Hansa-cogs. After a disastrous sea-battle south of Bergen against a Hansa fleet they were no longer mobilized. I suppose that the equipment in the churches was finally thrown out.

Only the gilded *veðrviti* and the *flaug* could be of use — now reduced to weathervanes — and perhaps in some cases filled with the same symbolic meaning as the lion-heads on the stavechurches. In Høyjord the vane even survived on the top of a stavechurch.

Except for the Saga-writers and medieval poets few contemporary written sources tell about vanes on Nordic ships. In one case, at the beginning of the twelfth century, some crusaders tried in vain to conquer a port in Palestine. One day they saw a fleet approaching. The sun glittered on the gilded vanes. That was a North Sea fleet, and it helped to conquer the town.

More fanciful is the account by a monk of St Omer in the beginning of the 1040s in *Gesta Cnutonis Regis Anglorum et Danorum*, or *Encomium Emmae Reginae*.[14] He described the fleet Knut Svensson, later called the Great, assembled to conquer England.

"Who among the enemy would be able to look upon the figures on the stems, those lions sparkling terrifyingly with gold, those men of metal with menacing golden fronts, those dragons made of pure gold, those bulls which foretold death and ruin through their sparkling, gilded horns — and not be stricken by fear and be afraid of a king who commanded such a terrible armament".

We don't know how fanciful the St Omer monk actually was. Gilded three-dimensional heads and figures of metal may have existed at the side of wooden sculptures. The Sagas only mention the gilded vanes, and they must have been produced in quite a large number to fulfil the steady demand through several centuries.

NOTES

1. Falk, Hjalmar, *Altnordische Seewesen*, Heidelberg 1912, p. 42.
2. The latest thesis on the Ringerike style with literature about the vanes is Signe Horn Fuglesang, *Some aspects of the Ringerike style*, Odense 1980.
3. The vane from the Söderala church, Helsingland is in the possession of The Statens Historiska Museum, Stockholm, the vane from Källunge church, Gotland, is kept in Gotlands Fornsal, Visby, the vane from Heggen church, Buskerud, in the Universitetets Oldsaksamling, Oslo and the vane from Tingelstad church, Hadeland, in Hadeland Folkemuseum, Gran. The Swedish Grimsta vane, dated to the eleventh century, is omitted. It is an archaeological find, fragmentary but obviously rectangular in form, rather small in size and very crude in design. It could easily have been a "merki", a *signum* in Latin, which was fastened to a spearshaft, a "stong", and carried by hand. (Margaretha Björnstad, Spånga's *Förhistoria*, Stockholm 1966). I furthermore doubt that the rectangular, gilded metal object from the Winchester Cathedral with Ringerike design on it can be proved to have been part of a vane as A. W. Brögger proposed in 1925.
The primary literature about the vaines is: Brögger, A. W. og Anders Bugge, *Bronseflöyene fra Heggen og Tingelstad*; Bugge, Anders, "Gyldne flöyer", *Aarsberetning* 1927, Oslo 1929, pp. 33–48; idem. "The golden vanes of Viking ships", *Acta Archaeologica*, II, Köbenhavn 1931, pp. 159–184; Salin, Bernhard, "Forgylld flöyel from Söderala kyrka", *Fornvännen* 1921, Stockholm 1923, pp. 1–22; Roosval, J., Acta angående Källungeflöyeln, *Fornvännen* 1930, pp. 367–72, More recent summing up by Hallvard Trætteberg, "Merke og flöy", in *Kulturhistorisk Leksikon for nordisk middelalder*, B. XI, Oslo 1966, pp. 549–55 and by several authors in Vindflöy, B. XX, Oslo 1976, pp. 91–93.
4. It is possible that Hanns Swarzenski's dating of the Tingelstad vane is due to a wrong translation from Norwegian to English in Anders Bugge's paper in *Acta Archaeologica*. (Hans Swarzenski, *Monuments of Romanesque art*, London 1967, Sec. ed., Figure 216, pp. 54–55). In the two previous papers Bugge dated the vane to the middle or the second half of the twelfth century. His stylistic arguments and

parallels are the same in all three papers. One expects "about the middle or the second half of the 12th century" in *Acta* as well. Instead "about the middle or the second half of the 11th century" appears. The *Acta* paper is the only literature mentioned by Swarzenski.

5.   Graham, H. D., *Antiquities of Iona*, London 1850, Plate 15. Bugge's candelship is in the Urnes stavechurch. The similar candelship from Dale church, now in Historisk Museum, Bergen, is preferred in this paper.

6.   Herteig, Asbjörn, *Kongers havn og handels sete* , Oslo 1969, pp. 88–89, and 112. The dating is based on archaeological strata. A Runic inscription on the stick says: Here sails the sea-daring.

7.   The Saga passages in this paper are mainly taken from Bugge's paper in the Acta.

8.   When the Söderala vane was discovered it was in the possession of a farmer who reported that the vane originated from the Söderala church. The missing lion was found at the side of the church.

9.   I am indebted to Statens Historiska Museum, Stockholm for taking extra X-ray photographs of the Heggen vane for this paper, and to Tone Strenger, Universitetets Oldsaksamling for all the drawings.

10.   Brögger and Bugge, 1925, pp. 21-22.

11.   Theophilus, *De diuersis artibus*, translated by C. R. Dodwell, London, 1961, Book III.

12.   Bull, Edvard, *Leding*, Kristiania og København 1912, p. 42.

13.   *Idem*, p. 18, note 1.

14.   *Gesta Cnutonis Regis Anglorum et Danorum*, or *Encomium Emmae Reginae*, translated into Danish by M. Cl. Gerta, *Kong Knuds liv og Gærninger, Selskabet for historiske Kilderskrifters Oversættelse*, København 1896, p. 30.

I want to thank the owners of the vanes, Statens Historiska Museum, Stockholm, Gotlands Fornsal, Visby, Nationalmuseet, Copenhagen, and Universitetets Oldsaksamling, Oslo for permission to take the necessary samples for analyses, and the Oslo University for analysing them. The same thanks go to Forhistoriske Samlinger, Moesgard, Arhus for sending me a sample of the Lolland horse. All the photographs are taken by the photographers of my own museum, except the Källunge vane and the Lolland horse which were generously sent me from Visby and from Copenhagen.

VIKING STUDIES: WHENCE AND WHITHER?

C. Patrick Wormald

Lecturer in Medieval History, University of Glasgow

I

IT IS AN ironical comment on the "bad press" which the Vikings have allegedly received that they are probably now better known to the reading public at large than any other aspect of Europe's early history. This is partly the result of the prodigious publicity arising directly or indirectly from the major exhibitions held in 1980 at the British Museum and the Metropolitan Museum, New York; and partly of the enduring fascination of the wild and colourful men of the north, who have always had their fans as well as their critics. But it also reflects the very marked advances in the understanding of the Vikings which scholars have made in the last 20 years. What I have to offer here is not so much a professional review of these advances, as a layman's survey of the general trends they represent, together with some tentative suggestions as to the course that future advance might take. I am no specialist in either the language or the archaeology of Scandinavia. My knowledge is largely of the "victims" of the Vikings: the English, the Franks, the Irish; and I must confess that my awareness of works in the modern languages of Scandinavia derives mainly at second-hand from what has been written in English, French and German. This exercise may thus justly seem an impertinence to the real specialists. However, Peter Brown, in his brilliant study of the rise of the Holy Man in late Antiquity, used anthropological models to show how an outsider, simply by virtue of his peculiarity, can help to resolve the tensions of an inward-looking community. I make no claims to exorcistic powers, nor to being at home on top of a pillar. But, *as* an outsider, unfamiliar with the norms and taboos of Viking studies, I might perhaps have something to offer to what does often seem to be a rather closed world.[1]

The starting-point, undoubtedly, must be the publication in 1962 of Peter Sawyer's *The Age of the Vikings*. This brave and skilful essay has turned out to be one of those works which, however controversial, yet attracts almost all subsequent work into its orbit. French, Irish and even Scandinavian, as well as British, scholars, archaeologists and linguists as well as historians, have directed their own research towards the confirmation or rebuttal of Sawyer's arguments.[2] It is unnecessary to do more than briefly summarize these arguments here. The first is that we know about the Vikings, unlike most other early medieval peoples, only through the writings of their victims and enemies, the clerical scribes of north-western Europe. The Vikings emerge as wholly destructive agents, unlike their almost equally violent Christian contemporaries, because they alone attacked churches and churchmen; their violence was thus noted with hostility, while that of Christians passed unnoticed, or without adverse comment. Second, in their hysterical preoccupation with the advent of Antichrist, these chroniclers suffered more than usual from the medieval propensity to exaggerate numbers. The Vikings were actually more like warrior-bands in quest of plunder than migrating hordes in search of land. Third, and for the same reason, the extent of their destruction was also exaggerated. As a result, historians have blamed them for developments that were not their responsibility: the decline of the Carolingian or Mercian empires, the decay of monasticism and the Church in general, the collapse or atrophy of culture, and the disappearance of North Sea ports like Dorestadt. Finally, because of the "iron and blood" perspective of our sources, we have ignored more constructive aspects of Viking activity: landed settlements, for which there is copious place-name evidence; or trade, confirmed by archaeological investigation of hoards and markets, both in Scandinavia and in Viking territories overseas.

The most conspicuous general effect of the Sawyer thesis has been the sort of observation with which the British and American public were deluged last year. An eloquent sample is Magnus Magnusson's: "Today, there is . . . less emphasis on the raiding, more on the trading, less on the pillage, more on the poetry and artistry, less on the terror, more on the technology, of these determined and dynamic people, and the positive impact they had".[3] In short, the Vikings used to be thought, in the immortal terminology of *1066 and All That*, a "bad thing"; they are now considered a "good thing". To the extent that it has encouraged scholars to take the Scandinavian peoples of the early Middle Ages more seriously in their own right, this trend is obviously welcome, though it is part of my purpose here to suggest that it has been exaggerated. But Sawyer's main, and original, purpose was not to "whitewash" the Vikings, and in taking this as his book's primary message, scholars and laymen alike have removed the debate from where he sought to put it. His was an attempt to produce an explanation of the Viking phenomenon, by arguing that there was nothing very exceptional about it. Viking movements were essentially warband raids of a type familiar in *Beowulf*, and other Germanic contexts. It was the development of the Viking ship, *c.* 800, that at last enabled Scandinavian warbands to transfer their activities to the western European theatre, and it was only their ignorance of the taboos of Christianity which made them look exceptional there. To quote: "Once the prejudices and exaggerations of the primary sources are recognized, the raids can be seen not as an unprecedented and inexplicable cataclysm, but as *an extension of normal Dark Age activity* [my italics] , made possible and profitable by special circumstances".[4] Any attempt to suggest that Sawyer's thesis is misconceived must nevertheless acknowledge its recognition of the need to relate the Vikings to the history of barbarians in sub-Roman Europe as a whole. What follows is not only a critique of the trends to which the thesis has given rise, but also an attempt to show that the Vikings can indeed be understood, if in a different way, by setting them in a wider chronological and geographical perspective.

II

I take first the question of sources. It is possible that scholars are now too pessimistic about the contemporary European sources for the Viking Age, and that there has been something of a failure of nerve with regard to the Scandinavian sources themselves. If one takes western Europe as a whole, the information for the ninth century is not so much worse, and may in some respects be considered better, than that for the barbarian invasions of the fifth and sixth centuries. The Irish annals, and more especially the *Anglo-Saxon Chronicle*, have obvious limitations of general bias and detailed knowledge as accounts of the Vikings; but, after all, we have no near contemporary record of the Anglo-Saxon invasions save that of their enemy, Gildas, and a comparison between the two sets of sources hardly favours Gildas.[5] On the continent, the superb series of Frankish annals may not be sympathetic to the Vikings, but are at least extremely full down to 900; again, they compare favourably with annalistic sources for fifth-century Gaul and Spain, just as the letters of Servatus Lupus and Hincmar compare with those of Sidonius Apollinaris.[6] Among hagiographical sources, the *Vita* of the Frankish missionary, St Anskar, which was written by St Rimbert, one of his Danish converts, gives at least as lively and as apparently reliable a picture of internal Scandinavian conditions, as does Eugippius' description of the experiences of St Severinus with fifth-century barbarians on the Danube. St Anskar was the founder of the archepiscopal see of Hamburg, which sought to retain responsibility for Scandinavian Christianity until the late eleventh century. Its historian, Adam of Bremen, said some undeniably daft things about Scandinavian history and geography. Yet Adam resembles Gregory of Tours in reflecting the outlook of a prestigious cathedral community on barbarians with whose conversion it had been closely involved; both Adam and Gregory had spoken with barbarian kings, and both used lost sources.[7] Such comparisons suggest to me that it is not enough to write off contemporary sources for the Viking Age as biased by bitter experience. Apart from anything else, the extraordinary range of Viking activity, quite literally from one corner of Europe to the others, means that we can compare one biased account with another, and an accumulation of similar accounts, however hostile, must be suggestive.

However, one respect in which the historian of the Vikings does seem worse off than his counterpart for the earlier barbarian invasions lies in the Scandinavian failure to produce apparently reliable retrospective accounts of their achievements. Bede and the *Anglo-Saxon Chronicle* for the English, Jordanes for the Goths, Paul the Deacon for the Lombards, and Widukind for the continental Saxons certainly look more respectable than the Scandinavian sagas, or the saga-like histories of Dudo for the Normans and Saxo Grammaticus for the Danes. Once again, this contrast may be more apparent than real. No one nowadays would try to write the pre-Viking history of Scandinavia from Saxo or the *Ynglingasaga*, but then historians are nowadays sceptical about the historical, as opposed to the mythological, value of the early sections of Jordanes.[8] For the Viking Age itself, Saxo and Snorri may be vitiated by deficient information or tendentious prejudice, but modern studies of Bede himself are increasingly aware of the way that his history was shaped by the genre in which he was writing, and his pastoral purpose in doing so.[9] Similarly, the early Scandinavian law codes have certainly, in their extant form, been systematized and interpolated, but we are nowadays less confident about the precise historical relevance of all early medieval legislation; the Scandinavian texts may not necessarily be more misleading than their Irish, Frankish or Anglo-Saxon counterparts.[10] Granted that Bede and *Lex Salica* are more reliable than Saxo and *Gragas*, historians of the Vikings could be more aware that their problems are not unique; and if historians of earlier barbarian invasions could still learn from the scepticism of students of the Vikings, the latter can take courage from the achievements of the former. Is it right, for example, for scholars to balk at the evidence of Ari Thorgilsson for the existence of Ragnarr Lothbrok, when their counterparts rarely show any such scepticism about the *Anglo-Saxon Chronicle*'s evidence for that of Cerdic? The time-lag between episode and evidence is similar in each case, and Ari strikes me at least as a sober historian in the traditional mould of early medieval "national" historians.[11] Indeed, though I am on shaky, not to say holy, ground here, I wonder whether it is justifiable to lump together all Scandinavian sources under the generic and historically pejorative label of "saga", or to have moved from a position of not believing everything, to one of not believing anything, in them. Analogy with equally problematic sources for other early medieval peoples would suggest that for certain issues, like the names of outstanding personalities, they may after all be trustworthy, especially if we cannot rationally account for what they say in terms of their writer's known preoccupations. If historians of the fifth and sixth centuries have nowadays managed to create a picture of the early Germanic invasions that makes sense, despite their similar problems, it should be possible to do the same for the Vikings, without falling back in despair on the archaeologists.

III

From these remarks about the evidence, I turn to the major issues of post-Sawyer Viking historiography, the questions of motive, of scale and of effect. Historians today stress "peaceful" considerations of settlement and trade in the Viking movements. Sawyer himself has argued that whatever loot the Vikings acquired, it rarely got home to Scandinavia. Prodigious quantities of eastern silver have turned up in Scandinavia, especially in Sweden and Gotland, but very little from the west. This itself argues that Vikings were not mere marauders. Sawyer suggested that the Norwegian sack of Lindisfarne and Iona in the 790s was a by-product of their settlement in the northern and western British Isles, and that when the Danes got in on the act in the 830s, they used their loot to *buy* land in the west.[12] It is hard to understand why Vikings were willing to use force to acquire silver, but not to acquire land. It has been pointed out that Danish and Norwegian hoards are anyway rare in the ninth century, so that no particular significance attaches to the absence of western coin.[13] It has also been argued that the monetary output of western Europe was much lower than that of the Muslim lands, which supplied the Swedish hoards, so that the ratio of eastern to western silver in Scandinavia simply reflects the fact that Sweden faced east and Norway and Denmark faced west.[14] There is no doubt that Ireland and Scotland, the areas where Norwegians were mainly active, were moneyless, and there *is* evidence in Norwegian graves that smart or precious "insular" objects were brought home.[15] Numismatists might not be so happy with the notion that coin-output was low in England and Francia. But in any case, the sources first record a substantial and specific payment to the Danes in 845, and such payments are not regularly attested, in England or Francia, until *c.* 860. By this time, the Frankish sources actually show that Danish armies were based in the west, though it should be noted that this was not so much out of concern with settlement as because their leaders were royal exiles.[16] The lack of western silver in Danish contexts is not then so surprising.

What needs particular emphasis, against any interpretation that puts settlement high on the list of Viking priorities, is the absence of *any* clear evidence for Viking settlement before the mid-ninth century. Archaeologists now date the first evidence for Norse settlers in the northern and western isles later than they did.[17] Wainwright's case for settlement there *c.* 800 depends on written evidence for *raiding* there, on the old archaeological consensus, and on place-names that could just as well be 50 years younger; indeed, Wainwright was mainly arguing that the settlement could not be *earlier* than 800.[18] The earliest unambiguous Frankish evidence relates to the Emperor Lothar's grant to Walcheren to the Danish royal exile, Heriold, in 841, which is also the date of the "foundation" of Dublin. Wintering in what are now England and France is first recorded a decade later.[19] Clear evidence of permanent settlement as opposed to winter garrisons comes in England with the armies of the 870s, and in Francia with Rollo in the early tenth century.[20] In other words, settlement does not seem to have been a primary, but a secondary, feature of Viking activity. This is surely a very powerful objection to the idea that the Viking invasions were caused by over-population and land-hunger.

Recently, however, the emphasis has shifted somewhat from settlement to trade as the "peaceful" dimension of Viking expansion. In 1962, Sawyer drew attention to the fact that there was a Norwegian trader, Ottar, at the court of King Alfred himself. In his most recent work, he has noted the commercial development of Scandinavia before and during the Viking Age, and the connection between the earliest Viking raids and the "wics" or trading centres of northern Europe: Dorestadt (attacked 834-7), Hamwih and Portland (840-2), Rouen (841), etc.; even Sheppey (835) and Noirmoutier (843), though famous mainly as monastic settlements, bestrode key commercial arteries.[21] The dramatic archaeological finds at York and Dublin overseas, and at Helgö, Birka, Hedeby, Ribe and Kaupang in the Scandinavian homeland, have powerfully highlighted the scope and scale of trade in the Viking period and area.[22] Indeed, Dr. Blindheim has argued that the insular objects in Norwegian graves were not loot but peacefully-acquired merchandise. Some (such as a bronze hanging-bowl with what could be a liturgical runic inscription, or a reliquary, bearing the name of a Norse owner, that still contained relics) seem to have had the same Christian significance in Scandinavia as they would have possessed in the British Isles, suggesting that they were not transferred by violence.[23]

Much of this argument commands respect. No one would now deny that Scandinavian expansion profoundly affected the economic development of north-western Europe, leading to the foundation of new towns, like Norwich, Dublin and the Scandinavian sites themselves; or the expansion of old, like, York, Rouen and probably London; introducing coinage to Ireland, and an improved silver currency to Northumbria.[24] Yet it is well to remember that experience of the West Saxon king's reeve at Portland some time between 786 and 802; he thought that the three ships of Northmen were traders, but he was wrong.[25] Scholars may now be making the same mistake, if with less lethal consequences for themselves. Some of Dr. Blindheim's grave-finds may well arise from trade, and some objects (whetstones, soapstone, leather) are not very likely to have been plundered or even given as presents. But in the first place, one cannot assume that weights and scales are necessarily the mark of a merchant. The Frankish annals record that the tribute paid to the Seine Vikings in 866 was 4,000 pounds, "according to their scales".[26] Scales were needed to assess the value of any precious metal, and would be as useful to a warrior-chief in distributing his loot as a trader. Secondly, the liturgical use of the hanging-bowl only *may* have been recognized, as Dr. Blindheim acknowledges (Professor Wilson has wondered whether hanging-bowls *ever* had liturgical uses).[27] Nor am I convinced that the devotional connections of the reliquary were known all along; unlike the catalogue of the 1980 exhibitions, I would not find it a "curious coincidence" if these connections were rediscovered at a later date through familiarity with other reliquaries.[28] But the third, and most important, point is that some of the insular objects have been removed from their original Christian context, like the mounts of book-covers or the panels of shrines, and these simply *must* have been looted at some stage in their history. Christians in the Dark Ages did not trade in sacred things, nor did they break them up to make a present for the wife. It required an act of sacrilege, if not violence, to transfer them from consecrated to secular purposes, whether this happened on a raid overseas or through robbery of a Scandinavian convert. Contemporary sources are quite specific about the looting and breaking up of books and shrines; when we find holy things in pagan graves, we really cannot ignore this evidence.[29] If a people who deposited such things in graves were not themselves raiders, raiding must stand somewhere in the background.

There is a further point here. It is convenient to apply the term "Viking" to all aspects of Scandinavian expansion in this period, including trade and settlement; but, whatever its much-disputed origins, its basic meaning seems to be "sea-borne military adventurer". An adventure does not need to be destructive, but it is obvious that the word has strong connotations of piracy, and "pirate" is a very common Latin term for the Vikings in Frankish sources.[30] Now, as Professor Wilson has observed, piracy is not always easily distinguished from trade, either in the skills involved, or in economic effect (at least for the beneficiary!) In the early Middle Ages, the distinction may have been even harder to draw than in the early modern Caribbean, and it is this problem which underlies the lively debate between Professor Grierson and his critics about the nature and extent of commerce in Dark Age Europe as a whole.[31] While Grierson may well have underplayed the importance of trade and traders as such, he did make the very important point that the circulation of goods was inherent in the activities of warbands themselves. Woden/Oðinn was, after all, god of both war and trade. Warriors in *Beowulf* acquired treasures by gift-exchange as well as plunder; and, in a moneyless economy, trade is often indistinguishable from gift-exchange.[32] This would suggest that raiding and trading could be different, yet related, activities of the same chieftain. Presumably, Ottar would not have been so welcome at King Alfred's court had he been recognizably a Viking, and I take it that St Anskar could tell the difference between the merchants with whom he set out from Hedeby to Birka, and the pirates who nearly captured him on his journey; but this does not exclude the possibility that the same seaborne warband would wear a trader's face in some circumstances, and a pirate's in others. Indeed, this is exactly what *Egils saga* implies on several occasions. Björn is said to have been "sometimes out raiding (*viking*), and sometimes on trading voyages (*kaupferðum*)". Thorolf and Egil won "immense wealth" harrying in the Baltic, and then put into Kurland for "a fortnight's peace and trading". Egil left a merchant-ship in the Vik, while he went raiding in the summer with Arinbjörn on the coasts of Germany and Frisia. The saga also casts a possible new light on Ottar's apparently innocent trading among the Lapps by revealing that those to whom the king of Norway entrusted the northern trade blended the collection of Lapp tribute with piratical attacks on others. I see no reason to believe that these details are thirteenth-century fictions; "at least", to quote the saga's latest translator, "they merit examination".[33] The lesson of this evidence, if evidence it be, is that it is as misleading to leave raiding out of Viking commerce as it is to leave trade out of Viking free-booting.

Moreover, if early Viking raiders could also be traders, the reverse applies to their descendants. To extend the analogy with the sixteenth-century Caribbean, slaving was as important for these prototype buccaneers as it was for Sir John Hawkins. Alfred Smyth has pointed to the prominence of *captivi* in Irish and Frankish records of Vikings. St Anskar and his biographer both redeemed slaves taken in the Baltic, and both Olaf Tryggvason and his mother were reportedly victims of the trade. Slaves are prominent in Ibn Fadlan's now notorious account of *Rus* activities.[34] It seems likely that towns like Dublin and Novgorod grew fat on trading slaves for which their inhabitants continued to raid in the hinterland, and there is evidence that York and Rouen owed at least some of their prosperity to the same source.[35] Whilst acknowledging that the Vikings brought new wealth to many of the areas in which they settled, one wonders whether their efforts were any more appreciated than were those of Hawkins in West Africa.

In short, I do not doubt the importance of the commercial angle to the Viking expansion, but the evidence suggests that there was an even more strongly predatory tone to Viking commerce than to that of the Robber Barons. In the light of the written evidence, which is not wholly belied by archaeology, I would prefer to take as the primary concept what the word "Viking" itself implies: the warband, albeit with an inherent commercial aspect. The existence of trade was a necessary condition of the emergence of the Vikings, as it is for all piracy. But the central *motif* of Viking history, from the contretemps at Portland to the martyrdom of the unransomed archbishop Aelfeah in 1012, was the quest for movable wealth, which was, as in *Beowulf*, the cement of a warrior-leader's following. The means employed did vary, from exchange, through the ransom or sale of prisoners and treasures, to the outright plunder of undefended concentrations of wealth and manpower in monasteries and markets. But we cannot ignore the clear implications of the evidence, whether sagas or Christian sources, that violence was basic to the making of Viking fortunes. Important as the Vikings were in the economic history of Europe, it is an illusion that their contribution was wholly, or even mainly, peaceful, and the illusion can only be encouraged by too much talk of trade.

IV

The argument thus far suggests, with Sawyer, that Vikings were essentially raiding warbands. But when we turn from the motives to the scale of the Viking movement, and from the earliest phases, in which settlement was apparently not involved, to the second half of the ninth century, when it did occur to some extent at least, we encounter new problems. Sawyer argued until recently that raiding warbands were what, in the ninth century, the Vikings remained. Even their largest armies should be numbered in hundreds rather than thousands, and settlement was never so dense as to argue the presence of peasant hordes rather than aristocratic landlords. Again, there is no need to rehearse at length his familiar and highly persuasive arguments: the exaggerations of all medieval chroniclers; the restrictions on numbers imposed by the maximum complement of an ocean-going ship like that unearthed at Gokstad, especially if horses, women and children – and, he could have added, prisoners – were also carried; and the sheer difficulty of keeping a large army in the field under early medieval conditions. But it now seems unlikely that, as a characterization of all, rather than most, Viking armies, the thesis will stand. Sawyer now concedes as much himself, but his argument has held the field for so long that the objections should be reviewed.[36]

In the first place, nearly all Sawyer's arguments prove that Viking armies *may* not have been large, not that the were certainly small: figures *may* be exaggerated; a *here* in English law was not *necessarily* more than 35 men; *if* horses, women and children were carried on *all* ships, numbers come down further; it would be *surprising* that a large army was controlled for so long; one does not *need* mass-migration to produce considerable linguistic impact; and so on. Moreover, only if all Sawyer's conditions are met do armies in fact fall below a thousand. If the army that attacked southern England in 892 really consisted of 200 ships or more, the figures would work out at about 1,500, even at seven or eight men per ship. If the size of the fleet is exaggerated by a factor of 100 per cent, but only half the ships carried horses and camp-followers, we should still have 50 ships with Gokstad's complement of 30 oarsmen, and an army of nearer 2,000. If some of the ships involved were larger than Gokstad — and, as a reviewer noted, Sawyer does not help his case by conceding that larger ships were used for comparable voyages in the second Viking Age — numbers would again go up. And if all these alternative conditions are met — that is, if only 50 per cent of a fleet of 200-plus ships was encumbered by "passengers", and 10 per cent of the ships were the size of *Skuldelev 2*, with a complement of 50 to 60, the size of the army would have to be pushed up to over 4,000; to this we should then add Haesten's Loire fleet of 80 ships, working out, on similar principles, at over 1,500 men.[37] Such hypotheses are no more a proof that Viking armies were large than are Sawyer's that they were small; but nor are they any more a set of hypotheses. Sawyer's case is an important warning of possibilities, not a demonstration of certainties.

Most of the criticism of Sawyer's arguments has come from philologists; it was their objections that dominated the sometimes-heated discussion of his "Two Viking Ages" paper in 1969, and also the review of work on the Vikings in England which Gilliam Fellows-Jensen published in 1975.[38] Most linguists flatly refuse to accept that the massive Scandinavian influence on the English language, and on the place-names north and east of the Danelaw's Watling Street frontier, could have been achieved by a few hundred settlers. To quote Professor Cameron: "I do not know of any student of the history of the English language who would accept that a small body of men could be responsible for influence *on this scale*" [my italics]. So strong is this conviction that, while accepting Sawyer's case for small *armies*, they have postulated a heavy peasant migration subsequently. Sawyer has reasonably objected that this is to substitute for a theory of large armies, supported by some historical evidence, a theory of unarmed migration for which there is no evidence at all; and in the second edition of his book, he argued that no one really knows what makes a language change.[39] Those lacking in the special skills of the toponomist are thus left in an impasse.

However, two points can perhaps be made. The first concerns the Danish place-names in England themselves.[40] It is now generally agreed that the earliest Danish settlements were on the best land; and because this land was already settled by Englishmen, Danish place-names are scanty (as around the "Five Boroughs" and York itself), and hybrid formations, like the famous "Grimston". What is sometimes called a second phase of Danish settlement is marked by purely Danish names, with suffixes in "-by" and "-thorp", on less good land, which had not previously been settled, and whose place-names therefore came to bear a stronger Danish imprint.[41] Now, the critical issue is really the date and nature of this "second" phase. In 1971, Sawyer argued that it was genuinely a second phase, subsequent to the initial settlement among the native population on good land; and he suggested that it reflected colonization, associated with the English economic "boom" of the tenth to twelfth centuries. Today, he sees it as a takeover by the Danes of existing settlements, previously the outlying vills of "discrete" estates.[42] But in either case, one would then surely have expected to find linguistic evidence of assimilation with the English in the form of more hybrids. To adopt the techniques of the syllogism: the absence of English elements in this second class of names argues *either* that Danish settlement was sufficiently dense to obliterate evidence of previous inhabitants, *or* that it was an unoccupied land. *But* the purely Scandinavian, if not the archaic, character of these names means that they must be early, before assimilation with the English set in; in fact, there is no evidence that, as a class, they are not contemporary with the initial settlement.[43] *Therefore*, these names are *either* evidence of relatively dense settlement on already occupied land, *or* evidence of relatively heavy and almost instant pressure on available landed resources, such that some settlers at least were pushed onto land of lesser quality. Either way, they are evidence of a significant influx.

The second point can be put more briefly and simply. Whatever the case with the history of the English language, it would also be hard to find parallels in the history of Germanic Europe for so much linguistic influence being owed by so many to so few. As against those of his critics who have pointed out that Scandinavian influence on English language and place-names was much greater than that of the Norman Conquest, Sawyer has observed that it was much less than that of the Anglo-Saxon settlement itself.[44] But it was also considerably greater, at least as regards language, than that of the Franks in Gaul or the Lombards in Italy, and few would number the Franks or Lombards in hundreds. Sawyer might argue that Scandinavian influence in England was stronger because Danish and English were much more similar than Latin and Frankish or Lombardic. Granted this point (and not every linguist would admit its relevance), the relative advantages enjoyed by Danish in England could have been cancelled out by the failure of its speakers to become permanent masters of their new environment, unlike the Franks.[46] I conclude that the linguists have won their case, if only on points.

Meanwhile, a *deus ex machina* for the whole dispute has recently appeared in the form of an article by Nicholas Brooks, which suggests that we can do without un-evidenced peasant migrations, and think of large armies after all. Brooks points out that contemporary Irish, Frankish and English sources are remarkably consistent in their estimates of what was sometimes the same naval force. Before 850, we rarely find over one hundred ships (and then only in such special circumstances as a fleet commanded by the king of the Danes). After 850, there are fleets of 150, 200 or 250, even as far away as Byzantium, and these numbers are exceeded only when there is some other reason to suspect exaggeration. The *Anglo-Saxon Chronicle* and Frankish sources each at some point number the fleet that was active on either side of the channel between 878 and 896 at 200 ships, and Haesten's Loire Vikings, who joined it in 810/1 at between fifty and a hundred. Such an ability on the part of unrelated sources to agree in "exaggeration" surely argues that there was no exaggeration at all.[47]

Brooks makes a further point, which is graphically confirmed by David Hill's newly-published *Anglo-Saxon Atlas*. Viking activity in the ninth century tended to concentrate in particular spheres at particular times. The 850s, years of perhaps only sporadic raiding in England, were a period of great pressure in Ireland and France. From about 865, Charles the Bald made headway against the Loire Vikings, and was undisturbed on the Seine; while Irish annals for the 860s and 870s have almost as much to say about Vikings in England and Scotland as of their depredations nearer home, and thereafter Ireland experienced its "forty years' rest". This was the period not only, as Sawyer pointed out, of the settlement of Iceland, but also of the *micel here* in England; and, as will be argued below, Alfred Smyth has made a powerful case that this army was led by a chieftain who was also active in Ireland. After Alfred's triumph in 878, Viking pressure on Francia resumed, then abated in the 890s, when the same army was attacking England, and picked up once more after Alfred's second victory.[48] The sources suggest how this came about. The Frankish annals show Viking fleets joining up and redividing, *secundum suas sodalitates*, and *per plures classes*, just as Haesten joined a larger fleet in 890/1 which itself divided in 896.[49] The *Anglo-Saxon Chronicle* sometimes names several leaders for the same army, and Viking armies fought in "divisions", both in England and France.[50] It therefore seems that even if many Viking enterprises were undertaken by small forces, they could unite to form much larger armies when the prospects looked promising, and these armies might then have been numbered in thousands, if not tens of thousands. If such armies were subsequently whittled down by long years in the field, they might still be reinforced from elsewhere in the west.

In the last resort, Viking expansion raises the same issues of scale of migration and settlement as the earlier Germanic invasions. There is no reason to suppose that ninth-century sources were any more prone to exaggerate than those of the fifth century. In England, if not elsewhere, the Viking impact on language and place-names compares favourably with that of the continental barbarians. The Vikings, admittedly, had to come by boat, but so did the Anglo-Saxons. They left little funerary evidence of their presence in their new homes, but fifth-century Frankish graves are also very hard to identify, and demonstrably ninth-century graves in Denmark itself are generally few and poor.[51] These comparisons matter because, though the evidence involved is itself comparable, even the latest, notably sceptical, estimate of barbarian armies in the fifth century speaks of "each group numbering at the most in the low tens of thousands".[52] Naturally, none of this proves that Viking numbers were similar. But it does make one wonder whether the scepticism about Viking numbers that has been fashionable since the publication of Sawyer's forceful arguments is wholly justified. It suggests, and Sawyer never proved otherwise, that we *may* after all have to think of a relatively large-scale movement, transcending the "normal" operations of Germanic warbands.

V

I come now to perhaps the best-known feature of the modern view of the Vikings, the argument that the scale and ferocity of Viking attacks on the Church were exaggerated by their clerical victims, who, because they alone wrote sources for the period, misled all subsequent historians into seeing the Vikings as a purely destructive force. This argument in fact has several parts. One is that Vikings saw churches not as temples of a rival faith to be destroyed, but as repositories of movable wealth to be looted; they differed from equally predatory Christians only in that they saw no distinction between secular and ecclesiastical treasure.[53] Another, especially associated with the work of Dr. Lucas on the Irish evidence, is that Christians also plundered churches, even before the Vikings came.[54] A third is that the decline of ecclesiastical life and culture in the aftermath of the Viking Age should be blamed on other factors: the secularization of monasteries, for example, was already apparent in England, Francia and Ireland.[55] Finally, it has also been urged that the Vikings attacked *only* churches, and were not necessarily as unwelcome to lay society.

The first thing to say about these arguments, in which there is much truth and indeed common sense, is that they are not wholly consistent. One cannot say that the Vikings stand out in the sources because only they attacked ecclesiastical targets, and then say that Christians also plundered churches. If the latter point is true, then there must still have been something especially cataclysmic about Viking methods to make them so much more noticeable. In fact, the *Annals of Ulster* for the year 833 do say that Feidhlimid plundered the sanctuary of Clonmacnoise "up to the church door", whereas they enter no such reservation about Viking efforts. However this may be, the late, lamented Dr. Kathleen Hughes has already dealt elegantly with Lucas's case, showing that, until *c.* 880, Viking desecrations were much commoner than Irish, and only thereafter do the Irish begin to catch up.[56] Again, if it be true that, before the Viking onslaught, the secularization of the Church was already far advanced, or, as I would prefer to put it, the Church was already impregnated with the values of lay society, one cannot then argue that Viking attacks on churches left society untouched.[57] It is certainly true that feuding dynasts and noblemen in England, Ireland and France sought Viking support, just as those of tenth-century Germany had recourse to pagan Magyars and Slavs, though such stratagems were rarely crowned with success, almost as if so shocking a *mésalliance* was in the long run counterproductive.[58] This does not mean that one can draw a clear line between the interests of Church and laity. A family monastery was, after all, a part of lay society by definition; for a family that had invested landed and movable wealth in a church, in return for benefits in this life as well as the next, its destruction was a personal disaster.[59] In England at least, laymen kept their charters in churches, and there are ninth-century cases of frantic families seeking to replace lost title-deeds to their estates.[60] The ninth century was not the sixteenth, and monasteries could not be dissolved without the most profound effects for society as a whole.

Nevertheless, these arguments have cumulative force, and must be met by more than logic-chopping. Some critics, notably Professor Wallace-Hadrill, have sought to meet them by going over the detailed evidence for the destruction of churches in the sources; but since the revisionist case starts with the view that these sources are distorted, their evidence is unlikely to carry conviction except for the already converted.[61] But more objective tests are available. Bishoprics were among the most durable institutions in medieval Europe; they were not lightly abandoned, even for a time, and were very resistant to change, even by ecclesiastical authority, In the Danelaw, the episcopal lists of all dioceses except the most prestigious, York and Lindisfarne, were interrupted for a matter of decades. This might just be a matter of deficient information; the earliest set of episcopal lists, from Mercia, was not kept up after 840–45, and the next set is West

Saxon from a hundred years later.[62] But what is in any case really significant is that the sees of Hexham, Leicester and "Dunwich" disappeared for good; indeed, we don't really know where the pre-Viking dioceses of Lindsey and East Anglia were based.[63] Such a dramatic disruption (and there is comparable evidence in Normandy) can hardly be explained in terms of slow ecclesiastical decay, and argues that the effects of Viking attack were very serious indeed: as serious, locally, as those of the Anglo-Saxon invasions.

Moreover, after the death of Bede, we know little about the histories of East Anglia or Mercia, and, but for the records preserved by York and St Cuthbert's community, we would know little of Northumbria. One would not necessarily expect to find a Mercian Bede or an East Anglian *Anglo-Saxon Chronicle*; but one would expect to find charters, and, apart from a few Lindisfarne and Peterborough records, there are none.[64] There is evidence of continuity on some ecclesiastical sites that have both Anglian and Viking-Age sculpture.[65] Nevertheless, the disappearance of charters argues that churches were disrupted, if not worse. The same goes for books and learning. It is highly unlikely that Mercian and East Anglian churches had no books like those which have survived from Kent and Wessex; and, even if we did not have his word for it, we would guess that the library which made Alcuin of York into the greatest teacher of his age must have been very impressive. Yet nearly all has disappeared.[66] In his famous preface to the translation of Gregory's *Pastoral Rule,* King Alfred wrote that learning admittedly was in decay, "before everything was ravaged and burnt". But, while idle Anglo-Saxon clerks might leave books on the shelves to be eaten by rats, they are most unlikely to have stuffed them into the monastic boiler.[67] The evaporation of almost the entire literate tradition of the pre-Viking Danelaw can only be the responsibility of the Vikings themselves.

This should perhaps prompt further thoughts about the view that Vikings were never systematically hostile to Christianity. It is true that Vikings were fairly rapidly converted once they settled in their new homes, though identifiable burials in Christian churchyards are not wholly impressive evidence of respect for local religious customs, and though, in the early eleventh century, Archbishop Wulfstan clearly felt the need for special measures against paganism in Danish areas.[68] It is also true that the attitude to Christianity suggested by *Egils saga* and Notker's *Life of the Emperor Charles* is rather one of coarse cynicism than fanatical intolerance; it reminds one of the enterprising Hedeby smith producing both crosses and Thor-hammers to order.[69] Yet there is an impressive unanimity about the way that the names given to the Vikings by Irish, English, Frankish and even Muslim sources all stress their paganism.[70] The Loire Vikings do seem to have stipulated that Pippin II of Aquitaine become a pagan as the price of their support; if this is true, it is an event without parallel in the entire history of Germanic relations with Christianity.[71] Dudo may not have invented the idea that his ancestors called on Thor as they went into battle.[72] It is worth remembering that conversion was longer resisted in Scandinavia itself than anywhere else in medieval Europe (the *Life of St Anskar* is almost the only Dark Age account of a mission that failed); that Scandinavian literature tells us 90 per cent of what we know about the Germanic pantheon, whereas *Beowulf* is uncompromisingly monotheistic; and that, unlike Anglian or Irish sculpture, Viking-Age sculpture in northern England leaves clear traces of pagan myth and legend. Granted that this *is* Christian sculpture, using traditional stories to make Christian points, it nevertheless draws on a pagan repertoire, whereas earlier Anglo-Saxon carvers had not. One could add that the Viking coinage of York is unique among western issues of the early Middle Ages in deploying a pagan iconography.[73] In the context of the Germanic invasions as a whole, it is not surprising to find some degree of continuity in churches and cemeteries. What *is* surprising is how far this continuity was, as it were, on Scandinavian terms.

Finally, there is the much-debated problem of Viking human sacrifices, attested not only by Adam of Bremen and Saxo Grammaticus but also, more importantly, by the earlier north German chronicler, Thietmar of Merseburg.[74] Alfred Smyth has recently resurrected the notorious blood-eagle, arguing that this grisly form of sacrifice to Oðinn was carried out both on King Aelle of Northumbria in 867 and on King Edmund of East Anglia in 869. The furor over the blood-eagle is a good illustration of the temper of modern Viking studies; scholars have been determined, not only that the evidence is uncertain (as it is), but also that the Vikings *could not* have perpetrated anything so ghastly. It is true that Smyth is not wholly straight with the evidence here; he shows that much of the saga of Ragnarr Lothbrok and his sons, the main evidence for the carving up of Aelle, was borrowed from the *Vǫlsunga saga*, but fails to note, as a further possible borrowing, that Sigurðr had carved the blood-eagle on *his* father's killer.[75] All the same, the story was established in both the east and west Norse traditions, and existed *c.* 1035, since it features in a praise poem for Cnut.[76] Smyth does answer the suggestion that the legend arose from a textual slip in the transmission of Abbo's *Life of St Edmund*; and even if Edmund was not despatched in this literally colourful fashion, Abbo's account of a scarcely less horrible death is without real parallel in western hagiography since the Acts of the Roman martyrs.[77] It is perhaps not surprising to have horror stories about pagans from potential victims; but what is unique about the blood-eagle is to find the practice described, if not gloried in, by the descendants of its perpetrators. Whatever the truth of the matter, the strangest thing is that it has seemed so important to deny it. Sawyer has observed that the blood-eagle is really no more appalling than hanging, drawing and quartering. One might add that one does not necessarily do a historical people a favour by denying the reality of what could have been among their most cherished religious rituals. We have, I think, to face the possibility that there *could* be something positive and petrifying about Scandinavian paganism, even if not all Vikings were fanatics (any more than all were like the Hedeby smith), regardless of what happened to their convictions once they settled in a Christian environment.

Undoubtedly, the destructive effects of Viking expansion *have* sometimes been exaggerated. The collapse of the Carolingian empire is too closely paralleled by that of its Merovingian predecessor for the Vikings to be accorded more than a contributory role, though the fall of Charles the Fat himself was clearly linked with his failure to defeat them. The Mercian empire, likewise, was probably undermined by dynastic disputes and the rising power of Wessex before the Vikings administered the *coup de grace*, though, again, they were responsible for King Burgred's resignation. Quite apart from the question of secularized monasteries, the cessation of the English Church's conciliar tradition may have been caused by resentment of the rise of Wessex rather than external assault.[78] A further point, not made often enough even by Viking apologists, is that Alfred's success against them was not unique. Frankish defences ultimately withstood their attacks, and it is easy to forget that Rollo was granted Normandy after a defeat at Chartres.[79] The Irish drove the "Gentiles" out of Dublin in 902, and, thought they returned, repeatedly defeated them, even before the famous battles of Tara in 980 and Clontarf in 1014; Dublin survived at least as much because it was useful to Irish kings as because it could not be eradicated.[80] The emerging Scottish kingdom, like the West Saxon, profited from the Vikings' elimination of its rivals, and then went on to mop them up.[81] Talk of Alfred's saving Europe from heathen hordes can be overdone.

But when all this has been said, it remains true that the Vikings had a drastic, and by no means always positive, effect on the political and cultural map of Europe. In England, three ancient and not necessarily effete kingdoms lost their independence and most of their literate tradition. On the continent, a mighty dynasty's prestige was badly dented, and the intellectual ferment of the Carolingian Renaissance, bubbling merrily until late in the ninth century, came to an abrupt end.[82] If Irish politics and culture emerged relatively unscathed, that was perhaps because of their own resilience rather than for want of Viking effort. Such effects have a bearing on the question of Viking numbers, and also on that of Viking fanaticism. There is some reason to believe that Viking paganism was more strongly rooted than that of other Germanic peoples. Evidence of continuity and early conversion has not persuaded historians that the fifth- and sixth-century invasions were other than seriously disruptive of Christian life and culture, and it may be even less justifiable to argue this way with the Vikings. If churches did usually recover from early Viking raids, the cases of the Danelaw and Normandy suggest that they were lucky to survive Viking settlement; and this in turn suggests that conversion was no so rapid and automatic after all.

VI

So far, I have been trying to argue that some of what has become accepted wisdom about Vikings since Sawyer's important book may need qualification. Before concluding my survey of these trends, I want to change tack and suggest that the most important and original work on the Vikings to appear since 1962, at least in English, has not yet had the recognition it deserves: Alfred Smyth's *Scandinavian Kings in the British Isles, 850-80*, with its companion volumes on *Scandinavian York and Dublin*.[83] Smyth's books mainly concern identifying the leaders in different spheres of Viking activity with each other, and with figures in Scandinavian sagas. The central thesis is that Inwaer and Healfdene, who appear in English sources as leaders of the 866 *micel here*, are the same as Imhar and Alband in the Irish annals, and as the Scandinavian heroes, Ivarr *inn beinlausi*, son of Ragnarr Lothbrok, and his brother.[84] The tenth-century kings of Dublin were Ivarr's descendants, and their repeated attempts to conquer Northumbria aimed at the reconstitution of his York-Dublin empire. Smyth is in fact offering us in Ivarr a Viking Clovis, invincible, cunning and cruel, albeit one who spoiled his chances of emulating Clovis's fame by dying remorselessly pagan; and his case, if it stands, that the chief rivals of Alfred's dynasty for control of Northumbria were the family of the Danelaw's founder, ranks as the most significant contribution to Anglo-Saxon political history since Sir Frank Stenton established the "Supremacy of the Mercian Kings" over sixty years ago.

Yet his case has not been well-received, to put it mildly; among recent English works on the period, perhaps only John Morris's *Age of Arthur* (1973) has aroused such a chorus of outraged experts.[85] Like Morris, Smyth was unwise. He posed an outright challenge, on matters of principle as well as fact, to an especially cautious branch of the learned profession; and in an age obsessed with methodology, he failed to establish his method. He was also unlucky. In the interval between the completion of his thesis and its emergence in print, Rory McTurk published an admirably thorough, methodologically unimpeachable, and ultimately negative, review of the evidence for Ragnarr Lothbrok and his sons in the British Isles, which seemed to pre-empt all his conclusions.[86] Nevertheless, James Campbell's positive judgement on Morris's book can also be applied to Smyth's: "It is brave, comprehensive and imaginative. These qualities outweigh the flaws which are inevitable when a powerful and sensitive historical imagination is inadequately controlled, and waxes dogmatic and over-specific on particulars".[87] There is more that can be said, both for Smyth's use of evidence, and for his basic case.

Smyth's method is in fact detectable, and not necessarily misconceived. He does not use later Scandinavian evidence on its own, without asking whether there was any reason to invent it. His approach is an intellectual equivalent to the principle that there is no smoke without fire. Thus, he does reject Saxo's general account of Ragnarr as king of the Danes, but he notes that many of its details would make sense if Ragnarr's was a "sea-kingdom", based on the islands and coasts of the Kattegat. He dismisses Ragnarr's death in King Aelle's snake-pit, but wants to know why Saxo describes "Hella" as king of the *Galli*; he suggests that, in some unspecified way, Saxo had access to an Irish source on Ragnarr's activities, since the Irish called the Norsemen *Gaill*. He may be wrong on both points, and has certainly not solved all the problems that arise; but to say that Saxo simply invented these details raises just as many problems. (Is it quite inconceivable that he used some early poem on Ragnarr? Professor Turville-Petre has persuasively argued for a connection between Irish poetry and the development of skaldic verse.[88]) For other points, like the Mediterranean expedition of Ragnarr and/or his sons, Ivarr's skill in sorcery, or the death of Halfdan/Agnerus, Smyth can cite similarities between Scandinavian and English, Irish or Frankish sources. It is true that the significance of these similarities is somewhat diminished by Smyth's argument that the relevant legends in the *fornaldarsögur* were first elaborated in England and Ireland; but they do at least push the origin of such traditions much nearer to the time of the alleged events.[89]

Above all, critics of Smyth's use of late evidence do not always seem to have asked themselves what better evidence we can expect. Ari's *Islendingabok* is, however late, the first coherent narrative we have from the "Viking side", and Adam of Bremen's *Gesta*, however unreliable, is the first outsider's attempt to write Scandinavian history. If Adam is the first to talk of *Ivar filius Lodparchi*, and Ari the first to say that Edmund's slayer was *Ivarr Ragnars sonr Loðbrokar*, this is depressing but also inevitable; one could in fact reverse the argument and say that Ivarr, son of Ragnarr Lothbrok, is attested by the earliest native sources![90] For the English side, on the other hand, one should note the limits of the evidence. Until the 870s, the *Anglo-Saxon Chronicle* is fragmentary and largely retrospective; it also concentrates on events in Wessex, and, though it does name Viking leaders, it seems that this was only, as in Francia, if they later concluded a treaty with the native authorities. By 871, when the West Saxons first encountered the Great Army, Inwaer was out of the way on Smyth's own reckoning, so we should not expect to find him in the *Chronicle*.[91] Even so, it does refer obscurely to the death in 878 of an unnamed "brother of Inwaer and Healfdene", which is important evidence of West Saxon awareness that the well-attested Healfdene had two brothers, one called Inwaer.[92]

Beyond Wessex, there is no contemporary English source, but not all subsequent evidence is wholly suspect. In particular, the *Life of St Oswald* was written *c.* 1000 by Byrhtferth, a reputable historian, at the abbey of Ramsey, which Oswald had founded, and it says that Oswald's own grandfather had come over with the Great Army, which was led by "Huba and Hinwaer"; this looks like oral tradition of a pretty high order. Ramsey, moreover, was the home for a time of Abbo of Fleury, whose *Life of St Edmund* makes Ingwaer the conquerer of East Anglia, and was probably the source of all subsequent English knowledge of this role.[93] In these circumstances, we are hardly entitled to better evidence that the army of 866 was led by three brothers, Inwaer, Healfdene and Huba, and that Inwaer was identical with Ivarr, son of Ragnarr Lothbrok (whoever he may have been). It is worth noting that the evidence for Rollo's foundation of Normandy would not have been much better, had the duchy shared the fate of Ivarr's empire.[94]

McTurk has attacked in detail the case that Inwaer/Ivarr, identical with the Imhar who appeared in Ireland in the 850s, returned to Dublin from the sack of Dumbarton "with a great booty of Englishmen, Britons and Picts" in 871, and died there as "king of the Norsemen in all Ireland and Britain" in 873; and the case that Healfdene was the same as "Alband, king of the Danes", who attacked the Dublin Norse in 875 and was killed by them in 877. According to Aethelweard's Latin version of the *Anglo-Saxon Chronicle*, "Iguuar" died deservedly shortly after Edmund's killing, and the man killed in 878 was in fact "Healfdene, brother of the tyrant Iguuar"; Ivarr can then hardly be identified with the man who died in Ireland in 873, nor Healfdene with the man killed there in 877.[95] Aethelweard certainly used a lost text of the *Chronicle* with some superior information, but he was also translating (with difficulty) and interpolating his own views. In the case of the 878 entry, the extant *Chronicle*'s *Inwaeres broður 7 Healfdenes* is certainly a strange phrase; but, as against Aethelweard's version, it surely deserves all the credit of a *lectio difficilior*; it is much easier to see how Aethelweard could have misread or mistranslated what is now in the English text, than how an English scribe could have made anything so obscure out of an original corresponding to Aethelweard's text. As regards Aethelweard's account of Iguuar's death, is it not a hagiographical commonplace that the perpetrators of such deeds as the slaughter of Edmund met their just deserts?[96] If what Aethelweard says about Iguuar and Healfdene can be dismissed, they may still be identified with their near-namesakes in Ireland; and, taking the evidence as a whole, they probably should be.

It is understandable that Smyth's books have irritated other scholars. He made mistakes; his approach to evidence looks audacious; he ignored cautious counsels issued in the past about such theories as his, and indeed those who had already put forward his theories.[97] He may be wrong in important aspects of his thesis, if not about the critical role of Ivarr's dynasty in Viking history.[98] But his efforts really cannot be dismissed outright, and should at least inspire others to ask the same questions. Apart from the way that his case for the coherence of Viking activity bears on the whole question of its scale, two features of his approach are especially important. One is that he does not ignore any available evidence on principle. Scholarly caution is all very well, but, if carried to excess, will obstruct any further advance in Viking history (as opposed to archaeology); indeed, we can hardly prove that semi-legendary high-medieval sources do *not* contain genuine memories of the Viking Age, unless we investigate the possibility with an open mind. Second, Smyth is interested in the leadership of Viking armies.

It is strange that, while students of other Germanic peoples have been obsessed with the identity and office of their leaders, Viking scholars have said very little of such things — a literal case of *Hamlet* without princes of Denmark! This is all the more remarkable in that Scandinavian evidence was once thought to have a significant bearing on the history of Germanic kingship in general.[99] The English, Irish and Frankish sources do distinguish between Viking "kings", like Healfdene, on the one hand, and "earls", "lords" or "dukes" on the other.[100] This in itself suggests that the word "king" was used consciously, because it expressed a quality which set some Viking leaders apart from others, and which was recognizably royal in European terms. Smyth's book points to another respect in which Viking studies might be more closely related to the study of the rest of early medieval Europe; in any case, "kingship" can surely not be left out of their remit for much longer.

VII

Throughout this paper, I have had the nerve to differ from the established school of Viking studies, notably from the ways in which it has been influenced by Sawyer's *Age of the Vikings*. I have argued that neither contemporary, nor even later Scandinavian, sources are necessarily wholly tendentious; that Viking expansion was originally inspired by the predatory instincts of the warband, which initially dominated, and were never quite eclipsed by, commercial concerns; that though earlier raids were carried out by relatively small numbers, interested in movable, not landed, wealth, later attacks consisted of larger numbers who did settle; and finally that the Vikings may have been almost as disastrous for Carolingian Europe as earlier barbarian invasions were for the Roman Empire. But Sawyer's book was above all an attempt to explain, not to excuse, the Vikings. It is unfortunate, and no fault of his, that it has concentrated attention on the effects of Viking attacks overseas, rather than their causes in the internal development of Scandinavia; it is unfortunate too that the critique of Smyth's factual and methodological errors appears to obscure his invitation to consider one aspect of that development, the growth of military kingship. What we have for Viking-Age Scandinavia at present is a vast wealth of archaeological evidence, whose exact historical significance has yet to be fully worked out, plus an essentially static analysis of Scandinavian society, which rarely transcends the classifications of the *Rigsþula*.[101] If I am to undermine Sawyer's own explanation, the least I can do in conclusion is try to put something in its place, in the hope of suggesting lines of research to experts. My tentative model owes much to Sawyer's own recent researches, as well as to the stimulus of Smyth's ideas. It is based on the conviction that a knowledge of historical patterns in early medieval Europe as a whole has a place in the understanding of the Vikings. Like Anglo-Saxon and early Irish history (and for much the same linguistic reasons), Viking studies tend to be pursued by specialists exclusively in the area. But the gulf between our historical and archaeological knowledge of ninth-century Scandinavia might be partially closed by finding analogies for the trends revealed by the intractable written evidence in the experiences of other "barbarian" peoples. This is not to say that whatever happened in the rest of Europe must also have happened in Scandinavia, still less to resurrect the nineteenth-century concept of a single *Germanentum*. But it is to accept the possibility that peoples with basically the same political and social vocabulary would be affected in similar ways by similar social forces.[102]

Scandinavia in the pre-Viking Age had not been unaffected by the turbulence of the *Völkerwanderung*. It had possibly spawned migrations, and the uprooted riches of the Roman Empire flooded back to it.[103] But eighth-century Scandinavian society had no direct experience of migration, so far as we know; and the flow of wealth from central and eastern Europe dried up after the Avars cut the traditional routes.[104] It is thus no surprise to find evidence that early Viking society shared significant features with pre-migration Germanic society as described by Tacitus. Like the kings of the *Germania*, for example, Scandinavian kings may have been beholden to a tribal assembly and its officers. King Olaf of the Swedes told St Anskar that he could not, alas, accept his mission until he had consulted his people in assembly; and, when their reservations had been overcome (by one of the king's senior supporters, not the king himself), he still could not give permission to preach without convoking an assembly in another part of the country. The *Heimskringla* illustrates a later King of Sweden's dependence on an assembly; as late as the thirteenth century, Swedish laws described how kings were made in a series of local "things", where law-speakers played prominent parts.[105] But the clearest evidence of Scandinavia's archaic political structure is, of course, the Icelandic "constitution", since the Icelanders believed that they had migrated precisely to escape the rising power of Norwegian kingship; Sawyer has recently suggested that the Icelandic *goði* represented the ancient type of Scandinavian tribal chief, which Harald Finehair was displacing.[106]

Sawyer's suggestion implies another possible feature of early Scandinavian rulership. *Goði* is often translated "priest", because it is cognate with Gothic *gudja*, which has that meaning, and because *goðar* have been linked with cult-centres. But the significance of the relationship may be only that the ancient Scandinavian secular office was in some sense priestly, or "sacral". The "sacrality" of Germanic kingship in general is much debated, and that of the Scandinavian kingship is now no less controversial.[107] All the same, there are interesting parallels between the Scandinavian evidence on this point, and that for the notoriously "sacral" kingship of the early Irish. Like Irish kings, and those of other Germanic peoples, Scandinavian rulers probably were thought to be descended from gods; the *Life of St Anskar* may reflect this when it tells how the Swedes of Birka agreed to organize a temple and sacrifices for a dead king, whom, they were told, the gods would elect to their college instead of Christ, if the people must have a new god![108] There is evidence, in Scandinavia as in Ireland, of royal inaugurations on sacred stones in places hallowed by religious cult and the burial of ancestors.[109] Like Irish sagas, Scandinavian tradition has many stories of the relationship of kings with thinly-disguised gods, of the mysterious deaths of kings (for example, by drowning in a vat), and even of the outright sacrifice of kings and their offspring.[110] Saxo and Snorri are almost as explicit as Irish sources about the connection between good kings and fertility, bad kings and famine.[111] Whatever one makes of the evidence on kingship, it does at least underline the strongly-rooted paganism of Scandinavian society, and this is a point further emphasized by the long struggles of Christian kings to eradicate it, as recounted by Adam of Bremen and the *Heimskringla*.[112]

But Tacitus also implies that the primitive pattern of Germanic society was beginning to break up. Romans, like nineteenth-century imperialists, preferred to deal with effective chieftains, and their diplomacy did all it could to promote monarchical power. Roman trade and subsidy created clearer distinctions of rank and wealth; and, as in other societies, economic growth promoted predatory as much as commercial activity, leading to the formation of groups of warriors under the leadership of a military adventurer, the famous *comitatus*.[113] In the long run, such developments inevitably disrupted traditional social structures. To hold his warband together, a leader had to be able to reward its members continuously with movable wealth, and perhaps ultimately, as they grew old, with land.[114] The sustained aggression required might set off a chain-reaction in society, as social nuclei were broken up by attack, and their individual particles flew off to form new warbands themselves, with similar consequences. With the support of a warband, a king, or even a *parvenu*, could achieve the real power that the Romans wished to see; but as kingship became more powerful, so it was increasingly open to competition, and unsuccessful aspirants became exiles, with their own warbands.[115] Caesar's account of the Gauls reflects these changes, with traditional kingship collapsing, and large numbers rallying around chiefs of various status.[116] Among the Germans themselves, two of the earliest leaders to confront Rome, Ariovistus and Maroboduus, were what German scholars call *Heerkönige*: leaders not of tribes, but of the detritus of tribes, extended and very large warbands, who needed loot but also land. Both men were treated by the Romans as kings, and one founded a dynasty.[117] It was probably changes of this sort that led to the formation of the new *gentes* of the third century and later, and to their invasion of the Roman Empire in numbers which may have been exaggerated, but were still considerable.[118] Finally, settlement in the Roman Empire completed what Roman wealth and diplomacy had begun: kings immeasurably increased their power and responsibilities, with Roman resources and advisers; warrior society developed along "feudal" lines; and the religion of the old homeland was displaced by that of the new.[119]

This brief, and of course grossly over-simplified, account of early Germanic social development may offer a clue to what lay behind Viking expansion. The *comitatus* and its lifestyle were probably known in Scandinavia before the Viking Age: its terminology is established in archaic levels of north-Germanic, and Vendel and Valsgärde are nothing if not *Adelsgräber*.[120] But Tacitus shows that the *comitatus* could co-exist with traditional tribal structures for a time, and lack of contact with south European wealth could have stunted its further development in the north. However, in the eighth century, there is evidence of renewed, and marked, economic expansion in Scandinavia: the intensive exploitation of its vast iron ore resources, which perhaps explains the settlement-expansion that some have seen as evidence of overpopulation; the development of urban concentrations with far-flung commercial contacts at Helgö, Ribe and Kaupang; and the growing flood of eastern silver down the Russian rivers, to whose significance Sawyer originally drew attention.[121] The *Life of St Anskar*, and the sagas also, show that, as trade expanded, so too did the number of sea-borne warbands preying on it.[122] As Sawyer suggests, the earliest raids on the west can be seen as the overspill of Baltic piracy, made possible by the coincidental, and related, development of the ocean-going Viking ship.[123] Muslim silver and European trade may thus have played the same role in Scandinavia as did Roman gold and Roman merchants for early Germanic society. But the earlier parallel suggests that warband activity would tend to escalate by geometrical progression, as ever larger numbers were uprooted and felt the pull of the adventurous life. This is what may lie behind Saxo's account of how Ragnarr recruited the most worthless sons and least-trusted slaves to serve in his army.[124]

1. Hogback stone monument; Lowther, Cumbria, England.

2. Free-standing stone cross; Aycliffe, Co. Durham, England.

3. Niederdollendorf stone, Rheinisches Landesmuseum, Bonn.

4. Viking era warrior; free-standing stone cross; Middleton, North Yorkshire, England.

5a. Tapestry fragments associated with the Oseberg ship burial; the Viking Ship Museum, Bygdøy, Norway.

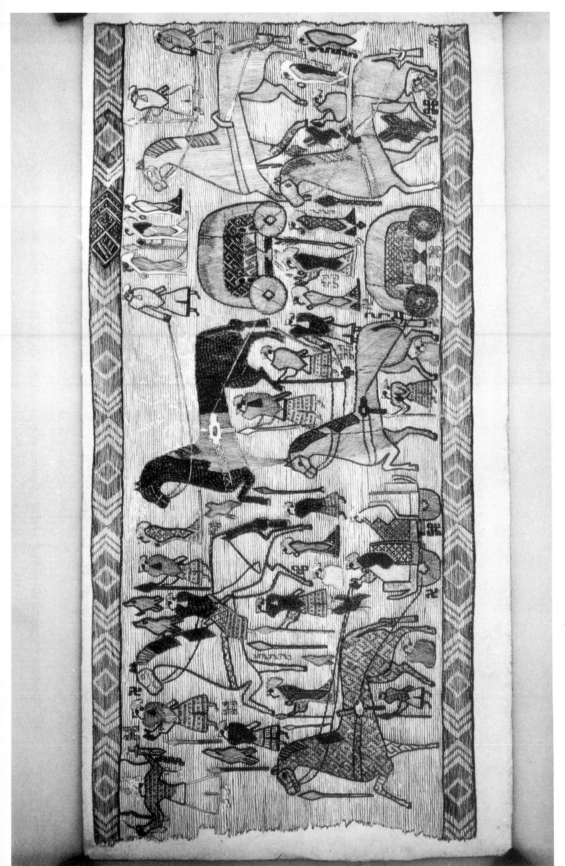

5b. Facsimile of Oseberg ship burial tapestry; the Viking Ship Museum, Bygdøy, Norway.

Hollow-cast silver pendant in form of a human head, Aska, gebyhöga, Östergötland, eden.

7. Sculptured stone fragments; St Mary Bishophill Senior, York, Yorkshire, England.

8a.   Free-standing stone cross; Halton, Lancashire, England.

8b.   Picture-stone; Lillbyärs, Stenkyrka, Gotland, Sweden.

9. Sculptured stone fragment in Tees Valley portrait style showing a warrior wearing a pointed cap; Sockburn-on-Tees, Co. Durham, England.

10. Sculptured stone fragment in Tees Valley portrait style showing a warrior wearing a bowl-like helmet; Sockburn-on-Tees, Co. Durham, England.

12b. Figure of a winged man under a draped arch—an angel or Wayland?; free-standing stone cross, Brompton, North Yorkshire, England.

12a. Figure of an ecclesiastic or saint standing under an arch and holding a scroll and maniple in the ninth century Anglian tradition; free-standing stone cross, Brompton, North Yorkshire, England.

11. Sculptured stone fragment in Tees Valley portrait style showing a warrior; Kirklevington, Cleveland, England.

12c. Birds cut by stencil in the Anglo-Scandinavian tradition; free-standing stone cross, Brompton, North Yorkshire, England.

12d. Plant scroll in ninth century Anglian tradition; and spear tip of armed Viking show below; free-standing stone cross, Brompton, North Yorkshire, England.

13. Late Pictish sculptured stone; Dunfallandy, Perthshire, Scotland.

15. Free-standing stone cross showing seated profile figure; Nunburnholme, East Yorkshire, England.

14. Free-standing stone cross showing a bound figure in the Anglo-Scandinavian manner; Gosforth, Cumbria, England.

17. Depiction of a mounted god on free-standing stone cross; Gosforth, Cumbria, England.

16. Free-standing stone cross showing profile figure in the Irish manner; Banagher, Co. Offaly, Ireland.

18. Sculptured stone cross-shaft with figure in distinctive 'mythological' dress; St Peter's, Kirkgate, Leeds, West Yorkshire, England. *(Photograph: James Lang.)*

19. Free-standing stone cross depicting the Crucifixion; Castledermot, Co. Kildare, Ireland.

20. (*left*) Local Anglian style; Ilkley, West Yorkshire, England; (*centre*) Local Anglian style; Otley, West Yorkshire, England; (*right*) Viking figural sculpture of the tenth century illustrating the influence of the local Anglian style; Weston, West Yorkshire, England.

21. The Franks Casket: a general view.

22.   The Franks Casket: a view of the front.

23. The Franks Casket: a view of the left side.

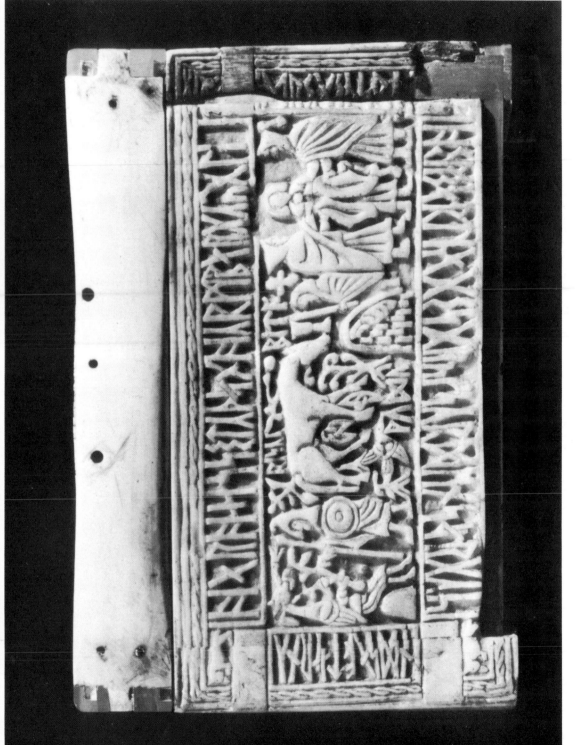

24. The Franks Casket: a view of the right side.

25. The Franks Casket: a view of the back.

26. The Franks Casket: a view of the lid.

26a. Late antique ivory reliquary casket:
Brescia, Italy.

27. The Luke symbol from the Echternach
Gospels.

28.   The David/Christ Triumphant figure treading on a beast from the Durham Cassiodorus.

29. Sculptured stone cross-shaft showing birds in the Northumbrian style; Aberlady, East Lothian, Scotland.

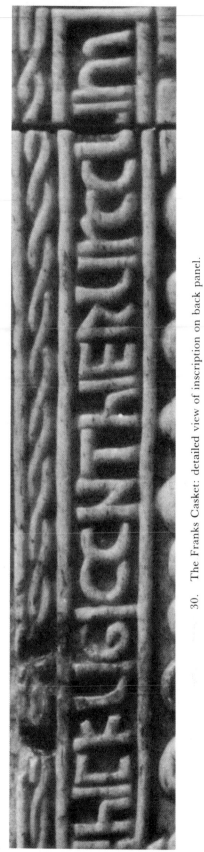

30. The Franks Casket: detailed view of inscription on back panel.

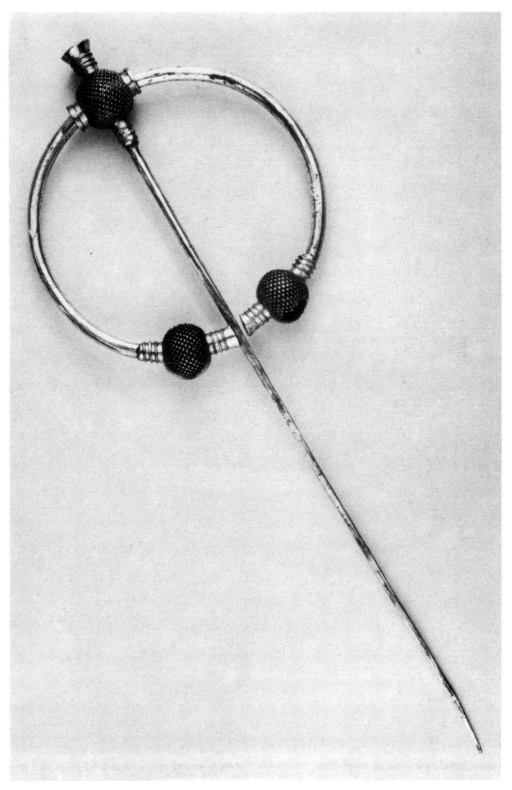

31. Tenth-century silver 'thistle-brooch' found in 1785 on Newbiggin Moor, Cumbria.
(British Museum)

32.   Ninth-century gold hoard from Hon, Vestfold, Norway, containing a variety of rings and pendants.

(Universitetets Oldsaksamling, Oslo)

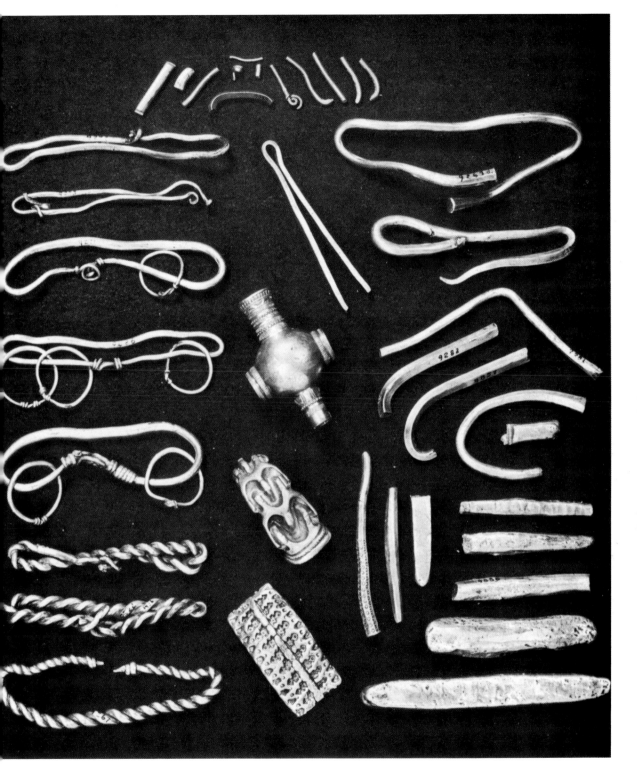

33. Rings, ingots and hack-silver forming a tenth-century silver hoard from Lahell, Lier, Buskerud, Norway.
(Universitetets Oldsaksamling, Oslo)

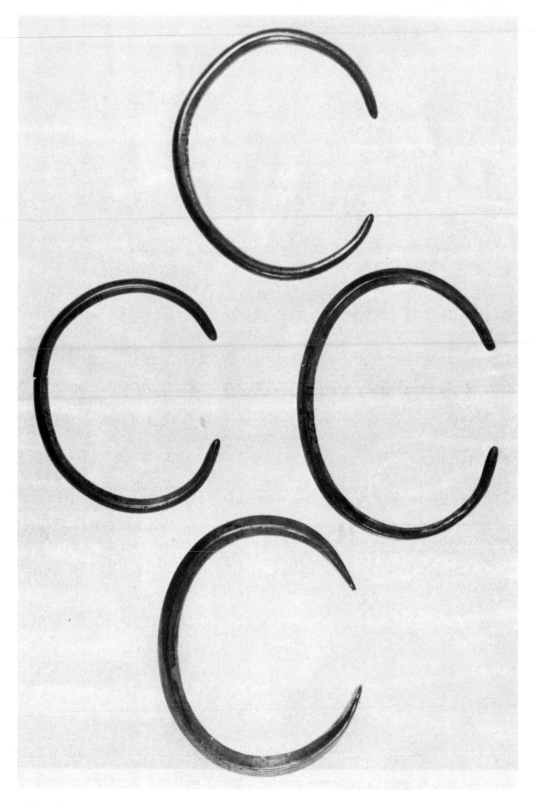

34.   Silver 'ring-money' hoard from Tarbat, Ross and Cromarty, Scotland, of tenth/eleventh-century date. (Scale 1/1) *(National Museum of Antiquities of Scotland.)*

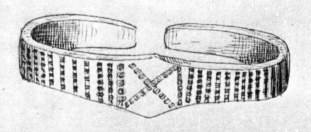

Original size
Silver Bracelet.

Weight 1 oz 11 dwts 2 gr

Ornamenting punched

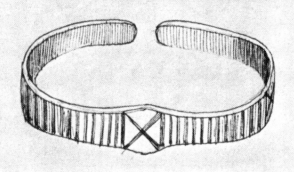

Weight 18 dwts 19 gr
5 Compartments are crossed.

Presented to Rich.d Sainthill Esq
by Aquilla Smith Esq M.D.
Nov 1848
J Windele Pinx.t

35. Silver arm-rings of Hiberno-Viking type of ninth/tenth-century date from Ireland. (Scale 1/1) *(Librarian, Royal Irish Academy, Dublin.)*

36. Norwegian bronze pen-
annular brooch imitating
silver 'thistle-brooches' (as
Plate 31), from Telemark.
(Scale 1/1)(*Universitetets
Oldsaksamling, Oslo*)

37. *(below left)* Silver filigree-ornamented pendant from Bredsätra, Öland, Sweden,
in the form of Thor's hammer. (Scale 1/1) (*Antikvarisk-topografiska arkivet, Stockholm.*)

38. *(below right)* Silver pendant from Goldsborough, Yorkshire, hoard deposited
*c.*925. (Scale 2/1) (*British Museum*)

39. Part of the largest-known mixed hoard of Viking silver, buried *c.*903 in North-West England, at Cuerdale, Lancashire. *(British Museum)*

40. Aerial view of part of Freswick Links, Caithness, Scotland.
(Crown copyright)

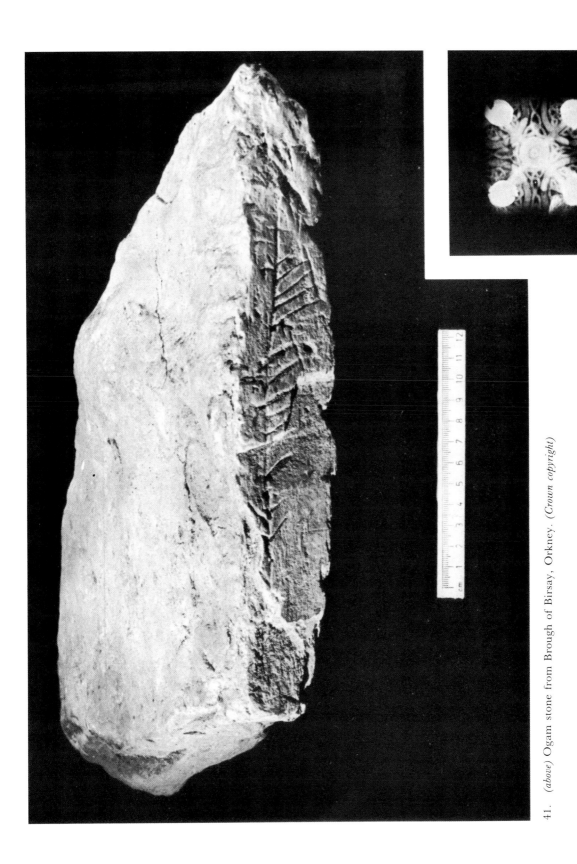

41. (above) Ogam stone from Brough of Birsay, Orkney. (Crown copyright)

42. (right) An X-Ray photograph of a bronze mount with cross-design from Brough of Birsay, Orkney. (Crown copyright)

43. Figure-of-eight shaped building under excavation, Brough Road, Birsay, Orkney.
(Crown copyright)

44.   Grave below cairn under excavation, Brough Road, Birsay, Orkney.
(Crown copyright)

45. Buildings under excavation, Beachview, Birsay, Orkney.
(Crown copyright)

46. Openwork ship vane of gilt copper from Söderala Church, Hälsingland, Sweden. *(Statens Historiska Museer, Stockholm, Sweden)*

47. Gilt bronze or copper ship vane from Källunge Church, Gotland, Sweden. *(Gotlands Fornsal, Visby, Gotland, Sweden)*

48. Vane of heavily gilt bronze, possibly from Heggen Church, Modum, Buskerud, Norway. *(Universitetets Oldsaksamling, Oslo, Norway)*

49. Ship vane of gilt bronze or copper from Tingelstad Church, Oppland, Norway. *(Hadeland Folkemuseum, Gran, Norway)*

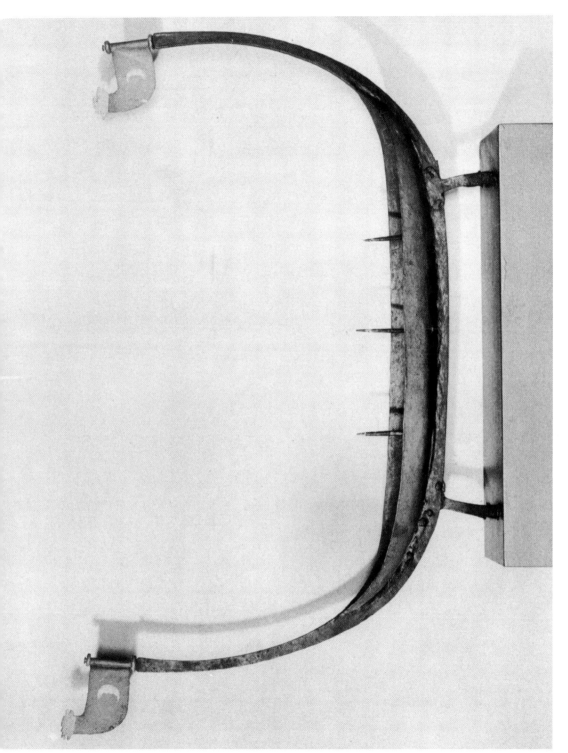

50. Boat-shaped candle-holder from Dale Church, Sogn, Norway. (*Historisk Museum, Bergen, Norway*)

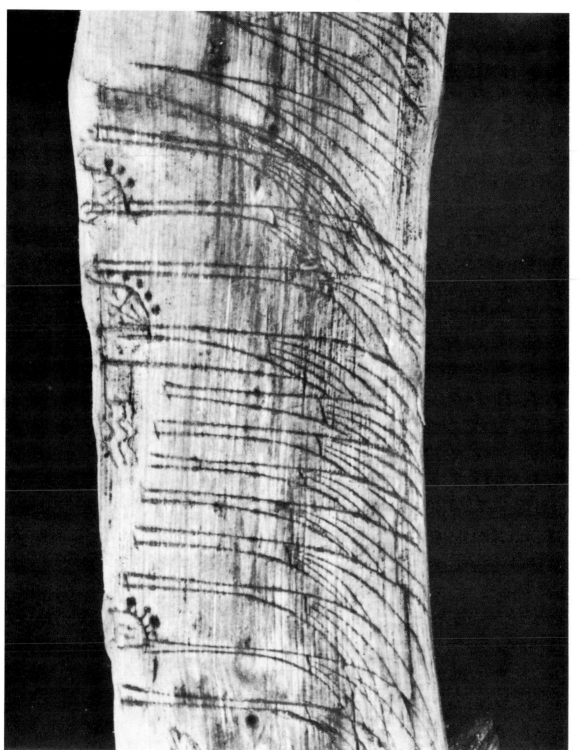

51.   Graffiti incised on a stick, recovered during an excavation. (*Historisk Museum, Bergen, Norway*)

52. 'Flaug'-style ship-vane from thirteenth/fourteenth centuries now located at Höyjord Stave Church, Vestfald, Norway.

53.   Detail of gilt vane at Söderala Church: cast lion riveted to upper edge of vane; Söderala Church, Hälsingland, Sweden.

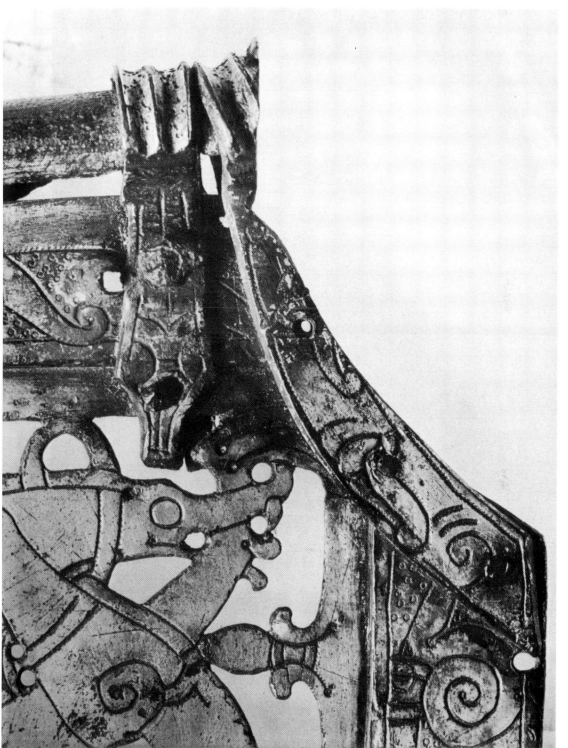

54. Detail of gilt vane at Söderala Church: bottom corner showing mounting socket;. Söderala Church, Hälsingland, Sweden.

55.   Detail of ship-vane at Tingelstad Church: griffito of ship stem (5 × 6 mm.); Tingelstad Church, Oppland, Norway.

It is also possible that the supply of eastern silver to the Baltic temporarily receded in the mid-ninth century, making it all the more likely that a pirate would seek his fortune in the west.[125] It would not then be surprising to find evidence for increasing Viking numbers c. 850.

Nor does the parallel with the earlier period end there. It is probable, and to some extent evident, that the Franks, like the Romans, sought to introduce order into their turbulent borderlands by encouraging stable kingship. They certainly thought that they were dealing with a single Danish kingdom, and there is evidence that Jutland at least had been united by a strong monarchy.[126] One would expect the Danes to imitate the ever-looming Frankish example, as earlier Germanic kings loved to adopt the panoply of imperial rule (and one would like to know what, if anything, is the significance of the fact that Saxo has Ragnarr introducing the Frankish *inquisitio* to Denmark![127]) But, as earlier, one effect of rising royal power was to make royal succession more competitive, and rootless warbands offered the means of competition. The *Life of St Anskar* tells how Anound, exiled king of the Swedes, recruited Danish followers with the prospect of the plunder that could be had in Birka by restoring him; and, ironically in view of Frankish efforts to stabilize the frontier, the Frankish coasts suffered badly from armies led by unsuccessful competitors for the Danish throne, apparently trying to build up their followings for another attempt.[128] Ivarr and his family may likewise have been disaffected offshoots of the Danish royal house, with whom they had names in common.[129] Against this Danish background, we may set the remarkably clear evidence of *Egils saga* and the *Heimskringla* for the growth of Norwegian royal power. There is nothing at all improbable about their picture of Harald Finehair and his successors forming a united kingdom for themselves by demoting local kings to the status of earls. Clovis did so, as did Offa and the Irish Ui Neill.[130] The sagas' stress on the importance of his warband in the making of Harald's power is again what we would expect.[131] Significantly too, perhaps, the kings who pursued this policy most vigorously, after Harald, were all Christians with experience of foreign models: Hakon the Good, Olaf Tryggvason and St Olaf.[132] But once again the effects of the concentration of royal power were, paradoxically, disruptive. Representatives of the old order, like Egil's family, took off as Vikings elsewhere (there is no reason to suppose that all such people went to Iceland); and fueds within the royal dynasty itself drove Eric Bloodaxe to Northumbria, and both the future King Olafs to participation, as exiles, in England's second Viking Age. The Viking Age saw Scandinavian kingship grow from *Volkskönigtum* to *Heerkönigtum*, as that of other Germanic peoples had earlier, and this growth was both cause and effect of Viking activity.

Sawyer's new explanation of the Viking phenomenon in this volume, with its focus on the economic development of Scandinavia as the key to the explosion of Viking piracy, is obviously close to the one put forward here.[133] But his causes are essentially causes of *raids*, and they depend, like his previous approach, on the belief that nothing more was involved. I have argued that there may have been large numbers of settlers, under men who would be recognized as kings, and that their pagan convictions can perhaps be underestimated. Sawyer is still thinking of "normal Dark Age activity, made possible and profitable by special circumstances". In my view, what we are seeing is an *abnormal crisis* in Scandinavian society, albeit one which other "barbarian" peoples also experienced. Not just the lure of western wealth, but profound changes in a hitherto fairly "traditional" society, sent increasing numbers careering out of their environment, and gave them leaders of regal status, who, if they were not to reign at home, would seek to do so elsewhere. In such circumstances, it is no surprise to find a mixture of cynicism with devout traditional belief; nor, given the Vikings' emergence from a previously stable background, compared to that of other invading barbarians, is it surprising that their paganism could be relatively militant; nor, once divorced from that background, is it strange that, like other Germanic peoples, they were soon enough converted.

My hypothetical model, in short, amounts to the proposition that the Viking Age was caused by the same sort of forces that produced the *Völkerwanderung* itself, but delayed for four centuries, and perhaps given a more pagan flavour, by Scandinavia's relative isolation. Whatever the reaction to this model, I would still suggest three points of method for any alternative. First, we should be less sceptical of the overwhelming testimony of a wide range of sources about the nature, scale and even leadership of Viking invasions; I am dubious about the historian's right to reject his evidence, unless it is provably wrong, even in favour of common sense, let alone of archaeology. Second, I think it is helpful, if not necessary, to set Viking history in its wider European context, if only to see what we may expect to believe in the sources, and what questions to ask of them; it is not really very likely that Scandinavian society would have followed a quite different evolutionary course from that of the rest of northern Europe in the early Middle Ages. Finally, let the current bout of Viking jubilations be the last in which the main issue is whether the Vikings were good things or bad things. There is more to history than the award of red and black marks. The importance, and the interest, of studying the development of Scandinavian society in the Viking Age is in no way diminished if one believes, as in the last resort I do, that though the Vikings may not have been mad, they were probably bad, and certainly dangerous to know.

NOTES

1.   Brown 1972. For the enduring popularity of the Vikings, *see* Mjöberg, 1980; books in English on the Vikings frequently run to second editions, and Hollywood has favoured them more than most early medieval societies. For their criticism of the first draft of this paper, and their encouragement to proceed, I thank Professor Farrell himself, and Professor Peter Sawyer — in view of what follows, this was especially generous of Professor Sawyer, and I should add that, had I seen his forthcoming book (Sawyer 1982) before this article was effectively in the press, I would have wished to modify my critique in several respects. I also thank my colleague, Mr. Leslie Collier, for help with Old Norse texts; my Glasgow students, Charles Duncan, Charles Johnston and Tom Wallace, for stimulation and, indeed, insights; and finally Dr. Jenny Wormald for far more than merely conjugal support.

2.   Sawyer 1962 (all future references are to the 2nd edition, Sawyer, 1971). Many of the works influenced positively or negatively by Sawyer are cited below, and no purpose is served by listing them here. I must stress again that this is a review of what I detect to be trends, not a comprehensive bibliographical survey; nor can it pretend to do justice to work in modern Scandinavian languages. My excuse on this last point is that Scandinavian contributions have been largely linguistic, literary or archaeological, and that a high proportion of the historiography of the Vikings has been devoted to their effects in western Europe by western European historians. My concern in this paper is with what western European historians have come to think about Vikings, and I write as one myself. For Sawyer's impact in Scandinavia, *see* Roesdahl 1970-3, 403.

3.   Magnusson 1980, 7.

4. Sawyer 1971, 202-3.

5. On sources for the sub-Romano-British period, *see* Dumville 1977; on the *Anglo-Saxon Chronicle*, cf. Whitelock 1979, 123-4, with references, and Davis 1971; for the Irish Annals, *see* Hughes 1972, 148-59.

6. The comparison emerges from *Wattenbach-Levison* 5 vols. 1952-73.

7. *Vita S. Anskarii* (1829); Adam *Gesta* (1917). I have used these editions, being unable to get access to Trillmich-Buchner 1968.

8. Saxo 1979, 1980; (these English translations — the latter with facing reproduction of the *editio princeps* — are used for convenience); citations of *Ynglingasaga*, and other constituents of *Heimskringla*, are from *Islensk Fornrit*, Vols. 26-7, 1941, 1945. On Jordanes, cf. Hachmann 1970.

9. Wormald 1978, 32-4, 58-63, 68-9, with references to recent literature.

10. A convenient and up-to-date survey of Scandinavian legislation, now beginning to attract more attention than in the past, is badly needed by the "outsider". On the problems of early Germanic legislation, cf. Wormald 1977; on Irish law, *see* Binchy 1943, 1975.

11. Citations of *Islendingabok* are from *Islensk Fornit*, Vol. 1, 1968; cf. Turville-Petre 1953, 90-105.

12. Sawyer 1971, 99-101, 206-11.

13. Randsborg 1980, 137, 152-3.

14. Klindt-Jensen 1969, 195; Dolley 1969, 181; Skaare 1975, 43-53.

15. *See* below, pp. 132-3 and n. 23.

16. *Ann. S. Bert.* 49, 75, 86, 125; for exiles, *see* nn. 19, 128 below.

17. E.g. Graham-Campbell 1980, 68-9.

18. Wainwright 1964, 126-40.

19. *Ann. S. Bert.* 39; *Ann. Fuld.*, 39; *Chron. Font.* 303; *A/S. Chron.* 188; *Ann. Ulster.* 344-7.

20. *A/S. Chron.* 195-6; Douglas 1942, 417-36; Musset 1975, 40-54.

21. Sawyer 1971, 35-6; Sawyer 1978a, 23-31.

22. Summarized in the relevant chapters of Barley 1977; cf. Hall, 1978; McGregor 1978; Graham-Campbell 1980, 86-111, and Smyth 1979, 191-242.

23. Objects originally assembled by Petersen 1940; cf. Blindheim 1976, 1977.

24. *See* n. 22; plus, for Norwich, Campbell 1975a; for Rouen, Breese 1977, 55-7; for London, Brooke 1975, e.g. 264-5; for coins, Dolley 1965, 1966.

25. *A/S. Chron.* 180; cf. *Chron. Aethelweard* 26-7.

26. *Ann. S. Bert.* 125.

27. Blindheim 1976, 14; cf. Wilson 1969, 13.

28. Graham-Campbell and Kidd 1980, 34. It may be noted that the relics in the casket were *not* original.

29. *Ann. Ulster* 278-9, 330-1, 348-9; *Vita S. Anskarii*, xvi, 700, xviii, 701; cf. Harmer 1914, 12-13; cf. also, Bakka, 1965, 32-40, esp. 39-40.

30. *Ann. Reg. Franc.* 110, 128, 153; *Ann. S. Bert.* 24-5, 34, 37 etc.; *Ann. Fuld.* 39, 45; *Ann. Xant.* 14; *Chron. Font.* 302; *Vita S. Anskarii* 697; cf. Sawyer 1978a, 29.

31. Wilson 1970, 94 (and cf. Eldjarn, in this volume); Grierson 1959, esp. 137-9, and for the major (not the sole) critique Metcalfe 1967.

32. Wallace-Hadrill 1971, 13; Sawyer 1977, 141, 144-5.

33. *Egils saga* (cited here and subsequently from *Islensk Fornrit*, Vol. 2, 1933), 27-8, 41-2, 83, 114, 217; cf. Fell and Lucas 1975, viii.

34. Smyth 1977, 154-68; *Vita S. Anskarii* viii, 696, xv, 700; xxxxv, 719; *Vita S. Rimberti (ibid.* 1829 — *see* n. 7) xvii-xviii, 773; *Heimskringla (Olafs saga Tryggvasonar)* 230-1; and, for Ibn Fadlan, Smyser 1965.

35. Pelteret 1980, 106-10.

36. Sawyer 1971, 123-31 (and *see* references in nn. 38-9, 42-4). As against Sawyer's observation that a mere 400 Norsemen could inflict immense damage on important Frankish forces, it may be noted that Regino of Prüm, who probably had west Frankish sources, shows that the decisive deaths of counts Robert and Rannulf were in essence accidental: *Regino Chron.* 92-3.

37. *A/S. Chron.* 201; cf. Sawyer 1971, 131-2; Roesdahl 1970-3, 408; McGrail, 1980, pp. 46-9.

38. Sawyer 1969, 176-9, 185-7, 196-201, 203-7; Fellows Jensen 1975, 181-206.

39. Sawyer 1969, 168, 176-9, 196-201, 204: Sawyer 1971, 167-71.

40. This line of argument has been well put by Bailey 1980, 37–40.

41. Cf. Fellows Jensen 1975, 193-201, with references.

42. Sawyer 1971, 158-67; Sawyer 1978b, 161-3.

43. Sawyer 1971, 160-5; Fellows Jensen 1975, 200-1. It appears that, while there *is* evidence that names in "-thorp" are, as a class, younger than names in "-by", *no* evidence (other than the poorer quality of the land involved) is cited by Sawyer or anyone else that names in "-by" are younger than "Grimston hybrids".

44. Sawyer 1969, 169.

45. Gamillscheg 1970; Gamillscheg 1935, 52-229; Lot 1945, 289-98.

46. Sawyer 1969, 177; Fellows Jensen 1975, 201-2.

47. Brooks 1979; for the Byzantine experience of 860, which he does not mention, cf. Obolensky 1971, 182-3. But for a critique of Brooks on this point *see* Sawyer 1982, Chapter 4.

48. Brooks 1979, 8-9; Hill 1981, 32-5; Smyth 1977. It is fair to add that Sawyer's most recent work has done much to develop this point.

49. *Ann. S. Bert.* 86, 89; *Ann. S. Vaast* 69; *A/S. Chron.* 194, 201, 205.

50. *A/S. Chron.* 193, 194, 210-11: *Ann. Fuld.* 99; *Chron. Font.* 303, 304.

51. James 1978, 70-1; Brønsted 1936.

52. Goffart 1980, 5, 231-4; cf. Brooks 1979, 3. However exaggerated the Ostrogothic numbers in Italy, they must indeed have been substantial to hold down for more than fifteen years a Byzantine army which we know to have been sizeable and better-equipped.

53. Sawyer 1971, 138, 145-6, 203-4; cf. d'Haenens 1969, 246-60.

54. Lucas 1966, 1967; cf. O'Corrain 1972, 85-9; For comparable Frankish evidence, *see Ann. S. Bert.* 222.

55. Sawyer 1971, 143-5; O'Corrain 1972, 83-5. Cf. Graham-Campbell, 1978-9 for an argument that Irish art was actually stimulated by the Viking advent.

56. *Ann. Ulster* 332-5; Hughes 1972, 152-8. For a Frank's ability to distinguish between two kinds of violence, *see Regino Chron.* 121.

57. This is argued in Wormald 1978, 50-8.

58. Famous cases are the aetheling Aethelwold, *A/S. Chron.* 207-9, and Pippin the Younger of Acquitaine, *Ann S. Bert.* 74, 105, 113; on the Irish evidence, *see* Hughes 1966, 203-5, and Smyth 1977, 129-53.

59. *See* the literature on the *Eigenkloster* cited in Wormald 1978, 51-4, and nn. 91-112.

60. Sawyer 1968, Nos. 367, 371 (two texts), 225, 395; cf. Sawyer 1979, 4-5, for the problems to which these charters give rise. References to the destruction of charters by fire are not found before the Viking period, and Sawyer himself is prepared to see a connection with Viking activity, *loc. cit.*

61. Wallace-Hadrill 1975.

62. Dumville 1976, 39-43. Our information on sees north of York depends largely on the northern annals incorporated in the *Historia Regum*, 3-66, which effectively break off in the early ninth century.

63. For the location of the Lindsey bishopric, *see* Ralegh Radford 1946; for East Anglia, Rigold 1961, and Scarfe 1972, 116-27; for Normandy, *see* Musset 1965, 218-22.

64. Brooks 1979, 13; on the Lindisfarne "charters", *see* Morris 1977, 91-3. The survival of Lindisfarne is not, of course, in doubt, but it is not easy to accept the argument that the community's "freedom" to wander about the north for seven or nine years means that they were not seriously threatened by the Vikings!

65. Bailey 1980, 76-84; Smyth 1979, 262-3.

66. Cf. Ker 1957, No. 319 for a rare example of a MS that apparently survived the ninth century in the north, before being transferred to the south; cf. also the Durham Cassiodorus (Durham B II 30), which Professor Bullough argues in his forthcoming study of Alcuin, to have been a product of the school at York. The Durham collection in general shows, of course, that a certain portion of the original Lindisfarne library survived, but this exception merely highlights the norm.

67. Whitelock 1979, 889; cf. Shippey 1979, 351-4.

68. For Viking burials in Christian churchyards (identifiable only, of course, because they *were* still to some extent pagan), *see* Wilson 1967, 1968. For Wulfstan's legislation, e.g. VI Aethelred 7, ed. Liebermann 1903, 248-9.

69.   *Egils saga*, 128-9; *Notker*, 90; Graham-Campbell, 1980, 187.
70.   Wallace-Hadrill 1975, 222; Smyth 1977, 222.
71.   *Ann. S. Bert.* 105, 113; cf. Wallace-Hadrill 1975, 226.
72.   de Vries 1956, 296.
73.   Bailey 1980, 101-42; for coins, Smyth 1975, 104-5; 1979, 95-6.
74.   *Thietmar Chron.* I. 17, 23-4; Adam *Gesta*, IV 26, 257-9; Saxo 1979, 73; cf. also *Heimskringla (Olafs Saga Tryggvasonar)*, I, 286; *(Olafs saga helga)*, II, 256.
75.   Smyth 1977, 38-53, 189-94, 209-13; *Edda* 1962, I, 179.
76.   Saxo 1979, 292; Whitelock 1979, 337; cf. Smyth 1977, 189-90. It may be noted that Ivarr's savagery was already notorious for Adam: *Gesta*, I 39, 40.
77.   Smyth 1977, 209-13; *Abbo Passio*, 10, 78-9. In view of general West Saxon ignorance of events beyond their borders, no real significance attaches to the phraseology of *Asser* c. 33, 26.
78.   This point is argued in my chapter on "The Ninth Century" for Campbell 1982.
79.   Vercauteren 1936; Douglas 1942, 427.
80.   O'Corrain 1972, 95-6, 101-4, 106-7; Byrne 1973, 267-9.
81.   Smyth 1977, 101-2, 149-53; Duncan 1977, 27-8.
82.   The point emerges powerfully from the source survey for later ninth-century Francia in *Wattenbach-Levison* V, 1973.
83.   Smyth 1975, 1977, 1979; it is also worth drawing attention to Smyth 1975-6 and Smyth 1978.
84.   Smyth solves the problem of Halfdan's absence from Scandinavian sources by identifying him with Saxo's Agnerus; there are certainly some suggestive coincidences: Smyth 1977, 260-3.
85.   The most significant reviews so far are those of Frank 1979; O'Corrain 1980; and McTurk 1980 *(see also next note)*; Smyth has generally fared better at the hands of English historians.
86.   McTurk 1976 — a critique which clearly influenced Frank and O'Corrain.
87.   Campbell 1975b, 177.
88.   Smyth 1977, chapters I–III, VI; cf. Turville-Petre 1953, 36-8.
89.   Smyth 1977, 52-3, 62-6, 196-200, 260-3.
90.   Adam, *Gesta*, I 39, 39-40; *Islendingabok*, 1, 4.
91.   *A/S. Chron.* 193, 194, 196: in each case, a peace-treaty follows rapidly, whereas in 893-6, there is no treaty, and there are no names, apart from that of Haesten, whose children were baptized in his absence under English sponsorship.
92.   *A/S. Chron.* 195.
93.   *Vita S. Oswaldi* 404; *Abbo, Passio* 4-6, 71-9; on Byrhtferth's authorship and general stature, cf. Lapidge 1979, and Lapidge forthcoming on his responsibility for the early sections of the *Historia Regum*. Note that the *Historia de Sancto Cuthberto*, 202, in what is probably a tenth-century part of the text (Craster 1954, 177-8) has "Ube Dux Frescionum", leading the attack on York, which suggests that the traditions recorded by Symeon of Durham and the Annals of Lindisfarne in the twelfth century may have some validity: cf. McTurk 1976, 96.
94.   Douglas 1942, 425-30.
95.   McTurk 1976, 117 ff. *Ann. Ulster* 366-7, 368-9, 372-3; 382-5, 386-7, 387-9, 390-1; *Chron. Aethelweard* 36, 43. On Aethelweard, *see* Winterbottom 1967, and Campbell 1978, 257 and n. 21.
96.   The same considerations apply to the reported death of "Reginheri" after his attack on Paris in 845, which apparently rules out his identity with Ragnarr Lothbrok (cf. McTurk 1976, p. 97). Hagiographical literature apart, Reginheri's death is recorded only by *Ann. Xant* 14; not by the equally contemporary *Ann. S. Bert.* 50-1, nor by *Ann. Fuld.* 35, nor even by *Chron. Font.* which preserves much otherwise circumstantial detail about Viking activities on the Seine.
97.   Not least Stenton 1970, 244, and Byrne 1962-3, 269. Though many of Smyth's identifications have been made before, it must be said that they have never been put with such force.
98.   The most striking of Smyth's other identifications is that of (i) Amhlaibh of Dublin in the Irish Annals, with (ii) the *Landnamabok*'s Olaf the White, with (iii) the *Ynglingatal*'s Olaf Geirstaþaalfr,, with (iv) the recipient of the Gokstad ship-burial. The links between (i) and (ii), and even between (iii) and (iv) may seem plausible, but that between (ii) and (iii) poses more problems; there is late evidence that Olaf the White's family was Christian, and the Icelanders used the sobriquet "white" for the baptized: Cleasby-Vigfusson, s.v. But the recipient of the ship burial was assuredly no Christian!

99. It featured prominently, e.g. in the "constitutional" histories of Dahn and Waitz. *See* Albani 1969, for the traditional view revived.

100. Cf. *Ann. Ulster* 339–40 (Saxulph *toisig*) with *ibid.* 382–3 (Amhlaibh et Imhar *duo reges Nordmannorum*); *A/S. Chron.* 193; *Ann. Fuld.* 108.

101. Foote and Wilson 1970 is among the most successful of these. This is not of course to belittle what Scandinavian archaeologists have been able to deduce about the social and political transformation of Denmark in the Viking Age. For an ambitious, if somewhat, eccentric, recent example in English, *see* Randsborg 1980.

102. My model in much of what follows is Thompson 1965, and behind him, the astonishing insights of Chadwick 1912. In my view, the exaggerations of past scholars, and the difficulties of the evidence do not entitle us to deny the reality or relevance of Germanic *Kulturgeschichte*. Wenskus 1961 is a notable, if long-winded, example of caution and constructiveness combined, which has also influenced what follows.

103. E.g. Wilson 1970, 45–62.

104. Jankuhn, in Barley 1977, 359.

105. *Vita S. Anskarii* xxvi-xxvii, 711–13; *Heimskringla (Olafs saga helga)*, II, 109–17; cf. Hoffmann 1976, 12–14.

106. Sawyer 1981; cf. Karlsson 1974–7.

107. The classic exposition of Germanic sacral kingship is O. Höfler, who depends heavily on Scandinavian evidence; cf. his views summarized in Höfler 1956. Cf. also, de Vries 1956. For an admirably careful review on the Scandinavian angle, *see* McTurk 1974–7.

108. *Vita S. Anskarii* xxvi, 711.

109. Hoffmann 1976, 180–5; cf. Byrne, 1975, pp. 15–22, 27, 39–9.

110. Saxo 1979, 171–2, 225–6, 243, 283; *Heimskringla (Ynglingasaga)*, I, 26, 31-2, 38, 47–50, 74; *(Olafs saga Tryggvasonar)*, I. 312–14. Cf. Byrne 1973, 18–19, 51–5, 59–64, 74–5, 97–9, 166–7, 184–9.

111. Saxo 1980, 90–5; *Heimskringla (Ynglingasaga)* I, 26, 31–3, 74; *Halfdanar saga svarta*, I, 93; *(Haralds saga ins harfagra)* I, p. 128: *(Hakonarmal)* I, p. 197; *(Haralds saga Grafeldar)* I 203, 221; *(Olafs saga Tryggvasonar)* I, 241–3. Cf. also, Hoffmann 1975, 63–4, and, for the Irish model, Byrne 1973, 24–6. With both Irish and Scandinavian evidence, one is of course arguing that the prescription may *once* have been valid, not that it still was at the time of writing.

112. Adam *Gesta* II, 55–9, 117–22; *Heimskringla (Hakonar saga góða)* I, 166–73; *Olafs saga Tryggvasonar)* I, 302–32; *(Olafs saga helga)* II, 72–83, 176–94 etc.

113. Thompson 1965, 17–28, 48–60, 72–108; Chadwick 1912, 344–65, 432–63. The *comitatus* has been a special target of modern sceptics, but this is once again to say that older views were exaggeratedly institutional and nationalist, rather than that they had no basis: *see* the reply to critics in Wenskus 1961, 347–73, and also Green 1965.

114. Tacitus makes no mention of land-grants, leaving open the question of what happened to warriors when they reached retiring-age. Land-grants are nevertheless attested in heroic poetry (cf. references in John 1960, 53–6), and in pre-Carolingian Frankish evidence: Magnou-Nortier 1976, 13–27, 49–57.

115. Thompson 1965, 72–84, 93–102. For exiles in early Anglo–Saxon England, *see* Campbell 1979, 9–10.

116. *Caesar, De Bello Gallico* 8–9, 26–9, 90–1, 160–1, 168–9, 308–9, 332–3, 334–5, 338–41, 384–5, 426–7, 438–9; cf. Wenskus 1961, 416–19.

117. The classic account is Schlesinger 1956, esp. 116–18.

118. Wenskus 1961, 429 ff; Todd 1975, 209–12; Wallace-Hadrill 1971, 8–14, esp. 11: "War-bands are tribes in the making".

119. I have discussed this with regard to law in Wormald 1977, 125–30, 136–8. On the displacement of "tribal" religion, cf. Thompson 1966, 127–32.

120. Lindow 1976, 17–41; cf. Wenskus 1961, 373. For this interpretation of Vendel and Valsgärde, *see* Wilson 1970, 52.

121. Sawyer 1969, 166; Sawyer 1978a, 124; Sawyer 1971, 86–119, 210. *See also* n. 22 above.

122. *Vita S. Anskarii*, viii, 696; *Egils saga* (as n. 33), plus 118–19, 121.

123. Sawyer 1978a, 28–9.

124. Saxo 1979, 283. For the parallel with Gallic *Heerhaufen*, *see* Wenskus 1961, 349.

125.   *See* the graphs in Sawyer 1971, 226-9, and Randsborg 1980, 152-60. But *see also* the forthcoming discussion in Sawyer 1982, chapter 6.

126.   This emerges especially from *Ann. Reg. Franc.* 138-9.

127.   Saxo 1979, 283.

128.   *Vita S. Anskarii* xix, 702-3; cf. *Ann. Fuld.* 45; *Ann. S. Bert.*, p. 70.

129.   E.g. Halfdan and Sigfrid: *Ann. Fuld.* 78; cf. McTurk 1976, 110-17.

130.   Wenskus 1961, 448; Wenskus 1964, for Clovis; for Offa, *see* Stenton 1971, 205-10; for the Ui Neill, O'Corrain 1972, 29-32.

131.   *Egils saga* 14-15; *Heimskringla (Haralds saga ins Harfagra)* 98, 100-1 etc., cf. Lindow 1976, 42-83.

132.   The *Heimskringla*'s account of St Olaf's pursuit of criminals, supported as it is by Sigvat, is strongly reminiscent of the vigorous policy of tenth-century English kings: *Heimskringla (Olafs saga helga)* II, 328-30. I hope to return to this subject in a forthcoming book on Anglo-Saxon kingship and law-making.

133.   *See* Sawyer, "Causes", pp. 1-7 above.

II: LITERATURE

ELEGY IN OLD ENGLISH AND OLD NORSE

A Problem in Literary History

Joseph Harris

Professor of English, Cornell University

RECENT ANGLO-AMERICAN scholarship seems to have given up the effort to write a real literary history that includes Old English poetry, and this is especially true of the elegies, which we appreciate, analyse, and edit but are content to see as a genre without a history. Stanley B. Greenfield seems to have taken the next logical step: "If the elegies are a genre in Old English, they are so by force of our present, rather than determinate, historical perspective; that is, by our 'feel' for them as a group possessing certain features in common".[1] The caveat is well taken, but for me the "feel" is strong enough still to demand the construction of a common literary history for as many as possible of the texts embraced by this "feel". So far no literary history has succeeded.[2] For example, Herbert Pilch's straightforward derivation from Welsh is not persuasive, and the Ovidian and Vergilian origins argued in a confusing fashion by Rudolf Imelmann and more simply by Helga Reuschel are no more convincing than P. L. Henry's claims for the milieu of Celtic Christianity and specifically its penitential aspects.[3] What *has* been accomplished for the Old English elegies is the establishment of lateral sources and influences that provide more or less probable histories for particular motifs and expressions, and especially for many important ideas. Thus the *ubi.sunt* topoi and the *sum* catalogues are understood as having a firm home in Latin-Christian thought, while the ruined hall and cuckoo are somewhat less securely considered Celtic-Classical or purely Celtic borrowings.[4] But among all these plausible "influences" we sense no mainstream, no old generic core to be developed and absorb the lateral contributions; we need to remind ourselves that the Old English genre consists predominantly of dramatic monologue in which a human speaks in the first person about the past, mostly his own past life, and (in Greenfield's phrase) "expresses an attitude towards experience".[5] The past may have been happy or unhappy or both, but the contrast with the speaker's present, a contrast invested with sadness, is constant.

The most successful literary histories of this genre stem from German-language scholarship and connect the Old English poems with a pre-invasion Common Germanic literary culture and with the rich evidence for various kinds of poetry associated with the dead. Rudolf Koegel's basic discussion (1894) was expanded and refined by L. L. Schücking in 1908 and by Georg Baesecke and Gustav Ehrismann in the interwar years.[6] However, Andreas Heusler's *Die altgermanische Dichtung*, the proper starting point for every consideration of the history of Old English secular poetry, fails us here, and Heusler leaves the Old English elegy hovering on the very edge of his great map of

Old Germanic verse.[7] He is uncertain about the connection to native funeral lament and to memorial poetry and seems surer of the outside influence from Ovid — but influence on what?[8]

I believe that Schücking was on the right path and that the several kinds of funeral verse form the true ultimate origin, though many links will remain missing. However, the immediate predecessor of Old English elegy would have been a Common Germanic heroic elegy. Heusler shied away from postulating such a genre because of his convictions, discussed below, about elegy in Old Norse and, more generally, because he was writing in a tradition that trusts too rigidly in a development from heroic to "novelistic" plots and from honour to sentiment as motives. I want to argue that the features common to elegy in Old English and Old Norse can be ascribed to a Common Germanic elegiac genre just as we use comparative reconstruction in linguistics; such reasoning is universally accepted when it leads to the idea of the Common Germanic alliterative line and to the Common Germanic form of the heroic lay, though it has rarely been suggested for elegy. Ernst Sieper's 1915 book on Old English elegy seems to be the only major work to embrace the derivation from ritual lament and to discuss Old Norse elegy in the same context.[8]

Elegy in Old Norse can be divided into two groups of texts. First there are skaldic *erfikvæði* or memorial poems, like Egill Skallagrímsson's *Sonatorrek*. I do not intend to discuss these memorial poems by historical poets in praise of the dead, but they are regarded by Heusler, Sieper, and others as having Common Germanic roots in laments for the dead. The second group includes six heroic elegies in the *Poetic Edda* and seven similar poems in sagas of ancient times found in Icelandic and in Saxo Grammaticus' Latin paraphrases.[9] In addition there are a number of passages in other Eddic heroic poems that can be considered more or less elegiac.[10] The generalizations of the present paper have been tested in detail only against the Eddic elegies proper but should also hold for the elegiac passages and the non-Eddic poems listed. Like the Old English poems, the Eddic elegies are in large part retrospective narratives in the first person. The major difference is that all these poems are firmly tied to particular heroic legends and replete with proper names — in Old English there are only four comparable names.[11] The chronology of events is stricter in the Old Norse poems, probably because they are still so firmly rooted in a story, and the burden of ideas is proportionally greater in the Old English, as if progressive loss of story has made room for the lateral sources and influences from Latin and Celtic literatures. Triangulating backward, then, from the surviving examples of Old Germanic elegy in Old English and Old Norse, we can imagine the general form of the Common Germanic elegy.

It was a dramatic monologue spoken by a figure from a known heroic story who told, in the first person, about the joys and especially the griefs of his life. If the speaker was a woman, and it often was, she might be in the midst of her life like Guðrún in the first Guðrún poem, or at its end, like Guðrún in *Guðrúnarhvǫt* . If the speaker was a man, he was most likely to be an old retainer, like the Wanderer or Starkaðr , who had outlived his lord and comrades; but *Deor* and the *Seafarer* suggest that this characterization may be too narrow. In any case, he has been through a great deal, and his speech may come close to the end of his life. In fact, so insistent is the association with the death of a male speaker that the well-documented deathsong type must be considered a subgroup of retrospective elegy in general.[12] The intellectual content consisted of a contrast of Once and Now, a sense of the *lacrimae rerum* or loss and sometimes, it seems, of consolation. There may have been room for some conventional wisdom or at least generalization, especially near the beginning and end. It is not clear whether our model should provide for the possibility of a narrative frame; *Wulf and Eadwacer*, the *Wife's Lament*, the second Guðrún poem, and most of the extra-Eddic poems like *Víkarsbálkr* are pure monologues, but *Guðrúnarhvǫt*, the first Guðrún poem, and *Oddrúnargrátr* have developed frames, while the *Wanderer*, the "Lament of the Last Survivor", and the "Father's Lament" in *Beowulf* have more or less brief frames. One solution is to assume that informal introductory and concluding prose originally formed a saga-like matrix for a monologue and that the two elegy traditions have independently shared a development toward framing the speech in narrative verse.

This model of a Common Germanic heroic elegy is, of course, a hypothetical construct which could not be compared seriously in degree of certainty with the proto-Germanic form of a word reconstructed from attested forms in North and West Germanic and supported by the entire apparatus of comparative Germanic grammar. However, both are unreal constructs which serve the purpose of establishing a history for the real reflexes, and the poetic development of elegy in Old English can be clarified as a progression toward generalization and finally allegory. *Wulf and Eadwacer* would, then, be our most archaic text, still close to a specific heroic legend and offering little or no generalizing philosophy. The development from *Wulf and Eadwacer* to the *Wife's Lament* preserves the basic generic form and remains based in a certain — if not quite ascertainable — story, but loss of all proper names and an increase in the gnomic content makes this second stage of Old English elegy perhaps the most characteristic for the genre in its English development. To the latter part of this stage belong also the "Father's Lament" and the "Lament of the Last Survivor": in addition, both of these elegies included in *Beowulf* have developed a narrative framework which was lacking or lost in the stage or stages represented by *Wulf and Eadwacer* and the *Wife's Lament*. In the *Wanderer*, a third stage, only those elements of an underlying autobiography are retained that allow themselves to be interpreted in terms of human life in general; the poem progresses from the life of an individual to the life of man, to man the microcosm, and finally to the macrocosm itself; the framing narrative, already quite general in the *Beowulf* passages, is also reduced to a few general remarks, and of course there is a quantum leap in philosophical content. Finally, in a fourth stage the elements of individual autobiography are further reduced and revised to accord with the larger symbolic purpose; this can be seen in an early phase in the *Riming Poem* and in a late phase in the *Seafarer*. In these poems the vestigial narrative setting of the *Wanderer* is gone, and all the information we need is conveyed by the monologue itself. The development from heroic autobiography to allegory of the life of man is accompanied by a steady growth in the amount of gnomic and homiletic material, in "ideas", until at the end of the *Seafarer* every trace is lost of the old generic core — that original, fictional, human voice complaining about the situation of experience in time.

In North Germanic the starting point was the same Common Germanic form, but the development was quite different. Briefly and tentatively, I see three stages. The most primitive poem of the group is *Guðrúnarkviða in forna*. There is no poetic frame, though the introductory prose of *Codex Regius* tells us Guðrún is speaking to þjóðrekkr (Dietrich, Theodorich) — a setting that almost all scholars consider to be an invention of the literary man responsible for the arrangement of the manuscript.[13] The first-person speaker looks back over the disasters and the few joys of her life from a point after her forced marriage with Atli. The wandering mind and combination of passionate ferocity and passive suffering bear close comparison with *Wulf and Eadwacer* and the *Wife's Lament*, but the underlying story is realized in a much clearer form, and the story is more complicated here than we must imagine for the original type; however, this complication is not an aspect of the history of the literary form itself but of the growth of the story complex (*Sagengeschichte*). In this first Norse stage, the Common Germanic model has evolved toward narrative complexity and perhaps toward specificity, and certain motifs from later sources have been added; but the old generic core is intact. In a second stage we find four poems which have developed a situation framing the elegiac monologue proper. *Guðrúnarhvǫt*, for example, opens with Guðrún "whetting" her last remaining sons, sending them out to meet certain death in an attempt to avenge their sister; then the tragic mother settles down to a long elegiac rehearsal of her life experiences that agrees in every way with our model. To this stage, then, belong also *Helreið Brynhildar, Guðrúnarkviða I*, and *Oddrúnargrátr*, which provide more and more developed frames for the heroine's elegiac retrospective. Finally, in *Guðrúnarkviða III* the narrative-dramatic frame has won out over the elegiac monologue, which is here reduced to one or two stanzas. We could see the old genre pass into verse homily in the *Seafarer*; here in *Guðrúnarkviða III* it passes into medieval, novelistic narrative. In English the development was from heroic story to psychology and general life patterns then on to allegory and homily — in other words, from experienced events to experience itself and thence to ideas little connected with experience. In Old Norse, on the other hand, the old core of traditional experienced events becomes surrounded with a second growth of pure story and finally overgrown with new events, not now filtered through an experiencer.

Admittedly, a more elaborate plan is required to fit in all the relevant Old Norse texts, but I want to make it clear that in all this I am speaking of a typological development and not of the dates of surviving texts or even their actual relative chronology. For the Norse poems are all considered by consensus to have originated in a time later than even the manuscripts of the Old English poems, and I must now turn to this problem. Heusler had no faith in a Common Germani heroic elegy because he believed the Old Norse poems to be the product of an Icelandic *Nachblüte* or poetic renaissance of the later eleventh through twelfth centuries; and not only were the extant texts composed there, but the genre of heroic elegy itself was invented in Iceland. He made this argument in very brief form in a paper of 1906 and then enshrined his view in both editions of *Die altgermanische Dichtung*.[14] But this view of the Eddic elegies is unconvincing because Heusler, while elaborating on the milieu and on the materials, failed to provide any models or to show how this completely new poetic type came into existence *ex nihilo*. Most of the early paper is concerned not with the elegies but with other poetry of the Icelandic *Nachblüte*, and I think a close look at his argument concerning one of these poetic types, the heroic catalogue or *þula*, would show that Heusler was confusing the date and provenance of a particular text or group of texts with its generic provenance and history. For he rightly claims the majority of the preserved *þulur* as learned codifications of the Icelandic renaissance; but when his overall presentation implies that the genre itself is a product of this milieu, the results contradict the well-known Common Germanic origin which Heusler himself affirms in *Die altgermanische Dichtung*.

Despite such potential objections, Heusler's view of the elegies held the field until Wolfgang Mohr's two learned, diffuse, and difficult monographs of 1938 and 1939.[15] Mohr's starting point is a comparison of the language, motifs, and spirit of the Eddic elegies with the much later Danish ballads. The rich hoard of coincidences leads him to derive the Icelandic texts from lost eleventh- and twelfth-century predecessors of the ballads. These were heroic elegies which themselves derive from a revitalization of heroic poetry through the international wave of novelistic fictions of ultimately southern origin. The milieu of these lost heroic elegies was Danish and north German, and the Icelandic poets of the twelfth and thirteenth centuries find their roles severely limited in Mohr's theory. Mohr's lead has been followed with modifications by other recent scholars, including especially Jan de Vries, Hanns Midderhoff, and Robert J. Glendinning.[16] Mohr's investigations were, I believe, on the right track, but a large number of problems in his method, some noted by de Vries, remain. I cannot give these problems the full airing they deserve here, but one group of difficulties is raised by the reconstructed oral sources. The novelistic poems which provided the model for the Danish heroic elegies are deduced; none survive. Presumably, their content was international tales and not Germanic heroic material; yet contemporary ballad scholars keep pushing the date of the origin of ballads as a genre later into the High Middle Ages, while Mohr's theory requires at least proto-ballads in the eleventh and certainly by the twelfth century.[17] Above all, I find it contradictory that Mohr, while making free use of early west Germanic material from the *Heliand* and Old English poetry for his linguistic comparisons, nevertheless excludes the very similar elegies in Old English from his derivation of the proto-forms of the Old Norse poems. Mohr himself looked this objection in the eye in the last brilliant pages of his second article, where he cites some of the evidence for an old, Common Germanic elegy, especially evidence from *Beowulf* and the *Heliand*, but he fails to recognize or at least to conclude that this earlier evidence for the same basic generic structure demands to be integrated into the overall evolution. My suggested modification of Mohr's theory would project the old generic core and some of the language and motifs that flesh it out (but of course no individual poem now extant) back into the Continental period before the Anglo-Saxon invasions. From that starting point the novelistic influences Mohr has demonstrated from proto-ballad poetry can be absorbed in the same way that the Old English elegiac genre absorbed lateral influences. For as literary history, Mohr's plan is liable to objections similar to those that met studies of the Old English elegies: an accumulation of influences is accounted for, but his model for the creation of the genre itself is either implausible or omits similar and related documents.

Mohr collected his coincidences of motif and language by a systematic comparison with the much larger corpus of ballads. I have emphasized instead more general considerations of literary history and generic structure, but I believe a systematic comparison between the heroic elegies in Old Norse and Old English will support the general theory with agreements also at the level of plot-type, theme, motif, and language. Such a catalogue is a major undertaking for another occasion, but I will conclude with a concrete example which is peculiar enough, I think, to demand a genetic, rather than a typological, explanation — we might call it elegiac exaggeration.

This takes the form of extravagant numbers of sad examples in *Deor* and *Guðrúnarkviða I* (which have been compared by F. P. Magoun)[18] or the list of superlative griefs in *Guðrúnarhvǫt*, stanzas 16-17. In *Hamðismál*, st. 4-5, Guðrún exaggerates her isolation when, in fact, she has two sons left to her — if only she would not send them out to die. Tones of a similar exaggerated isolation may be audible in the *Wife's Lament* and the *Wanderer*, and Egill in *Sonatorrek*, st. 4, is certainly exaggerating with "... my line is at its end like the withered stump of the forest maple".[19] For Egill had a surviving son as well as daughters and grandchildren.

But truly striking examples of a conventional "plural of grief" are found in *Beowulf* and *Guðrúnarkviða II*. In the "Lament of the Last Survivor" the shift from singular to plural is not illogical but nevertheless arresting:

                              Nah, hwa sweord wege
          oððe fe(o)r(mie)   fæted wæge
          . . . .
                    feormynd swefað (2253b-2256b).[20]

          (I have no one to bear the sword or to
          polish the decorated cup ... The
          polishers are sleeping [in death].)

Note the repetition of the verb as plural verbal noun. In the "Father's Lament" the lone son "rides" on the gallows ("... þæt his byre ride / giong on galgan", 2445b-2446a), but eleven lines later in the paraphrased "sorrowful song" the father declares: "ridend swefað, / hæleð in hoðman" ("the riders are sleeping, heroes in the grave", 2457b-2458a). Whether these are gallows-riders or equestrians or a bit of both,[21] the shift to the plural is probably not a scribal error but an elegiac convention parallel to *feormynd swefað*. Finally, in the second Gudrún poem, the one called "the old", the heroine meets the horse of the slain Sigurðr ; Grani has returned home with an empty saddle stained with blood: "Weeping and wet-cheeked I went to talk with Grani, I asked the steed the news; Grani then drooped, hung his head to the grass. The steed knew this: his owners were not living."[22] This closing plural in *eigendr né lifðot* is distinctly illogical but also effective if we know the convention.[23] Grani, of course, had only one owner, and in this context only Sigurðr's death can be referred to, but the plural carried conventional tones of elegiac ruin like the *waldend licgað* ("the rulers are lying [dead] ") of the *Wanderer* (l. 78b) and the *betend crungon, / hergas to hrusan* ("the rebuilders have fallen, [whole] armies have fallen to the earth") in the *Ruin* (ll. 28b-29a).

The similarity between a line like *gedroren is þeos duguð eal* ("fallen is all this company") in the *Seafarer* (l. 86a) and the sublime exaggeration of Henry Vaughan's "They are all gone into the world of light" (from *Silex scintillans* [1655]) must, of course, be due to a typological, not a historical, association; but in genetically-related literatures — closely related traditional literatures such as Old English and Old Norse secular poetry — a shared minor feature such as the convention of elegiac exaggeration and the subordinate form I called the plural of grief seems to be based on a common heritage. Like the common structural core of the elegiac genre in these sister literatures, the major feature by which the genre is defined, this minor motif is not a literary universal or even linked to a common story; instead it seems to be genre-bound, likely to be produced by the genre even when in violation of logic, and the prevalence of present-participial nouns here seems to point to a common dictional ancestor as surely as the common structural features do. It will be a formidable task to excavate and evaluate the many similar coincidences on all the levels between the two bodies of elegy, and Mohr's work requires a much more extended critical scrutiny than I have been able to give it here, but I believe this is the way to a better literary-historical understanding of the elegy in Old English and Old Norse.

NOTES

1. Greenfield 1972, 135.
2. For reasons that will become plain *The Ruin* and probably *The Husband's Message* must be omitted from the usual inventory of elegies in standard treatments such as Greenfield 1966, 142-75. *The Ruin* is imbued with *elegiac sentiments* but is not, according to the structural definition offered in this paper, itself an *elegy*. *The Husband's Message* contains some elegiac retrospective, but the best contemporary opinion is that it belongs structurally (and therefore generically) to the poetry of speaking objects (prosopopoeia), in this case a cross; cf. Kaske 1967, 41-71 and Goldsmith 1975, 242-63.
3. Pilch 1964, 209-24; Imelmann 1920, especially 187-238; Reuschel 1938, 132-42; Henry 1966.
4. Cross 1956, 25-44; Cross 1958-59, 77-110; Cross 1961, 63-72, especially 68-72; Sieper 1915, 70-77. For further references and a complete review *see* Leslie 1966, 25-37 and Leslie 1961, 61. Dietrich 1966, 20-22 offers still further caveats (beyond those of Leslie) to the Celtic cuckoo.
5. Greenfield 1966, 143.
6. Koegel 1894; the discussion of *Totenlieder* is pp. 47-55, but Koegel's derivation of the extant Old English elegies is different and independent, pp. 62-63; *see also* Schücking 1908, 1-13; Baesecke 1940, 358-65; Ehrismann 1932, 35-44.
7. Heusler 1957. *See* especially 143-50; for a thorough review of origin theories and a further development of Heusler's views, *see* Dietrich 1966; another recent survey — Göller 1963, 225-41 – is more general.
8. *See* Sieper 1915, 3-31 and 78-106; compare Neckel 1908, 495-96 ("Anhang: die altgermanische Heldenklage" which partly contradicts his discussion of "Egil und der angelsächsische Einfluss", in Neckel 1908, 367-89). Stray comments touching this subject may be found in Kershaw 1922, e.g. p. 6 and in notes; Phillpotts 1931, 66-67; Dronke 1969, 184.
9. Neckel and Kuhn 1962: *Guðrúnarkviða I, Guðrúnarkviða II (in forna), Guðrúnarkviða III, Helreið, Brynhildar, Oddrúnargrátr,* and *Guðrúnarhvǫt*. Heusler and Ranisch 1903: *Víkarsbálkr, Hrókslied, Hiálmars Sterbelied, Hildibrands Sterbelied,* and *Qrvar-Odds Sterbelied.* From Saxo Grammaticus 1866: *Starkads Jugendlied* (parts of pp. 182-99) and the fragment in Heusler and Ranisch 1903, No. XI, D, and *Starkads Sterbelied* (pp. 269-73). (For the exact contents of *Starkads Jugendlied*, the Latin prose resolution of a lost [Icelandic?] poem, compare Heusler and Ranisch 1903, XXXI-XXXII, and Herrmann 1922, 424-42 and references there; for *Starkads Sterbelied*, Heusler and Ranisch 1903, XXXI, and Herrmann 1922, 557-67.) This list of Old Norse elegies is taken over, along with their titles, from Heusler 1957, 183-86.
10. Parts of *Helgakviða Hundingsbana II, Grípisspá, Sigurðarkviða in skamma, Atlamál,* and *Hamðismál* in Neckel and Kuhn 1962 and of the *Innsteinslied* and *Qrvar-Odds Männervergleich* in Heusler and Ranisch 1903.
11. "Wulf", "Eadwacer", "Deor", "Heorrenda".
12. Lönnroth 1971, 1-20.
13. The prose passage represents the "collector's" hypothesis about the occasion of *Guðrúnarkviða II* and is based on his reading of *Guðrúnarkviða III,* but *see* Glendinning (forthcoming) who reverses these relationships, taking the prose as integral to *Guðrúnarkviða II* and *Guðrúnarkviða III* as a further development of the prose-verse complex. However, when *Vǫlsunga saga* introduces *Guðrúnarkviða II* it is as a soliloquy spoken in the lady's bower (ch. 32), and *Norna-Gests þáttr,* which alludes to the poem, knows nothing of Þjóðrekkr.
14. Heusler 1957, 183-89, and Heusler 1969, 165-94, especially 168-69.
15. Mohr 1938-39, 217-80 and Mohr 1939-40, 149-217.

16.   De Vries 1958, 176–99; Midderhoff 1966, 243–58; Midderhoff 1968–69, 241–78.
17.   For a recent review *see* Holzapfel *et al.* 1978.
18.   Magoun 1942–43, 1–15; compare Phillpotts 1931, 66.
19.   "þvíat ætt mín / á enda stendr, / sem ´hrǽbarnar / hlinnar marka´"' (text from Turville-Petre 1976, 310).
20.   Klaeber 1950.
21.   Compare Klaeber's note and Schücking 1908, 10–11, where, however, the convention cited is different from the one I propose.
22.   *Guðrúnarkviða II*, 5: "Gecc ec grátandi við Grana rœða , / úrughlýra, ió frá ec spialla ; / hnipnaði Grani þá, drap í gras hǫfði; / iór *þat* vissi: eigendr né lifðot."   (text from Neckel and Kuhn 1962).
23.   Most commentators pass over this plural in silence; Dahlstedt 1962, 40 refers it to Sigurðr and his slayer, who in some versions is slain by the dying hero; Detter and Heinzel 1903, notes to *Vǫluspá* 6, 5 and esp. to *Hávamál* 28, 5, cite many instances of plural forms for singular concepts, not all convincingly explained; Bugge 1965, 423, thought of Sigurðr and his son Sigmundr; de Vries 1958, 168, n. 25: "Die Redensart ist etwas verschwommen, vielleicht soll der Plural die harte Realität, dass es hier nur Sigurd betrifft, verschleiern".

THE CONFESSION OF BEOWULF AND THE STRUCTURE OF *VOLSUNGA SAGA*

Thomas D. Hill

Professor of English and Medieval Studies, Cornell University

ONE OF THE traditional problems of *Beowulf* scholarship concerns the characterization of the hero. To quote Klaeber: "Those readers who, impressed by Beowulf's martial appearance at the beginning of the action, expect to find an aggressive warrior hero of the Achilles or Sigfrit type, will be disposed at times to think him somewhat tame, sentimental, and fond of talking".[1] There have been various responses to this view of the characterization of Beowulf. One has been to assume that the contrast between Beowulf and the other great figures of Germanic heroic epic is deliberate and meaningful — that the *Beowulf*-poet knew Germanic heroic literature well and intended to present a quite different type of hero. This view is current in the critical literature on *Beowulf*, but it has never received much elaboration. In this paper I would like to compare Beowulf with the protagonists of one of the great cycles of Germanic heroic legend, the Volsung cycle. I propose to begin this comparison by looking closely at the passage in which Beowulf summarizes his own life. I then intend to argue that the paradigm of Germanic heroic life which is defined in the Volsung cycle contrasts markedly with Beowulf's definition of his own career, and that this contrast is intentional and meaningful. I will conclude by exploring the implications of this contrast for the structure of the poem as a whole.

I

After Beowulf has slain the dragon and realizes that he is dying, he looks back on his life and his reign, and comments upon it. He begins by lamenting that he has no son to whom he can give his armour and then continues:

> Ic ðas leode heold
> fiftig wintra;   næs se folccyning,
> ymbesittendra   ænig ðara,
> þe mec guðwinum   gretan dorste,
> egesan ðeon.   Ic on earde bad
> mælgesceafta,   heold min tela,
> ne sohte searoniðas,   ne me swor fela
> aða on unriht.   Ic ðæs ealles mæg
> feorhbennum seoc   gefean habban;
> forðam me witan ne ðearf   waldend fira
> morðorbealo maga,   þonne min sceaceð
> lif of lice (2732–43)[2]

This is obviously an important passage, yet as far as I am aware, it has received relatively little attention. One might begin by noting that Beowulf, as is appropriate, faces death quite differently than such specifically Christian heroes as Bede or Byrhtnoth. Rather than repenting for sins which he might have forgotten to confess and to atone for, Beowulf serenely enumerates his accomplishments. And the list of his achievements raises another problem. Beowulf's major positive achievement is having kept well his ancestral lands; his negative achievements are that he has avoided false oaths and aggressive wars,[3] and has not slain any of his close kin. The modern reader, at least, is tempted to reflect that Beowulf has hardly defined for himself a very demanding ethical ideal. It might seem that any human being who had any concern for the moral significance of his actions would avoid false oaths, and, at the very least, refrain from killing people closely related to him. Beowulf's claims may seem to be rather moderate in themselves, but there is a marked contrast between his summary of his own life and the definition and characterization of the hero in other relevant Germanic heroic legends.

The text which I wish to use to illuminate this question is the Old Norse–Icelandic Vǫlsunga saga. There are of course immediate problems with this comparison. The date of Beowulf is unknown, but it is conventional to date it as the "age of Bede", i.e. around 725. There are reasons for being hesitant about accepting such an early dating,[4] but it is clear that Beowulf can hardly be later than c. 1000, the accepted date of the manuscript in which the poem is preserved. Vǫlsunga saga however, is preserved in one vellum and a variety of paper manuscripts of which the oldest (the vellum) is dated around 1400. And the most plausible account of its origins is that it is a late thirteenth-century prose reaction of Eddic poems dealing with the matter of the Vǫlsungs.[5] It could thus be legitimately objected that it is hardly appropriate to explicate an eighth-century Old English poem by comparison with an obviously derivative thirteenth-century Old Norse prose text. But in defence of this procedure, I would insist upon the archaic character of the material which the author of Vǫlsunga saga gathered. We know something of his sources and how he worked, and his very failure as an artist, his inability (or unwillingness) to shape and restructure his material into a new artistic creation, makes his book all the more valuable for the student of heroic legend and Germanic myth. The author of Vǫlsunga saga was very much concerned with respecting the integrity of his sources, to such an extent that he preserved obvious inconsistencies and discrepancies in his narrative.[6] And he was also concerned with compiling the "whole book" of the Volsung legend. Thus, if Vǫlsunga saga does not faithfully reflect the language of its sources, and does not perhaps reflect in every detail the Volsung legend as it was known in ancient Scandinavia, it is none-theless a very useful gathering of heroic legend. And the poet's sources were archaic — perhaps as archaic as Beowulf, in some instances perhaps even more so.[7] Again, the fact that the author gathered all the Volsung material into one book permits one to see patterns and similarities in this material which are less evident when one is attempting to survey the often difficult and sometimes discordant poems dealing with the Volsung legends in the Poetic Edda.

In approaching Vǫlsunga saga, then, I propose to ignore the traditional problems concerning the relationship of the material in this saga with other and more famous works which deal with the Volsung legend. These essentially diachronic questions have been extensively discussed, and I have no particularly new insights to offer.[8] What I propose instead is to treat Vǫlsunga saga as if it were a discrete and individual work, to see whether I can discern any consistent concerns or themes in the work, and then to turn again to the problem of Beowulf's confession.

One's first impression upon reading through *Vǫlsunga saga* is that it is extremely sanguinary. One's second is likely to be confusion at the plethora of incident which is narrated. The author of the most recent English-language edition and translation felt it necessary to provide a summary. Even an extremely compressed, bare summary of *Vǫlsunga saga* runs to about three closely-spaced printed pages. Essentially, the author of the saga turned heroic narrative verse into bare prose without elaborating or expiating upon his sources. He rarely makes any attempt to motivate or to characterize the various figures. The women are all beautiful, the men handsome, proud, and utterly indifferent to physical danger. Repeatedly in the saga, men set out to certain death, without hesitation or even apparent concern. In this saga, at least, the popular clichés about the literature of the Vikings are amply fulfilled.

But the relative simplicity of the saga and the plethora of incident permit us to discern certain basic concerns of those heroic poems which are narrated here in bare prose. The opening of *Vǫlsunga saga*, which is somewhat less spare than the remainder of the work, defines one of these themes explicitly and one symbolically. The saga begins with the founding of the Volsung line and speaks of how the "Volsungar hafa verit ofrkappsmenn miklir".[9] The phrase *ofrkappsmen miklir* is difficult to translate succinctly. Finch paraphrases it as "autocratic inflexibility of purpose", which strikes me as quite good.[10] Kapp is cognate with OE *camp* and means "energy", "contest", or "eagerness". To "deila kappi við einhvern" is "to contend or contest" with someone. Thus to be an *ofrkappsmaðr* is to be too energetic in contending, too ready to fight, whether or not it is necessary. And this is clearly a major theme in the Volsung matter. The first named Volsung — Sigi, King Volsung's grandfather — begins his career by slaying a *þræll* who had bested him in hunting, thus simultaneously showing himself to be violent, zealously competitive, and keenly aware of class distinctions. When Sigmund obtains the precious sword from the tree, he not only refuses to sell the sword to his brother-in-law Siggeir, but insults him as well, thereby preparing the stage for the next episode in the saga, the treacherous attack by Siggeir upon his father-in-law and brothers-in-law. Before this attack, King Volsung is warned by his daughter but refuses to leave for safety because "... ek mælta eitt orð óborinn, ok strengða ek þess heit at ek skylda hvárki flýja eld né járn fyrir hræzlu sakir, ok svá hefi ek enn gert hér til, ok hví munda ek eigi efna þat á gamals aldri? Ok eigi skulu meyjar því bregða sonum mínum í leikum þeir hræðisk bana sinn, því at eitt sinn skal hverr deyja, en má engi undan komask at deyja um sinn. Er þat mitt ráð at vér flyjum hvergi ..." (p. 6).[11] This speech, among other things, provides a brief definition of what being "ofrkappsmenn miklir" entails. One might define it as the refusal to accept limitations, to grant one's own or other's merely human weakness.

At any rate, King Volsung remains and is slain in battle, and the next part of *Vǫlsunga saga* concerns Signy's revenge on her husband for the death of her father and brothers. I do not propose to go through *Vǫlsunga saga* citing instances of *ofrkapp* episode by episode. It would be tedious and unnecessary, since few readers of the saga would, I believe, be prepared to doubt that the characteristic heroic posture of the main characters of *Vǫlsunga saga* is precisely that reckless defiance of common sense and human weakness exemplified by King Volsung's speech.

The theme of *ofrkapp* is explicitly defined in the opening scenes of *Vǫlsunga saga*, whereas the other great theme of the saga is defined symbolically. In King Volsung's magnificent hall, there is a great tree whose trunk is within the hall and whose branches and flowers extend over it. The tree is called *barnstokkr* or "child trunk"; we still speak of a "family tree" in English and there are comparable Icelandic idioms.[12] I would suggest that King Volsung's tree "child-trunk" is a symbol for the family, specifically King Volsung's descendants. The name itself suggests some such meaning, and various editors and commentators have already interpreted it as a fertility symbol.[13] At any rate, at the feast when Siggeir has come to ask for Signy's hand in marriage, Odin appears, plunges a sword into the tree, offers it to the man who can draw it out, and abruptly leaves. A sword plunged into "child-stock" is, I would suggest, a suitable emblem for violence "within" a given family. And the suggestion that this episode does bear some such meaning is confirmed by the fact that Odin's brief visit occasions the quarrel between the two brothers-in-law, Sigmund and Siggeir, which results in the death of all the male Volsungs except Sigmund. The sword plunged into *barnstokkr* thus results in violence between close kin.

I would define this theme in *Vǫlsunga saga* as "kinship violation", failure to respect the ties of kingship. Kinship violation in the Volsung cycle involves, as in the Oedipus story, a symmetrical pattern. Various of the Volsungs "undervalue" kinship; they deliberately murder their close relatives. By contrast, Signy and Sigmund "overvalue" their kinship bond; they commit incest.[14] And it is hard to exaggerate the importance or the frequency of kinship violation in these stories. Sigi, the grandfather of King Volsung, is murdered by his brothers-in-law. His son Rerir kills his uncles in response. Rerir's son Volsungr is not directly responsible for his mother's death, but her death *is* a prerequisite for his birth. Siggeir , of course, kills his father-in-law and brothers-in-law, and in turn is killed by his wife, brother-in-law and nephew. Even within the Volsung line itself, when Sigmund and Sinfiotli are in the forest, living as wolves and waiting for a chance to obtain vengeance on Siggeir, they quarrel over their respective valour, and Sigmund seriously wounds Sinfiotli. It is an extraordinary moment when the uncle and father nearly kill his nephew and son. In addition to nearly killing his own child, Sigmund kills two of his sister's children by Siggeir; and Sinfiotli, of course, kills two more of the children Siggeir has begotten on Signy. Of Signy's five sons, four are killed by members of her family. And Sinfiotli finally dies when poisoned by his stepmother. The central portion of *Vǫlsunga saga*, the story of Sigurd Fafnisbani, begins with a patricide when Fafnir slays his father to obtain treasure all for himself; and it continues with a fratricide when Regin contrives the death of his brother, Fafnir. The famous story of Sigurd, Brynhild, Gudrun and Gunnar involves, of course, the betrayal and murder of one brother-in-law by his wife's brothers, and at least the suspicion of a quasi-incestuous relationship between Sigurd and Brynhild, a brother-in-law and sister-in-law.

After the murder of Sigurd the next episode involves a reiteration, as it were, of conflict between brothers-in-law, when Atli traps and slays Gunnar and Hogni. In return, Gudrun slays her own children by Atli, feeds them to their father, and then slays Atli. Gudrun's final marriage, to Jonakr, again involves conflict between in-laws. Jormunrek asks for Svanhild, Gudrun's daughter in marriage; and Svanhild is sent to him to be married. But on the (false?) belief that Randver, his son, has seduced Svanhild, Jormunrek has them both killed. Gudrun sends two of her three remaining sons to take vengeance for their half-sister's death. On the way they meet Erp, their brother, and ask him how he will help them. His reply is succinct — "Like hand helps hand, or foot helps foot". Displeased with his answer, they kill him, coming to realize only later that his answer was actually a good one. Without the assistance of Erpr, they succeed in maiming but not killing Jormunrek, and are themselves killed. This final episode in which Gudrun's sons hastily slay their brother neatly juxtaposes the two great themes of the cycle of legends. Hamdir and Sorli are *ofrkappsmenn*; they quickly and arrogantly respond to what they perceive as a challenge, and they do so with utter disregard for the bonds of kinship.

The fact that the Volsungs and their successors (Sigurd is the last male Volsung to feature in the story) are *ofrkappsmenn* does not require elaborate comment. The theme of the overreaching hero is a universal one. But the theme of kinship violation perhaps requires more comment. To begin with, the prevalence of stories in *Volsunga saga* concerning kinship violation does not mean that the authors of the anonymous poems which *Volsunga saga* summarizes were somehow liberated from conventional attitudes about the value of kinship. When Brynhild is advising Sigurd as to how he should conduct himself, the first matter she speaks of is kinship: "Ver vel við frændr þína ok hefn lítt mótgerða ｜við þá ok ber við þol, ok tekr þú þar við langæligt lof". (pp. 39–40).[15] And at several points in the saga the author injects moralizing comments about the impropriety of some killing which a given Volsung or Volsung heir has performed. The brief story of Hamdir, Sorli, and Erp at the end of *Volsunga saga*, which I have already mentioned, might be taken as a brief *exemplum* warning against the dangers of reckless contempt for fraternal bonds. If the Volsungs disregard the normal ties of kinship, it is because they are set apart from ordinary people by cruel destiny, not because those ties are not meaningful.

It is, of course, hard to say why the poets and their audiences were as fascinated by the theme of kinship violation as they appear to have been. Perhaps one reason for their particular concern over the problem of conflict between brothers-in-law, a situation which occurs five times in *Volsunga saga*, is that that relationship is crucial to the order and stability of any patriarchal society in which kinship is important. The natural family is in a sense a given — a father, mother, and their children. But any extension of that relationship is in a sense conventional and symbolic, particularly in a patrilinear society. In such a society, elaborate chains of kinship rest upon the unprovable and ultimately perhaps dubious assumption that all of the women in a given nexus of relationships conceived their "lawful" children as a result of intercourse with their "lawful" husbands. At any rate, one way of defining the social structure of the Germanic-speaking peoples during the early Middle Ages would be to see society as a whole as comprised of individual patriarchal "natural" families forming themselves into larger social structures by exchanging "the gift of a woman", to use Levi-Strauss's phrase.[16] And of course the crucial juncture in establishing these larger structures is the link between the males of the family which gives the woman, and the male who receives her. If a son-in-law does not respect the bond of kinship between himself and his father-in-law, or a brother-in-law that between himself and his brother-in-law, more distant relatives will hardly respect their obligations. All of the evidence, however, is that kinship, often quite extended kinship, was a very important aspect of early Germanic society. Thus, violent conflict between brothers-in-law is not simply a domestic, private tragedy. It threatens, potentially, the whole fabric of society.

Yet another reason why kinship violation might have seemed a suitable topic for those poets who elaborated the Vǫlsung legend is a paradox implicit in the political structure of early medieval Germanic society. For the ordinary man and woman, and even for the ordinary aristocrat, kinship was a dominant feature of the social structure. One tilled land, worked at a trade, or served as a warrior, at a given place and on given terms; and the place and the terms were in a large part determined by family relationships. Nothing was more usual than for a boy to inherit his father's position, or to obtain a given position because of various family ties and obligations. It therefore followed that in ordinary circumstances, the larger and more distinguished one's family, particularly one's immediate family, the more fortunate an individual might be presumed to be. One of the reasons why Njal was so respected was that of his three sons, one was among the greatest warriors in Iceland, and the other two were unquestionably very brave and very accomplished men. When they brought Kari, one of the great warriors of the north into the family by the "gift" of one of Njal's daughters, this was a formidable family indeed. And the stature of each of these individuals was enhanced by his association with the others. But at the very apex of early Germanic society, the royal families exhibited in practice, if not in theory, a radically different attitude towards the bonds of kinship. The principle of primogeniture was not so firmly established that a younger brother might not challenge an older one for control of the kingdom; early Germanic kings often divorced and remarried several times, and the quasi-official practice of concubinage meant that there were often a number of legitimate and illegitimate contenders for the throne. And one of the great commonplaces of early Germanic history is dynastic warfare between two or more closely related aspirants to the throne. Eric Blood-Axe, for example, the son of Harold the Fair-Haired, was responsible for the death of no less than five of his own brothers. Thus the recurrent episodes of kinship violation in the Volsung legend had a quite real counterpart in the history of the royal families of the north.

To summarize my argument, then, I am suggesting that *Vǫlsunga saga*, and by inference the Volsung legend in the north, interweaves two great themes, the hero as *ofrkappsmaðr* who refuses to accept limits, and the theme of kinship violation. I do not see how anyone could reasonably argue that these concerns are not thematically important in the Volsung legends; but I can see a potential objection, which may have more force. The overreaching hero is a common theme in heroic literature throughout the world. In the context of medieval literature, one thinks of Byrhtnoth, Roland, Grettir, Gunnar of Hliðarendi, Farinata (perhaps) and a variety of others. Similarly, the theme of kinship violation is a great commonplace. To cite two prominent extra-medieval examples, both *Hamlet* and *King Lear* are concerned with this theme — as well as with much else. Thus a potentially serious objection to my argument might be that the themes I have identified are universal ones which would be as conspicuous by their absence as by their presence.

There are two answers to this objection. First, even if these themes are universal ones, the emphasis which they receive in this cycle of legends is remarkable. Over and over again, the Volsungs and their successors go to meet hopeless odds lest they be thought cowardly. And time and again, a marriage which should lead to peace and harmony becomes the occasion of further strife. Finally, *ofrkapp* and kinship violations are interwoven to a remarkable degree in these stories. The legends concerning the Volsungs are not simply about violent conflict within a given family but rather about how this conflict continues, since the parties involved cannot accept any compromise. And, as far as I am aware, the interweaving of these themes is not a universal. The first part of the *Chanson de Roland* may be about an *ofrkappsmaðr* , but the poem is not concerned with kinship violation in any significant way. *Hamlet* is concerned with the crime of fratricide, but neither Hamlet nor the King is notably or rashly unyielding.

If this analysis of *Vǫlsunga saga* seems at least generally cogent so far, the next question is to what degree all of this is relevant to *Beowulf*. I would suggest that the *Beowulf*-poet knew that the Volsung legend in a form at least generally similar to the legend as it is preserved in the Eddic poems summarized in *Vǫlsunga saga*. To begin with, the *Beowulf*-poet alludes to the Volsungs in an extended passage in which a *guma gilphlæden*, after following the tracks of the dying Grendel, begins to praise Beowulf in song to his fellows. He first speaks of Beowulf's great dead, and then proceeds to compliment Beowulf by comparing him implicitly with the greatest hero of the north, Sigemund the son of Wæls — i.e. Sigmund the Volsung.

                 Welhwylc gecwæð
þæt he fram Sigemundes   secgan hyrde
ellendædum,   uncuþes fela,
Wælsinges gewin,   wide siðas,
þara þe gumena bearn   gearwe ne wiston,
fæhðe ond fyrena,   buton Fitela mid hine,
þonne he swulces hwæt   secgan wolde,
eam his nefan,   swa hie a wæron
æt niða gehwam   nydgesteallan;
hæfdon ealfela   eotena cynnes
sweordum gesæged.   Sigemunde gesprong
æfter deaðdæge   dom unlytel,
syþðan wiges   heard wyrm acwealde,
hordes hyrde.   He under harne stan,

æþelinges bearn,   ana geneðde
frecne dæde,   ne wæs him Fitela mid.
Hwæþre him gesælde   ðæt þæt swurd þurhwod
wrætlicne wyrm,   þæt hit on wealle ætstod,
dryhtlic iren;   draca morðre swealt.
Hæfde aglæca   elne gegongen
þæt he beahhordes   brucan moste
selfes dome;   sæbat gehleod,
bær on bearm scipes   beorhte frætwa,
Wælses eafera.   Wyrm hat gemealt.
Se wæs wreccena   wide mærost
ofer werþeode,   wigendra hleo
ellendædum   (he þæs ær onðah). . .
                          (874–900)

This digression in the poem has received considerable comment. I wish to touch briefly on some of the points of correspondence which are relevant to my argument. To begin with, the name *Sig(e)mund* is the same in both *Beowulf* and the Old Norse texts, and while the correspondence between *Wæls* and *Vǫlsung* and *Fitela* and *Sinfiotli* is not exact, the similarity is unmistakable. Secondly, the reference to the "wide siðas", involving "fæhðe ond fyrena", which Sigmund and Fitela experience together, corresponds exactly (so far as it goes) with those episodes in *Vǫlsunga saga* in which Sigmund and Sinfiotli live together in the forest, plundering and slaying innocent travellers.

In addition to living as outlaws, they even become beasts taking on the shape of wolves. The phrase "fæhðe ond firena" is a charged one in the context of *Beowulf* as a whole, the poet twice uses the identical phrase to refer to the depredations of Grendel (lines 137 and 153), and the terms *fæhðe* and *fyrena* are both used separately in connection with Grendel's and his mother's assault on Heorot.[17] During this episode in their careers, Sigmund and Sinfiotli are very reminiscent of Grendel in their relationship to the world of ordinary men. They live on the margin of society — in the forest where nothing but wild creatures live — and they prey upon innocent passersby. The question of whether they are human or bestial is at least ambiguous in that when they put on "úlfhamir" they are in appearance wolves. And although the author of *Vǫlsunga saga* does not lay emphasis upon this aspect of their degradation, the fact that they fight as wolves implies that they, like Grendel, drink human blood and taste human flesh. Later in the saga this point is made explicit in Sinfiotli's flyting with Granmar.[18]

Again, the *Beowulf*-poet knew that the Volsung legend involved a famous dragon fight in which a great hero won much treasure. In contrast to the version of the Volsung legend known in the north and on the continent, the *Beowulf*-poet thought that Sigmund rather than his son Sigurd won the treasure; but this contrast is, I think, less significant than it might appear. One of the characteristics of the matter of the Volsungs is that the poets told, in effect, the same story over and over, ascribing it, however, to different generations of the Volsung line, and then to their successors. This argues a gradual expansion of the legend, a gradual accretion of episodes which in turn occasioned a demand for new generations of Volsungs to act out an extended story line. The *Beowulf*-poet knew the Volsung legend when it was presumably shorter and less diffuse than the narrative preserved in *Vǫlsunga saga*, but this does not necessarily mean that the character of the legend had changed as it evolved.

If this passage in the poem shows that the *Beowulf*-poet knew something of the Volsung legend, the next question is whether this body of heroic legend is relevant to the poem in any way other than providing material for an extended digression. And at this juncture in the argument I return to my point of origin — Beowulf's confession. As I have said, the problem with this speech is that it seems curiously pointless and bland. Beowulf's claims for himself, as he faces death, are rather what one might expect from a respectable, prosperous farmer than from a great hero and king. But if one assumes that the poet and his original audience knew the Volsung legend in a form which exhibited the essential thematic patterns of the Eddic poems which were redacted in *Vǫlsunga saga*, Beowulf's speech is meaningful indeed.

Beowulf is, in effect, defining himself as an anti-Volsung, as a hero and king who has avoided the heroic faults which are so large a part of the story of the Volsungs. To begin with, Beowulf prides himself upon having kept his inheritance well; no neighbour has dared to attack him (2732-37), but he says nothing of any conquests. Among the Volsungs, Sigi and Helgi carve out new kingdoms for themselves, Rerir expands upon his royal inheritance by constant warfare, and Sigmund has to regain his inheritance by driving out the king who has ruled in the interregnum between Volsung's death and the return of Sigmund. The Volsungs characteristically gain their thrones by violence and maintain it by constant, aggressive warefare. Beowulf, by contrast, inherited his land in due succession, and kept it so well that no one dared attack him. His reign was a peaceful one.

This emphasis on Beowulf's relative pacificism is supported by Beowulf's next claim that he "ne sohte searoniðas" (2738a). The term *searonið* occurs only in *Beowulf*; there it is used three other times. Klaeber offers two glosses, the first being "crafty enmity" or "treacherous quarrel", and the second "battle" or "conquest". It seems to me, however, that there is one quite simple gloss for the term which fits all contexts. The primary meaning of *searo* is "skill", "art", or "craft". A *searo* is a body of knowledge or a skill which a man has devised. The primary meaning of *nið*, however, is "hostility", "strife", or "conflict". Thus an immediate interpretation of *searonið* is a "conflict which a man has devised", i.e. "devised", "chosen", or in certain contexts "aggressive" conflict. This meaning is appropriate in the various contexts in which the word occurs in *Beowulf*. In lines 581 ff. Beowulf concludes his account of his swimming match with Breca by remarking that he has not heard that Unferð performed any such *searoniðas* as this. The point is that while Beowulf and Breca voluntarily, and from one perspective perhaps even rashly, ventured their lives on the ocean, Unferð has never risked his life in such a freely chosen conflict − indeed even when his lord's hall was invaded by Grendel, Unferð avoided combat. The next occurrence of *searonið* is in lines 1187 ff., in the poet's brief allusion to the "Brosinga mene", where he says that Hama fled the *searoniðas* of Eormenric.[19] Klaeber suggests glossing the term as "crafty enmity", but as far as I can see "aggressive hostility" would be as appropriate in context. We know relatively little about this episode in Germanic heroic legend, and there is no particular reason why Eormenric's hostility towards Hama was necessarily crafty. The third example of the term *searonið* in *Beowulf* occurs in Beowulf's confession, where I would interpret Beowulf's claim that he has not "sohte searoniðas" to mean that he has not sought "deliberately chosen" or "devised" conflict. And the final instance of this term occurs in the conclusion of the poem, in the beginning of that much-disputed passage, where the poet comments upon the curse on the gold which Beowulf won from the dragon. The poet says that when Beowulf sought out the dragon he "sohte searoniðas" (3067); and this usage accords with the gloss I have suggested for this word. The battle with the dragon was a conflict *(nið)* which Beowulf sought deliberately, which he in a sense contrived.

Given the fact that the word *searonið* occurs only four times in Old English, it is of course difficult to be certain of its meaning. I know no way of proving that my interpretation of the compound is right and Klaeber's wrong. But my interpretation of the term has at least the advantage of simplicity. Whereas Klaeber found it necessary to propose two quite different meanings for *searonið* to account for its use in *Beowulf*, my gloss, which is based upon the primary meanings of the two elements of the compound, fits the various contexts where the word occurs in the poem quite well. It also explains why Beowulf, in his dying speech, should boast of never having "sohte searoniðas", whereas the poet explicitly says that Beowulf "sohte *searoniðas*" when he attacked the dragon and when Beowulf implicitly disparages Unferd for never having sought such "searoniðas" as Beowulf encountered when he swam with Brecca. The point is that although Beowulf aggressively sought out conflict with monstrous enemies of humanity, among men he was quite pacific. He defended his own, but he did not seek searoniðas, "deliberately devised quarrels".

Beowulf's third claim, that he never swore false oaths, seems less pointedly relevant to the Volsung legend. It is of course true that the central dilemma of Sigurd Fafnisbani is his double commitment to Brynhild and Gudrun; and it is stated in *Volsunga saga* and elsewhere that he swore oaths to Brynhild when they first met.[20] Again, Gunnar and Hogni who eventually murdered Sigurd, first swore with Sigurd that they all shall be "í brœdralag, sem þeir sé sambornir brœðr" (p. 47).[21] But even so, breaking oaths does not seem to be as prominent a theme in the Volsung legend as either kinship violation or *ofrkapp*. I suspect that Beowulf's reference to his probity in keeping his word is meant to contrast with the characteristic faithlessness of the kings of the north, who like their divine patron, Odin, did not hesitate to lie when it suited their purpose.[22]

At any rate, Beowulf's final asseveration, that he has never slain close kinsmen, contrasts markedly with the usual fate of the Volsung hero, who characteristically either slays or is slain by, and in some instances both slays and is eventually slain by, persons closely related to him. Beowulf's respect for the bonds of kinship is such that he refused the crown rather than usurp the inheritance of Heardred, Hygelac's son. Thus, in his dying speech Beowulf defines himself as a pacific though strong king, and as a man who has never offered violence to his kin; and the contrast between this mode of Germanic heroism and that exemplified in the Volsung legend is both so sharp and so specific that I believe the poet is deliberately contrasting his hero with those whose deeds are celebrated in the Volsung cycle. Brodeur remarks in *The Art of Beowulf* that "Beowulf is a hero of finer mold and nobler spirit than other champions of Germanic story",[23] and he offers this observation not as a particularly novel insight, but as a paraphrase of a widespread critical consensus. I agree with Brodeur's sense of the sharp contrast between Beowulf's mode of Germanic heroism and that of the more usual hero of Germanic legend, but I am attempting to argue that this contrast is more meaningful and more sharply focused than has been widely realized.

II

If this argument — that Beowulf's mode of heroism contrasts meaningfully with that of the Volsung heroes — seems cogent, the next question is whether the concerns which are expressed in Beowulf's confession are relevant to the poem as a whole. I think they are. Tolkien has taught us that *Beowulf* is not simply fabulous, but is rather symbolic. In addition to this aspect of his interpretation of the poem, which has proven very influential, Tolkien also emphasized that *Beowulf* is a poem of contrasts. Beowulf's glorious youth is set against his glorious but tragic last venture against the dragon. The building of Heorot is the apex of the glorious reign of Hroðgar, but a few lines later the poet mentions the tragic feud in which Heorot was destroyed by fire. Tolkien's observation that the poet was concerned with contrasts — that the narrative structure of the poem reflects the structure of the Old English poetic line — has on the whole attracted less interest than his comments on the symbolic significance of the monsters whom Beowulf fights. One exception, however, is R. E. Kaske's discussion of the theme of *sapientia et fortitudo*, which both elucidates a number of passages and explains much about the pattern of the poem as a whole.[24]

In particular, Kaske's argument that the court of the Danes is characterized by *sapientia* yet lacking in *fortitudo*, while that of the Geats is exuberantly brave and strong yet demonstrably lacking in *sapientia*, is particularly relevant to my argument here. Kaske is not simply arguing that these courts are flawed — an argument which would hardly be very controversial — but that these flaws are related and contrasting. I have suggested that the two major themes of the Volsung legend are respectively *ofrkapp* and kinship violation — that the *Vǫlsunga saga* and thus presumably the archaic poems upon which it is based interweave these themes again and again. And it is generally recognized by *Beowulf* scholars that Beowulf performs his great heroic feats in two courts which are both endangered. Beowulf manages to kill Grendel and his mother while at Hroðgar's court, but Hroðgar's palace will be burnt as a consequence of the failure of his attempt to establish peace with the Heaðobards. And the family succession, the assumption of Hroðgar's sons to his throne will be forestalled by Hroðulf's violent assumption of power.[25] Thus the dignified and apparently serene court which Beowulf visits and frees from the threat of Grendel and his mother will be disrupted by internal dissension. And significantly — in terms of this argument at least — this dissension involves the violation of kinship. The most immediate threat to Hroðgar's rule, Ingeld, is Hroðgar's future son-in-law, and thus bound to him by the bonds of kinship as well as by the terms of their settlement. And Hroðulf is Hroðgar's nephew, bound by blood kinship as well as the memory of Hroðgar's kindness. And thus one of Hroðgar's opponents is a relative by marriage, the other a blood relative, exemplifying the full range of modes in which men may "under-value" kinship.

The importance of this theme in the first part of the poem is underscored by the fact that Hroðgar's opponent Grendel is a descendant of Cain, whose crime the poet specifically defines as the violation of kinship:

> Grendles modor,
>
> ides, aglæcwif,   yrmþe gemunde,
>
> se þe wæteregesan   wunian scolde,
>
> cealde streamas,   siþðan Cain wearð
>
> to ecgbanan   angan breþer,
>
> fæderenmæge;   he þa fag gewat,
>
> morþre gemearcod   mandream fleon,
>
> westen warode.   þanon woc fela
>
> geosceaftgasta;   wæs þæra Grendel sum,
>
> heorowearh hetelic . . .   (1258–67).

In the court of Geats, by contrast, the Geats and Beowulf himself value kinship appropriately. After Beowulf has told Hygelac of his adventures at Hroðgar's court, he gives Hygelac a sword which Hroðgar has given him to take to Hygelac; he then gives Hygelac the horses and the treasure which Hroðgar gave him for cleansing Heorot. The poet then comments on Beowulf's generous respect for the ties of kinship which link him and Hygelac:

Swa sceal mæg don,

nealles inwitnet   oðrum bregdon

dyrnum cræfte,   deað ren(ian)

hondgesteallan.   Hygelace wæs

niða heardum,   nefa swyðe hold,

ond gehwæðer oðrum   hroþra gemyndig (2166–71).

The death of the Geat, Herebeald, at the hands of Hæðcyn, his brother, might seem to violate this pattern, but Hæðcyn's death was, according to the text of *Beowulf*, an accident. And perhaps more importantly, Hæðcyn's death is a personal but not a national tragedy for the Geats. There is no suggestion that this event affects the Geatish people as a whole. But if the Geats respect kinship, they seem, apart from Beowulf, to be infected by that reckless disregard for consequences which the Old Norse poets called *ofrkapp*. The political consequences of Beowulf's death will, according to the messenger's speech, be disastrous. And the decisions which have led to this situation are not merely unwise; they are unwise specifically in that the Geatish rulers who made them were too proud in their strength and thus were, as the Icelanders would say, *ofrkappsmenn*. Thus the terms of *ofrkapp* and kinship violation are relevant to the thematic structure of *Beowulf* — these terms are part of that complex and variegated texture which John Leyerle has called the interlace pattern of the poem as a whole.[26]

In concluding I would like to touch briefly on the relevance of this theme to the greatest continental Germanic epic, the *Nibelungenlied*, a work which like the *Vǫlsunga saga* is based upon earlier poems concerning the Volsungs. While the related themes of *ofrkapp* and kinship violation are not as prominent as they are in the *Vǫlsunga saga*, these terms are nonetheless relevant. The first part of the *Nibelungenlied* is concerned with the death of Sîvrit at the hands of his brother-in-law Gunther, and thus concerns kinship violation. The immediate motivation for this murder is that Sîvrit has shamed Prünhilt by revealing that he was the man who wrestled her into submission on her wedding night; and the irrefutable signs of his conquest are Prünhilt's ring and girdle which Sîvrit takes from her that night, because of, the poet suggests, "sînen hôhen muot".[27] The second part of the *Nibelungenlied* concerns the treacherous destruction of the Burgundians by their sister Kriemhilt — again, violence within the family. And in coming to Etzel's court, the Burgundians exhibit that sort of imprudence which the Icelanders would call *ofrkapp*. The poet explicitly comments that if the Burgundians had explained to Etzel what they feared from Kriemhilt, he would have prevented the disaster. But "durch ir vil starken übermuot ir deheiner ims verjach".[28] At certain crucial junctures, then, the *Nibelungenlied*, too, reflects this theme, as indeed one might expect in any work closely associated with the legend of the Volsungs.

This paper began with a few lines of *Beowulf*; in attempting to explain them, I have had to cite texts written hundreds of years after and hundreds of miles away from any reasonable surmise about the dating and location of *Beowulf*. But the absence of any appropriate Old English heroic texts makes such a procedure necessary, for *Beowulf* exists and can be understood only in the context of Germanic heroic literature as a whole. In the Volsung cycle, poets told of the deeds of the Volsungs, whom they admired but at the same time thought tragically flawed. The *Beowulf*-poet, by contrast, rejected the implicit pessimism of these old stories and instead chose to depict a much gentler and more admirable hero. Klaeber, in a famous and much discussed comment, thought the idealization of Beowulf so marked that it best could be understood by assuming the poet intended to depict Beowulf as a Christ figure. Whatever one makes of this suggestion, it is important, I believe, to see that when the *Beowulf*-poet has his dying hero say that he has not sought *searoniðas,* and has respected the ties of kinship, the asseverations are not pointless banalities, but rather implicitly contrast this hero with the heroes of the most famous cycle of heroic legend of the Germanic world, the Volsungs. The *Beowulf* poet does not say that his hero was stronger, or braver, or wiser than the heroes of old; but he does imply that he was better. It has occurred to me that the Christian significance of *Beowulf* (assuming with Klaeber that the poem might bear such significance) is latent rather than explicit — that it is simply the contrast between Beowulf and the archaic heroes to whom the poet alludes which is suggestive. Thus Beowulf, who is certainly not a Christian, might not so much be a Christ figure as a hero who suggests, by his gentleness and wisdom, as well as his strength, what a specifically Christian heroism might imply to the Germanic world.

There are of course a variety of other problems to which my discussion of these themes might conceivably be relevant. The *Vǫluspá* poet, for example, speaks of kinship violation and violence as characteristic of the final times before *ragnarǫk*:

Brœðr munu beriaz	skeggǫld, skálmǫld
ok at bǫnum verðaz,	skildir ro klofnir,
muno systrungar	vindǫld, vargǫld
sifiom spilla;	áðr verǫld steypiz;
hart er í heimi,	mun engi maðr
hórdómr mikill	ǫðrum þyrma.[29]

And, of course, one wonders about the relevance of these themes to the other works associated with the Volsung cycle or to various digressions in *Beowulf*, particularly the Finnsburgh and Ingeld episodes. But if this paper is incomplete in a sense, if the argument I have outlined is open-ended, this is after all what one might expect. For I have been arguing that *Beowulf* does not simply celebrate one of the ancient heroes, but that its subject is ultimately the tradition of Germanic heroic literature as a whole.

NOTES

1.   Klaeber 1950, 1.

2.   All quotations of Old English poetry are from the *ASPR* by line numbers. For the convenience of the reader I provide translations of the more extended passages of Old English poetry. The translations from *Beowulf* are, with the exception of the translation of lines 2732-44, quoted from Clark Hall 1950, with minor revisions. *Beowulf* lines 2732-44: "I held this people for fifty years. There was no king of the neighbouring peoples who dared approach me with weapons or threaten me. I awaited in my home what was destined for me in time, I held my own well and I did not seek out *searoniðas* [for translation *see infra*] nor did I swear unjustly any oaths. In all this I may, sick with deadly wounds, have joy; because the lord of men does not need to reproach me with the murder of kinsmen, when my life departs from my body."

Beowulf lines 874-900: He related almost everything that he had men say of Sigemund, his deeds of valour, many untold things, the struggle of the son of Wæls, his wanderings far and wide, the feuds and treacheries — things that the sons of men knew nothing of. But Fitela, who had been with him, knew them, since the uncle used to tell something of such a matter to his nephew, as they had always been friends in need in every struggle, and had felled with their swords many of the race of monsters.

There arose no little fame to Sigemund after his death-day, since he, hardy in battle, had killed the dragon, keeper of the hoard. Under the grey rock, he, son of a price, ventured the perilous deed alone — Fitela was not with him.

Yet it befell him that the sword pierced through the wondrous snake, so that it, the sterling blade, stuck in the rock, — the dragon died a violent death. By valour had the warrior secured that he could enjoy the ring-hoard at his own will; the son of Wæls loaded a sea-boat, bore the shining treasures into the bosom of the ship. The dragon was consumed in its heat.

In deeds of bravery he, the protector of warriors, was by far the most renowned of adventurers among the tribes of men — he had prospered because of that . . .

Beowulf lines 1258-67: Grendel's mother, monstrous among womenkind, brooded over her misery — she who must needs inhabit the dread waters, chilling streams, after Cain slew by the sword his one brother, — his father's son. Cain then had gone forth outlawed, branded for murder, to flee the joys of men, — lodged in the wilderness. From him were born numbers of fateful spirits, of whom Grendel was one, a hateful outcast-foe, who at Heorot . . .

Beowulf lines 2166-71: So should a kinsman do, and never weave a cunning snare for another, or contrive death for his bosom friend by secret craft. His nephew was most true to Hygelac, the brave in battle, and each was mindful of the other's good.

Trans. of *Voluspá* stanza 45: "Brothers shall fight and slay each other. Sisters' sons [or daughters] shall spoil kinship [i.e.commit incest?]. It is hard in the world, great whoredom, an axe-age, a sword age — shields are cloven, a wind age, a wolf age before the world totters. No man will spare an other".

3.   For discussion of *searoniô*, see *infra*.

4.   *See* Klaeber 1950, cvii and following for discussion; briefly, the only firm argument for the early dating of the poem is that a poem "evincing the most sympathetic interest in Danish affairs cannot have well been composed after the beginning of the Danish invasions"(*ibid*.). This argument would have more cogency if we were concerned with dating a corpus of epic poetry such as the *chansons du geste*. But the *Beowulf*-poet may have been idiocentric in his antiquarian interests or have lived at a particular Old English court, monastery, or household more sympathetic to the Danes than Klaeber would allow.

5.   On the date and provenance of *Volsunga saga*, see Finch 1965, xxxvi-xxxviii.

6.   *See* particularly Chapters 22-29, which conflate several different accounts of Sigurd's relationship to Brynhild.

7.   The dating of the Eddic poems is a notoriously difficult problem; but it can be ascertained that the matter of the Volsung cycle was current in pre-Christian Iceland in poetic form. And of course the evolution of the matter of the *Nibelungenlied* is one of the great and traditional problems of Germanic scholarship. *See* Andersson 1980 for a recent discussion of these problems.

8.   For a very detailed discussion of the relationship of the *Volsunga saga* and its sources, *see* Wieselgren 1935-36.

9.   "... how the Vǫlsungs have been great *ofrkappsmen*". All quotations from *Vǫlsunga saga* are from Finch 1965, by page numbers. For the convenience of the reader I will quote Finch's translation, slightly modified in some instances.

10.   *Ibid.* p. 6.

11.   "While yet unborn I spoke one word and swore an oath that fear would make me run from neither fire nor iron. Up to this moment I have acted accordingly, and why should I not keep to it in old age? And when the games are on there'll be no young women pointing a finger at my sons for fearing to meet death, for everyone must die sometime — There's no escape from dying the once. And my decision is that we do not run. ..."

12.   Thus for example *aett-kvísl*, "family *branch*"; *kyn-kvísl*, "kin-*branch*" are attested in Old as well as modern Icelandic; and *aettargrein*, "family-*branch*", is current in Modern Icelandic. In Old Norse-Icelandic myth the human race was created from two tree trunks, *askr* and *embla*; see *Vǫluspá* stanza 17, Jón Helgason 1952, I, 5. Egill Skallagrímsson uses the phrases *aettar askar*, "ash tree (i.e. member) of my family" and *kynvior*, "family-tree" in *Sonatorrek*, stanza 21. See Turville-Petre 1976, 21 for a convenient edition and translation. I am indebted to Mr. Charles D. Wright of Cornell University for pointing this passage out to me.

13.   Finch 1965, XXXV.

14.   For this formulation, *see* Levi-Strauss 1963, 215. Levi-Strauss is, of course, discussing the Oedipus myth.

15.   "Behave well towards your kinsmen and take but scant revenge on them for their offences. Bear with them, and you will win lasting praise".

16.   Levi-Strauss 1969, *passim*.

17.   *Beowulf*, ll. 1333, 1340 in which the term *faehðe* occurs, and ll. 164, 750, 811 in which the term *fyren* occurs.

18.   Finch 1965, 16.

19.   *Beowulf*, ll. 1197-1201.

20.   Finch 1965, 40 and 44.

21.   *Ibid.*, 47.

22.   *See* for example *Hávamál*, stanza 110, Helgason 1952, I, 30.

23.   Brodeur 1971, 76.

24.   Kaske 1958, 425-56.

25.   The assumption that the court of Hroðgar will be endangered by internal dissension and again that the Geats are in grave danger after the death of Beowulf is widespread in criticism and discussion of the poem. This assumption has been challenged by Sisam 1965, 51-59; 80-90; Sisam is correct in asserting that these events are only suggested — not explicitly predicted. But he does not consider what purpose those suggestions bear if they do not point to impending trouble.

26.   Leyerle 1967, 1-17.

27.   Bartsch 1965, 10, 680; 116.

28.   *Ibid.*, 31, 1865; 294.

29.   *Vǫluspá*, stanza 45, Helgason 1952, 10-11. This paper was delivered before the Harvard Medieval Seminar on 17 April 1980 and (in an abridged form) for the Cornell Viking Lecture Series on 13 November 1980. I would particularly like to thank Professors William Alfred of Harvard University, Joseph S. Harris of Stanford University, and R. E. Kaske of Cornell University for their comments and suggestions.

BEOWULF AND THE NORTHERN HEROIC AGE

Robert T. Farrell

Professor of English, Medieval Studies and Archaeology, Cornell University

BEOWULF IS without doubt the single most important text in Anglo-Saxon to have come down to us. While the chronicles and series of laws, the sermons and penitentials give us a much more detailed account of life, society and customs in Anglo-Saxon England, *Beowulf* is not only an outstanding technical achievement in a complex tradition of poetry, but also a first-rate manifestation of heroic or epic spirit.[1] In addition, *Beowulf* provides a prime source of information about the life and customs of Anglo-Saxon England, and is a document of major importance for the early history of Scandinavia. In the course of this investigation, these aspects of the poem will be addressed not only because they are of great interest in themselves, but also because there is a curious and interrelated series of problems associated with the poem precisely because it *is* so important. Historians, cultural historians and archaeologists have mined the poem for evidence about both early England and early Scandinavia, and the conclusions they have reached often feed back into the interpretation of the text, with the end result that the poem is in due course called upon to elucidate itself. By this I mean that an historian or archaeologist will use *Beowulf* as a source of information, and will construct a model of early Anglo-Saxon society based on his survey of the poem. This study will then serve in part as the basis for the comments of a literary historian. Alternately, a literary critic, overjoyed by the new evidence archaeology provides, will make too many demands on archaeological material.[2] This example is a reduction to crudity of a complex problem, but it is nonetheless valid.

The purpose of this essay is to survey current opinion on Scandinavian contact with England during the period 400–1100, as a basis for a better understanding of the literary text, and to show in turn how *Beowulf* is at least in part a predictable outcome of this contact. If this work opens up more extensive and more fruitful communication among literary critics, cultural historians and archaeologists, in such a way that the exchange of ideas can take place more swiftly, the writing of it will be fully justified. Much of the evidence presented here is already well known among archaeologists and historians, but needs to be reasserted for at least some literary critics.

Before turning to the complex problems of scholarly inter-influence, dealing with the poem as literature is of the first importance. It is not my prime purpose to direct attention either to the questions of the poem's *genre*[3] or to its metrical and rhetorical structure, but rather to address the question of the importance and meaning of the poem's concentration on Scandinavia. In simple terms, there is a paradox central to *Beowulf*: all of the action of the poem and all of the major characters are Scandinavian, for the most part men and women of the *Dene*, the *Geatas* and the *Sweon*. These tribal names are first cited in Old English because the modern cognates "Danes", "Swedes" and "Geats" carry too heavy a weight of fixed nationality and social custom. If one fact about early Scandinavian history is clear, it is the local allegiances and quickly-shifting alliances of very small groups. States develop only at a very late date, close to the millennium. Unless this fact is borne in mind, the names of these major tribes will be given too much weight, and there will be great difficulties in the understanding of both the age in which the poem was written and the age in which its action takes place. Denmark alone shows signs of relatively early consolidation into a kingdom.[4]

A brief review of the cultural and geographical contents of the poem will make its Scandinavian bias clear, and show, too, how free were the exchanges among the peoples of pre-Viking Scandinavia. Beowulf, through his mother, is of the Geats. His father Ecgtheow is a wandering warrior, who presumably served among the Geats long enough to win a bride, and who certainly served at other courts as well.[5] Beowulf visits the Danes to rid them of a monstrous affliction, both out of a sense of the propriety of such noble action and because Hrothgar, king of the Danes, had taken Ecgtheow and his young son Beowulf into his court in a time of great need. Warriors of several nationalities are present at Hrothgar's court, with Wulfgar, a lord of the Wends,[6] perhaps the most highly placed of them. After affairs are settled in Denmark, Beowulf goes home to serve his maternal uncle Hygelac, who now holds the throne. After Hygelac loses his life in a raid on the Frisian coast, Beowulf serves as guardian to Hygelac's son, Heardred. Ignoring good advice, Heardred takes up the support of rebels against the king of the Swedes, and loses his life.[7] After coming to the kingship, Beowulf undertakes a difficult battle in which he kills Ongentheow, king of the Swedes.

One of the major points of this paper is a re-assessment of the nature of this section, all of which centres on the mid-part of the sixth century, roughly speaking 525–575. The Finnsburh Episode covers an even earlier age, probably *c.* 450, a very early period indeed in the Migration Age. A corollary is a close examination of the date at which *Beowulf* was written, and the social and political environment which gave rise to it. From the standpoint of the implications of the text, even a cursory reading (or initial hearing) leaves one with the firm impression that we are expected to view Hrothgar, Hygelac, Freawaru and Beowulf himself as noble representatives of an heroic past and role models for future actions. To an early Medieval auditor or reader, Beowulf and the other heroes in the poem would almost certainly have served as spiritual ancestors, to be revered and followed. They are bold and resolute in action, strong in adversity, and particularly careful to avoid rash or immoral actions. The kind of life they lead would almost certainly have been approved of in any society that had produced heroic literature.[8] What is significantly different here is the relation between heroic literature and the heroic age from which the literature springs.

Many civilizations have had heroic poetry — Greek, Albanian, Indian, Russian, Celtic, Germanic, Scandinavian and Anglo-Saxon; all have a tendency to find heroes in an age that is past.[9] For the Germanic peoples, heroes from the fifth and sixth centuries have an important place: Eormanric, Theodoric the Ostrogoth, Theodoric the Frank, and Attila are leaders in a large cast. While the *Beowulf* poet uses heroes from the same period, those who receive most attention at his hands are Scandinavians.

Given the date at which Beowulf was preserved for us, *c.* 1000, and the place, England, this stress on Scandinavian heroes is little short of astonishing. Unfortunately, we have no

firm notion of where or when the poem was composed.[10] The times could hardly have
been worse for recording a poem peopled with heroes from Scandinavia. The evidence
of the *Anglo-Saxon Chronicle* is very clear on how terrible these men of the north were.
One disaster after another crowds the pages of the later *Chronicle*, with the worst decades
on either side of the millennium. King Edward was slain in 978/79, and the chronicler
states, "No worse deed was ever done the English than this was, since the time they
first reached this land".[11] But one person, even though a king, does not count for much
in the face of national calamity involving much of the population. The Vikings were
systematic in using up the portable property of England. £10,000 was paid over to the
Vikings in 991, £16,000 in 994, £24,000 in 1002. In 1010, the invaders hit East Anglia
so hard that they could not be withstood; the English were utterly demoralized:

> When the raiders were in the east, the home forces were in the west; when they were in the
> south, the English forces were in the north. Then all councillors were ordered to the king, that
> he might be advised on how to protect the homeland. But whatever advice was given, it didn't last
> a month. Nor, no head man would gather an army, but instead fled as fast as he could, and no
> shire would help the next.[12]

The perspectives on the Vikings in texts of other kinds were equally dark. Three
important texts bracket the millennium, and these parallel exactly the date of *c.* 1000
for *Beowulf*. *The Battle of Maldon* was certainly composed after 991, the date of the
battle, and probably not long after that date. In *Maldon*, the Vikings are arrogant and
insolent tricksters who destroy Byrhtnoth, a most pious and valiant nobleman, and his
battle force. They bring about his end partly by force and partly by guile.[13] The poem
is a poignant celebration of courage and sustained effort by the English, who continue
to fight though they are doomed to fall. The second document is the most famous of
all the sermons of Wulfstan, Archbishop of York and Worcester. It is his warning to the
English (*Sermo Lupi ad Anglos*) about the nature of the afflictions they are experiencing,
and the worse sufferings that are to come. In the piece, Wulfstan accounts, among other
offences, the way in which churches are despoiled of their treasures to pay off the
Vikings. These terrible visitants from the north are instruments of God's anger:[14]

> Often two or three Vikings will drive the multitude of Christian men from sea to sea, out through
> the provinces enslaved together, to our common disgrace, if we would understand rightly in aught.
> Yet for all the frequent reproach that we endure, we return honour to them that abuse us. We con-
> tinually reward them, and they daily oppress us. They harry and smite, bind and insult, spoil and
> raven [*sic*], and carry away on shipboard; and lo, what in all these disorders is plain and manifest
> save the wrath of God upon this nation?

The third text is Ælfric's sermon on the Martyrdom of St Edmund, King of East
Anglia. This last piece was also composed around the millennium. The picture of Hingwar
"suddenly stealing on the land like a wolf, and slaying men, women and innocent
children, and humiliating the poor Christians" is particularly striking after the studied
assonance of Ælfric's poetic style in the opening of the sermon.[15]

Thus, in the context of what has come down to us from the mainstream of contemporary literature and history, the *Beowulf* poet was odd man out, in that he provides
an interested and sympathetic account of the heroes and peoples of Scandinavia. These
nobles lead virtuous lives, and are presented not as crude pagans, but rather as cultivated
pre-Christians.[16] In what follows I will attempt to show that this picture of noble
Scandinavian ancestors is not only justifiable, but virtually predictable, in the context

of cultural and artistic exchange, partly as the result of conquest and partly by means of trade, among Germanic peoples from early to late Middle Ages. It will be necessary to approach the question of Scandinavian heroes in *Beowulf* from a number of perspectives. The first of these is *genre*, that is, the mode and tradition in which the poem was composed.[17] Perceptive and careful critics have described it as tragedy, as elegy and as epic. Despite these particular comments, most would agree that the poem is a prime example of the heroic in literature, and this aspect of *Beowulf* is the point of nexus between literature and culture.

Beowulf *as Heroic Poetry*

Beowulf centres on the long life and illustrious career of a hero from among the Geats, who for the epic 50 years of his kingship managed to keep peace within all Scandinavia, primarily by taking an active part in the affairs of the Danes, the Swedes, and his own tribe. This aspect of the poem, in which a hero embodies all that is best in the way of virtue in his society, and who performs deeds not possible to ordinary men, is found in almost every manifestation of the heroic tradition. Though somewhat backward in his youth, Beowulf accomplishes the cleansing of Heorot both because he has superhuman strength, and because he chooses, through a sense of fairness (which in the event proves providential), to fight Grendel without weapons or armour. *Beowulf* is different from other manifestations of the heroic in that it is one of the briefest poems in the *genre*. The Homeric epic with its tens of thousands of lines and the early Indian epics of even more massive size are more typical. It is a mark of considerable skill that the *Beowulf* poet manages to evoke heroic and epic spirit, without resorting to amplitude. Comparisons more close than the Greek and Indian heroic poems make clear both the bases of *Beowulf*, and the nature of the heroic age in which its central characters act.

Both the Celtic and Germanic heroic literatures are closely cognate with *Beowulf*, with the Germanic further divided into Old and Middle High German, and Old Icelandic. Each of these traditions sets its action in an age long past. The *Táin Bó Cúalinge*, which deals with the fall of Cuchulainn, has come down to us in manuscripts of the twelfth and fourteenth centuries, but it deals with events that in view of the modes of life, dress, weapons and warfare have by some scholars been placed around the beginnings of the Christian period.[18]

When we turn to Germanic manifestations of the heroic, many of the major poems in Old High German and Old Icelandic centre on the actions of Attila, Eormanric, Theodoric the Ostrogoth and Theodoric the Frank, all of whom flourished in the fourth to sixth centuries. Strict historical chronology is of little interest to those who composed heroic poetry; they were too much interested in pitting character against character in order to make points about proper conduct of one's life. Jan de Vries made this point in a particularly striking way in his important study, *Heroic Song and Heroic Legend*:

> In later years, when Medieval Europe had consolidated itself, people looked back on the past centuries to find event pressing on event, one figure jostling another. It was like looking from a distance at a mighty range of the Alps in which the steep giants seem to stand in a row against the horizon although in reality great distances separated them. The migration period was telescoped so that the figures came to lie in one plane. Eormanric, Attila and Theodoric became contemporaries, and their relative positions no longer accorded with actual history.[19]

In sum, then, those who wrote heroic poetry in Celtic and Germanic society had a goal in common. They set out to demonstrate heroic values and virtues in a richly evocative way. Not only was the reader's (or auditor's) intellect to be moved to an understanding of right action, but he was to be deeply moved in his emotions as well. The *Beowulf* poet accorded fully with his colleagues in other cultures. But the *Beowulf* poet — and indeed the entire tradition of Anglo-Saxon heroic poetry — differed widely from the closest Germanic cognates. Eormanric, Attila and the two Theodorics, so important to the general Germanic tradition, have at best a marginal importance in the corpus of Old English poetry.

The *Beowulf* poet has chosen a particular context for his poem which is best described in aggregate as a northern heroic age, and he has chosen a different group of heroes to celebrate. I will spend some time showing how the material is shaped and used, and I will call upon a wide variety of evidence in trying to discover why the poet chose this stress, and how it functions in his hands. As I hope to show, his picture of the north is is different from that presented by Scandinavian sources in the medieval period, in that the characters of Danish, Geatish, and Swedish stock are *more admirable* in the English accounts than they are in such early Scandinavian versions of history as have come down to us. The evidence of cultural history, particularly what may be described in the broadest sense as archaeology, gives some clear indications as to why the *Beowulf* poet made this choice, and why he sought his matter in the north, rather than accepting the events and characters of general Germanic heroic tradition. As a final point I will attempt briefly to show how this basis works as literature, and I will discuss some aspects of what we call the literary effect of the poem. It is my belief that the force and richness of *Beowulf*, both for its original audience and for modern readers, is in large part based on the implications of the northern heroic age.

The Old English Tradition and General Germanic Figures

Beowulf is best studied in the context of Old English poetry as a whole, and the use the Anglo-Saxon writers made of the great heroes of Germanic legend who flourished in the fourth to six centuries. The only way to cover the evidence adequately is to discuss each relevant document in detail. Since the term "heroic" has been applied to Old English literature in a number of ways, I stress that for the present purpose *only* those poems which make some use of general Germanic heroes will be discussed in detail. Thus, important texts such as the *Battle of Maldon* and *The Dream of the Rood* will not be dealt with here, though they clearly are rich manifestations of an heroic ethic.

The Franks Casket

Though the text is short and difficult to sort out, it cannot be denied that the lines on the Franks Casket, left side, are a poem telling of the death of a whale cast up on shore:

> fisd flodu ahof   on fergenberig
> warþ gasric grorn   þaer he on greut giswom.

Dr. Page, in his *Introduction to English Runes,* translates the lines:[20]

> The fish beat up the seas, on to the mountainous cliff.
> The king(?) of terror became sad when he swam on to the
> shingle.

Since in this text we have a pair of lines that follow the rules of Germanic alliterative poetry, it is valid to study the *context* of that poem, a well-wrought box of cetacean bone, most of which came to the British Museum in the nineteenth century. Linguistic and art historical evidence allow us to view the casket as one of the earliest manifestations left to us of the taste of Germanic peoples in England during the early Christian period.[21] It is safe to see it as a product of the early eighth century, and it may well come from the seventh. The iconography (or perhaps it is more appropriate to say the decoration) of the casket is quite important in the present discussion, because it is excellent evidence for the kind of mixture one would expect from a period of open-ended and broad-minded intellectual and artistic exchange. Classical legends (Romulus and Remus), the Judaeo-Christian tradition (Titus and the Jews, the Nativity), and scenes from northern legend (Egil, Weland, and perhaps others) are found on the object. The juxtapositions of these scenes are of particular interest. Such a mix would not be unusual in a tenth-century context, for it is now generally accepted that the Vikings, particularly in the tenth century and after, were quite as ready to assimilate northern legends with Christian traditions as they were to produce offspring with the tribes or peoples who first inhabited the territory they settled. It is all the more remarkable, therefore, to find an Anglo-Saxon carver displaying the same catholicity of taste several centuries earlier, when the great monastic centres of Lindisfarne and Wearmouth–Jarrow were following separate paths and different traditions of craftsmanship in manuscript illumination and the other arts.[22] If any aspect of the iconography of the Franks Casket is particularly striking, it is the presence — even the dominance — of scenes from northern legend.

On the front, for example, Weland the Smith is found with the body of one of Nithad's sons at his feet. This panel is juxtaposed with the adoration of the Magi. On the top of the casket is a figure generally taken to represent Egil.

It is my own belief that the Franks Casket is a particularly attractive indication of the kinds of juxtaposition one would expect in a renaissance. By this I mean a period of intense cultural and intellectual activity, during which new juxtapositions are tried, and new balances sought after. The most famous "renaissance" episode in the development of Anglo-Saxon literature is the career of the poet Cædmon, who was the first to apply the traditional Anglo-Saxon poetic mode to Christian materials. This "miracle", in which an old servant of a monastery, hitherto incapable of *performing* poetry or song at a feast, turns out great poems on Creation, Biblical history and the life of Christ, is indeed remarkable.[23] But the Franks Casket — and its two scant lines of verse — is even more remarkable, for it is not the super-imposition of an old poetic over a new material, but rather a juxtaposition of several kinds of material — pagan legend, Biblical history and classical legend — all in the same context. The language, the decoration of the casket and its closest parallels suggest that if we seek a localization for the renaissance which produced it, we can hardly avoid putting it into the Golden Age of Northumbria. If this be so, then we must accept the consequence that the iconography of this piece shows without doubt that Christ and Weland can appear not only on the same objects, but as parallel scenes on the same side. *Pace* Alcuin's famous indignant statement, in which he questions the juxtaposition of Ingeld and Christ. In one of the best-known letters of the early Middle Ages, Alcuin writes to Hygebald, Bishop of Lindisfarne, in 797:

> Let the word of God be heard, not the musician, the sermons of the Fathers, not pagan poetry. What has Ingeld to do with Christ? The House is narrow — it cannot hold both. . . . The eternal king reigns in Heaven, the lost pagan cries out in hell.[24]

This letter has on occasion been seen as an attack on all secular poetry, but there is clear evidence that both Alfred and Charlemagne made use of — and apparently enjoyed — such pieces. Alcuin's injunctions are entirely proper in a monastic setting, but cannot be taken as appropriate for a seventh- or eighth-century patron who had eclectic tastes.

Mr. Wormald has certainly made a very strong case for Alcuin's letter as a statement of the orthodox position in the eighth-century and ninth-century church; monks and bishops should not have read, heard, or countenanced such literature. But noble persons clearly *did* relish it, and one influential segment of the Insular church — the early Irish tradition — was remarkably enthusiastic about heroic pagan ancestors and the literature about them, and very optimistic indeed about their chances for salvation. It is my stance that while Mr. Wormald's defence of Alcuin and his definition of the context in which he flourished is almost certainly correct, *Beowulf* represents an alternative which, though unorthodox, was certainly attractive.[25]

Widsith

When one turns to *Widsith*, to quote Dryden praising Chaucer, "here is God's Plenty!" This poem almost certainly comes from an early stratum of Anglo-Saxon literature, and is a source of continual vexation to critics who try to explicate its cryptic references. One major component of the poem is a roll-call of heroes; it is significant, and vexing, that the majority of those mentioned are unknown to us from other contexts. As is the case with the creator of the Franks Casket, the author of *Widsith* had broad interests. Eormanric's court is the centre of the action, and was the place in which the *scop* held himself *ealle ðrage* (roughly speaking, "most of the time") (l. 88). But the poet also seeks out such splendidly exotic peoples as the Medes, Israelites, Persians, Egyptians and Scots. The poem is of interest to the present study for several reasons. In most Germanic versions of his life, particularly in later Scandinavian sources, Eormanric is portrayed as a rather vicious character. The first reference to him in *Widsith* is in line 8, where his name is collocated with *wraðes wærlogum*. The glossing of this phrase has generally been taken as "fierce breaker of treaties". Since this one note is entirely out of context both with the account of the hero in *Widsith* and with his character as it is displayed in the earliest sources, Kemp Malone some years ago proposed a nominal emendation to *wraðes wærlogum*, translating the phrase "vengeful on those who break treaties", and held that Eormanric, as he appears in *Widsith* and the other early sources, is a stern, but just, ruler.[26] Thus, both the basic text and the stratum of legend are in congruence as early manifestations of heroic legend.

The references made to northern kingdoms and their rulers in *Widsith* are still more striking. What we have left to us of Old English poetry is for the most part mere chance preservation. No clearer evidence of this exists than the name-catalogue in *Widsith*. It is, therefore, all the more significant that *Widsith* supports (and possibly prefigures) the major interests of *Beowulf* in a surprisingly close way. A parallel — or base — for the Finnsburh *Fragment* and Episode is found in lines 26 to 29, where Finn and Sighere, Hnaef and Helm are mentioned:

> Oswine weold Eowum 7 Ytum Gefwulf,
> Fin Folcwalding   Fresna cynne.
> Sigehere lengest   Sæ-Denum weold,
> Hnæf Hocingum,   Helm Wulfingum, . . .

The three tribes central to *Beowulf* are mentioned in a geographically appropriate order in ll. 57-58:

> Ic Waes hid Hunun   7 mid. Hreð-Gotum
> mid Sweom 7 mid Geatum   7 mid Suþ-Denum.

An Offa is set against an otherwise unknown king of Denmark in a long passage, which is immediately followed by a brief account of Hrothgar and Hrothwulf, who are praised for keeping peace for a very long time; placement and dating of *Beowulf* has sometimes been attempted on the congruence of a name for a continental Offa and Offa, King of Mercia.

> 35 *Offa weold Ongle,   Alewih Denum:*
>   *se wæs* þara manna   modgast ealra;
>   nohwæþre he ofer Offan   eorlscype fremede;
>   ac Offa geslog   aerest monna
>   cniht wesende   cynerica maest;
> 40 naenig efeneald him   eorlscipe maran
>   onorette   ane sweorde:
>   merce gemærde   wið Myrgingum
>   bi fifeldore: heoldon forð siþþan
>   Engle 7 Swæfe,   swa hit Offa geslog.
> 45 Hroþwulf 7 Hroðgar   heoldon lengest
>   sibbe ætsomne   suhtorfædran,
>   siþþan hy forwræcon   Wicinga cynn
>   7 Ingeldes   ord forbigdan,
>   Forheowan æt Heorote   Heaðo-Beardna þrym.

The point of all these collocations should be clear. The kings, the peoples and the events dealt with in these passages support the interest in things Scandinavian that we have in *Beowulf*.[27] It is certainly important to note that the twenty-odd lines of *Widsith* cited here constitute only a small part of the poem, and that many other heroes (including the traditional Theodoric, as well as Eormanric) also play parts in the text. But in the major stratum of *Widsith* outlined here, a distinct northern heroic age is referred to in bare outline, and it is the background for the central interests in *Beowulf*. It is very significant that insofar as any dates can be assigned to these figures, c. 500 is accurate — that is, precisely the same date for the "historic" and legendary figures in *Beowulf*.[28]

The Finnsburh Fragment *and Episode, and* Deor

No matter how one chooses to relate the Finnsburh Episode (ll. 1063-1160) in *Beowulf* to the short fragment discovered by Hickes in the Lambeth Library sometime before 1705 and subsequently lost, it is clear that both have conflicts between Danes, "Half-Danes", and Frisians as central to their action. Though it is difficult and probably fruitless to guess at the original size, content and purpose of the *Fragment*, and equally fruitless to guess at its original date or place of composition, the congruity of central focus — Danes in conflict with continental Germanic peoples — remains strong. It is equally clear that the *Beowulf* poet put forth a certain sympathy for the hopeless Finn. The Episode is of far greater importance than the *Fragment*, for it occupies an important place in *Beowulf*. This tragic account of peoples and blood-relatives bound to slay one another by the constraints of a rigid code of ethical conduct serves as the "entertainment" at the celebration which follows Beowulf's conquest of Grendel. The central focus is on the terrible anguish of the Danish queen Hildeburh, who must suffer the death of her son and brother, and watch them burn on the same pyre. The Episode, and its northern Germanic perspective, will be treated below, in the context of *Beowulf*.

Deor

Though *Deor* must be dealt with in this account, it is by almost any standard an anomalous piece.[29]

In *Deor*, Eormanric is presented in a much darker light than elsewhere in Old English poetry, in a brief portrait that is in closer accord with general Germanic tradition. Perhaps this piece, like the *Waldere* fragment and such "Christian Heroic" pieces as *Genesis B*, is derived from a late continental tradition. As is the case with almost all Old English poems, it is virtually impossible to date the poem on internal evidence. Kemp Malone posited a date of *c.* 900, but did not hold very strongly for that date.[30] *Deor* is unusual for many reasons; for one, its use of a refrain is virtually unique. It is also difficult in that a number of heroes are dealt with in a peculiarly elliptical way. Despite the apparently traditional presentation of Eormanric as a cruel and much feared ruler, the poem looks to the north for inspiration. Weland leads the group; Beaduhild, Maethild and Geat follow. These are clearly heroes from northern legend, and the temptation to connect Geat with the *Geatas*, inhabitants of south-west Sweden, is strong, though the association is not directly made in any literary source known to me.

General Germanic Heroic Tradition in Beowulf

I have attempted to show that *Widsith* gives a concise and accurate account of northern heroes whose period of activity is *c.* 500, the time of central interest to the *Beowulf* poet. Following Malone's minimal emendation, the presentation of Eormanric is close to that of other early sources. He is a splendid ruler, a just but stern king. This picture differs considerably from the later Germanic sources.

It is extremely significant that the *Beowulf* poet has little interest in general Germanic heroes. Weland is mentioned briefly as an arms maker (l. 445); Eormanric is cited as displaying *searoniðas,* ("deadly hostility") to Hama, because he carried off the Brosing neck ring (*Brosinga mene*) (ll. 1197-1202), but this brief episode serves only as an introduction to the subsequent loss of the torque at Hygelac's death. The whole passage dealing with Eormanric is quite elliptic, and we are left with the enigmatic detail that Hama, the retainer who stole the necklace, "chose eternal counsel"(?) (*geceas ecne raed*).[31]

It is now appropriate to turn to the question of the historicity of *Beowulf*. I have elsewhere proposed the view that the poet is writing heroic history, that is, an account in which the moral and ethical implications of the action in the poem are far more important than an account of accurate chronology and the presentation of events in such a way that modern readers would accept them as fact.[32] If a poet in this mode seems to write history as we would define that term, he does so because the process adds lustre to an ethically satisfying narrative. The important point is that when the *Beowulf* poet *does* accord with other sources, his account seems to be surprisingly accurate.

From the standpoint of Germanic heroes, more central to the interests of *Beowulf* is the account of Sigemund's exploits in ll. 874-900, as background and parallel to the celebration of Beowulf's victory over Grendel. Both Beowulf and Sigemund are monster-slayers, both triumph over dragons. In fact, as Tolkien pointed out long ago, these are the only dragons that exist in Germanic legend, save for the *Miðgarðsormr*, the dread beast that circles the earth under the expanse of the waters, and awaits its part in the destruction of the world. But it is *Sigemund*, the father who is celebrated in *Beowulf*, not Siegfried, his son, who is famous through the ages in later Germanic legend, and in traditions which extend to Wagner. How are we to account for the dragon-slaying being attributed to father, rather than to son? In this instance, C. L. Wrenn's suggestion seems quite a good explication of a difficult point. He held that we have the earliest version in the Old English text, since *Beowulf* was written down some hundreds of years before any other Germanic version of the legend was recorded. By Wrenn's reasoning, the earlier text (*Beowulf*) reflects a tradition which is more trustworthy because it is older.[33]

We have another striking example of an early Germanic poem being closer to history than its later literary relations in the Old High German *Hildebrandslied*. In almost all continental sources, Theodoric the Great must do battle with Eormanric to gain his throne. In history, Theodoric's actual enemy was Odoaker, and this historical ruler rightfully appears in the early *Hildebrandslied*. So far, then, there are two references to Germanic heroes which can be taken as early, that dealing with the history of Eormanric as a stern but just king in *Widsith*; and the father, Sigemund, rather than the son, Siegfried, being the dragon-slayer in *Beowulf*. The notion that earlier texts are closer to history is further supported by a similar instance in Old High German.

The Death of Hygelac — Historical Validation

We have in *Beowulf* a most unusual, most fortunate, and most over-used circumstance, the death of Hygelac, who is in the poem king of the Geats. Elsewhere, by historians as reliable as any medieval writer can be, he is called *Chochilaicus*, and a Dane. The philological equivalent of Hygelac = Chochilaicus has never been in question, and though the racial attribution "Dane" is incorrect, no one seriously contests that it was Hygelac who met his death at the hands of Theodobert, son of Thedoric, king of the Franks, towards the end of the first quarter of the sixth century.[34] Indeed in the *Liber*

Monstrorum, another validating source, even his tribe is stated correctly, for there (in an expuncted variant) he is described as a Geat (*Rex gotorum*).

The several passages in *Beowulf* that deal with this event are surprisingly accurate in detail. The Franks are mentioned, as well as the Frisians, and another specific tribe, the Atuarii, who lived further inland, apparently along the River Niers, 12 miles south of Nijmegen in Holland, are also brought in. In his lament for his lord, Wiglaf, Beowulf's kinsman-retainer, the last of his line, cites the *Hugas* (= Franks) and the Merovingians as potential destroyers of the Geats. With respect to Hygelac's fall and the events surrounding it, we are faced with a broad spectrum of historically accurate specifying detail. Peoples, tribes and relationships are clearly and accurately seen and represented by the *Beowulf* poet. It is curious, and significant, that though both Theodoric the Frank and his son were to have independent careers in Germanic legend, they are not mentioned by name in *Beowulf*, and no trace of their later roles can be discovered in the text. One way to account for this lack is to hold that the central events of *Beowulf* and the forming of their relationship to history and legend took place at a relatively early date, early, that is, in comparison with the state of legends in Germanic literature composed centuries later. If such was indeed the case, the Frankish kings had not yet assumed the heroic proportions they were later to be accorded. Thus, both the fall of Hygelac and the substitution of father for son in the Sigemund episode are indications that the central interests of *Beowulf* were fixed at an early date. Whether this thesis is accepted or not, the central event for the *Beowulf* poet at this stage in his work is the tragic fall of Hygelac, king of the Geats, and Beowulf's kinsman-lord.

It is necessary at this point to sum up my arguments so far. *Beowulf* and *Widsith* agree on some essential points, most especially in their respective accounts of northern heroes and peoples. The Franks Casket and *Deor* further support this northernly perspective. It is possible to see the *Widsith* poet's treatment of Eormanric, the *Beowulf* poet's identification of Sigemund as dragon-slayer, and his highly circumstantial account of Hygelac's fall as indications of earliness of date, or perhaps more accurately earliness of legend-formation. We may, therefore, reasonably conclude that some of the major strands of Old English heroic tradition became set well before the general Germanic tradition *as it has come down to us* had in other cultures formed its cadre of heroes and their deeds.

The Finnsburh Episode

There is a close link between the fall of Hygelac and the Finnsburh Episode in *Beowulf*, for both Hygelac of the Geats and Hnaef of the 'Half-Danes' were fated to fall on the coast of Frisia, across the Channel from England. In the Finnsburh Episode, the central battles involved Danes, "Half-Danes", Frisians and Jutes.[35] The story provides an ethical conflict for Hengest, who loses his lord Hnaef, and must swear an oath and make a peace with Finn, his lord's *bana*.[36] He finally achieves his revenge by killing Finn, king of the Frisians, and taking Hildeburh, his queen, back to her Danish homeland. She has had to suffer the terrible loss of brother and son, killed as they fought on opposite sides; Hildeburgh has had to watch them burn together on the same pyre, in a most grisly scene.[37] Subsequently, her husband is murdered by Hengest, her kinsman. Thus, both the Episode and the account of Hygelac's fall celebrate the fall of valiant Danish heroes, and the terrible sufferings of a Danish princess, all participants in the highest kind of heroic tragedy. This is the ethical and emotional centre of the Finnsburh Episode; the ethical and emotional centre of *Beowulf* is the struggle of a great Scandinavian hero to maintain peace among its three great Northern peoples, who, previous to his dominance, had engaged in frequent conflicts.

The Nature of Warfare in Early Germanic and Scandinavian Society

The conflicts between Swedes and the Geats have occasioned extensive commentary of the darkest kind in critical literature; R. W. Chambers, over half a century ago, spoke of the conflicts between the Geats and the Swedes as Beowulf's revenge against a "hated Swede", Onela, king of the Swedes.[38] Adrien Bonjour provided an even more highly coloured version of the same conflict in which Onela, a villain who ravages the land of the Geats, establishes himself as king by destroying his nephews, who were the rightful rulers of the land.[39] In recent years, Kenneth Sisam pointed out that there is no evidence *whatsoever* in history for the destruction of the Geats at the close of the sixth century, but rather many indications that the Geats were flourishing at the millennium and beyond.[40] In 1972, I cited the evidence of both the text of *Beowulf* and its cultural context to show that the situation with regard to tribal conflict was quite fluid in the Germanic past, and that this looseness of structure is found both in historical accounts and in the literature of the period.[41] In *Beowulf*, the hero is remarkable because he keeps the peace both with the Swedes *and with the Danes*, despite the hostilities that had existed between the *Danes* and the *Geats* before Beowulf saved the kingdom of Hrothgar.[42]

Despite this evidence to the contrary, Professor Eliason has recently re-stated the traditional dark view of Geatish/Danish conflict. Beowulf could not be related to the Swedes through his father Ecgtheow, Professor Eliason tells us, because a terrible hatred separated the two tribes.[43]

Professor Eliason views the conflict between the Swedes and Geats as a struggle to the death between two peoples, in which national allegiances are firm, clear, and exclusive. It is accurate to say that Professor Eliason is following a tradition in this respect, one in which R. W. Chambers and Adrien Bonjour participated. Such a view provides very satisfying literary highlights, but it simply does not accord either with the realities of life in the Germanic heroic age or with the literature of that age as it has come down to us. As early as the beginning of the present century, H. M. Chadwick presented very strong evidence to show the relatively fluid nature of society in the heroic age.[44] Peoples could join together for a short time to meet a common enemy, as did a confederation of Scandinavian, Hiberno–Scandinavian and Celtic princes who tried to defeat King Athelstan at *Brunanburh* in 937.[45] Individuals could take up service with kings of other nationalities, and gain honour in that way. Beowulf himself became Hrothgar's man for a time, and Wulfgar, *Wendla leod* (= Lord in Sweden?), held high office at the same court. Such temporary allegiances were also seen in history as well. Sometime towards the end of the ninth century, Alfred took the Norwegian lord Ohthere into his court for a time, apparently as an honoured visitor, and gained an invaluable account of travel in northern waters from him to include in his reworking of Orosius' geography. Clearly, though Alfred had very nearly been destroyed by Vikings some few years before, he received this Norwegian into his court with no less honour than that with which he took in *peregrini* from Irish monastic houses. Fostering at another court was a common practice; two Northumbrian kings of the early Anglo-Saxon period indulged in it. Oswald's son and two sons of Oswiu were in the care of Penda at various times. In the tenth century, Hakon, son of the great Scandinavian king Harold Fairhair, was proud to carry the title *Athalstéin's fostri*, as the foster-son of Athelstan.

It is evident that we should, therefore, have a much more open approach to cultural and social relations not only in the fourth to sixth centuries, but beyond, perhaps into the late Saxon period. What we now call Denmark, Norway and Sweden cover a geographical area in which peoples saw themselves as belonging to much smaller cultural and social entities than countries. These districts could form loose alliances for trade, or be brought together by strong rulers by conquest, but no arrangements were fixed for long periods until rather modern times. The limited social structure is reflected in the size of the group who went to "war".

The question of *scale* is important here. In a seminal piece now over 20 years old, Professor Sawyer commented on the referent for the word *here*, usually translated as "host" or "army".[46] In Anglo-Saxon, *here*, "enemy force", is used in contrastive distribution with *fyrd*, the group of locals who stood against the invading force. Sawyer cites the seventh-century laws of Ine: "we call up to seven men thieves; from seven to thirty-five a band; above that is a *here*". It is certain that the referent for *here* increased in size as the raids and invasions of the Viking period went on; if the raiders came in some 30-odd ships, as they are said to have done in 836, 840, and 843, something like a thousand men were on board — but a thousand is not *tens* of thousands, the figure the modern words "host" or "army" carry with them in connotation. Even if the host of critics who attacked Sawyer for suggesting that figures in medieval chronicles should be taken *magno cum grano salis* have made some telling points, and we must view the later Danish invasion fleets as involving many hundreds of men, this larger figure still does not accord with modern resonances of the words for army. Far more importantly, we must posit significantly smaller numbers for the fifth- and sixth-century war bands, on the basis of both law codes and the text of *Beowulf*.

When we turn back to the heroic age, it is noteworthy that Beowulf himself leads a group of *fifteen* in his voyage to Denmark; this seems to be a goodly and sufficient expeditionary force, and the Danes recognize and accept it as such. As Girvan pointed out in 1935, "in early times, and especially in northern Europe, the body [of warriors] could not have been really large".[47] Girvan further cited Ammianus Marcellinus as telling us of one army numbering two hundred and more, but Girvan held that such a large force would be exceptional for the north. If we wish to bring our understanding of early literature into accord with the realities that existed in the period 400 to 1000, it is clear that we should have quite limited and modest understandings of the Anglo-Saxon words for king, nation, and army, especially in the earliest periods.

These are not the only areas where changed perception is called for. It is perhaps even more important to re-assert the political and economic fluidity among the peoples of Scandinavia before the millennium. It is, therefore, entirely inappropriate to view the conflicts among small bands of warriors in tribal groups in *Beowulf* as mobilization and deployment of sixth-century Scandinavians on the model of World War I. This notion seems to underlie the literary criticism espousing the "total war" philosophy.

I hope to show that the central theme of heroic Scandinavian ancestors in *Beowulf* stems from a tradition of Anglo-Scandinavian contact which was fruitful and productive, and which can be traced in continuity from the earliest part of the migration period to the Norman invasion. As far as the relation between Swedes, Geats and Danes within the poem, I will briefly restate and amplify the case that I made some few years ago. It is my contention that Beowulf himself is presented as a great hero precisely because he could make peace among the major tribes of the north. It may well be that he is able to accomplish this difficult task because he is related — by blood or by adoption — to all three tribes; but this is a relatively minor consideration, for his accomplishment is far more significant than his means of gaining the desired end of peace throughout Scandinavia.

The Traditional Interpretation of the Vikings

Our views on the events and culture of the early Middle Ages are deeply coloured by the perspectives of those who wrote the chronicles and histories which have come down to us.[48] Even St Bede, a towering figure in historiography, had predispositions and even perhaps prejudices which have seriously affected our understanding. As Mr. Wormald recently demonstrated, we have lost a good deal by Bede's suppression of evidence on the nature of secular literature and society in his own time. Bede's failure to report on certain aspects of the times, Wormald holds, is the prime cause of the failure of historians even of so imposing a stature as Sir Frank Stenton to deal with culture and literature adequately.[49]

Our narrowness of perspective in contrast with Scandinavia at *all* periods is coloured by the semantic overtones of the title — or more properly the epithet — *Viking*, and by the universal tone of outrage and horror of contemporary Christian and Moslem commentators who report on the violations of the peace carried out by bands of Scandinavian warriors from the eighth century onward. Alcuin's comments ring throughout history not only because he gave one of the first statements on the Vikings, but because he sets a tone which is maintained by virtually all commentators from the eighth century onwards, whether we read the Anglo-Saxon *Chronicle*, Irish chronicles, or continental sources.[50] As Professor Sawyer has pointed out, there is a noticeable improvement in the image of the Vikings when one consults the tradition in the north of England.[51] Valuable traces in the Peterborough and York Chronicles, and in the histories of the twelfth-century writer Simeon of Durham, show both tolerance for and acceptance of neighbours of northerly origin. The more we look at the general run of commentaries, most of which were produced in the south of England, the less acceptable the central action of *Beowulf* becomes. To see the contrast more clearly, I supply an analogy. If we want to have both *Beowulf* and anti-Viking comments accord purely on the basis of literary evidence, it is as if some reader in the thirty-third century had left to him a major novel in English on the glory of ancient German heroes as one of the few sustained literary monuments of England in the period 1900–1925. World War I would provide a block to comprehension.

It is my contention that the question is best addressed by looking at Scandinavian contact with the rest of Europe specifically *including* both late classical Rome and the

the eleventh-century Byzantine court, putting aside the term "Viking" and its resonance, and forgetting for a time the many verbal attacks against the Scandinavians by European commentators in the period 800–1000. At a stroke, we have thus put aside a great deal of evidence, in fact the vast majority of written evidence, but enough remains to give us a field for fruitful surmise. As we deal with the period 500–1000, we are confronted by a wealth of archaeological and cultural evidence, which gives testimony not only about the fact of contact between Scandinavia and England (*inter alia*), but also about the kind of influence that Scandinavia had on the rest of Europe. This survey will show that though some aspects of Scandinavian contact give rise to the supposition that the Vikings were the scourge of God, there is ample indication that in many instances Scandinavian impact was positive, adding to cultural richness rather than destroying civilization. It is probably accurate to say that even in the most terrible times of raid and conflict, we see the Scandinavians from our perspective as more terrible than their contemporaries saw them, because our vision has been based primarily on the horrified perceptions of those who wrote chronicles.

What we are surveying, then, is *Scandinavian* contact, 500–1000, with particular emphasis on *peaceful* Anglo-Scandinavian contact, 700–1000. For those who are primarily interested in Scandinavian culture, art history, and archaeology, much of what I present here is already well known, but a review of the field is necessary, because the full thrust of recent research in early Scandinavian studies has yet to make an impact on some recent literary criticism of *Beowulf*.

Scandinavian Contact with the Classical World

From any standpoint, it can hardly be held that the peoples of Scandinavia were unknown to the classical world. The earliest account of voyages so far north was that of Pytheas of Marseilles at the end of the fourth century B.C., in a work now lost to us. Such northern peoples as the Cimbri and the Teutones came into violent conflict with Rome in the pre-Christian era, and they were by no means always the losers in battle. In the first four centuries of the Christian era, there was certainly some interest in the northern peoples, as Tacitus' *Germania* and the map of Ptolemy show. There are also a goodly number of indications that Scandinavian peoples traded with the Roman Empire. One might question what the Romans would *want* from the north — but answers quickly come to mind with amber, walrus ivory and furs leading the list, and leather, cattle, and slaves as other desirable items. Unfortunately, such goods rarely survive in archaeology, and we must validate this contact in the main from the appearances of Roman goods and coins in the north.[52] Glass beads and drinking vessels — the latter being specially prized — seem to have been of very great importance to early Scandinavians of high stature, especially in the fourth and fifth centuries.[53] Other kinds of Roman goods have been found in some abundance (dishes, ladles, bowls, etc.), but it is probably quite safe to follow Gwyn Jones' characterization of the period: "Silver and gold poured north, masses of coin into Gotland, Skåne, Bornholm, and the Danish isles . . . Southwards in exchange went skins and furs, amber, sea-ivory, and slaves".[54]

But what of specific contact between England and Scandinavia before the Viking raids? Though there has been much dispute on the settlement of England, every discussion must in due course return to Bede, who tells us that Saxons, Angles and Jutes were the settlers — the last tribe being somewhat difficult to locate and to account for. They have been located both in East Holstein and in Jutland. In a series of publications on the pottery of Anglo-Saxon pagan burials and their continental parallels, J. N. L. Myres concludes that though pottery that parallels material in both East Holstein and Jutland exists in England, there is a very heavy concentration of pottery of Jutland type in Kent, which is where Bede said the Jutes took up residence. In a passage far less commonly quoted, Bede lists a number of tribes from whom the Angles and Saxons in Britain derived their origins — this list includes, among others, Danes and Frisians. Myres cites a number of pottery examples that have parallels for English materials in southern Sweden and Norway, as well as the Jutland peninsula itself.[55]

There is danger here of circular argument, but the congruence of Bede's account of the settlement and the pottery evidence is further supported both by the mode of the early settlement itself, and by the text of *Beowulf*. One of the very clear aspects of Dark Age archaeology is the evidence for the *gradual* process that led to the settlement of England. The northerly peoples sailed down the coast of modern-day Germany and Holland. Their presence is attested — very clearly so — in the raised up mounds (*terpen*) along the coast of Frisia.[56] There were many reasons for coasting, as opposed to making a direct crossing. In a fascinating study, Charles Green spelt out the terrible dangers and difficulties of a direct crossing in a fourth- or fifth-century boat.[57] Though more recent opinions on the sailing characteristics of early vessels may somewhat lighten Green's dark picture, the passage from Jutland and East Anglia could have been hair-raising, and Green showed how even a successful coastal voyage could take two to six months. The movements from north to south seem on occasion to have been leisurely affairs, extending into years or even decades.

The congruence of very firm archaeological evidence with the events which underlie the Finnsburh Episode in *Beowulf* is remarkable. One would expect a certain amount of friction, and also some fusion, of races because of common interests in the kind of leisurely migration that led to the settlement of England. Difficult as the Finnsburh Episode and *Fragment* are, the general outline of the conflict in this part of *Beowulf* text is quite clear. The Frisian king Finn had married a Danish princess, Hildeburh; Hnaef, her brother, visits the court, and is killed in a battle that was apparently started by the Jutes.[58] Finn and his Frisians are brought into the battle, and fight to a stalemate; a peace is made, and both Danes and Frisians (and presumably Jutes) draw together under a truce. But Hengest, the Danish brother of Hnaef, in due course takes his revenge for his brother's death by slaying Finn.

This story is told at the gathering which celebrated Beowulf's victory over Grendel. It is clearly an account of heroic history (in the sense in which I have explained that term above), and it is told because it highlights the Danes, both through the noble sufferings of a Danish princess, and through the ethical conflicts of Hengest, who must endure a long time before taking revenge for his lord's death. If we date-back these events from the fall of Hygelac, which is recorded in historical sources as having taken place *c.* 525, then it is safe to assume that the Danish–Frisian conflicts alluded to in the Finnsburh *Fragment* and Episode took place in the fifth century. From my point of view, the way in which this account of the movement of peoples and their conflicts in the poem accords with a large body of archaeological evidence is *more* significant than the several mentions of Hygelac, king of Geats, in early Scandinavian sources. Archaeology and the evidence of *Beowulf* combine to give a picture of Scandinavian peoples in place, on the coast of Frisia, and ready to move across the Channel as settlers in England. If this were all we had to go on, the case would be tantalizingly incomplete, suggestive as it is. We must turn to East Anglia, to the early dynasty there, and to the splendid treasure-trove of Sutton Hoo for proof-positive that other Scandinavian settlers were established in England before the seventh century, and maintained very close contact with their homeland.

East Anglia and Sutton Hoo: the "Swedish" Connection

The Sutton Hoo ship burial was discovered in the summer of 1939, and was quickly excavated and put into safekeeping for the duration of the Second World War. This collection of artefacts discovered in a ship that was buried *c.* 625 is certainly the most significant discovery in early European archaeology to have come from the ground in the present century. The list of publications on this find and its interpretation comes to many hundreds of items, not a few of which attempt to elucidate *Beowulf* by direct relation with Sutton Hoo material, or to clarify artefacts by quotations from the text of the poem. Such exercises have often led to overstatements and misinterpretations — but they are not important to the present discussion. The Sutton Hoo find and its context throws a great deal of light on relations between England and Scandinavia in the sixth century, and is thus of prime importance for our present discussion. Some scholars — British and Scandinavian both — have held that the ship and its contents are wholly Swedish.[59] In a series of careful and detailed analyses written over the course of some 30 years, Dr. Rupert Bruce-Mitford has made the nature of the find, its importance and its relationship with Scandinavia far more clear.[60] He holds that such items as the sword, helmet and shield have very close affinities with East Scandinavian materials. His arguments are convincing, though we must await publication of the fourth and last volume of the Dr. Bruce-Mitford's definitive study of the Sutton Hoo ship burial for the most complete statement on what he has chosen to call "the Swedish Connection". It is quite possible, as Bruce-Mitford posits, that the dynasty ruling East Anglia in the sixth and seventh centuries, the *Wuffingas*, were of Scandinavian origin.[61]

In a paper entitled "The Sutton Hoo Ship-Burial: Comments on General Interpretation", Dr. Bruce-Mitford adduced reasons for linking the royal line of East Anglia with the royal line of the Swedes. Such a connection had already been made by Sune Lindquist in 1948 — when he went so far as to equate *Wehha* in the geneaology of the tribe found in British Museum Ms. Cotton Vespasian B VI with the *Weohstan* who appears in *Beowulf*.[62] This is bringing together archaeological and literary evidence with a *very* strong hand. It should be noted that Anglo-Saxon genealogies are notoriously jumbled documents, with mythical, historical and legendary name-forms, all brought together into a splendid structure that often extends back through the names of pagan gods to Noah.[63]

Despite the best efforts of J. N. L. O'Loughlin, the relationships among the Wuffing genealogy, the Sutton Hoo ship burial and Sweden are still by no means fully clear.[64] On the basis of archaeological evidence, there is no doubt about direct and sustained contact between England and Scandinavia, but the dynastic question is still very much an open one, and must remain so until new evidence comes to light.

The only objection I have to Dr. Bruce-Mitford's arguments to date is that his points of inspiration and parallels for the Sutton Hoo materials seem strangely precise in view of the evidence. The sword pommel at Sutton Hoo is paralleled by a piece found at Hög Edsten Kville parish, Bohuslän and elsewhere (clearly *West* Scandinavia); other items from the Sutton Hoo ship are similar to pieces from the islands of Gotland and Öland, which had cultures that differed markedly from the mainland.[65] Decorative motifs found on the Sutton Hoo helmet and purse are paralleled not only in Scandinavian contexts, but also in Kent and Lincolnshire.[66] We must await Dr. Bruce-Mitford's last volume, and weigh both his conclusions and the discussion of other scholars, before a final determination can be attained. At present, it seems to me that the parallels for Sutton Hoo extend beyond the old kingdom of the Swedes in Scandinavia, and that the Scandinavian influence is found in more places in England than East Anglia. We *can* come to a *provisional* conclusion, however.

Given the generally scant nature of the archaeological and historical evidence for the period *c.* 400–700, we have fairly clear indications of early and sustained contact between Scandinavia and England. Not only does the pottery and other specific material evidence support it, but the grave goods found at Sutton Hoo, and perhaps the affinities of the East Anglian royal line, give us sufficient indications that at least some settlers from Sweden and Norway migrated to England, as well as a comparatively large number from the Jutland peninsula. The text of *Beowulf*, supported by historical sources, shows that at least one (unsuccessful) pre-Viking raid took place, when Hygelac of the Geats was slain in the course of a raid on the Frisian coast at the beginning of the sixth century, and that the Danes maintained an officer to challenge visitors as to their origin and intent (ll. 229–257). This congruence of poetry and history gives us a validation in written sources of precisely what we would expect to find on the basis of the archaeological evidence. Northern peoples coasted southward, and only after long periods of passage sometimes marked by conflict, sometimes peaceful, made their way to England. Thus, if we take the events of the Finnsburh Episode as happening in the fifth century, follow through the death of Hygelac, and weigh carefully the extensive evidence from Sutton Hoo for Scandinavian contact, we have a picture of a link between Scandinavia and England from perhaps as early as the beginning of the fifth century to about the first quarter of the seventh century, when the Sutton Hoo ship was laid in the mound. The Sutton Hoo material and its parallels in England and Scandinavia are clear indications of actual sustained contact, while the Finnsburh Episode shows Scandinavian peoples in close proximity to England.

The Seventh and Eighth Centuries

We are hard-pressed to follow this trail for the next several hundred years. There is no recorded evidence that a raid such as Hygelac's struck England until the sudden and dramatic attack on a host of major centres of culture towards the end of the eighth century. But peaceful contact and the everyday business of trade seldom, if ever, got the kind of attention chroniclers give to raids and atrocities, so no great case against the possibility of at least some contact can be made. One thing is certain: voyages of settlement were being made across the North Sea with frequency, and with some reasonable chance of success. Generally speaking, such vessels as have survived from the early period had been seen as rather poor stuff. The testimony of Roman commentators on Early Germanic vessels certainly contributed to this view, which was confirmed by the early evaluations of such vessels as the Nydam ship. Dating from the early migration period, this vessel was excavated in the early 1860's. When scholars evaluated its seaworthiness in the 1920's, they found the ship a poor sailer indeed, and estimated that over a ton of ballast would have been necessary to keep it from overturning. It turns out that this view was based on a misinterpretation of the excavated materials, which did not allow sufficiently for shrinkage whilst the ship was buried. On the basis of more recent research, it appears that the ship actually had a sound design, and would have sailed very well indeed.[67] This opens at least the possibility of return or multiple voyages; if the ships were as horrific as early commentators would have us believe, they would have been abandoned on the beaches, as settlers landed — but such was clearly not the case.

But the written record is silent on these aspects of early English society; the interest of historians centred on other matters for this period: the Celtic and Roman Christianization of the island, the internal conflicts between the various kingdoms within England, and the Germanic tribal chiefs' conflicts in the process of becoming heads of dynastic houses and dealing with their Celtic enemies.

793–878

The Viking raids scandalized all Europe in the late eighth and early ninth centuries. Raids became bases for settlements, in England and on the continent, and serious land-taking began in the last third of the century. Edmund of East Anglia was murdered most foully in 869, and by 878 Mercia and Northumbria were in Scandinavian hands, and Alfred was hiding in a marsh. Alfred's remarkable military skill managed to save Wessex, but his victory left more than half the country under Scandinavian control — the "Danelaw". The business of peaceful settlement and co-existence had begun, though Viking raids were by no means over.

There are many aspects of this whole process of raid, conquest, and settlement that are unclear, but the focus of our interest must remain on the conditions which could have caused *Beowulf* to be produced. Were the late eighth and ninth centuries a period of unremitting horror, with total disruption of all social, economic and artistic systems, or was the whole process rather less destructive than that. The thrust of the archaeological evidence clearly supports the latter view.[68]

Let me parallel the terrible raids on the 790's with another kind of evidence. The place is Sumburgh Head, the southern tip of mainland Shetland, or, according to the romantic name accorded the spot by Sir Walter Scott, *Jarlshof*. The site, which shows the super-imposition of a Viking settlement over a Celtic one, is rightly described by its excavator, J. R. C. Hamilton, as "one of the most outstanding archaeological sites ever excavated in the British Isles".[69] The importance of this site is put most succinctly: "The site shows that the Norsemen are already settling west over sea in the initial phase of Viking raids which witnessed the sacking of many monastic establishments in the West. . . . Behind the Viking raider we can discern at Jarlshof the more prosaic figure of the peasant farmer crossing the North Sea not in search of loot but of land in the sparsely populated Scottish Islands".[70]

Two further aspects of this site have ramifications for this discussion. The first is the evidence for peaceful exchange and perhaps intermarriage with the Celtic inhabitants, and the second is the complete linguistic dominance of a Scandinavian language over the Celtic base. We have a close parallel for what happened here in the later Viking settlement on the Isle of Man.[71]

In the Shetlands, and elsewhere, such peasant farmers as these seem to have caused little trouble. Their tracks are thus harder to trace. Mr. Morris surveys the evidence (pp. 70-94) and concludes that in the Orkneys and elsewhere at least some Viking settlements appear to have been accomplished with minimal disruption to earlier peoples. Fortunately, we have an account of the visit of the Norwegian noble and trader Ottar (*Ohthere*) to the court of King Alfred. Ohthere's profitable trading voyages to the far north were of such interest to the English king that he incorporated them into his reworking of Orosius' *Geography*.[72] One swallow does not make a summer; but the account is so rich, so detailed, and so striking, in view of Alfred's perilous balance with the Danelaw and the constant Viking raids on his kingdom, that it must be allowed considerable weight. It is quite clear that the ninth-century English court, and therefore probably the ninth-century English farmers, could and did identify not social origin, but *intent*. A trader was accepted as such, even though he was a Norseman; raiders were dealt with in appropriately vigorous ways.

At this point, I stress that I do *not* wish to make a case for the Vikings as gentlemen of leisure on a cultural tour, or to lessen in any way the atrocities they perpetrated. But as Peter Sawyer points out,

> The Chronicles and other writings of the Christian West are generally content to record the outcome of battles or wars by noting the success or failure of a king. Only rarely in the writing of such men as Gregory of Tours or Bede is there a chance of glimpsing the destruction, the suffering and the misery such conflicts entailed. Much remains concealed and we can never know what bloodshed lay behind such brief annals as "And that year (776) the Mercians and the people of Kent fought at Otford". This ignorance does not, however, entitle us to assume that internal strife before the Vikings came was little more than cattle rustling. We are, of course, very thoroughly informed about much of the destruction wrought by the Vikings but this was not because the Vikings did more damage. The simple reason is that the Vikings were not Christians but pagans, who attacked the churches which their Christian counterparts, in general, treated with respect.[73]

Another assumption on the basis of the *Chronicles* is that if a site were raided, it was ruined and emptied. Lindisfarne was struck in 793, Jarrow in 794. There were communities at both places for a considerable time after they were first attacked. According to the Chronicle of St Bertin, the famous town of Dorstadt, a trading centre in Frisia, was plundered in 834, wasted in 835, depopulated in 836, with tribute exacted in 837. There were three *more* attacks before 863 when the town was destroyed not by the Vikings, but by the changing course of the river. There are clear indications that monks on the continent more greatly feared a bad abbot than they did the Vikings; a community could repair, or rebuild, after a raid, but if lands were sold off by a corrupt leader, the economic base of the community could be destroyed.[74]

The Vikings as Town Builders

The image of the Vikings as the destroyer of civilization is very firmly fixed, but archaeological evidence will not accord with that image as the fair representation of Scandinavian influence in the west. One of the most striking aspects of recent research in Viking studies is their contribution to urban development. Thanks to the discoveries and research of the past 30 years, a convincing case can be made for the Scandinavians as builders of new towns.[75] Dr. Blindheim surveys the richness and complexity of Viking urban development, primarily in the Scandinavian homeland, on pp. 42–69. Not only are there a goodly number of important centres of trade and manufacture in Scandinavia itself – Birka, Ribe, Kaupang and Helgö among them[76] – but there are a large number of towns in Ireland *and in England itself* which were either founded by Scandinavians, or made into new and thriving centres by their efforts. Dublin and York were prime members of a thriving economic community, the first largely a Viking foundation, the second a town brought to a new standard by a vigorous Anglo-Scandinavian community.[77] On the basis of the most recent excavations, it is clear that *both* were major centres of manufacture, as well as trade.[78]

As for *new* towns, a case has recently been made for the Scandinavians as pioneers in the establishing of new kinds of urban centres, based on models totally different from those of the Roman Empire. These places grew from small markets in the early period, to more formal market places (*emporien*) in the sixth century, to fully-fledged urban centres (*vici*) in the tenth century.[79] Viking town building extended into England. Norwich, Stamford and Thetford were heavily built up *after* Viking visitations, with the latter an impressive place, possessed of earthen fortifications, paved roads, cloth and metal manufactories, and perhaps as many as a dozen churches. The positive case for Scandinavian influence is summed up by Susan Reynolds in the following way:

> Despite contemporary lamentations, the undoubted injuries to churches, and the belief of some modern historians that the Vikings dealt a heavy blow to town life, no English town is known to have been destroyed by the Northmen. Hamwih was plundered in 842 but archaeological evidence suggests that it continued to be inhabited for almost a hundred years afterwards. On the contrary there is a good deal to suggest that the impact of the Danes on town life in England, at least after the first shock, was a stimulating and constructive one. According to Domesday many of the largest towns in the country lay in the Danelaw in 1086, while phenomena like streets described as "gates", church dedications to St Olave, and (more doubtfully) the institution of lawmen, point to a considerable Danish influence on many of them.[80]

In the face of such evidence as this, the Vikings as raiders and plunderers clearly represent only a small part of the Scandinavian influence on England. There is archaeological evidence for contact between England and Scandinavia roughly 425–625, ample evidence that the Shetland "Jarlshof" settlement was not necessarily a bloody conquest, and that even in England's dark hours at the end of the ninth century, King Alfred (and presumably his subjects) could and did clearly distinguish between a noble Norwegian trader and a thug who had come to raid. But more important is the pre-eminent effect of the Scandinavians not only on the place names of the country, but also on the structure and growth of the English language.

The Linguistic Evidence – I. Place-Names

The study of place-names in England is one of the most exciting and rapidly advancing fields of scholarly endeavour. Spurred by what one major contributor to the fields has described as a "middle age revolution", the subject has advanced very rapidly in the past 20 years.[81] Professor Kenneth Cameron's Israel Gollancz Memorial Lecture in 1976 was both a brilliant statement of principles, and a significant contribution to the field,[82] and Margaret Gelling's *Sign-posts to the Past* (1978) provides an eminently readable general account. Though much work remains to be done, the place-name evidence shows the great extent of the Scandinavian element in English culture and tells us much about the precise nature of the settlement. Three types of names are of particular importance. The first is the place-name ending in the Scandinavian element *-by*. Kenneth Cameron finds 303 such names in the *Domesday Book*; the number increases to 360 if later appearances of the name are counted. 207 of the *Domesday* examples had personal names as their first element, 192 of them Scandinavian. The most important point about these names is that *-by* settlements tend to be in rather second-rate places. Place-name scholars have proposed that instead of pushing out the local inhabitants, a significant number of Scandinavian settlers sought a peaceful accommodation with the neighbours by settling in less fruitful area., The names ending in *-thorp* have the same meaning in English as in Danish, that is, a secondary settlement, or outlying small hamlet. More difficult are names consisting of a Scandinavian personal name and the OE-*tun* (farmstead, village), as in *Flixton* — Professor Cameron in 1976 suggested that such names are records of at least a few of the men of the Danish army that partitioned the land in 877.[83] It is interesting to consider Professor W. F. H. Nicolaisen's summary statement on Viking place-names in Scotland: "it is worth remembering that these Scandinavians were people who were in need of land and who were ready to settle down and lead their lives in a society governed by law, wherever they had the opportunity to do so. The Scandinavian place-names of Scotland certainly are proof of that attitude".[84]

Whether this be true or not is not particularly important for our present purpose; what *is* significant is the clear evidence for extensive Scandinavian settlement, which was on occasion accomplished peacefully and with minimal disruption.

It seems appropriate here to add a *coda* on personal names in England at this time, and Scandinavian influence on them. In an extremely valuable study, Dr. Gillian Fellows-Jensen has surveyed Lincolnshire and Yorkshire.[85] It appears that Scandinavian name forms began to appear *c*. 880, but their popularity was very strong even as late as 1066–1150, when nearly five hundred names of Scandinavian origin are noted. The acceptability of such names in high-ranking Anglo-Saxon families is of particular interest. Earl Godwin of Wessex had eight children — five of whom had Scandinavian names.[86]

Scandinavian Effects on the English Language

Many years ago, Otto Jesperson produced something of a *bon mot* in his statement on this topic in *The Growth and Structure of The English Language*: "An Englishman cannot *thrive*, or be *ill* or *die* without Scandinavian words, *they are* to the language what *bread* and *eggs* are to the daily fare".[87] All the words in italics are of Scandinavian origin. John Geipel has recently provided us with a thoughtful and far-ranging study of Scandinavian impact on the English language in *The Viking Legacy*.[88] He provides much information on the heavily Scandinavian orientation of northern dialects, both modern and medieval, as well as useful insights on the broad-ranging impact of general Scandinavian origin. But when frequency of use is taken into account, they are very important words indeed. Most significant are such words as *take*, *die* and *window*, where words of Scandinavian origin replace the Old English words of the same meaning but of different form. It is rather wonderfully ironic that though Wulfstan of York provided us with the brilliant rhetorical account of Viking attacks cited above on p. 182, that very sermon is very liberally seasoned with Scandinavian words. The curious English glosses added in the tenth century to the Lindisfarne Gospels seem to show that where Scandinavian English contact was most intense, the morphological system of English, already greatly simplified by phonological reduction, was further reduced by the English and Scandinavian grammatical systems rubbing against one another.[89]

A most marked example of Scandinavian influence is the third person plural pronoun. OE had h-forms (*hie*, *hem*, etc.), ON th-forms (*their*, *theira*). Chaucer's English was on a balance-point with such forms; he used th-forms as subject, and h-forms in oblique cases. The weight of evidence is in favour of the contention that the sounds, inflections and words of Modern English are significantly and pervasively affected by Scandinavian influence. This influence is particularly remarkable, because speakers of Scandinavian languages seem to have had no great investment in their language. Elizabeth Okasha's *Hand-List of Anglo-Saxon Non-Runic Inscriptions* shows that texts produced in areas heavily affected by Scandinavian influence for people with very Scandinavian name-forms were very little influenced by Scandinavian language.[90] A pious Scandinavian who built a church or erected a monument to a relative or friend was quite happy to have his inscription in Old English.[91] As Geipel points out, the Vikings who settled in France adapted to Old French rather quickly, and Scandinavian settlers in Canada and America gave up their language with much greater ease than Italians, Germans, or Slavic speaking peoples.[92] This trend towards easy surrender, as it were, makes the heavy influence of Scandinavian on English all the more remarkable. From the standpoint of finding an application for the Scandinavian thrust of *Beowulf*, it does not particularly matter whether the Scandinavian influence on English language was the super-imposition of a ruling class, as was to happen with Norman French,[93] or the effect of large-scale association through extensive settlement. The archaeological evidence seems to support the latter view, but the evidence is by no means all in.

Finally, a very bold argument for strong Scandinavian influence on Late Old English and Early Middle English is being put forward by Dr. Poussa of Helsinki. In a paper soon to be published in *Studia Anglica Posnaniensia*, entitled, "The Evolution of Early Standard English: The Creolization Hypothesis", she argues that a Midland Creole dialect grew in the Old English period, and perhaps stabilized during the rule of King Cnut. This Creolization, Poussa argues, is the primary cause of the loss of grammatical gender and extreme simplification of inflections. The Norman French influence is less significant than previously thought. The terms "Creole" and "Creolizations" need explication. In the narrow sense, a true Creole is a secondary development upon Pidgin. Pidgin is a "stripped" language, with very few words (a few hundred), and a minimal syntax. A Creole arises when this greatly reduced language is expanded once more into a full-scale language. In my interpretation at least, Dr. Poussa uses Creole in a less narrow sense, using the word to indicate that the Old Scandinavian language is more pervasive in its effects on English than previously thought. For further details on the meaning of the terms, *see* Robert A. Hall, Jr., 1966, especially xii–xiv.

Evidence of Sculpture

Though there are always differences on the dating of certain pieces, it is clear that the Anglian tradition of carving continued, strong and productive, throughout the period of Scandinavian settlement. Scandinavian elements were added as time went on; Mr. James Lang reaches this conclusion in a study of Anglo-Saxon and Viking-Age sculpture in the York school: "Nothing redeems the Viking reputation more than the Yorkshire carvings since of the five hundred pieces nearly 80 per cent belong to the Anglo-Scandinavian period (c. 875-1066) and the mixed population of York and its Ridings was responsible for a great flowering of stone sculpture, developed in a succession of local schools, whose art remains distinct both from the styles of the Scandinavian homelands and from neighbouring insular art in Ireland, Man, or even Northumbria north of the Tees".[94] And Mr. Christopher Morris cites some 70 pieces of sculpture in the Tees valley which continue earlier traditions, and which show a marked interest in Viking themes, elements, and motifs. Morris states: "Whatever the impact of the Scandinavians on the area, it certainly did not include a destruction of the native traditions of stone-carving. Rather, it was accepted, if not revitalized by the introduction of new ideas and even possible new forms such as the hog-backed grave monuments."[95] Those ponderous monuments are numerous in modern England and Scotland, and can be related to Scandinavian house-styles.

Evidence of English–Scandinavian Assimilation

The thrust of Mr. Morris' paper is that a survey of the evidence in several fields shows that "Viking" and "Native" are not two entirely separate and unrelated groups, and that there was at least "reciprocity, if not integration" between them. Mr. Morris would have us view stone sculpture in the Tees valley as "Anglo-Scandinavian". He has provided us with a careful account of a small area, and has marshalled an impressive array of evidence to support his thesis, which I think is entirely acceptable. David Wilson has made a series of more broad-ranging comments on the settlement of the Vikings, in papers which span more than a decade.[96] He holds for rapid cultural and artistic assimilation of Scandinavians. His comment on the relationship between the two peoples in the north of England is of particular interest:

> One can trace quite clearly in the art of the north-east the successful blend of two different artistic traditions, a blend which illustrates the congruity of two different artistic traditions, English and Scandinavian. The mixture illustrates the similarity of outlook of two different people, talking closely-related languages, living in the same area, worshipping the same god and having a certain continuity of political and even ecclesiastical organization.[97]

There is little doubt about the extremely important role played by the Church during even the most trying of times. First of all, figures of power, like Wulfstan, quite clearly held for Northumbrian interests, even if alliance with Scandinavian forces was necessary to maintain them. Noble Northumbrians saw southerners as their primary enemies. As Professor Sawyer points out, "the relationship between the church and the Scandinavians was complex and by no means entirely hostile" (Hall, 1978, 7). The Scandinavians were even welcomed by some leading Englishmen, including Archbishops of York, because they helped preserve the traditional independence of Northumbria from rule by Southerners.

On the basis of archaeology, art history and linguistic evidence, it seems quite safe to claim that a large proportion of the Scandinavians who settled in England managed to take up their land and make peace with their neighbours in a remarkably short time, thus creating conditions that would be highly favourable to the production of a poem celebrating northern ancestors. The ability to adjust to new conditions was very much a hallmark of Scandinavian settlers and traders, and the job of settling in was easier because of the closeness in language and culture that existed between Anglo-Saxons and Scandinavians.

As a kind of distant coda, we have a striking confirmation of the close similarities between Anglo-Saxons in the way in which recruits were treated in the famed Varangian Guard of the late Byzantine Empire. Through its history, the guard consisted almost exclusively of foreign mercenaries. At first Russians dominated, then Scandinavians, and finally Englishmen. In a recent study clarifying the role of both the English and the Scandinavians in the late Byzantine Empire, Jonathan Shepard cites Greek sources to show how the term "Varangian" had as its referent English and Scandinavians — but *not* other Germanic peoples — in the late eleventh century. Shepard goes on to show that though both Scandinavians and English were granted ranks in the Byzantine service that were based on their position in their native societies, the English formed "a hard and permanent core of the imperial guard", and that the Scandinavians also had high positions.[98] At this point, the devil's advocate must enter, and the nature of the review of Scandinavian-English contact presented above made clear. There is abundant archaeological evidence to support the textual Jeremiads on Viking raids, Viking destruction of social and economic order, widespread gloom among the English, and what were at the time cataclysmic changes in the institutions and the quality of life. The monks of Lindisfarne did not wander for seven years on a whim, the great ecclesiastical centre at Whitby seems to have suffered a blow from which it could not recover fairly early in the period of Viking incursion, and I don't suppose that many of those who were wrenched from their homes or religious communities to be sold into slavery had a lively appreciation of the finer points of Scandinavian culture. But this side of the Scandinavian impact on England, and on Europe, is well known, and needs no detailed discussion here. *Beowulf* has come down to us, a text that deals entirely with Scandinavian affairs and Scandinavian heroes; on the basis of the survey I have presented, there is a cultural context in England from the settlement period through and beyond the Conquest which serves as a basis for this pro-Scandinavian bias of the poem.

Conclusions, and Reflections on the Impact of Beowulf *as a Literary Text*

There are some conclusions that can be drawn on the nature of *Beowulf*, on the basis of the evidence here. First of all, it is now possible to see the central argument of the poem directly related to what we are beginning to see are the facts of early Scandinavian history, and the heroic history derived from that factual basis. Some men of the north clearly had peaceful dealings with England from the Migration Period to the Norman Conquest. Given the manuscript context of *Beowulf*, Cotton Vitellius A.xv, it is clear that the compiler of that manuscript, his intended audience and, to some extent, the intended audience of *Beowulf* poet were interested in wonders. But the Scandinavian affairs of the poem must be seen as a basic context in which the action of the poem, and its heroes, function. Much as one would hope to provide a date for the composition of the poem on the basis of this survey of Scandinavian contact with England, there is no firm evidence for any particular date. Paradoxically, it seems that one would be hard-pressed to have *Beowulf* originate in the South of England around the time it was written down, because evidence for Viking raids is very strong in the period 980–1015, and it would be harder to find an audience (in southern England at least) interested in a Scandinavian-based story. But during the earlier part of the tenth century, when Edward and Athelstan conquered the Danelaw, the trade and diplomacy flourished mightily, such a poem would have been appropriate. There is a strong probability that an English poem on Scandinavian heroes would have had an international currency; Athelstan was a respected figure throughout the northern world. Just *after* the millennium the poem would have been entirely appropriate in the courts of the Scandinavian rulers in England. It was a time for close contact and ready exchange between the English and the men of the north. Prominent Englishmen quickly came to terms with the new rulers, and such men as Wulfstan quickly took up service under Cnut.[98a]

When one looks further back in time, it is hard to find a time in which *Beowulf* could *not* have been enjoyed. Schücking's theory that the poem could have been composed as a lesson in how to rule for princes in an Anglo-Danish kingdom in the Danelaw, and thus dated to the end of the ninth century, cannot easily be dismissed.[99] Certainly, *Beowulf* would have been an ideal piece of propaganda for someone who wished to bring Scandinavians and Anglo-Saxons closer together on the basis of their common heritage. There are no insuperable objections for seeing the poem as the product of the eighth[100] or even the seventh century.[101] The striking fact is the broad range of times in which *Beowulf* could have been composed. It is more fruitful to approach the question of a placement for the poem in a broader perspective; what are the most likely contexts for this work, points at which culture, circumstance and acceptance for the men of the north would have obtained? It is evident that Northumbria in the seventh and eighth centuries could easily have been the place of origin for a poem which celebrates noble pre-Christian ancestors.[102] The Franks Casket almost certainly arose in the Northumbrian milieu, and the thrust of the iconography of the Casket and the moral implications of the poem are quite similar, in that both are products of open-ended and receptive traditions, which could easily incorporate elements from pagan Christian and classical bases. The open-ended nature of the Insular Christian tradition which had its origin in Ireland would have seen no great difficulty in bringing together admirable figures from northern history with Biblical scenes and scenes from classical legend.[103] The poem is so set that the major characters meet the tastes of a Christian audience who expected their pagan ancestors to act with prorpriety and decency in a pre-Christian age. But equally important is the fact that the poem and its ethical sub-stratum would have been almost as acceptable to a pagan audience. It is my belief that its centre, the history of heroic and noble ancestors, can be read either way.

If we look for a placement for the poem other than in the north of England, the East Anglian culture which produced the splendours of Sutton Hoo clearly would have found the poem a moving and compelling story. If we wish to hold that the poem is early, then East Anglia is a *more* likely setting than Northumbria, for the connection with Scandinavia at an early date is proved to have existed there by very hard archaeological evidence; but this is not to say there was no connection between Scandinavia and the north of England at the same period.[104] Given the gradual and generally tolerant nature of the conversion of the Scandinavian community, in which the Christian God was first accepted as a kind of *primus inter pares*, and pious Northmen were for a long time "prime signed", rather than baptized, the balance in the poem between Christian and pagan ethics would have been brilliantly appropriate.[105] East Anglia, then, has a strong but by no means exclusive claim as the place of origin for *Beowulf*.

If I were to put forward my own view, it is that *Beowulf* is designed to serve as an almost perfect instrument for bringing Scandinavian and Anglo-Saxon together, on the basis of a glorious shared past. It is, I think, very significant that the picture of the early kings of Scandinavia is far more brilliant in *Beowulf* than it is in the literature of the northern world.[106]

One other likely place for the origin of *Beowulf* is in the kingdom of Offa, who ruled from 757 to 796. He was *bretwalda*, and had recognition and power far beyond his own kingdom. As Sir Frank Stenton evaluates him, "He was the first English king to play an independent part in Continental affairs, and he was not overshadowed by [Charlemagne] the greatest ruler of the whole Dark Ages. He understood that it was the duty of a king to encourage foreign trade."[107] Offa's trade might well have been in part with Scandinavians. It is interesting to note that the first recorded Viking raid in England hit the kingdom of Beortric, Offa's son-in-law, and that Beortric's customs officer lost his life when he tried to treat the raiders as if they had come to trade — clearly the motive he expected when they appeared.

In writing this piece, it has been my intent to provide a context for the apparent paradox of the Scandinavian centre of *Beowulf*. A survey of literary and archaeological evidence shows that an interest in Scandinavian affairs among Englishmen (despite the vicious attacks of Viking raiders) was possible at almost any time in the period 400–1100, and was particularly apposite if one's attention is not centred on southern England. It should be clear from the literary evidence that there is a strain of interest in Scandinavian heroes which runs through Old English literature, and further that the celebration of the northern heroic age is found *only* in the major English poem. It is hoped that this study will help to *broaden* the appreciation of the poem. In pointing out the most likely contexts for a poem dealing with figures from Scandinavian heroic history who would have been attractive to Englishmen and Scandinavian alike, it has *not* been my intention to fault, or to contradict, any other interpretation of *Beowulf*. The greatest test of the art of the tradition — and the individual *scop* — who made this poem is its richness, and its open-endedness. I hold only this: that though *Beowulf* could serve many other purposes, for ancient and modern readers alike, the stress on Scandinavian affairs was natural and even predictable in the light of the sustained and fruitful contact between England and Scandinavia throughout most of what some are still pleased to call the dark Ages. It is particularly significant, and not a little ironic, that the Old English poem gives a brilliant and elevated picture of the early kings of Scandinavia. There is no account to equal it in writings which have come down to us from the north. Dane and Geat, Swede and Saxon would all have found much to ponder in this early English poem. Pagan, prime signed and Christian could have found it a useful source of instruction, and a model of behaviour for members of a warrior class.

NOTES

This study has been in progress for half a dozen years. In the course of working on it, I have had advice and useful commentary from a number of colleagues. Dr. Bruce Mitchell of St. Edmund Hall, Oxford, read an early draft, as did Professor Fred Robinson of Yale. Dr. Lucy Collings of Stonor, Henley-on-Thames, also read an early draft, and provided me with many useful details on general Germanic literature. Almost every contributor to this collection has been kind enough to help in one way or another, with David Wilson and Joe Harris in particular providing a great deal of good counsel. The Humanities Faculty Research Fund and the English Department at Cornell provided funding for photographs, maps, and manuscript preparation.

I gratefully acknowledge all of this help, and resolutely claim such faults as may be present in the work as my own. Though a formal dedication of so slight a piece would be improper, their study is intended to honour the memory of Charles Donahue, who brought me into the field of early medieval studies whilst I was a student and junior colleague of his at Fordham University. *He wæs betra ðonne ic!*

1 Ker 1897 sets the poem neatly in context; the mastery of metre the *Beowulf* poet displays has been discussed by a host of scholars, with Bliss 1967 and Cable 1974 of particular importance. For a very useful brief review of criticism and interpretation of the poem, *see* Shippey, 1978.

2 To start with my own base discipline, Charles Wrenn made far too many direct associations between the ship-burial at Sutton Hoo and the wealth of artefacts it contained when in 1958 he added a chapter on "Sutton Hoo and Beowulf" to the third edition of R. W. Chamber's *Beowulf: An Introduction.* (Chambers 1958). The new reconstructions of many of the objects invalidate much of what he said. Lindquist (1948) presented a paper on "Sutton Hoo and *Beowulf*", the English version of which was translated by Rupert Bruce-Mitford. The paper was an attempt to elucidate the poem by means of the find, and *vice versa*, in which he held that Sutton Hoo was "wholly Swedish". It did not gain acceptance either by archaeologists or by literary historians. Dr. Rupert Bruce-Mitford, who has contributed so much to our understanding not only of Sutton Hoo but of Dark Age archaeology in its entirety, takes the text of *Beowulf* too far, particularly when he brings together the ship-burial at Sutton Hoo with Scyld's funeral in *Beowulf*. In the poem, Scyld's body is set adrift in a treasure-laden vessel. There is no burial, such as was the custom in ancient Scandinavia. Cameron (1969) pointed out a parallel for Scyld's funeral is found in the disposal after death of St Gildas. There are striking parallels in *Celtic* tradition for setting bodies adrift, but none in Scandinavian contexts. *See* further Bruce-Mitford 1975 and Cameron 1969. Most recently, Dr. Bruce-Mitford again returns to the over-enthusiastic claims of Charles Wrenn for Sutton Hoo by holding that once the full impact of the Scandinavian material is properly understood, "it may perhaps be seen that the contribution of Sutton Hoo to *Beowulf* studies, in addition to close analogies between the archaeological material and the text, offers something deeper, a clue perhaps to the transmission of the Scandinavian elements of the poem to the Anglo-Saxon world. This hope it is which led me to say, on the extravagant-seeming dictum of Professor Wrenn, cited earlier [to the effect that Sutton Hoo may be as important to the poem as the Thorkelin transcripts of the manuscript], that it might well in the long run prove justified" (Bruce-Mitford 1979, 35). Once again, a *single* text is compared to a *single* find — which leads to strains on both literary and archaeological evidence.

3 Two first-rate studies of *genre* are Tolkien 1936 and Greenfield 1962.

4 As even a cursory reading of such works as Jones 1968 or Foote and Wilson 1970 indicates, nationality — or any identification or participation in affairs beyond a very local level — was not usual until rather late in the early medieval period. The general outline seems to be somewhat as follows. The Swedes around Uppsala rose to power sometime in the sixth century, but throughout the entire period there was a clear tendency for tribal groups to re-form allegiances among the various peoples of what we now know as Denmark and Norway, and the peoples of Sweden, the Geats and the Swedes.

In addition to the power and wealth centred around old Uppsala, there is a heavy concentration both of iron age strongholds and of Roman trade goods in south-west Sweden, the territory of the Geats. The islands of Gotland and Öland were particularly well favoured in the early medieval period, and a very great density of strongholds and Roman trade goods and other treasures are found there.

The situation in Denmark is significantly different. The figure of Gotfred, who assumed the rule of Denmark *c.* 800 was a formidable one, for he jealously guarded the trade rights Denmark had enjoyed for many centuries, and also fought Charlemagne to a standstill. In addition to the sensitivity of Denmark to trade shown by Gotfred's career, it is certain that Denmark must have been in some sense a consolidated kingdom long before Gotfred for the *Danevirke*, long attributed him, has recently been dated to *c.* 737, on the basis of very strong dendrochronological evidence. Dr. Wilson has recently studied this fortification and other structures in "Civil and Military Engineering in Viking Age Scandinavia" (Wilson 1978), and concluded "The people who many consider as piratical rabble were in fact effective and serious leaders, sometimes with technical abilities hitherto largely ignore or unknown".

5   Ecgtheow certainly took up service under Hrothgar of the Danes (see ll. 459–484), and Beowulf himself tells us that his fame – and perhaps his experiences – spread among many nations (ll. 262–266). For an ambitious and absorbing reconstruction of Ecgtheow's career, *see* Kemp Malone's "Ecgtheow" (Malone 1940).

6   Though the OE *wendla leod* could have several other meanings, I follow C. L. Wrenn in finding his origins in Vendel, Sweden. *See* Wrenn 1973, 300. (*N.B.*: The 1973 edition was revised by Professor Bolton, but in this instance Wrenn's helpful note was allowed to remain.)

7   My justification for this outline of events, in which Heardred is seen as at best ill-advised, is set out in Farrell 1972.

8   From the standpoint of heroic tradition, the principal characters in *Beowulf* are quite properly concerned with honour and ethical conduct in extremely trying conditions. Many of the poem's central actions are accounts of such conflicts: the suffering of Hildeburh, who must watch son and brother burn on the same pyre, is one of the most horrifyingly realistic passages in the poem. The plight of both Finn and Hengest caught up in a feud not of their making, and the anguish of Beowulf himself, who must kill the rightful king of the Swedes in order to avenge Heardred, are examples of this. Despite the many contributions to the scholarship, which cast Beowulf's dragon battle and his dealings with the treasures in dark light, it is my view that the stratum of heroic, ethical conflict is absolutely basic and of overriding importance.

9   The most useful and concise statement about these traditions is De Vries 1963. On Germanic figures and their backgrounds, Chambers 1912 is most useful, though superseded in some respects in Malone 1962. Chadwick 1912 is still first-rate.

10   There is strong controversy at present on the date of composition of the poem; two lengthy studies appeared in 1978 which build rather detailed cases for particular contexts in time, place and culture for *Beowulf*.

The first is W. R. Bolton's entirely unconvincing *Alcuin and "Beowulf": An Eighth Century View* (Bolton 1978), and the second is Patrick Wormald's "Bede, *Beowulf* and the Conversion of the Anglo-Saxon Aristocracy" (Wormald 1978). On attending a conference on the date of composition of *Beowulf*, held at the Centre for Medieval Studies at Toronto in April 1980, I discovered that the combined efforts of scholars from a number of disciplines produced little new on the date of the poem, either in the way of new or previously overlooked evidence, or in a revised consensus of opinion. A sub-group held that the poem was composed late (tenth or early eleventh century), but this stance was balanced by scholars who held very firmly for an eighth-century date, and a Mercian or Northumbrian context for the poem. The end result of the meeting was that the dating of *Beowulf* is more open than it was before the conference, when the majority of scholars had held for an eighth-century date. It will require a great deal of evidence to confute Mr. Wormald's solidly structured case for an eighth, or perhaps early ninth, century context for the poem. Among his points of reference are, first, the life of St Guthlac, who is presented, as Wormald puts it, as a "saintly hero in something of a traditional mould", and a saint whose aristocratic background and style of holiness puts him firmly in the class of *Adelsheilige* (*op. cit.* 56).

Second, there is the penchant for Scandinavian ancestors in the genealogies of the period, and the names in the Mercian line of Kings, Offa, Beowulf, and Wiglaf, echo of names central to Beowulf. Dr. Poussa of Helsinki kindly provided me with a pre-publication copy of her extremely interesting paper on the date of *Beowulf* (Poussa 1981). Her summary is as follows, as she makes a case for a tenth-century date: "Historical evidence for the number of Scandinavian immigrants to England in the 9th and 10th centuries, and their political significance, is reviewed. It is proposed that the *Beowulf-*

poet may be Anglo-Dane, in touch with both the oral literature brought over by the Scandinavian settlers, and, by education, the literary culture of Anglo-Saxon England. The model for the society of *Beowulf* may be found in the tenth-century Viking trading towns of the Baltic. The Norman Conquest, with its anti-Danish policy in history-writing and destruction of the OE literary language, is responsible for the misunderstanding of *Beowulf* in later centuries." In sum, then, the current state of scholarly opinion seems to be that the date of *Beowulf* is very much an open question, though there is a very interesting series of arguments currently being presented for a tenth-century date.

11   All citations from the Chronicle come from *Two of the Saxon Chronicles Parallel*, ed. C. Plummer and J. Earle (Oxford 1892). The text is translated from the curious panegyric found in the Laud Ms. (I. 123).

12   This is a rather free translation of part of the Laud Ms. for 1010. The OE Reading:

> "þonne hi wæron be easton. þonne heold man fyrde be westan. þonne hi wæron
> be suðan. þonne wæs ure fyrd be norðan. þonne bead man ealle witan to cynge.
> man þonne rædan sceolde hu man þisne eard werian sceolde. Ac þeah man
> hwæt thonne rædde, þæt ne stod furðon ænne monað, æt nyxtan næs nan
> heafod man þæt fyrde gaderian wolde, ac ælc fleah swa he mæst myhte. Ne
> furðon nan scir nolde oðre gelæstan æt nyxtan."

13   The arrogance of the Viking raiders is clearly seen in their demand for tribute (ll. 29–41); the very *lytegian*, referring to the Viking request to pass over the causeway (l. 86), is generally glossed "use guile". For first-rate recent studies of the poem, see Gneuss 1976 and Robinson 1978.

14   The translation is from George Sampson, *The Cambridge Book of English Verse and Prose* (Cambridge 1974). I cite the original from Whitlock 1963.

> "Oft twegen sæmæn, oððe þry hwilum, drifað þa drafe cristenra manna fram
> sæ to sæ, ut þurh þas þeode, gewelede togædere, us eallum to woroldscame, gif
> þe on eornost ænige cuþon ariht understandan; ac ealne þæne bysmor þe þe oft
> þoliað we gyldað mid weorðscipe þam þe us scendað: þe him gyldað singallice,
> 7 hy us hynað daeghwamlice; hy hergiath 7 hy bærnað, rypaþ 7 ræfiað 7 to scipe
> lædað; 7 la, hwaet is ænig oðer on eallum þam gelimpum butan godes yrre ofer
> þas þeode swutol gesæne?"

15   *See* Ælfric, *Lives of Three English Saints*, ed. G. I. Needham (London, 1966). The Sermon on St Edmund is on pp. 43–59, and the passage translated on p. 46.

16   Charles Donahue, in two very important essays (1948, 1965), developed a background for the poem in "Insular" Christianity. By this he meant an open-ended, pragmatic kind of faith, in which it was possible to admire and emulate the good example of pre-Christian ancestors.

17   The two most significant essays are Tolkien 1936, published also as a pamphlet (Oxford, 1958), and De Vries 1963, especially Chapters 3–7.

18   On the date and setting of the *Táin Bó Cúalinge, see* J. X. W. P. Corcoran, "The Origins of the Celts: the Archaeological Evidence" 17–41, in Chadwick, *The Celts*, 1970, and Aodh de Blácam, *Gaelic Literature Surveyed* (Dublin and Cork, 1928), especially 31. In her 1970 edition of the *Táin*, Cecile O'Rahilly points out that the earliest version of the tale, "a conflation of two 9th century versions, is found in a manuscript written about 1100" (ix). The tale existed in the eighth century and perhaps as early as the seventh. Despite these relatively late firm dates, there are very strong affinities between Celtic matters described by early classical commentators, and the setting of the *Táin*.

19   De Vries 1963, 196–197.

20   The text and translation of these lines are taken from Page 1973, 176–177.

21   On the inscriptions of the Franks Casket, Napier 1901 is still of primary importance. The collotype plates are of particularly high quality. Napier dates the inscription on linguistic considerations to the very beginning of the eighth century (381). Campbell 1961 holds that the inscription "can be assigned to the eighth century without hazard", 4, n. 2. Beckwith 1972 posits the same date on the basis of art historical evidence. Both Beckwith and Kendrick 1939 relate the piece to decorative elements in the Lindisfarne Gospels, and Kendrick further holds that there is a strong northern influence in the piece 1938, especially 122–125. Karl Schneider proposes a date of 550 for the casket and holds that it came into being in the Merovingian kingdom, but was produced by a heathen Angle named

Domgisl. Though the early date is tempting, the evidence Schneider presents is not strong (Schneider 1970). The most recent discussion of the entire question of dating OE texts on linguistic bases is Amos 1980, who concludes (following Becker 1973) that 650-750 is about as closely as we can date the inscription, Mrs. Webster's dating of "the years around 700" (above, p. 30), is about as accurate a date as can be offered).

22   As Alexander 1975 points out, in a comparison of Codex Amiatinus (a Jarrow product) and the Lindisfarne Gospels, the technical modes of the two books are quite at variance; while the Amiatinus artist strove for effects of perspective and contrasts of dark and light, the illustrator of Lindisfarne uses abstract colour, and is not at all interested in illusionistic presentation of figures. This is just one in a series of major differences between the two scriptoria. *See* further Rupert Bruce-Mitford 1969.

23   Cædmon's "Miracle" is perhaps best explained as the felicitous and new combination of traditional Germanic poetic forms with Christian subject matter.

24   Golden age of Northumbria — roughly speaking, the period 650-750. For the original text of the letter, *see Alcuini Epistolae* 124, ed. Dunmler, *MGA Ep. Ser. Karolini Aevi*, II, 183. On the more inclusive Irish Christian tradition, *see* Donahue, 1948 and 1965. *See* Wormald 1978 for his careful arguments on the context of Alcuin's letter.

25   Wormald 1978.

26   Kemp Malone, *Widsith* (London, 1936), 65 and 141-144. He bases his case both on the consistency of the poem *Widsith* itself, and on the early sources (notably Ammianus Marcellinus and Jordanes). Malone does not change his argument significantly in his 1962 version of *Widsith*. As Wormald 1978 has pointed out, Hermanneric had a rather grim reputation for Archbishop Fulk of Rheims (822-900). Fulk had strong English contacts. Malone is convinced that language evidence "leads us to conclude that *Widsith* was composed and reduced to writing in the latter part of the seventh century" (62, 116), and that the metrical evidence supports the same date range. If Malone is correct, then *Widsith* and Franks Casket are of approximately the same date, but Amos 1980 in a thorough review of language evidence as a basis of dating OE texts does not support Malone.

27   *See* further Farrell 1972.

28   Our dating centres on the one certainly historical figure in the poem, Hygelac, and his death at the hands of a Frankish army early in the sixth century. If we date Beowulf's life from this event, and allow some years for the short and ignoble reign of Heardred, Hygelac's son, Beowulf, would have been born *c.* 500, done his monster slaying in Denmark before 525, and ruled *c.* 525-575. *See* above, 189-90.

29   On *Deor* and its interpretation, *see* further Kemp Malone 1965.

30   His view is put as follows: "There are indications favourable to A.D. 900 or thereabouts, but these are only indications and do not warrant positiveness in our conclusions". Malone, *Deor, op. cit.,* n. 29, 22. Amos 1980 further points out the uncertain nature of linguistic evidence for dating.

31   The word *raed* may have the connotation "divine counsel" in this and other instances in the poem. Clearly, that glossing would be appropriate in l. 1760, where Hrothgar uses the word in the course of his "sermon". On this glossing for *raed, see* further Farrell 1968.

32   Farrell 1972.   33   Wrenn 1973, 47.

34   The most often cited source is Gregory of Tours, *History of the Franks*. Since Gregory died in 594, he wrote very close to the event indeed. The attack of Chochilaicus (Hygelac) is also reported in the *Liber Historiae Francorum* (*c.* 727). For further discussion, *see* R. W. Chambers 1958, 3-6. Gotfried Storms has studied "The Significance of Hygelac's Raid" at some length in *Nottingham Medieval Studies* 14 (1970), 3-26. His interpretation is at variance with mine; he proposes that the expedition was "not primarily a plundering raid but a military, tactical move in the struggle for hegemony of Western Europe between Theodoric the Ostrogoth and the Franks" (16). Despite my very great respect for the range and learning of this article, I cannot follow Professor Storms' interpretation either of the archaeological material, or the linguistic evidence of *Beowulf*. To have a king of the Geats acting as a third major power in the first quarter of the sixth century is to posit a degree of political sophistication and a tactical and economic base of a much greater sort than we can at present discern. In addition, his opinions on the England–Scandinavian relationship need revision in the basis of recent archaeological publications.

35   D. K. Fry's edition of *Finnsburh — Fragment and Episode*, in *Methuen's Old English Library* (London and New York, 1974), provides a useful summary of scholarship as well as some interesting new insights on the poem.

36   *Bana* means "slayer" and can refer either to the person who killed someone, or to the slayer's lord, who caused the deed to be done.

37   After Hnaef and his nephew were laid on the pyre together, "The greatest of pyres mounted to the heavens, roared before the mound; and gashes, deadly cuts to the body, burst whenever blood welled out". (ll. 1119–1122a).

38   Chambers 1958, 5.

39   Adrien Bonjour's spirited and sensitive defence of *The Digressions in Beowulf* (1950, re-printed Oxford, 1965) led him to misinterpret details. His handling of the death of Heardred and Beowulf's foray into the land of the Swedes is marred by inaccuracy. As an instance, on the basis of a close analysis of the text, it is simply not possible to hold, as Bonjour does, that "the rightful heirs to Ohthere are indeed deprived of the throne by their uncle Onela" (32). Storms, *op. cit.* note 34, bases part of his argument on an absolute antipathy between Swede and Geat.

40   Kenneth Sisam 1966, 51–59.

41   Farrell 1972.

42   The crucial evidence for prior discord between the Danes and the Geats is found in ll. 1855–63, a speech by Hrothgar. The old Danish king speaks of the peace which Beowulf brought between Danes and Geats — where there had previously been terrible enmities (*sacu . . . inwitniþas*). Since the passage is often overlooked, it seems best to cite it in full; in ll. 1853 to 63, Hrothgar praises *Beowulf*:

> Dear Beowulf, your spirit pleases me more and more as time goes on. You have brought about a peace between two nations, Spear-Danes and Geats; wars will end, the terrible enmities which they have endured in the past; while I rule this great kingdom, there will be an interchange of gifts, and many a man will greet another with good things across the expanse of the sea, the gannet's bathing-place; the ringed ship will bring gifts and tokens of regard over the seas.

43   Eliason 1978 holds that some major elements — such as Wiglaf's being Beowulf's sister's son — are suppressed "to preserve the mood of unmitigated gloom at the end of the poem" (104).

44   Chadwick 1912, 1–109.

45   On "Brunanburh" and its context, *see* further A. Campbell 1938.

46   Sawyer 1971, 123. Sawyer's notion of small-scale Viking armies in the later Anglo-Saxon period has been often attacked. The most recent sally to have reached me is that of N. P. Brookes (1979). Since in the present instance I am citing Professor Sawyer as an indication of smaller groups functioning in a much earlier period, it does not seem appropriate to present all the arguments question-ing his conclusions on the late Viking period in England.

47   Ritchie Girvan, 2nd ed. 1971, Ammianus is quoted on 45–46. Girvan's incisive review of the nature of Germanic society deserves reading in full.

48   Professor Sawyer made this point eloquently and elegantly in the chapter entitled "The Written Sources", *The Age of the Vikings*, 12–47.

49   Wormald 1978.

50   Gwyn Jones (1968), 194–95, translates Alcuin's comment on the first Viking incursion as follows:

> "It is some three hundred and fifty years that we and our forefathers have inhabited this lovely land, and never before in Britain had such a terror appeared as this we have now suffered at the hands of the heathen. Nor was it thought possible that such an inroad from the sea could be made."

51   Sawyer 1071, 14–15.

52   Two recent studies by Lotte Hedeager serve both as useful surveys of recent scholarship, and as contribution to the field. In the first of these (Hedeager, 1980a), she gives an interesting picture of Germanic and specifically North Germanic contact with the Roman Empire:

> It may be suggested that political centralization occurred several times in several local areas in Free Germany throughout the period in question. But these developments were soon followed by political decentralization. Thus we may regard the whole of Free Germany as one regional system, composed of dozens of local political systems linked together through changing political and economic alliances — a continuous and conflicting process of evolution and devolution. The

focus of evolutionary interest is then to determine when this process transforms the regional system as a whole. This supposes a reconstruction of the local social systems, their political and economic interdependence and their relations to the Roman Empire.

In a second piece (Hedeager 1980b), the relationships between communities in Denmark are discussed, and the author posits a unified Eastern Denmark *in the Roman period*, the dissolution of which played a role of central importance in the settlement of England:

In "Danmarks Oldtid" Brønsted connected the migration of the Jutes with a supposed invasion of the Danes from the east, based on a historical myth (Brønsted 1966: 271 f.) It may now seem that the core of historical truth in this myth was the formation of the first "Kingdom" or "State" which for a period of some generations unified Eastern Denmark. It would also seem reasonable if this Eastdanish [*sic*] Kingdom had attempted to extend its power further to the west, an attempt which failed. But this could hardly have any direct connection with the later migrations. Indirectly, however, a new development had been triggered off. A new military and political state of affairs had been established, which in several cases may have stimulated suppressed tribes to migrate. Thus from the Roman Iron Age, it seems reasonable to add this factor along with overpopulation and ecological degradation, as a possible cause of migrations.

53   *See* Eldrid Straume, "Glass-gefasse mit Reparatur in norwegischen Grabfunden der Volker-wanderungzeit" in *Festschrift zum 50 jahrigen Bestehen des Vorgeschichtlichen Seminars Marburg, Marburger Studien zur Vor- und Frugeschichte*, ed. Otto-Herman Frey und Helmut Roth, *Band* 1 (Gladenbach 1977), 273–282. *See* further Note 56 below on glass.

54   Jones 1968, 23.

55   The clearest statement is found in Myres 1977, 114–117. His most interesting comment explicates Bede's referent for "Danes". "By the Danes Bede probably meant to imply the people of southern Scandinavia in general including the near parts of Norway and Sweden including Sjaelland and Fyn. ... Contacts with Sweden, whatever their nature, played a large part in the culture of East Anglia exemplified in the Sutton Hoo ship burial of 620–30, and there are indications in the pottery of the previous centuries to support the claim that Swedish influence, not necessarily confined to East Anglia, was present at an earlier date" (116). *See* further Myres 1970, and 1969. In book Five, Chapter 9 of the *Ecclesiastical History*, reference is made to Frisians, Rugians, Danes, Huns, and Old Saxons, from whom the Angles and Saxons resident in England were known to have derived their origin; this is an account of the life of Egbert, [Qui]

noverat esse nationes, a quibus Angli vel Saxones, qui nunc Britanniam incolunt, genus et originem duxisse noscuntur;unde hactenus a vicina gente Britonum corrupte Garmani nuncupantur. Sunt autem Fresones, Rugini, Dani, Hunni, Antiqui Saxones, Boructuarii . . .

56   In her account of *The Fifth Century Invasions South of the Thames* (London, 1965), Vera Evison provides a survey of scholarship of the settlement period. She held that in the process of settlement "tribes were inextricably mixed already on the continental seaboard before they even embarked for England". Myres' more recent work gives good support for a certain amount of mixing, but the pottery evidence shows even more clear linkages between England and southern Scandinavia. Traces of early Scandinavian settlement and inter-influence between England and Scandinavia in the Migration Period are found elsewhere. In a study of the early disc brooch, Dickinson 1978 suggests that the brooches of this type that appear in Scandinavian contexts in the sixth and seventh centuries are either copies of English originals, or direct imports from England. Sonia Chadwick Hawkes 1978 holds that "The early Vendel Period bow-button brooch found is most likely to have been brought to Kent by a Scandinavian bride; probably she came from Gotland but, in view of Kent's continuing connection with south Scandinavia at this period, she may have come from Denmark. Lack of precision in Scandinavian archaeological chronology makes it impossible to date her coming with any certainty, though one would suggest not before *c.* 570" (93). George Speake addresses the question of general relations in art between England and Scandinavia, and holds that "the case for a Scandinavian origin for both Anglo-Saxon styles I and II is strong . . ." (Speake 1980, 94, following Holmquist 1955). Significantly, he further holds that Kentish Style II finds close parallels in west Scandinavia, Denmark and southern Norway (*ibid.*, 85). We must await further publication in this field before the full extent of Scandinavian participation in the early settlement of England can be appreciated.

It is interesting — and curious — to note that though the Sutton Hoo ship burial is, as Dr. Bruce-Mitford 1975 puts it aptly, "Mysteriously without glass" (135), a blue glass vessel was found in Mound 2 (also a boat grave). This object has parallels at Cuddleston, Oxfordshire, Aylesford, Kent, and Broomfield, Essex. Significant for the Scandinavian connection are the examples found at Løland, Vigmostad, Vestagder and Tu i Klepp, Joederen, Norway, both now in Oslo (Universitetets Oldsaksamling). Dr. Bruce-Mitford points out that this sort of vessel is not found in the Rhineland, and "may well be of Anglo-Saxon manufacture, perhaps connected with a blue glass and trailed jar industry based on Faversham . . . (*ibid.*). The most recent connection in glass finds known to me is Speake 1980 (53), who discusses glass as one aspect of English connections with west Scandinavia:

> Further confirmation of contacts between Norway and Kent are the blue glass bowls (Harden's Class VIIIa iv) which have been found in two finds from Norway and five sites in England and which belong to the same chronological horizon as the jewellery under discussion. In view of the likelihood that vessels of dark blue glass were made in Faversham, Kent, and that the Norwegian glass bowls seem to have been Kentish exports, we appear to have evidence for trade and mutual influences between south-east England and Norway.

57   Charles Green, *Sutton Hoo: The Excavations of a Royal Ship-Burial* (New York, 1963), especially 103–114.

58   Jutes. I follow here the glossing Professor Fry (Fry 1974, 81) provides for OE *Eotan*, a people "originally from Jutland" who "migrated near the Frisians, where they fell under Frisian hegemony".

59   Maryon 1946 and Nerman 1948.

60   The most useful introduction to the Sutton Hoo material is Bruce-Mitford's *The Sutton Hoo Ship-Burial — A Handbook*, 3rd edition (London, 1980). Two volumes of the definitive publication of the find are now out, Volume I (1975), dealing with Excavations, Background, the Ship, and Inventory; and Volume II (1978), dealing with Arms, Armour, and Regalia. For further bibliography, *see* Bruce-Mitford, 1976. Scandinavian — specifically east Scandinavian — connections are cited *seriatim*, but especially in the concluding paragraphs on the Shield and Helmet (Bruce-Mitford 1978, 91–99, 205–219).

61   Bruce-Mitford 1974, 1–72.

62   For the Lindquist piece, *see Aspects of Anglo-Saxon Archaeology* (London, 1974), 1–72.

63   After a careful study of a number of texts and genealogies, Kenneth Sisam concluded: "As historical records, all the genealogies in their early parts fail because fact, fiction and error cannot be distinguished", Sisam 1953, 329.

64   O'Loughlin 1964.

65   For a distribution map of Sutton Hoo parallels and further discussion, *see* Farrell 1972, 44–48.

66   The purse has one panel with a man flanked by two beasts. The closest Swedish parallel Dr. Bruce-Mitford cites comes from Torslunda, in the island of Öland. It is a die for impressing metals. A similar iconography is found on a band of bronze sheet-metal which decorates a bucket found in the cemetery at Hough-on-the-Hill, Lincolnshire. On one panel of the helmet is a human figure carrying two spears, and wearing a horned helmet. A helmet from Boat Grave 7 at Valsgarde, Uppland has a similar iconography, as does another die at Torslunda, Öland; but the same iconography is found on a belt buckle from the cemetery at Finglesham, Kent. Jacqueline Simpson in " 'Wendel' and the Long Man of Wilmington", *Folklore* 90 (1979) attempts to relate the supposed earlier version of this massive outline figure both to the Torslunda dies, the embossed plaques on the Sutton Hoo helmet and the Finglesham Man. Her conclusions are in the main based on an 1851 engraving of the figure, done before the "restoration" of 1874, when the figure was outlined in brick. *See* further Bruce-Mitford 1978, especially 203–223, Chadwick-Hawkes *et al.* 1975, and Fennell 1969. For further bolstering of south or west Swedish elements, *see* Speake 1970 and 1980. Bruce-Mitford 1979 has at last extended the points of reference for the East Anglian material beyond a north-eastern Swedish context. In speaking of the helmet found in Öland, the long island off south-east Sweden, which have direct parallels in the decoration of the Sutton Hoo helmet, he states:

> These dies are not stray finds, but come, as we now know, from a settlement site and from a house where there were hearths and certain signs of industrial activity, such as fragments of a crucible.

They seem to show clearly that helmets like those from Sutton Hoo and Vendel were not being manufactured exclusively (if indeed at all) in Uppland, that is, in the territory of the Svear — north of Lake Mälar, where they have mostly been found, but also much further south, in the Baltic, on the island of Öland. It raises the question whether the helmets found in the boat-graves of central Scandinavia, and particularly of the Uppland area, are not perhaps all spoils of war, captured from warriors of the south. Or perhaps the weapons and armour of Svear and Geatas were the same, made by the same itinerant craftsman. This single example underlines the danger of associating the dramatic affinities we see at Sutton Hoo between the archaeological material of East Anglia and that of East Scandinavia, with precise geographical areas or specific tribes, such as the Svear, or the Geats, or any other. The archaeological situation in Sweden is complex (pp. 34-5).

As I pointed out at the beginning of this paper, he clouds the issue by holding that the excessive claims made by Charles Wrenn (Wrenn 1959) for the importance of Sutton Hoo "may in the long run prove justified". Once again, the pattern of over-extension of evidence shows itself, and the broader relations between archaeology and medieval literature are bypassed.

67   For the re-evaluations of the Nydam ship, *see* Akerlund, 1963. For a good discussion of the ships of the Anglo-Saxon period, *see* further Bruce-Mitford, 1975, especially Chapter V, "The Ship". Valerie Fenwick *et al.* (1978) provides a useful survey of Anglo-Saxon vessels and their cognates, and S. McGrail's (1974) account of the Gokstad *faering* is a piece of absorbing interest. A point too often stressed — and strained — is whether or not a particular vessels had sails. Angela Care Evans makes the practical point that "anything that floats can be intelligently wind assisted", and in my own experience a scrap of sail little larger than three by four metres serves to move a 30-foot craft quite nicely through the Gulf of Mexico. Projecting keels and reinforced keelsons are evidence for relatively sophisticated sailing engineering — but one cannot imagine *anyone* choosing to row when any alternative was possible. After all, on the testimony of Caesar (*De Bello Gallico* III, 13 f.), there were sails used by the Veneti in their ships of the first century, which were in many respects stronger and more seaworthy than Roman ships, and which used skins for sails. The Roman vessels of this period certainly had sails.

68   In this context, one must weigh carefully the very first account of a Viking raid in the Anglo-Saxon *Chronicle* for 789. King Beortric's reeve rode up to three ships of Northmen, who promptly killed him. As Professor Sawyer points out (Sawyer 1972, 17-19), there is more to this brief episode than is apparent at first glance. First of all, some manuscripts of the *Chronicle* identify the raiders as from Hörthaland, i.e., a specific locale in south-west Norway. Second, the king's minister died trying to lead the visitors to the king. In the tenth-century *Latin* version of the *Chronicle*, written by Aethelweard, we are told much more about this event. The servant is described as *exactor*, which can mean official in general, but which was the overtone of collector of taxes (*customs* in this case?), and *he rode up to the ships because he thought they carried merchants*. The importance of this commentary can hardly be overstressed; at least one late tenth-century English noble had the notion that when a shipload of foreigners showed up (in this case from Scandinavia) the normal expectation was that they were intent on trade.

69   Hamilton 1956, 3.   70   *Ibid.*, 5.

71   On Man, *see* further D. M. Wilson 1974. Wilson gives evidence for significant inter-influence between Celtic and Scandinavian communities. A later publication (Davey 1978), gives much more detail. In a study of "Norseman and Nature in the Kingdom of the Isles", Basil Megaw concludes: "A true estimate of conditions in Man has to balance substantial evidence of a powerful and persistent Scandinavian element in the ruling circle and the chief landowners against a background of native continuity, presumably with widespread bilingual ability in much of the population" (Davey 1978, 228). Margaret Gelling holds for a more pervasive Norse influence, with "the number of the newcomers relatively high, and the social status of the majority of them relatively low" (*ibid.*, 260). Gillian Fellows-Jensen, in an attempt to accord these views, holds for "a quite considerable Norse settlement on the island", with Man as a "melting pot for Vikings of various national origins, most of whom had a period of evidence in one or more of the other Scandinavian colonies before their arrival in Man". *Ibid.*, 316, 318.

72   On the *Orosius*, *see* further D. Whitlock, "The Prose of Alfred's Reign", in Stanley, especially 89-94. At least one scholar, Charlotte Blindheim, holds that we can find a local habitation for the port of which *Ohthere* told King Alfred. Kaupang, she maintains, is a "port of trade", i.e. as Kare Lunden defines such a place, a "meeting place for foreigners and potentially hostile groups". Mrs. Blindheim holds (Blindheim 1973):

The archaeological evidence indicates that southern Vestfold already possessed considerable economic resources during the Roman Age and the Migration Age, and that in the course of time these resources were concentrated in fewer hands — the Oseberg Find should suffice as an illustration — and as a result, administered and organized trade of the type sketched by Lunden developed, in keeping with events in the North Sea and the Baltic region. To my mind "port of trade" must be the best technical term to describe the trading centre at Kaupang. And thus we have returned to our point of departure, to the term Alfred employed in the *Orosius*: Port.

73   Sawyer 1971, 203–4.

74   *See* further Crocker 1974; for a still more forceful statement on the positive influence of the Vikings, *see* Riché 1976.

75   *See* Herbert Jankuhn, "Die Anfange des stadwesens in Nordeuropa", *Festschrift fur Richard Pittioni* II., ed. Herbert Mitscha-Markhein *et al.* (Wein 1976, 298–321). On very early trade, *see* Vierck 1972, and Bakka 1971.

76   Helgö is perhaps the most exciting of the trading centres. The site was totally unknown until a quarter of a century ago, and even now only a small portion of it has been excavated. Among the amazing finds are an Irish crozier, and an Afghan statue in bronze of the Buddha. Helgo's contact with the outside world began probably in the first century A.D., and a hoard of some 70 coints of fifth and sixth century date has been recovered. *See* further Holmquist 1978; he views this site as a "flourishing Scandinavian oasis in a chaotic Dark Age Europe" (132). This is a forceful view, but smacks somewhat of nationalism and is perhaps excessively dramatic. On the towns elsewhere in Sweden, Denmark, Norway, and Germany, *see* further M. W. Barley, *European Towns: Their Archaeology and Early History* (London and New York, 1977).

77   *See* further Smyth 1975, Cramp 1967, and Radley 1972. On the pre-Viking settlement of Dublin, *see* Clarke 1977. Two settlements (Ath Cliath and Dubblinn) almost certainly came into being before the Vikings arrived.

78   *See* further Delaney 1977, Brooke and Hill 1977, and O'Riordáin 1971.

79   Jankuhn 1976, 298–306.

80   *See* Reynolds 1977, quotation 37. The background and content of Scandinavian influence is set in Chapter 1 and 2. Asbjørn Herteig extends the range of Viking foundations in the British Isles still further:

The Vikings and the Anglo-Saxons each took a part in the creation of such towns as Lincoln, Stamford, Leicester, Derby, and Nottingham, and it is within the bounds of reason that the Vikings had a great deal to say in the creation of Dublin, Waterford, Wexford, Limerick, and Cork.

Herteig 1975, 18.

81   Gelling 1979, Introduction 15.   82   Cameron 1976

83   *See* further Cameron 1971.   84   Nicolaisen 1976, 120.   85   Fellows-Jensen 1968.

86   The names are Sveinn, Haraldr, Tosti, Gyrthr and Gunnhildr, with the OE strain represented in *Leofwine, Eadgyth* and *Ælfgifu*. Godwine was married to Gytha, sister of Jarl Ulfr and aunt of Sveinn Ulfsson of Denmark (Fellows-Jensen 1968, LXIII).

87   O. Jespersen 1955, 83. Jespersen's account of Scandinavian influence is still first-rate.

88   Geipel 1971.

89   The Lindisfarne Gospel book was glossed in the tenth century by Aldred. While the series of glosses — often only truncated forms intended primarily as lexical indicants — can hardly be called a language, a great deal can be learned from such material.

90   Okasha 1971.

91   An example of this conservatism and respect for English is found at Kirkdale, Yorkshire, where Orm, Gamal's son, is reported to have rebuilt St Gregory's church. *See* Okasha 1971, 87–88.

92   *See* further Geipel 1971.

93   On Norman French influence, *see* Baugh and Cable 1979, especially Chapter 5.

94   Lang 1978, 11; *see also* Lang 1979, 145–172. In his excellent *Viking Age Sculpture* (London, 1980) Professor Bailey makes a point about how sculpture functions as one element of the complex yet fruitful relation between church and new dwellers in England of Scandinavian origin. In his view, these carvings "show the adjustment which had been the key to the assimilation and the successful conversion of an earlier wave of Scandinavian settlers" (204).

95   I am greatly indebted to a pre-publication copy of Mr. Morris' "Viking and Native in Northern England: A Case Study", from which I quote. On the hog-back monuments, *see* further James T. Lang,

"Hogbacks in North-Eastern England" (unpublished M.A. thesis, University of Durham, 1967), and Holger Schmidt, "Vikingirnes husformede gravsten", *National museets arbegjdsmark* (1970), 13–28, and "The Trelleborg House Reconsidered", *Med. Arch.*, 17 (1975), 52–77; On the economic importance of hogbacks, *see* Higham 1979. Morris 1976 and 1977 are important corollary studies. One could parallel the Viking influence on sculpture in the other arts without great difficulty.

96   *See* Wilson 1967, 1968, and 1976.

97   Wilson 1976, 399. It must be noted that Dr. Bailey interprets the way in which the Vikings took up sculpture rather differently. First of all Bailey cites evidence to show that "there was very little sculpture around the graveyards of most villages in 876" (p. 81). Such sculpture as there was Bailey contends, was monastic, and therefore esoteric and allusive. The very great increase in sculpture produced in the Viking period shows, in Bailey's view that "stone carving did not just continue into the Viking period but was enthusiastically taken up, both at sites where it had been established previously and at other places where it had not" (*ibid.*).

98   Shepard 1973, 91. On the Scandinavian and English in Byzantium, *see* further Blondal 1978, Ellis-Davidson 1976, and Nicol 1974.

98a   Professor Kevin Kiernan, in a new study (Kiernan 1981), holds that the *Beowulf* MS is "the archetype of the MS as we now have it". His justification of the poem's function in an Anglo-Scandinavian society is surely a plausible one, and deserves serious consideration:

> It is not hard to imagine how Anglo-Saxon poems like *Beowulf* might have emerged during the reign of Cnut the Great, as an aesthetic aftermath of the Danish Conquest. On its most basic level, the subject matter is thoroughly Scandinavian, and the poem begins with a dedicatory salute to the founding of the king's royal Scylding dynasty. Surely Hroðgar, the dominant power in Scandinavia, who received exiles like Hunferð and Ecgþeow; who married a foreign queen —worried about the succession of her sons — and who was honoured by heroes like Beowulf, could have been modeled on the latest Scylding king, Cnut the Great. The Anglo-Saxon poet who created the exploits of Beowulf in Denmark was content to suggest that even the mighty Scyldings, led by a wise and noble king, were not immune to irrational disaster. Cnut could not have been embarrassed by the implication that everything in this life is transitory, or that God rules the universe. (p. 278)

99   *See* "Wann entstand der *Beowulf*? Glossen, Zweifel and Fragen", *Beitrage zur Geschichte der Deutschen Sprache*, xlvv (1917), 347–410.

100   On an eighth-century date, *see* above, (footnote 10).   101   *See* further Girvan 1935.

102   The Christian societies which were swayed by a Christian Irish culture were remarkable in their ability to tolerate ancestors who were not Christian, but who acted well under the Old Law. *See* further Donahue 1948 and 1965.

103   Ellis Davidson 1969, studied the juxtaposition of icons on the casket, and had this to say of the face which had Beaduhild and Mary on it (*see* Plate 00): "The use of the new Christian and classical leaning to present native themes from an heroic past points to a time when the cult of the warrior god was still active in England and flourishing in Scandinavia, while at the same time Christianity had made sufficient impact for its symbols and its teaching to be used with confidence and accuracy". On the Insular tradition, *see* above note.

104   On the East Anglian placement, *see* Rupert Bruce-Mitford 1971; and Bruce-Mitford 1975, especially 683–717.

105   Gwyn Jones (1968), 315, note, gives the following translation of a quotation from *Egil's Saga*, Chapter 50, as the best explication of prime signing. The sign of the cross was made over the pagan in question, and thus cleansed him of evil spirits, and permitted him to attend Mass; as the Saga goes, "This was a common custom of the time among traders and those who went on war-pay along with Christian men; for those who were prime signed held full communion with Christians and heathens too, yet kept to the faith which was most agreeable to them". The conversion of Iceland in the year 1000 was marked by the same kind of open liberalism; the Law Speaker decreed that all Iceland would be officially Christian, but citizens could do what they wished at home.

106   *See* Farrell 1972, especially 37–39.

·107   Stenton 1971, 224. I see Offa's court as a possible place of origin for *Beowulf* on the basis of the international prominence of this very great Mercian ruler; to my mind, the mention of Offa, apparently the ruler of the Continental Angles, is strained a great deal by using it as a basis for a connection of *Beowulf* to the eighth-century Mercian court.

III: THE VIKINGS IN NORTH AMERICA

THE VIKINGS AND NORTH AMERICA

By Gwyn Jones

Professor Emeritus, University of Wales

THE NORSE DISCOVERY and attempted settlement of some part of the North American continent was an event of little practical consequence, for long retentive of its mysteries, and destined to be overtaken by later discoveries of an altogether more bruited and significant kind. Yet for those who made the first landfalls and stay-overs there is fame, and for the peoples that sent them forth an ineffaceable notch cut on the talley-stick of human achievement. No wonder there is no shortage of claimants. The three best-known of them are, as expected, small, gallant, and loquacious westward-facing peoples: the Irish, who have a good claim but bad evidence; the Welsh, who have a bad claim *and* bad evidence; and the Scandinavians, more particularly the Norwegians and the Icelanders, who have a good claim and good evidence.

There may be others. But it was St Brendan, Prince Madoc, and the progeny of Eirik the Red, who, whatever they found or did not find in foreign parts, discovered good publicity men at home, and are therefore the only names that count. Even so, the first two don't count for much. *Írland it mikla* and the *Madogwys* — Ireland the Great and the Welsh-speaking Indians — belong with the wraiths and hallucinations of history. They may distort or foreshadow, as in a glass darkly, but they do not mirror forth, and cannot record.

Which brings us to the Norsemen, and very quickly thereafter to the Viking Movement West-over-Sea, and more particularly to those North Atlantic voyages that resulted in the discovery and lodgement within a Norse orbit of the Faroes, Iceland, Greenland and Vinland-America. Hindsight confers upon this an aura of inevitability, but there had to be the right compulsions at the right time: political strains and economic needs, personal desire and public circumstance. There had to be both means and opportunity: ocean-going ships, manageable climatic conditions, seaways and the seaman's all-embracing art. And there had to be, what for want of a more precise phrase we may call the Spirit of the Age, that "willingness to have a go" which here, there, or somewhere else — Carthage, Normandy, Castile, England, America — drives men to expansion and conquest, to triumphs in the arts and sciences, to fabulous wealth and far-reaching deeds, to fabled shores and the unimaginable parabolas of outer space.

Such an age was the so-called "Viking Age", and some such concatenation of circumstances brought it forth. The term is a flexible one, but we are not much astray in our present context if we apply it to the internal and external history of the Danish, Norwegian, and Swedish peoples during the period 780-1080. Between those dates — and not forgetting to remind ourselves of the Norse (Viking) outpourings east and south-east to the Baltic lands, Russia, the Black Sea and Byzantium, and south and south-west to the British Isles, the Frankish Empire, and the Mediterranean — that sinewy Midgarðr-snake of trade-routes, piracy, and armed endeavour equal to anything wrought out west — with that reminder murmuring in our ear, we may now turn to the story of how the *Insulae Aquilonis*, the Island Countries of the north, brought into the light of history the Island Countries of the west.

The story falls into three sections: first, Norse migration into the Faroes, Iceland and Greenland, which established the pattern that would eventually include America; second, the significance of the Norse settlements in Greenland for Norse contact with the American littoral both north and south of latitude 64° N.; and third, the literary and archaeological evidence for a Norse presence in "Vinland" itself.

I. Faroes, Iceland, and Greenland

The isolated tangle of fjords, tide-rips, fishing-grounds, grazing grounds, fogs and storms known as the Faroes, Faereyjar or Sheep Islands, was the indispensable first stepping-stone in the Norsemen's ocean-leap west. The first Norse settler was a chieftain named Grim Kamban. He was as likely to have gone there by way of Ireland or the Hebrides as from Norway, for remote as they were — and indeed because they *were* remote — they had already been the haunt of Irish religious, or *peregrini*, for almost a hundred years. We have this on the authority of the Irish monk Dicuil, who further tells us in a work written in 823 that the Islands, because of the activities of Norse pirates, were by then once more empty of anchorites though, true to their name, full of innumerable sheep.

Nor is this the only information relevant to our purpose to be found in Dicuil. He mentions *Iceland* under the name *Thule*:

"It is now thirty years since priests (*clerici*) who lived in that island [that is, Thule] from the first day of February to the first day of August told me that not only at the summer solstice, but in the days on either side of it, the setting sun hides itself at the evening hour as if behind a little hill, so that no darkness occurs during that very brief period of time, but whatever task a man wishes to perform, even to picking the lice out of his shirt, he can manage it precisely as in broad daylight. And had they been on a high mountain, the sun would at no time have been hidden from them . . . "

He has other good news, too, for all save north-bound lice. They deal in fallacies, he says, who speak of a six-month day followed by a six-month night. Nor is it as cold there as has been reported — though one day's sailing to the north you *will* find the frozen sea.

So by the year 790 or so Irish hermits in search of solitude had more than a passing acquaintance with this still remoter island-refuge 240 miles north-west of the Faroes. Obviously, where an Irish monk could go a Norse trader or land-hunter could follow. This duly happened, about 860, and might well have happened earlier but for the sharp upsurge of Viking activity in western Europe after 830, with its creaming-off of acquisitive venturers on the plunder-routes south and south-west.

This is what the "Father of Icelandic History", Ari Thorgilsson, in his *Íslendingabók* or "Book of the Icelanders", has to tell us about the first settler, the revered Ingolf Arnarsson. Ari was writing in the 1120s.

"A Norwegian named Ingolf is the man of whom it is reliably reported that he was the first to leave Norway for Iceland, when Harald Fairhair was sixteen years old, and a second time a few years later. He settled south in Reykjavik. The place is called Ingolfshofdi . . . where he made his first landing, and Ingolfsfjall west of Olfus river, where he afterwards took land into his possession".

This dry and bony statement is elsewhere much fleshed out with entertaining but all-too-familiar motifs of folktale, saga, and romance: three wandering mariners, three voyages, three ravens, three land-namings, love-vows and slayings, supernatural intrusions, onomastic invention, even a tribute to the land's benignity and butter-laden grass — a circumstance highly relevant to the discovery of Vinland-America in its turn. But for the moment we are not looking that far ahead, and there is more to say of Iceland. The settlement, once started, proceeded apace, and by the year 930, we are informed, all the habitable land had been taken. For all the talk of Icelandic democracy, it was taken, very properly — for how else?— by men of rank or family, supported by their kinsmen, followers and slaves. And what they took they aimed to keep. The compulsions which brought them from their estates, holdings, even territories in Scandinavia, Ireland, and the Hebrides, were the familiar ones: expulsion by a hornier hand, land shortage, provision for their children, grazing for their stock, restlessness, ambition or emulation, prospects of trade and hopes of easy pickings. It must have helped, too, that the decades either side of the year 900 were propitious to colonization. Hammered in Brittany and France, pounded in Wessex and Mercia, thrown out of Dublin, Anglesey and the Hebrides, bereft of their leaders in Scotland and Orkney, many a riever and robber would be glad to set sail for the butter-laden grass, the unculled hunting-grounds and fishing-banks rumoured, and with reason, to be for the taking "up there".

Icelandic tradition in the saga-centuries made great play with the notion that the mostest and bestest of settlers came out to escape the tyranny and constraints of the kings of Norway; and while this is far from being the whole truth, certainly the five generations from Ingolf to the end of the Söguöld or Saga-Age in 1030 were rich in men of resource, creative intelligence, and high endeavour. They explored and made the most of their sundered and barricaded new-found land, made poetry first and prose-narrative later a common pursuit and national industry, practised litigation and the blood-feud with almost equal zest, threw out Red Thor and brought in White Christ, and at much the same time colonized those parts of Greenland from which the American voyages would in turn be mounted. And not least — and not least surprising, in respect of the Norse expansion west — they stayed the course, and are still there.

Like the Faroes, Iceland when the first settlers rounded its alien headlands and nosed their creaking ships into tricky estuaries — Iceland too was empty of human inhabitants, save for a few Irish solitaries in the south-east and south-west. They found no one and nothing to subdue, save the land itself and the hither-and-thithering streams of ocean which at once kept them in touch with the known world they had left, and before the Saga-Age was out would put them in touch with Greenland and the eastern littoral of the North American continent.

This would be the place, had we room for it, to say something adequate about the Norse sea-going ship, the *hafskip*, or ship of burden, the *knörr*, without which the Atlantic voyages could not have taken place: about the North Atlantic itself and the problems it posed for such ships and the men who sailed them; and about those men, their skills, arts, and aids to navigation. But that would be a subject of its own. The Viking-sea-going ship was the most famed traverser of oceans and unlocker of distant lands known till that day — and I am not for one moment forgetting or belittling the craft that bore Carthaginian Hanno and his monkey-skins south to Sierra Leone, or carried Pytheas the Massalot north past Britain to the coagulate northern sea. It was probably towards the middle of the eighth century that Scandinavian shipwrights and ships' captains brought what we may call the Norse ship-of-all-work into existence. Fifty years later they had produced not only a gallery of longships and warships, but more important to our present purpose, vessels after the fashion of the Gokstad ship in Norway and Wrecks 1 and 3 from Skuldelev-Peberrenden in the Roskilde Fjord in Denmark, which could operate outside coastal waters, and as a sailing-ship with auxiliary oars carry men, animals, and goods of every description from Norway and Denmark to such havens and marts as awaited them around the North Sea, Baltic and Mediterranean, and over the stormy wastes of the North Atlantic to colonies and new homelands in the west.

The discovery, exploration, and settlement of Greenland, like the discovery and settlement of Iceland, presents the familiar picture of a rich embroidery of fiction over a spare fabric of fact. Both fiction and fact are attached to a man named Eirik the Red, from the favoured fields of Jaeren in south-west Norway. As with Iceland, the first sighting was accidental: the exploit of yet another storm-driven mariner, Gunnbjorn by name, who lived to tell the tale. But the credit of deliberately setting out for, finding, exploring, and making the first European settlement in Greenland is by the universal ascription of early Norse history and saga granted to Eirik. This is what Ari Thorgilsson has to say of him in his turn — that Ari who likewise told of the settlement of Iceland:

"The land which is called Greenland was discovered and settled from Iceland. Eirik the Red was the name of a Breidarfjord man who went out there from here and took land in settlement at the place which has ever since been called Eiriksford. He gave the land a name, and called it Greenland, arguing that men would be drawn to go there if the land had a good name. Both east and west in the country [that is, at both the Eastern and Western Settlement] they found the habitations of men, fragments of boats, and stone artefacts, from which it may be seen that the same kind of people had passed that way as those that inhabited Vinland, whom the Greenlanders call Skraelings. When he began to settle the land, that was fourteen or fifteen years before Christianity was introduced into Iceland [which means 985 or 986]."

This is our first glimpse of Vinland, but our tale yet awhile is of Greenland. The account of Eirik in his own saga, *Eiríks saga Rauða*, is altogether more elaborate, and we can safely take most of its detail with three pinches of salt. Eirik took part in three lots of manslayings, which had him turned out of three successive homes in Norway and Iceland. He was banished for three years, had three sons, explored south-western Greenland for three years, and by his land-taking at Brattahlid in Eiriksfjord (the modern Tunugdliarfik), his good luck and leadership, and the patriarchal authority that accrued to him with time, he became the Grand Old Man of Greenland. That his story is encrusted with legend need not detain us on our quest for Vinland. The thing to do is to keep our ear alert for error, and our eye open upon likelihood and impossibility. Early Norse historians are as unreliable as early historians everywhere, and the saga-writers were as free as historical novelists the world over to invent, adapt, reshape and recolour. Early Greenland sources tell of natives of cerulean hue, or 23 feet tall, or nearby virgins who grow pregnant by drinking water; but they tell, too, of calving glaciers, the glittering ice-cap, and the peril of icebergs to ships. The whale of error must never distract our attention from the minnow of truth.

Indeed, even the most sceptical modern critics of the literary sources do not question the basic facts that Greenland was first opened up to European settlement in the 980s, that against all apparent odds the settlement prospered, and that the two major areas of settlement were Eystribyggd, the Eastern Settlement, in the neighbourhood of today's Julianehaab, and Vestribyggd, the Western Settlement, in the general area of today's Godthaab — both of them, that is, despite their names, lodged on the south-west coast of the country. Eventually, it is estimated, there would be some three to four thousand Europeans resident there.

They sound very few for so huge and hostile an environment. But for a while things went not too badly. As the thirteenth century *King's Mirror* informs us — and as we can safely deduce and confirm for ourselves — the newcomers quickly occupied "the little strip along the water's edge", as attractive then as it is today. The same authority describes how they climbed the highest mountains in various places, and looked around for areas free of ice, but found none. What they did find were hunting grounds in the north, driftwood, sea-mammals, fish in every water, bear and fox for furs, caribou for hides, birds for down, narwhal for sea-ivory, falcons for the kings of Europe and princes of Arabia. They established a viable trade with Norway, fostered woollens, were soon converted to Christianity and allowed to pay tithes and in 1261 surrendered their independence to Norway and were permitted to pay taxes. What more could a colony ask for?

Eventually the answer would be, for continuance, an assured economy, for security in the face of a worsening climate, the encroaching Eskimo, the decline of Norwegian sea-power and eclipse of Greenland trade, the failure to adapt to circumstance and recognize the priorities, and the increasing forgetfulness and neglect shown by the Scandinavian homelands and the Hansa. In short, for survival, for existence itself. For Greenland was fated to fall out of sight, and the Greenlanders disappear: the Western Settlement by the middle of the fourteenth century, when the Norwegian cleric and official Ivar Bardarson would report that "the Skraelings hold the entire Western Settlement"; and the Eastern Settlement by about 1500. The process was dismal and prolonged, and such details as we have are macabre. As the stars in their courses fought against Sisera, so the revolving centuries fought against the Norsemen in Greenland. The decline and extinction of the Settlements is considered by Scandinavian historians to be the most sombre episode in the entire record of European colonization overseas.

II. *Norsemen and Skraelings in Greenland and Canada*

The voyages to the Faroes, Iceland, Greenland, and Vinland-America associated with the names of Grim Kamban, Ingolf, Eirik the Red, Leif Eiriksson and Thorfinn Karlsefni, all took place at a time when the northern lands and seas were enjoying a comparatively favourable climate, much like today's. During the years 800 to 1100 particularly so — but after 1200 it was growing colder, and would go on to grow very cold indeed. The evidence is plentiful, has been often rehearsed and much debated, but the conclusion stands. With the cold came the Eskimo. The Eskimos (Inuit) or Skraelings mentioned by Ari we assume to have been Eskimos of the Dorset Culture, who had vanished from south-west Greenland well before the Norsemen's arrival. But the Eskimos who now proceeded to infiltrate western Greenland were people of the Thule Culture, who had made their way across northern Canada from Alaska, and from Ellesmere Island entered the Thule area of Greenland sometime before 1200. As the Inugsuk folk they would take over the habitable strip of the western coast and, though this is not to our purpose now, some went round the top of Greenland and spread far down the east coast, too.

These two related circumstances, a colder climate after the year 1200, and the resultant struggle for the land's yield and substance between Norsemen and Eskimo, need to be emphasized because they bear closely on one area of guarded supposition and two ardent speculation in the "Matter of America".[1] But before broaching these let me first, invoking no authorities or recondite knowledge, express the opinion that the settlement of Iceland made the eventual discovery of Greenland certain; and in its turn the settlement of south-west Greenland made the discovery of the fronting coasts of North America certain. The Vinland voyages were not an isolated phenomenon, but the last, the most striking to the imagination, though on the whole the least durable or consequential of the Viking voyages west. The written documents which tell of them are not freakish and suspicious survivals existing in a vacuum: they are exactly what we should expect to find among the plenitude of documents in many languages which tell of Viking progress in the ninth and tenth centuries by land and sea and river, north, south, east, as well as west. To me it would be inexplicable if the Norsemen had not reached North America, and unthinkable that there should be no written records of the event.

Certain of these records — I am thinking particularly of the two sagas known to us all, *The Greenlanders' Saga* and *Eirik the Red's Saga*—are common to the story of Greenland and North America. Thus, all known voyages meant for the American continent were mounted in south-west Greenland, and the sons and relations of Eirik the Red dominated the Vinland as they did the Greenland scene. The sections of those sagas which tell of the Greenland voyages and those which tell of the American are similar in substance, nature, quality and tone — in short, they are all of a piece. Believe in the one and you have to believe in the other. The one significant difference is that the account of the Greenland settlement, for all its imperfections (and they are many) is visibly confirmed by the extensive Norse archaeological remains there — well over four hundred Norse buildings of different kinds have been excavated so far — whereas the story of Norse remains in North America — Newport Tower, Kensington Stone, Beardmore Find, Vinland Map, *et al.* — has been till very recently a story of deception or error which it would be as idle to rehearse as yet again to refute. Instead, to continue with my expressed opinion of a page or so back, once the Norsemen had plotted their homes and shared out pasture in the grassy areas of south-west Greenland, and were in process of exploring and exploiting their new surroundings, they would quickly feel assured that out west lay *something*. From their own mountain tops, from ventures out to sea, from all their lore of sea and sky and birds and fish and sea-mammals, from their experience of refraction and maybe of mirage, even from their vague yet indicative mythological world-picture, they would guess at the presence of yet more land to the west, and nothing would stop them going to investigate it.

It may therefore be reasonably assumed that the Norse settlers in Greenland soon acquired a degree of acquaintance with the islands and peninsulas of Arctic Canada. They had ships, resolution, land-hunger, and an urgent need to make a living by exploiting each and every natural resource within their reach. Some have argued that the Norsemen were almost immediately *au fait* with the Hudson Bay area, with Baffin,

Devon, and Ellesmere islands, and their intricate network of waterways. But unless the documents are interpreted with determined ingenuity they yield no trace of it. That the Greenlanders moved up their own coast as far as Disco and Upernavik, and once to Melville Bay, we know — but the full process took time. That they crossed the water and proceeded south by way of Labrador is our imminent theme — and it happened quickly. What happened in addition is unclear. As hunters, fishers, and garnerers of all good things, the Norsemen must have made many unrecorded but vaguely traceable, or at least deducible, voyages over a period of three or four hundred years, not only to regions in the general latitude of the two Greenland colonies, c.58–64° N., but farther north (of which two cairns discovered in Jones Sound 76° 35′ N., and two more on Washington Irving Island 79° N., may be the visible proof), and why not farther south (where we shall seek to follow them later)? They must at times have wintered away from home, doubtless at regularly frequented bases, and surely in moderate numbers; but that their journeyings were inconclusive in terms of settlement seems all too clear.

It was Jón Dúason's thesis, as prescribed in his huge *Landkönnun og Landnám Íslendinga í Vesturheim, "Exploration and Settlements of the Icelanders in the Western Hemisphere"* (Reykjavik, 1941–48) — cold-shouldered by his compatriots, but espoused by the Canadian Tryggve Oleson in his official history, *Early Voyages and Northern Approaches*, 1963 — that quite a number of Norsemen from Greenland went over to an Eskimo way of life in both Canada and Greenland, and that by intermixture with the Dorset people whom they found there became the ancestors of a new race, the Thule Eskimo, who eventually took over the whole of Greenland from the white man. Thus they see three Norse or part-Norse entries into Arctic Canada. The first was by way of Norse voyages of exploration and exploitation — something we have just discussed. The second was by way of a racial blending of Norse (Viking) hunters and trappers with the Dorset Eskimo, which produced the Thule people. The third was when the Thule people made life so difficult for the remaining white men in Greenland that they threw in their lot with the Thule Eskimo and departed across the Davis Strait into Baffin Island and became part, a fast-diminishing part, of the bloodstream of the inhabitants there before the next wave of European voyages and acquisition.

My comments on this are as follows. First, there is a wealth of probability and a few pieces of evidence for Norse voyages there. Second: archaeologists, anthropologists, and Arctic prehistorians will have nothing to do with the Dúason-Oleson theories of the origin of the Thule Eskimo and the subsequent movements of that people. There is one piece of literary-historical evidence, the well-known entry for 1342 in the Icelandic annals of Bishop Gisli Oddsson, written in Latin as late as c. 1637, but generally held to be based on documents destroyed in the fire at Skalholt in 1630. The bishop writes: "The inhabitants of Greenland of their own will abandoned the true faith and the Christian religion, having already forsaken all good ways and true virtues, and went over to the peoples of America (*ad Americae populos se converterunt*)". About this one can only say that the inhabitants of Greenland did *not* abandon the Christian religion — though their Christian bishops did abandon the inhabitants of Greenland — and that we simply do not know what the bishop meant by "the peoples of America". I think that like Ari Thorgilsson before him he meant Skraelings in general, that is, the native population of Greenland and America, and not of America alone. Otherwise there is nothing in

Scandinavian written sources that lends unambiguous support to the Dúason–Oleson theory, and there is much that contradicts it.

Again, from everything we know of the Scandinavians in Iceland and Greenland, they were uncompromisingly tenacious of their family genealogies and their status as Europeans. (We are not, of course, here talking about white hunters and sailors attaching themselves to native women, wherever found.) Also it would require the most compelling and incontrovertible evidence to make one believe that within a period of two centuries a fair proportion of Norse Greenlanders could depart the settlements, produce a hybrid race, and that this race could subsequently inherit the colonies of the fellow-countrymen of these same Norse Greenlanders, with apparently no one on either side aware of their blood-tie and family relationship. But as a reference to the literature of the subject shows, the evidence, whether archaeological, anthropological or linguistic, far from being incontrovertible, has been and still is the subject of keen debate and sharp division.

Finally, a number of Thule Eskimo folktales contain references to a mysterious people called the Tunit, or Tornit. Dúason–Oleson think these were the Norsemen, but just about everybody else thinks they were the Dorset Eskimos. Neither a Norse–Dorset nor a Norse–Thule miscegenation has established itself as an explanation of all such highly debatable phenomena as long or rectangular houses, bear-traps, cairns, nails and knives, fragments of cloth, wood or iron, eider-duck shelters, suspected correspondences of vocabulary, tall or blond or bearded Eskimos, whenever and wherever encountered in the Canadian Arctic. A vestige may be found, but a presence cannot be proved. Thus the claims first made in the 1960s and thereafter pressed with vigour by Thomas Lee for a Norse or part-Norse settlement or settlements in the Ungava Bay region of North Quebec have suffered an accelerating erosion. There are recent reports of small finds made since 1978 of Norse material (including cloth and chain mail sections) on Ellesmere Island 79° N., reinforcing the discovery of earlier fragments in the same general area. They are of the period A.D. 1190-1280-1310-1520, but at present even though their Norse nature is accepted it is not possible to say whether their presence on Ellesmere Island is attributable to trade between Inuit (Eskimo) groups in Greenland and Canada or between the Inuit and Norsemen.[2] In the present state of knowledge the mildest verdict possible upon the Dúason-Oleson thesis is "Non-proven".

III. Vínland ìt goða: Wineland the Good

And so at last our series of inconclusions and non-conclusions has brought us to the heart of the "Matter of America", i.e., the first chronicled European, which means Norse, acquaintance with those identifiable areas south of latitude 64° N., which I shall forthwith and summarily christen southern Baffin Island, Labrador, and northern Newfoundland. The evidence, until the last decade or so, has been almost entirely documentary, some of it of doubtful provenance, almost always circumstantial, and often merely allusive — and so a happy hunting-ground for scholars, explorers real and armchair, romancers, popularizers, ignorami, and other assorted seekers after truth or illusion.

It all began with that somewhat slippery ecclesiastical historian, Adam of Bremen, who, in his *Descriptio insularum aquilonis* or "Description of the Island Countries of the North", which forms the fourth book of his *Gesta Hammaburgensis ecclesiae pontificum*, of *c*. 1075, tells us he derived his information about Vinland, which we consider to be somewhere in North America, from Svein Estridsson, king of the Danes, who died in 1706.

> "He told me of yet another island, discovered by many in that ocean, which is called Wineland from the circumstance that vines grow there of their own accord, and produce the most excellent wine. While that there is abundance of unsown corn there we have learned not from fabulous conjecture, but from the trustworthy report of the Danes. . . . "

It doesn't sound all that trustworthy, but we can throw the adjective away, and the wine and corn after it, and still believe with Adam that a living king of the Danes believed in the eleventh century that there was a place called Wineland–Vinland. We have heard earlier the no-less-famous passage from Ari's "Book of the Icelanders" of *c*. 1122, with its reference to the Skraelings of Greenland and the inhabitants of Vinland. There is also the so-called *Geographical Treatise* in Arnamagnaean MS 194, written down in 1387 in the west of Iceland, but containing a section attributable to the twelfth century, which says: "To the south of Greenland lies Helluland, and then Markland, and from there it is not far to Vinland, which some people consider extends from Africa". This and its relationship to the Resen-Vigfusson cartographical evidence of the late sixteenth century (which is late, but honestly late), has been argued up hill and down dale, but apart from the reference to Africa (which can be fitted without violence into an Icelandic twelfth century word-picture), it is more or less true and approximately accurate — high praise, indeed, among Vinland sources — and antedates Columbus by a very wide margin.

And so we come to the all-important Icelandic narrative sources, and specifically to the two sagas which tell of the first voyages to Vinland a decade or two either side of the year A.D. 1000, and the two entries in the Icelandic Annals which afford us a tantalising glimpse of continued but enfeebled Norse contacts there.

The two sagas are *Groenlendinga Saga*, "The Greenlanders' Saga" (*c*. 1200), and *Eiriks Saga Rauða*, "Eirik the Red's Saga" (*c*. 1265). It would take the Yankee Stadium to house the libraries of disputation and conjecture written about them; and we can straightway admit that they are unsatisfactory as source material for the voyages of *c*. A.D. 1000, whether taken together or considered apart. For a start they weren't written down for at least two hundred years after the events they describe. But they are what we have and until a few years ago they were all we had. They are prodigal of unlikelihoods and impossibilities, contradictions and inventions. Among other oddities they retail biblical legend, Germanic folklore, and classical fable, and offer them all as truth, from Horace's *Insulae Fortunatae* to Isidore of Seville's uniped, from Thor's mixed blessing of a whale to Thorvald Eiriksson's (which were likewise the Icelander Thormod Coalbrow's Poet's) famous last words. And yet — greatest marvel of all — these sagas indubitably contain information about how ships sailed on a traceable course from Eiriksfjord in Greenland, north, west, then south, to northern Newfoundland, and maybe farther south — certainly to what we now call North America, and certainly centuries before the voyages of Columbus. When scepticism has done its best, and blind belief its worst, something of fact and rather more of tradition remains to direct us to persons, who are expendable, and localities, which are not.

Both the popular and the learned mind have now come to cohere on the likeliest course of events. Like Iceland, like Greenland, the new land was first sighted by a storm-swept mariner who lived to tell the tale. His name is given as Bjarni Herjolfsson. Several voyages of exploration and attempted settlement followed. Saga tradition ascribes the glory of the white man's first landing to Leif Eiriksson, and the honour of the first attempted settlement to the Icelander Thorfinn Karlsefni.

Leif, we are told by *The Greenlanders' Saga* (and I choose that here in preference to the deforming errors of *Eirík's Saga*), made a carefully planned voyage in the light of what Bjarni had to tell him, and put ashore in three identifiable areas: in a place he named Helluland (Flatstone Land), which most students agree is the southern portion of Baffin Island; in Markland (Wood Land, Forest Land), generally held to be Labrador south of the medieval tree-line (south of Nain, if you like); and finally in Vinland (Wine-land, *Vinland*, without question to the medieval world, though some modern rationalists have come to prefer Grassland, *Vinland*), a region whose northern extremity can reasonably be equated with the northern extremity of Newfoundland, but whose southern extension is a matter of unending argument based for the most part on next to nothing. Leif spent a winter in Vinland at a place where night and day were of a more even length than in Iceland or Greenland. On the shortest day of winter the sun was visible above the horizon from about nine in the morning until three in the afternoon. This place he named Leifsbúðir, Leif's Booths. The following summer he returned to Greenland, full of Vinland's praises, its mild winter, grass and grapes, its timber and salmon, the presence of sweet dew and absence of human beings.

A few years later the Icelander Thorfinn Karlsefni led an expedition to Vinland, either to Leifsbúðir (*Greenlanders' Saga*) or to places *Eiríks Saga Rauða* calls Straum(s)fjördr (Stream Fjord) and Hóp (which means a landlocked tidal bay). Once again an identification with the Belle Isle area of northern Newfoundland seems unavoidable, while our recognition of places like Cape Porcupine and the Strand on the Labrador coast grows more compelling. He took not only his men, but some of their wives, together with livestock, and settled in for two or three winters. They met, traded with, and eventually fought with the natives or Skraelings, and were forced to withdraw. Thorfinn's son Snorri was the first named person of European descent reported to be born on the American continent – that same Snorri who was the great-grandfather of Bishop Brand Saemundarson of Hólar in Iceland from 1163 till his death in 1201.

There are other voyages recorded in the Vinland Sagas. Another son of Eirik the Red, Thorvald, is reported to have met his death by an Indian arrow in the Hamilton Inlet–Lake Melville area of Labrador, where in true white-man fashion he had laid violent hands on the first natives he encountered. An Indian arrow-head found by Aage Roussell at Sandnes in the Western Settlement is one of the very few pre-Columbian links between Greenland and Vinland, though William Fitzhugh's team of searchers in the Hamilton Inlet and English River area (reports in the *Bulletin of the Canadian Archaeological Association*, 4 (1972) and 5 (1973)) found no evidence of Thorvald's journeyings or resting-place in that region "now heavily grown over with spruce with a thick forest floor of moss, birch, and alders" – a salutary reminder of the problems facing the seeker after genuine Norse remains.[3] Yet another son of Eirik, Thorstein, attempted a voyage, met with bad weather, was blown all over the ocean, and did not so much as set eyes on America. In the last recorded voyage, that of Eirik's in all ways dubious daughter Freydis, it is hard to place any credence whatsoever. This series of voyages was at an end by *c.* 1020.

There would be other voyages, a substantial number unchronicled and therefore unknown — and just two of which we are offered a brief but evocative mention. Two sets of Icelandic Annals for the year 1121 record that Bishop Eirik of Greenland went in search of Vinland, which is usually interpreted to mean that he sought to establish whether there were any Christians surviving there, and found there were not. Then in 1347 another two sets of Annals inform us, the first that "There came a ship from Greenland, smaller in size than the small Icelandic boats; she came into the outer Straumfjord on Snaefellsnes, and had no anchor. They had made a voyage to Markland (Labrador), but were afterwards storm-driven here". And the second that "At this time (1347) came a ship from Greenland, which had made a voyage to Markland, and had eighteen men on board". After that, from the ancient sources there is nothing.

Except, of course, their cherished directives, whose persistence in the human memory has helped produce the later saga of the men who during the last 70 years have done so much to determine the course and nature of the Vinland voyages and identify certain Norse place-names and places. It is a story that reaches back to such great names as Nansen, and beyond him Reeves, and beyond him Rafn, but inasmuch as our best hopes are now directed to L'Anse aux Meadows in northern Newfoundland, which we increasingly tend to see as the ancient Promontorium.

As for *Winlandiae*, it would seem ungrateful not to mention, however briefly, the names of four men: the Canadian Captain Munn, with his *Wineland Voyages* of 1914; the Finn Vaïno Tanner, with his *De gamla nordbornas, Helluland, Markland, och Vinland* of 1941, and his magisterial survey of the geography of Newfoundland–Labrador three years later; the Dane Jørgen Meldgaard, whose researches on the ground in the appropriate areas were recorded in *Fra Brattahlid til Vinland* in 1961; and finally the indefatigable Norwegian traveller and explorer Helge Ingstad, who has devoted 20 years of his life to the search for indisputable Norse remains over thousands of miles of the Canadian and American coast-lines, and with the help of the sagas and the assistance of his wife, Anne Stine Ingstad, has, we think, found them.[4]

This does not mean that we have necessarily found Leifsbúðir,Straum(s)fjörðr or Hóp. It is altogether more likely that we have not. But the Ingstads, overtaking and improving on the inquiries of their predecessors, have now not only identified a site of Norse habitation, but have excavated it, so that some eight or nine house-sites, with hearths, cooking pits, a smithy, bog iron, a ring-headed bronze pin and a single soap-stone spindle-whorl have come to light, some of which appear to be quite certainly Norse and if not of the central date A.D. 1000 unarguably within the overall period of Norse activity in Vinland. The artefacts are few and not impressive; there are no human skeletons and no weapons, no conclusive evidence of farming or husbandry, not even a Christian cross; but the whole complex has undergone critical scrutiny by Scandinavian, Canadian and American archaeologists and workers in the ancillary disciplines, Eskimo and Indian as well as Norse, and is by now just about universally accepted as authentic. The full claim and evidence are presented by Anne Stine Ingstad in *The Discovery of a Norse Settlement in America* (Oslo 1978).[5]

Such an identification of Norse occupation, however sparse or disjointed, in a saga-signposted area of the *Promontorium Winlandiae* in medieval times has at present an importance far beyond any hoped-for identification with a dwelling-site such as those attributed by the sagas to Leif Eiriksson or Thorfinn Karlsefni. It has been clear for a good while that the written records have nothing more to offer, the pen must yield to the spade, and only an authenticated archaeological find can advance our long-drawn-out state of high likelihood to full assurance. This seems now to have come about, and L'Anse aux Meadows encourages us to go on looking southwards for evidence of a medieval Norse presence in more genially habitable areas.

But whether our search prospers or not, the Norseman, the Viking, is now firmly established as the discoverer and first European explorer of North America. His arrival there was brought about by the cross-play of accident and design, and hindsight, as we said earlier, confers upon it the aura of inevitability. And yet his stay made so shallow a scratch, so faint a colouration on the surface of American history that it has taken almost a thousand years to find it; and maybe the most lasting consequence of his sojourn was the begetting of the begetter, three times removed, of a twelfth-century Icelandic bishop. As so often, the Vikings failed to clinch their undertaking. The unexpected presence of a hostile population, both Indian and Eskimo, the colonists' lack of manpower and a dominant weaponry, their long and chancy lines of communication, the fated recession of Norse sea-power, the increase of ice in northern waters, the decline and extinction of their springboard, base, and refuge in Greenland — these would prove fatal to the Vinland venture.

And yet it was a northern battle-honour, and they that wrought it "on Time's eternal bede-roll worthy to be filed". Equally satisfying to today's observer, it provides an aesthetic culmination to the Norseman's North Atlantic Saga. And yet it is hard to see the Vinland adventure as one of the wondrous might-have-beens of history. For the best Norse contribution to the United States and Canada had to wait on the Norse second coming, on those men and women who bear in their veins the blood of their Scandinavian ancestors, and in their hearts the warm sensation of their Scandinavian origin — but who, unlike their forebears of a millennium since, belong not with a remote and tenuous area of the American past but with the American present and the promise of its future. For a loquacious and westward-facing kinsman of the nowhere-ever Prince Madoc and the never-never Welsh-speaking Indians, it is a great privilege to congratulate all such on their past and present fortune and distinction.

NOTES

1   I have discussed all three on many occasions during the past fifteen years, and am grateful to the editors and owners of copyright who have permitted me to reproduce or adapt earlier words of mine to this new occasion. They are, in particular, the Oxford University Press, *The Beaver*, *The Geographical Magazine*, the Smithsonian Institution and Newberry Library, and the *Dictionary of American History*.

2   *See* Schledermann 1980. I am much indebted to Mr. Schlederman for supplying the Cornell Symposium on "The Vikings in North America" (October 23, 1980), with a proof of his then unpublished article, "Eskimo and Viking Finds in the high Arctic" *National Geographic*, 1981.

3   For a detailed summary of the present state of knowledge respecting the Norsemen in North America the reader cannot do better than consult Plumet 1978, and R. McGhee, "Norsemen and Eskimos in Arctic Canada" in *Vikings in the West*, ed. Guralnick, Chicago, 1982. *See also* Roussell 1972; Fitzhugh 19

4   Munn 1919; Tanner 1941; Meldgaard 1961; Ingstad 1978.

5   Ingstad 1978.

NORSEMEN IN AMERICA

A Select Bibliography, 1950-1980

Compiled by Louis A. Pitschmann

Cornell University Libraries

Adam, Paul, "Il n'y a pas de Mystère du Vinland". *Inter-Nord*, IX, 239-56.

Anderson, John Richard, *Vinland Voyage*. London: Eyre & Spottiswoode; New York: Funk & Wagnalls, 1967.

Anderson, W. R., "Norsemen in Medieval America: An Appraisal of the Evidence". *Inland Seas*, XXXIV, 190-99.

Berg, Henry, "Vinland og tidevannet". *Det Kongelige Norske Videnskabers Selskab Museet, Årbok for 1955*. Trondheim, 45-65.

Bird, Junius B., "Conservation Work at the L'Anse aux Meadow, Newfoundland, Archaeological Site". *National Geographic Society Research Reports . . . 1964*. Washington: National Geographic Society, 1969, 21-25.

Blegen, Theodore C., *The Kensington Rune Stone: New Light on an Old Riddle*. With a Bibliography by Michael Brook. St Paul: The Minnesota Historical Society, 1968.

Breckenridge, R. W., "Norse Halberds". *American Anthropologist*, LVII, 129-31.

Brøndsted, Johannes, "Norsemen in North America before Columbus". *Smithsonian Institution Annual Report for the Year Ended June 30, 1953*, 367-405.

——, "Problemet om Nordboer i Nordamerika før Columbus: En Bedømmelse af de Amerikanske Materiale. Med Bidrag af Karl Martin Nielsen og Erik Moltke". *Aarbøger for Nordisk Oldkyndighed og Historie*, 1950, 1-152.

Carpenter, Edmund, "Further Evidence on the Beardmore Relics". *American Anthropologist*, LIX, 875-78.

Collins, Henry B., "The L'Anse aux Meadows Archaeological Site in Northern Newfoundland". *National Geographic Society Research Reports . . . 1961-1962*. Washington: National Geographic Society, 1970, 39-49.

Erik den Rødes Saga: Med en Indledning om Nordboernes opdagelse af Vinland af Einar Storgaard. Copenhagen: Foreningen "Fremtiden", 1961.

Enterline, James Robert, *Viking America: The Norse Crossings and Their Legacy*. Garden City: Doubleday, 1972.

Foote, Peter G., "The Vinland Map, II: On the Vinland Legends on the Vinland Map". *Saga Book of the Viking Society*, XVII, Pt. 1, 73-89.

Gini, Corrado, *The Location of Vinland*. Institute of Economics, Norwegian School of Economics and Business Administration, Bergen, Norway. Papers, No. 13. Bergen, 1960.

Godfrey, William S., "The Archaeology of the Old Stone Mill in Newport, Rhode Island". *American Antiquity*, XVII, 120–29.

—, *Digging a Tower and Laying a Ghost: The Archaeology and Controversial History of the Newport Tower.* Thesis (Ph.D.), Harvard University, 1952.

—, "The Newport Puzzle". *Archaeology*, II, 146–49.

—, "The Newport Tower: A Reply to Mr. Pohl". *Archaeology*, IV, 54–55.

—, "The Newport Tower, II". *Archaeology*, III, 82–86.

—, "Vikings in America: Theories and Evidence". *American Anthropologist*, LVII, 35–43.

Hagen, S. N., "The Kensington Runic Inscription". *Speculum*, XXV, 321–56.

Haugen, Einar, "Bishop Eric and the Vinland Map". *Proceedings of the Vinland Map Conference.* Chicago: The University of Chicago Press, 1971, 137–44.

Haward, Peter J., *High Latitude Crossing: The Viking Route to America.* London: Coles, 1968.

Huntington, E. G., "An Historical Basis for Vinland". *Bulletin of the Massachusetts Archaeological Society*, XVIII, 61–63.

Ingstad, Anne Stine, *Excavations at L'Anse aux Meadows, Newfoundland 1961–1968.* The Discovery of a Norse Settlement in America, Vol. I. Oslo: Universitetsforlaget, 1977.

—, "The Norse Settlement at L'Anse aux Meadows, Newfoundland: A Preliminary Report from the Excavations 1961–68". *Acta Archaeologica*, XLI, 109–54.

—, *Det Nye Land med de Grønne Enger.* Oslo: Gyldendal Norsk Forlag, 1975.

Ingstad, Helge, "Archaeological Expedition to the Norse Sites at L'Anse au Meadow, Northern Newfoundland". *National Geographic Society Research Reports . . . 1963.* Washington: National Geographic Society, 1968, 145–49.

—, *Fridtjof Nansen and Vinland Research.* Fridtjof Nansen Minneforelesninger, XIV. Oslo: Universitetsforlaget, 1978.

—, "Vinland Ruins Prove Vikings Found the New World". *National Geographic Magazine*, CXXVI, 708–34.

—, *Vesterveg til Vinland: Oppdagelsen av Norrøne Boplasser i Nord-Amerika.* Oslo: Gyldendal, 1965.

—, *Westward to Vinland: The Discovery of pre-Columbian Norse House-Sites in North America.* Translated from the Norwegian by Erik J. Friis. London: Cape; New York: St. Martin's Press, 1969.

Jensen, Arthur, "The Norsemen in Vinland". *Anthropological Journal of Canada*, III, No. 2, 14–16.

Johansen, Margaret, *Voyagers West.* Illustrated by William Ferguson. New York: I. Washburn, 1959.

Jones, Gwyn, *The Norse Atlantic Saga: Being the Norse Voyages of Discovery and Settlement to Iceland, Greenland, America.* London, New York: Oxford University Press, 1964.

—, "Western Voyages and the Vinland Map". *Proceedings of the Vinland Map Conference.* Chicago: The University of Chicago Press, 1971, 119–29.

Kaups, Matti Enn, "Shifting Vinland—Tradition and Myth". *Terrae Incognitae*, II, 29–60.

—, "Shifting Vinland — Tradition and Myth: A Rejoinder", *Terrae Incognitae*, III, 97–105.

Landsverk, Ole Godfred, *Ancient Norse Messages on American Stones*. Glendale, Calif.: Norseman Press, 1969.

—, *Runic Records of the Norsemen in America*. New York: E. J. Friis; Distributed by Twayne Publishers, 1974.

Langenberg, Inge, *Die Vinland-Fahrten: Die Entdeckungen Amerikas von Erik dem Roten bis Kolumbus (1000-1492)*. Cologne, Vienna: Distributed by Böhlau, 1977.

Lee, Thomas E., "Ancient European Settlement Revealed at Payne Lake, Ungava, 1965". Travaux Divers, No. 16. Quebec: Laval University Centre d'Etudes Nordiques, 1967, 28-116.

—, *Archaeological Discoveries, Payne Bay Region, Ungava, 1966*. Travaux Divers, No. 20. Quebec: Laval University Centre d'Etudes Nordiques, 1968. Second Printing, 1970.

—, "Archaeological Investigations, Deception Bay, Ungava Peninsula, 1965". *Anthropological Journal of Canada*, V, No. 3, 14-39.

—, *Archaeological Investigations of a Longhouse Ruin, Pamiok Island, Ungava Bay, 1972*. Collection Paléo-Québec, Vol. II. Québec: Laval Université Centre d'Etudes Nordiques, 1974.

—, *Fort Chimo and Payne Lake, Ungava, Archeology, 1965*. Travaux Divers, No. 16. Québec: Laval Université Centre d'Etudes Nordiques, 1967.

—, "The Norse in Ungava". *Anthropological Journal of Canada*, IV, No. 2, 51-54.

—, "The Norse Presence in Arctic Ungava". *The American-Scandinavian Review*, LXI, 242-57.

—, "A Summary of Norse Evidence in Ungava, 1968". *Anthropological Journal of Canada*, V, No. 3, 41-48.

—, "A Summary of Norse Evidence in Ungava, 1968". *Anthropological Journal of Canada*, VI, No. 4, 17-21.

—, "The Ungava Norse: A Reply to Birgitta Wallace". *Anthropological Journal of Canada*, VIII, No. 1, 21-23.

Liestøl, Aslak, "Cryptograms in Runic Carvings: A Critical Analysis". *Minnesota History*, XLI, 34-42.

Løberg, Leif, "Norrøne Amerikaferders Utstrekning". *Norsk Historisk Tidsskrift*, XLI, 233-52.

Mahieu, Jacques de, *L'Agonie du Dieu-Soleil: Les Vikings en Amerique du Sud*. Paris: R. Laffont, 1974.

—, *Drakkars sur l'Amazone: Les Vikings de l'Amerique précolombienne*. Paris: Copernic, 1977.

—, *Le Grand Voyage du Dieu Soleil*. Paris: Editions et Publications Speciales, 1971.

Mallery, Arlington H., *Lost America: The Story of Iron-Age Civilization Prior to Columbus*. Introduction by Matthew W. Stirling. Washington Public Affairs Press, 1950.

Meldgaard, Jørgen, "Fra Brattalid til Vinland". *Naturens Verden*, 1961, 353-84.

Moltke, Erik, "The Ghost of the Kensington Stone". *Scandinavian Studies*, XXV, 1-14.

Mongé, Alf, and Ole G. Landsverk, *Norse Medieval Cryptography in Runic Carvings*. Glendale, Calif.: Norseman Press, 1967.

Mowat, Farley, *Westviking: The Ancient Norse in Greenland and North America*. London: Secker & Warburg, 1966.

Mulligan, Andrew A., "Viking Times". *Europe: Magazine of the European Community*, No. 221, 27-34.

Musmanno, Michael A., *Columbus Was First*. Introduction by John B. Duff. New York: Fountainhead Publishers, 1966.

Naess, Almar, *Hvor lå Vinland? En Studie over Solobservasjoner i de Norrøne Sagaer*. With a summary in English. Oslo: Dreyer, 1954.

Nielsen, Karl Martin, "Kensingtonstenens Runeindskrift". *Aarbøger for Nordisk Old-kyndighed og Historie*, 1950, 73-88.

Oleson, Tryggvi J., *Early Voyages and Northern Approaches, 1000-1632*. The Canadian Centenary Series, Vol. I. Toronto: McClelland and Stewart; New York: Oxford University Press, 1964.

——, "The Vikings in America: A Critical Bibliography". *The Canadian Historical Review*, XXXVI, 166-73.

Olson, Robert, "Was Our Biggest Historical Find Our Biggest Hoax?". *Maclean's*, 13 April, 1957, 30-31, 80-84.

Pistilli S., Vicente, *Vikingos en el Paraguay: La Aldea Vikinga-Guaraní en la Cuenca del Plata*. Asunción: Ediciones Comuneros; 1978.

Plumet, Patrick, *Archeologie de l'Ungava: Le Probléme des Maison Longues à Deux Hemicycles et Separations Interieures*. Contribution du Centre d'Etudes Arctiques et Finno-Scandinaves, No. 7. Paris: Sorbonne, 1969.

——, "Les Vikings en Amérique: La Fin d'un Mythe". *Les Vikings et leur Civilisation: Problèmes actuels*, 61-73. Edited by Régis Boyer. Paris: Mouton, 1976.

Pohl, Frederick J., *Atlantic Crossings before Columbus*. New York: Norton, 1961.

——, "Leif Erikson's Campsite in Vinland". *American-Scandinavian Review*, LIV, 25-29.

——, *The Lost Discovery: Uncovering the Track of the Vikings in America*. New York: Norton, 1952.

——, "The Newport Tower: An Answer to Mr. Godfrey". *Archaeology*, III, 183-84.

——, *The Viking Explorers*. New York: T. Y. Crowell, 1966.

——, *The Viking Settlements of North America*. New York: C. N. Potter, 1972.

Powell, Bernard W., "An Osseous Find at Follins Pond". *Bulletin of the Massachusetts Archaeological Society*, XVIII, 32-36.

Quinn, David Beers, *North America from the Earliest Discovery to First Settlements: The Norse Voyages to 1612*. New York: Harper and Row, 1977.

——, "The Vinland Map, I: A Viking Map of the West?". *Saga Book of the Viking Society*, XVII, Pt. 1, 63-72.

Redmond, Jeffrey R., *"Viking" Hoaxes in North America*. With a Foreword by Erik Wahlgren. New York: Carlton Press, 1979.

Rieth, Adolf, *Vorzeit gefälscht*. Tübingen, Wasmuth, 1967.

Schledermann, Peter, "Notes on Norse Finds from the East Coast of Ellesmere Island, N.W.T.". *Arctic*, XXXIII, 454-63.

Shippen, Katherine Binney, *Leif Eriksson: First Voyager to America*. New York: Harper, 1951.

Spjeldnaes, Nils and Kari E. Henningsmoen, *"Littorina Littorea*: An Indicator of Norse Settlement in North America?". *Science*, CXLI, 275-76.

Snorri Sturluson, *From the Sagas of the Norse Kings*. With an Appendix: "The Norse Voyages to Vinland about 1000 A.D.". Oslo: Dreyer, 1967.

Stromsted. Astri A., *Ancient Pioneers: Early Connections between Scandinavia and the New World*. s. 1.: Erik J. Friis, 1974.

Stoylen, Sigvald, "The Kensington Rune Stone". *American Book Collector*, XVI, No. 3, 6-9.

Travelier, G., *Amérique an mille*. Paris: Editions Fleurus, 1959.

Tornöe, Johannes Kristoffer, *Columbus in the Arctic? And the Vineland Literature*. Oslo: s.n., 1967.

—, *Early American History: Norsemen before Columbus*. Oslo: Universitets Forlaget; New York: Humanities Press, 1965.

Tushingham, A. Douglas, *The Beardmore Relics, Hoax or History?* Toronto: Royal Ontario Museum, 1966.

Verhoog, P., *De Ontdekking van Amerika voor Columbus*. Hilversum: C. de Boer, Jr., 1959.

Vilmundarson, Thórhallur, "Reflections on the Vinland Map". *American-Scandinavian Review*, LIV, 20-24.

Vinland the Good: The Saga of Leif Eiriksson and the Viking Discovery of America. With a Preface by Helge Ingstad. Translated by Joan Tindale Blindheim. Oslo: Tanum, 1966.

The Vinland Sagas: The Norse Discovery of America. Translated with an Introduction by Magnus Magnusson and Hermann Palsson. New York: New York University Press, 1966.

The Vinland Voyages: The Icelanders Discover America and Write the First Canadian History. Translated and edited by Roy H. Ruth. Winnipeg: Printed by Columbia Printers, 1965.

Wahlgren, Erik, "The Companions Bjarni and Leif". *Proceedings of the Vinland Map Conference*. Chicago: The University of Chicago Press, 1971, 131-35.

—, "Further Remarks on Vinland". *Scandinavian Studies*, XL, 26-35.

—, *The Kensington Stone: A Mystery Solved*. Madison: University of Wisconsin Press, 1958.

—, "The Runes of Kensington". *Studies in Honor of Albert Morey Sturtevant*. Lawrence: University of Kansas Press, 1952, 57-70.

—, and Marshall McKusick, "Vikings in America: Fact and Fiction". *Early Man*, Winter 1980, 7-11.

Wallis, Helen, *et al.*, "The Strange Case of the Vinland Map: A Symposium". *The Geographical Journal*, CXL, Pt. 2, 183-214.

This selection is from a forthcoming annotated bibliography by Louis A. Pitschmann.

IV. LATE REFLEXES

WILLIAM MORRIS AND SAGA-TRANSLATION:

'The Story of King Magnus, Son of Erling'

James L. Barribeau

Lecturer in Medieval Studies, Cornell University

I

VIKING INFLUENCE spread across continents: in the east, through Europe to Russia and Greece; in the west, to Britain, Ireland, Greenland, Iceland, and to the New World; all of these exploits have been addressed in greater or lesser detail elsewhere in this volume. But Viking influence also spread across time — in fact, across a millennium. The eighteenth and nineteenth centuries, already primed by their study of Old English and recently discovered manuscripts, attacked Old Norse with a characteristic vigour, but the two audiences differed: Old English was for scholars and clerics; Old Norse, for the adventurer, the romantic — for William Morris. The Victorians, too, fell to the Vikings.

This Viking conquest did not occur without a long period of preparation, however. The Spenserian imitators of the eighteenth century helped keep medieval ideals, at least as they saw them, fresh in the minds of the public. The Gothic novelists — Horace Walpole, Mary Shelley, Matthew Lewis, Anne Radcliffe; the romantic poets — Coleridge, Keats, Wordsworth; and the romantic novels of Sir Walter Scott sustained a popular interest in a sort of "medieval", though they often stretched the time limits and their interpretations to include whatever might imply darkness and intrigue.[1] In architecture, Strawberry Hill kept alive some notion of "medieval" until Ruskin and others took up the call much later. At the same time, many of the great manuscripts of medieval literature were being discovered,[2] and scholarship in most medieval matters was beginning to grow. In spite of all this activity, however, Old Norse scholarship was virtually non-existent. In fact, "Runick", as it was called, was often confused with Celtic, and considered very mysterious indeed. It was not until the great translators and editors of the nineteenth century presented Norse literature to the public that scholarship could begin to advance. Before the nineteenth century, the English literary world enjoyed no editions, no dictionaries, and no translations (unless one were to count the few north-inspired poems of Thomas Gray, who knew no Old Norse and got the material for his "translations" from the Latin of Bartholin and the French of Mallet's *Introduction à l'histoire de Dannemarc*.[3]

Whereas the literary men of the eighteenth and early nineteenth centuries faced an almost impossible task when confronting Norse literature, by the mid-nineteenth century the situation had totally changed, thanks mostly to the great pioneer translators of the 1840s and 1850s. Although Amos Cottle attempted to translate some of the *Elder Edda* in 1797, and William Herbert is generally considered to be the first English translator to have had a first-hand knowledge of Icelandic, as demonstrated by his *Select Islandic Poetry* of 1804–1806, the beginning of serious scholarly attention to Old Norse literature is marked by George Webbe Dasent's *Younger Edda* of 1842 and Samuel Laing's *Heimskringla* of 1844. Dasent followed his *Edda* with his translation of Rask's *Grammar of the Icelandic or Old Norse Tongue* in 1843, his translation of *Njáls Saga* (*The Story of Burnt Njal*) in 1861, and that of *Gísla saga* (*The Story of Gisli the Outlaw*) in 1866. In 1851 Benjamin Thorpe published his *Northern Mythology*, and in 1866 the *Elder Edda*.[4]

In 1869 that great translating team of the second half of the century, William Morris and Eiríkr Magnússon, published their *Story of Grettir the Strong*, followed in 1870 by the *Volsunga Saga: The Story of the Volsungs and Niblungs*. Morris paraphrased the *Laxdæla Saga* in his "Lovers of Gudrun" in 1870 as well, and the two went on to compile *The Saga Library*, including the *Heimskringla*, my subject here, in the last decade of the century.[5] The last three decades of the century saw the appearance of Edmund Gosse's *Egilssaga* (1879), another treatment by W. C. Green (1893), Cleasby and Vigfússon's *Dictionary* (1874), Vigfússon and Powell's *Icelandic Prose Reader* (1879), Henry Sweet's *Norse Primer and Reader* (1886) and Vigfússon and Powell's *Corpus Poeticum Boreale* (1883).[6] So within a hundred years of Thomas Gray, most of the work had been done to present the great literature of the north to the general public. In Samuel Laing's words, "The object [of this translation] has been to make it [the *Heimskringla*] ... not merely a work for the antiquary, but for the ordinary reader of history, — for the common man."[7]

II

Perhaps more than any other translator of the past century, William Morris has enjoyed his share of controversy. Doubtless, Morris's almost fanatical medievalism has furnished the critics with abundant ammunition. From early on, Morris's language was full of English criticized as "Wardour Street",[8] "the affectation of archaism", "pseudo-Middle English", and "specious nullity of false phrasing".[9] *The Defence of Guenevere*, according to one critic, is "the strangest collection of poetry not confessedly insane in the language".[10] Though at first applied only to Morris's poetry, these attacks were later directed toward all his works by popular critics, though not necessarily by skilled linguists. Such criticisms were levelled at Morris throughout most of his career, and continued into the twentieth century. In this century, his most noted detractors include D. M. Hoare, who said some years ago that Morris "cannot go deep enough", and "the intrusion ... of the *chevalresque* into the crisis [of *Laxdæla Saga*] is unpardonable";[11] and Lee Hollander, who maintained that Morris's translation, "because of the unfortunate misconception—not dead yet — that the sagas require an antiquarian language flavoured with English dialecticisms, is almost unreadable today".[12]

Nevertheless, Morris's supporters are many. The reviewers welcomed *The Earthly Paradise*, as did the public. *Sigurd the Volsung* was called "the one great epic of the nineteenth century".[13] Conrad Nordby, at the turn of the century, wrote of poetry "by the hand of the Master".[14] Several of the founding fathers of modern medieval scholarship were great admirers of Morris. For example, W. P. Ker referred to "The Lovers of Gudrun" as "the noble echo" of the original.[15] Later in this century, E. V. Gordon, another philologist, declared, "The greatest literary interpreter of the north that has been in England was William Morris. . . . He was better able than any other poet had been to apply poetic gifts to Norse subjects, and the result, when he did, was magnificent."[16] E. R. Eddison, shortly thereafter, in "Some Principles of Translation", compares Morris's translation with Samuel Laing's and concludes Morris's is "the more perfect achievement, . . . by comparison, living human speech". He is able "to produce a translation which has the life and freshness of an original composition and which preserves on the whole the very tone and accent of the saga . . .".[17] About the same time, in a letter to his brother, C. S. Lewis laments the fact that, after finishing *The Wood Beyond the World*, he has no more Morris prose-romances to read.[18] Five years later, in praising Morris, he says, "Morris invented for his poems and perfected in his prose-romances a language which has never at any period been spoken in England",[19] a language he later used in his translations. In the 'thirties and 'forties, Morris's most adamant supporter was Karl Litzenberg, of the University of Michigan, who wrote five articles on various aspects of Morris's northern inspiration. According to Litzenberg (like Ker, Gordon, and Lewis, a skilled philologist), "No other modern writer has re-created the temper of Old Norse literature so completely and so adequately".[20] In the 'sixties and 'seventies, though, critics seemed awkward, even embarrassed, in supporting Morris's work.[21] In most cases the trained philologists recognize the merit of Morris's artistry; only the somewhat short-lived, even "trendy", critics disparage it.

At the root of this controversy, of course, is Morris's medievalism, specifically his fascination with "the north". Although he expressed interest in medieval architecture while at the Marlborough School,[22] his dedication to Malory, Chaucer, whom he called his "Master",[23] and to the thirteenth century in general, did not begin until Morris was at Oxford (1853–1855), which according to Morris's primary biographer, J. W. Mackail, "still . . . breathed from its towers the last enchantments of the Middle Ages".[24] Though disillusioned with the academic life at Oxford, Morris was introduced to Thorpe's *Northern Mythology* by his friend, Edward Burne-Jones, though Burne-Jones himself would "never go further north than Hampstead", if he had his way.[25] Thorpe "opened to Morris a new world, which in later life became, perhaps, his deepest love".[26] "The literature of the north", as Morris called it, from that point on began to control Morris's literary production. In the course of his lifetime, he wrote over 50 pieces in some way related to northern influence.[27] Though Morris's early poetry, *The Defence of Guenevere* (1858), and *The Life and Death of Jason* (1867), shows a general inclination towards the medieval, his earliest prose shows definite signs of "Scandina-vianizing". *Gertha's Lovers*, *Svend and his Brethren*, and *The Hollow Land* all have characters with northern names. Yet, as Litzenberg points out, the influence goes no further than this. More important Scandinavian traits appear in Morris's poetry of the second half of the 1860s — *The Wanderers* (1865–1868), and *The Earthly Paradise* (1868).[28] These poems reflect Morris's efforts, beginning about 1860, to read translations of various Icelandic writings. During this period, however, Morris could rely only on translations, often inaccurate (or in the case of Laing, based on a modern Norwegian translation of the original Old Norse). But in 1868 came a meeting that was to affect profoundly Morris's feelings toward northern literature and enable him to deal with the material first hand: he was introduced to Eiríkr Magnússon, a native Icelander, and began to take lessons in Old Norse, which got him closer to the north than ever before,[29] providing him with the substance for some of his best poetry ("The Lovers of Gudrun" and *Sigurd the Volsung*), as well as training him for his later translations.

In the Icelander Eiríkr Magnússon, Morris met the ideal collaborator, and his equal — in enthusiasm, stature, temper, and quest for precision. May Morris describes him thus: "I remember him well at Cambridge, a short stocky man with a full face, light hair and bushy moustache. He spoke English with the exquisite precision I have noticed in other cultivated people of [Iceland]. He used to sing Northern folk song with a big voice that nearly blew the roof off their little sitting room in Cambridge. I remember he walked up and down the room, Icelandic fashion, as he sung. His enthusiasm over the literary matter of Iceland knew no bonds of space or time: only the other day I met someone who knew him in Cambridge who said, if one met him in the street, one had only to mention something about the literature of the North, and there Magnússon would stand talking, regardless of time or weather."[30] Bertha Phillpotts, student and long-time acquaintance of the Icelander, describing Magnússon's professional acumen, says, "This combination of scholarship with sympathetic insight together with his vigorous personality made Mr. Magnússon an unforgettable teacher .... Mistranslation or grammatical inaccuracy he regarded with much the same horror as actual untruthfulness .... A saga read with him remains in the memory as a living thing, and must always recall the enthusiasm for knowledge, the idealism, and the love of country which were characteristic of a unique personality."[31] These descriptions suggest a man well equipped to deal with an Englishman who "clung to [the topic of Iceland] like ivy to the oak", as Stopford Brooke unsympathetically remarked,[32] and about whom Magnússon himself was later to say, "From the very first day that I began work with William Morris on Icelandic literature the thing that struck me most was this, that he entered into the spirit of it not with the pre-occupied mind of a foreigner, but with the intuition of an uncommonly wide-awake native".[33]

That "very first day" occurred in the autumn of 1868. A mutual friend arranged a meeting between the two men. At his Queen's Square house, Morris met Magnússon "with a manly shake of the hand", according to Magnússon, and "with a bound" he led Magnússon to his second-floor study where "a very animated conversation ensued on Icelandic matters".[34] They arranged a schedule of reading Icelandic three times a week, beginning with *Gunnlaug the Wormtongue*, a work of about 50 pages, which they finished in two weeks.[35]

After *Gunnlaug the Wormtongue* and *Grettir the Strong*, their first translation, Morris and Magnússon began work on *The Story of the Volsungs*, published in 1870 with 13 poems from the *Edda*, and *Laxdæla Saga*, never published but later used by Morris as the basis for his "Lovers of Gudrun" episode in *The Earthly Paradise*.[36] These translations were followed five years later by *Three Northern Love Stories*, containing *Gunnlaugs Saga Ormstungu* (*The Story of Gunnlaug the Wormtongue*), *Friðþjófs Saga* (*The Story of Frithiof the Bold*), and *Viglundar saga væna* (*The Story of Viglund the Fair*), with some additional short stories.[37] About the same time, the pair was working on *Hænsaþóris Saga* (*The Story of Hen Thorir*), *Bandamanna Saga* (*The Story of the Banded Men*), and *Hávarðar saga Ísfirðingr* (*The Story of Howard the Halt*), as well as on the *Heimskringla*,[38] all of which were to appear, after a fifteen year hiatus in *The Saga Library*.

On 2 July 1890, Morris wrote to Bernard Quaritch that he would agree to do a Saga Library, and would begin work "at once on a prospectus".[39] In a letter to Lady

Burne Jones six days later, Morris writes, "I have undertaken to get out some of the Sagas I have lying about. Quaritch is exceedingly anxious to get hold of me, and received with enthusiasm a proposal to publish a Saga Library: item he will give me money (or perhaps I ought to say old books)".[40] *The Saga Library*, according to the prospectus, was to be 15 volumes. Only six appeared, the last a thorough collection of notes, indexes, genealogical tables, etc., compiled by Magnússon and published in 1905. Volume I included *Howard the Halt*, *The Banded Men*, and *Hen Thorir* (1891); Volume II, *The Eredwellers* and *The Heath Slaings* (1892); and Volumes III to V, the three parts of the *Heimskringla*. They completed this last volume at the end of April 1895, eighteen months before Morris's death, in a last burst of energy before Morris's final debilitating illness. Shortly after the completion of the volume, Burne-Jones lamented, "It is sad to see his enormous vitality diminishing".[41]

In a study of this scope, limited to but one manuscript of the dozens Morris produced, I could not hope to present a final report of Morris's method of translation; instead, using his manuscript for the *Heimskringla*'s *Story of King Magnus, Son of Erling*, I offer only a beginning, a first step towards a long-needed analysis of this great man's translation process, of his unflagging conscientiousness, and of the method usually followed by one of our most prodigious, if not always our most appreciated, translators of saga literature. His enthusiasm, coupled with the skills of a native Icelander, produced a corpus of poetic translations unequalled in the field.

Magnússon describes their method of translation in these words: "The work on it was divided between Morris and myself in the following manner: Having read together the sagas contained in the first three volumes [of *The Saga Library*], Morris wrote out the translation and I collated his MS. with the original. For the last two volumes of the Heimskringla the process was reversed, I doing the translation, he the collation; the style, too, he emended throughout in accordance with his own ideal."[42] The manuscripts of the first volumes, though somewhat indicative of Morris's views on translation, are not nearly as interesting as the last two, for which Morris and Magnússon reverted to their original method, when Morris implored Magnússon, "You be my grammar as we translate. I want the literature".[43] Magnússon, in fact, realized the important role these last two volumes play in any estimation of Morris's artistry. "Among the literary remains of William Morris", he writes, "the MS on which the second and the third vols. [sic] of Snorri Sturluson's *Heimskringla* (being the fourth and fifth vols [sic] of the *Saga Library*) are based, forms a particularly safe, indeed an indispensable basis whereon the future criticism of the great man's relation to old northern literature is to be based. The MS, extending to 800 pages, comprises the ten sagas of the Kings of Norway which cover a period of 163 years, from the accession of Olaf the Holy to the reign of King Magnús Erlingsson".[44]

Though much of this manuscript is lost, portions of it have reappeared over the past 50 years. Stefán Einarsson, in 1933, noted that Karl O. E. Anderson was working on pages, privately owned, containing *The Story of Sigurd the Jerusalem-Farer*, *Eystein*, and *Olaf* in Volume V of *The Saga Library*; however, that study has never been published.[45] In 1961, J. N. Swannell, a critic whose lukewarm appreciation for Morris's translation-style exemplifies the usual reaction in the past decades, included a brief study of the *Ólafs Saga* manuscript, owned by the Brotherton Library of the University of Leeds, in his article on Morris as an interpreter of Old Norse, but that study leaves the incorrect impression that Morris was an impatient translator, whose work was a game, or rather just an experiment.[46] Although one must agree that Morris's statement when he first began to study Icelandic, that he must have the story, suggests a student whose over-eagerness could lead to carelessness, an examination of the last saga of the final volume of *The Saga Library* — indeed, the last translation Morris was to do — demonstrates that Morris had fully outgrown the impatience indicated by his remark, "I must have the story. I mean to amuse myself".[47]

The Morris–Magnússon manuscript of *The Story of King Magnus, Son of Erling*, now preserved in The Huntington Library,[48] measures 12¾ by 8½ inches (Figure 1). The leather-bound, ruled notebook has 38 leaves with the translation on the rectoes only, except for Morris's verse translations of the three poems in the story and Morris's several questions directed at Magnússon (e.g., referring to Jón Kútiza, "What is the English name — Curtis? Very common"), which appear in the opposite versos. The verso of the first, unnumbered, leaf bears the following legend, possibly inscribed by W. Heffer, for the 1908 sale of the manuscript: "Morris/ The Original Manuscript, on 37 leaves, in the Autograph of Eirikr Magnusson [sic], filled with Alterations and Corrections in the hand-writing of William Morris, also with 3 verses of Poetry in his hand". The pages are numbered in Arabic numerals starting with the second leaf, the first page of translation, in the top centre (pp. 3, 4, and 10 also in the top right). Throughout are marginal notes in a fourth, rough hand, probably that of a foreman for the printer, dividing the text among typesetters and indicating the beginning of each four-folio gathering. On the rectos, the clear hand of Magnússon is crossed out, redirected, corrected, and emended in the bold hand of Morris. These alterations fall into four main categories:

1) corrections in translation (including corrections of Magnússon's English)
2) emendation to create syntax similar to the Icelandic (for example, verb/verb, noun/noun, etc.)
3) emendation to create word order similar to the Icelandic
4) substitution to provide cognates (the most substantial group).

Corrections in translation make up the smallest group. Though Magnússon was a conscientious and skilled linguist,[49] his Icelandic would occasionally interfere with his English. When he comes across the Icelandic *frændr* in Chapter II,[50] he confuses it with its English cognate and defines it incorrectly as "friends"; Morris corrects it to "kin". In Chapter I, Morris changes Magnússon's translation for *mundu*, "wood", to the correct "would". Morris also corrects more serious errors by Magnússon; for example, Magnússon translates "might want" for *þyrfti*, which in the context actually means "might need". Likewise, Morris guards against loose translation: Magnússon translates *nǫkkurr* as "some" and "several" (both correct) rather than Morris's "certain", as in "a certain haven", giving it the force of an indefinite article, non-existent in Old Norse (Chapters III, XX); *vǫkðu* as "kept watch" rather than the more literal "waked" (X); and *hafði* as "took", perfectly correct, rather than "had" (XII), the more literal translation. Morris also keeps the original tense, though it occasionally seems awkward, and alters Magnússon's material to match the original: "falling" becomes "fell" (*fellu*), and "leaping" "leapt" (*hljópu*) (VII). Morris eliminates the pleonastic "do" — an uncommon element in English before the sixteenth century: "did not fasten" becomes "made not the boat fast" (*festu þeir ekki bátinn*) (VI). However, Morris allows more leeway in the translation of names: he disallows Magnússon's "Heinrik" for *Heinrek*, and substitutes "Henry", surprising in light of his early works, in which he freely used northern names; on the other hand, he prefers "Roald Longtalk" to "Roald Longsermon" for *Hróaldr langtala* (III), but this revision may reflect Morris's preference for cognates rather than his thoughts about name-translation.

In the second group, more extensive than the first, Morris is very conscientious about retaining the syntax of the Icelandic; thus, when Magnússon inadvertently switches prepositions, Morris reinserts the original: "for king" to "to king" (*til konungs*) (I), and "took for king Sigurd" to "took Sigurd to king" (*tóku . . . Sigurð til konungs*) (IX). Morris also seems anxious to retain adjectival constructions: Magnússon's translation for *ef hann var ráðinn*, "if he had made up his mind", Morris changes to "if he were of mind". Verbs, though, seem to merit Morris's closest attention. When Magnússon translates a verb as a noun, Morris changes it back to a verbal structure; for example, *at gjalda*, an infinitive structure, is "awarded a fine" for Magnússon, but "to pay" for Morris (XIX). In Chapter V, Magnússon translates *fœri í milli* as a present participle, "passing between", which Morris changes to "fared between". Similarly, in the next chapter, the simple past *lá* is translated "was lying" by the Icelander; Morris prefers "lay". A few lines later the same thing happens — Magnússon's "were sitting" for *sátu* becomes "sat". Morris also prefers to retain the active voice. *þeir . . . áttu tal sitt*, "the counsel was taken" for Magnússon, becomes "they took the rede together" (I). Intransitive verbs stay intransitive for Morris, as well: *Ok leggja þá hvárirtveggju til orrustu*, rendered by Magnússon as "either side forthwith gave battle", is changed to "and then either side thrust into battle" (VII). Morris avoids periphrasis and "took to flight" becomes "fled" for *flýði* (III). Even more careful, Morris goes back to the impersonal roots of the construction and renders *þykki mér* "methinketh" rather than Magnússon's "I deem" (I). Adverbs, as well, receive careful treatment. Magnússon's "since ye fare in such a wild manner" for *er þit farið svá ákafliga* changes to "that ye fare so wildly" (VI). Morris's keen eye is always on the lookout for unfaithful syntax. Always faithful to the original, he was prepared to sacrifice the popular notion of "English", a fact appreciated by several of the great philologists, as mentioned above.

Morris's use of word-order to create parallel constructions comprises the third group of alterations. Of the numerous examples in the manuscript, a few must suffice here. In Chapter I, Magnússon translates *tóku margir vel undir þetta ráð* "for this many gave good cheer"; Morris rearranges the sentence to match the original more closely: "Many took well to this rede". In the same chapter, Magnússon translates *Allir játtu því at gera þetta samband með fullum trúnaði* "They all said yea to joining this fellowship in full good faith"; Morris again rearranges the sentence and changes the word order to match Snorri's line: "All yeasaid it to make that fellowship with full troth". Morris also holds to Germanic subject-verb inversion in his translation: *þá þynntisk lið á bryggjunum* for Magnússon "then the host on the bridge thinned", becomes for Morris "then thinned the host on the bridge" (III): so also, *ok fell þar mjǫk mart manna af Hákonar liði*, "and there fell much folk of Hakon's host". When Magnússon reverses *sunnan at eynni* (VI) to "towards the island from the south", Morris revises it to "from the south to the island". Again, in Chapter XII, he changes Magnússon's "the weather was cool with sleet falling" (*Svalt var veðr ok vátadrífa*) to "chill was the weather with drift of sleet".

Throughout the manuscript, Morris follows this pattern — he always changes Magnússon's construction to parallel the original.

The final area of correction represents the most substantial and most controversial of Morris's techniques for translation. To list Morris's use of Icelandic/English cognates and archaisms in this story would require scores of pages. Only a few representative examples can be discussed here. Perhaps the most obvious example of his technique is the use of "fare" for the Icelandic *fara*; one never "goes" anywhere in Morris's saga — one always "fares". Likewise, in Chapter I, Morris uses "bidding" for *boð* (Magnússon: "word") and "flock" for *flokkrinn*, which Magnússon usually translates "band". A well known Morrisism that comes up frequently is "rede", Morris's translation for *ráð* (Magnússon's "counsel" or "advice"). Also, *næst ... bana mínum*, "next to my very death" for Magnússon, becomes "next to my very bane" for Morris.

So far, the examples of cognates have been fairly acceptable to the common reader. We move now to an aspect of Morris's translations that has evoked admiration in some, but has provoked fury in many. Morris frequently extends his use of cognates to include extremely archaic, sometimes dialectal, often obscure English words. For example, he translates *týnt*, "lost", as "tyned", choosing a northern dialectism originally borrowed from Old Norse. *Harðráðr*, for Magnússon "hard-counsellor", becomes even more obscure with Morris: "hard-redy". So "enemies", *óvinir*, is translated literally by Morris (the Icelandic prefix *ó-* is a negative element) as "unfriends"; also, *ófrelsi* ("tyranny") becomes "unfreedom", and *ófriðr* ("war") "unpeace".[51] Similarly, he translates *mikit mannfall* as "mickle man-fall"; Magnússon translates this phrase as "great fall of men" (VI). *Heituðusk*, "vowed", Morris translates "behight" (VII); likewise, *heitir*, "called", becomes "hight", as in *sem heitir á Stǫngum*, "where it hight Stongs", going back to its Teutonic roots. At the same time, Morris worked to keep out Latinisms: Magnússon's "avail" becomes "help", and "vessels" becomes "ships" (VI, VII). One of the most extreme examples of Morris's persistence in maintaining cognates is his revision of Magnússon's translation of *kraptr*, as in *með fjanda kraptr*, "the power of the fiend", to "the craft of the fiend" — in this case somewhat confusing the actual meaning. Nevertheless, though one might not always agree with Morris's predilection for adapting cognates, the point is that Morris clearly watched his Icelandic original closely.

Any discussion of Morris's translation techniques must concern itself, however briefly, with his treatment of skaldic poetry, of which three examples occur in this saga (*see* Appendix B of this paper for a side-by-side presentation of the Icelandic and the three versions of translation), though in such a short paper it is impossible to communicate the intracacies of tone and style, on one hand, and the rugged charm, on the other, of this extremely rigid, yet deliberately obscure, form of poetry.[52]

Briefly stated, the rules of skaldic poetry are these: like the rest of Old Germanic poetry, skaldic poetry is alliterative; the difference is that skaldic poetry, unlike Old English poetry, for example, strictly counts syllables; it is also stanzaic. The predominant skaldic stanzaic pattern, to which the three examples in *Magnússaga* belong, called *dróttkvætt*, is comprised of two quatrains: each line (usually called a half-line, in opposition to the Germanic long line) must contain six syllables with three stresses, the last two syllables making up a trochaic foot (the other two feet are usually trochees, also). The first, stressed syllable of the even line springs back, as it were, and alliterates with two stressed syllables in the preceding line. Thus the two lines resemble the Old English long line, though the number of unstressed syllables is strictly regulated.

In addition, *dróttkvætt* requires a demanding pattern of internal half- and full rhyme (occasionally, end rhyme also appears): the odd lines must display consonance (called *skothending*); the even, full rhyme *(aðalhending)*. Both rhymes must involve the penultimate syllable of each six-syllable line. Thus, in the following stanza, the second poem in Appendix B, alliteration occurs three times in every two lines, ruled by the first, stressed syllable of the even lines *(gríðar: Greitt: gumna; Túnsbergi: trauðr: tenn,* etc.); the penultimate syllables of the odd lines control *skothending (dróttinn: Greitt: rjóða: trauðr,* etc.) and the same syllables of the even lines control internal full rhyme *(víou: gríðar; snúna: Túnsbergi):*

> Greitt frák, gumna dróttinn,
>
> gríðar fáks, í víðu,
>
> trauðr esa tenn at rjóða.
>
> Túnsbergi þér snúna.
>
> Hræddusk bjartra brodda
>
> býjarmenn við rennu.
>
> Uggðu eld ok sveigðan
>
> alm dynviðir malma.

As classical *dróttkvætt*, this stanza contains 48 syllables (in line three, *esa* would be shortened in delivery to fit the meter); 24 are metrically long[53] and stressed, 12 bear alliteration,[54] eight display *skothending*, and eight *aðalhending*.

Morris's translation also appears in an eight-line stanza, divided syntactically into two quatrains. Each line has three stresses, and usually ends with a trochee. Morris's lines, however, have more than the limited three unstressed syllables of classical *dróttkvætt*; yet his excess unstressed syllables are primarily prepositions and articles — following the metrical liberty allowed the skald, Morris's version, too, through resolution, could fit the six-syllable line of *dróttkvæt*. Morris's use of alliteration, however, strays from the required pattern, though alliteration is still fundamental to his verse: most of Morris's lines have two alliterative syllables (loath'st: Lord; teeth: troll-wife; lightly: luck; stems: steel-din; townsmen: meet; Adrad: steel-din). Sometimes Morris's alliteration connects two lines, though not by alliterating the proper *dróttkvætt* syllables, as in lines three and four: wide: went: with (Morris chose "wide" over Magnússon's "broad", presumably to achieve this link). In all three stanzas, the final couplets in Morris's versions are alliteratively linked (in stanza two, however, *st* would not alliterate with *sw* in *dróttkvætt*). In the first poem, moreover, lines four and eight resemble the classical pattern by alliterating a stressed syllable (though the first syllable is not stressed) with stressed syllables of the previous line; the same occurs in line eight in the third poem. Another requisite of *dróttkvætt*, internal rhyme, either full or half-, is only incidental in Morris's translation. Morris instead opts for simple assonance. In the first stanza, for example, "would" and "Onund" assonate, as do "Till" and "Sigurd", "folk" and "worthy", and "hard" and "thenceward" (Morris's word, probably chosen for this effect), and a visual rhyme appears, "should": "house" (*dróttkvætt*, however, was primarily aural). The same situation occurs in the second stanza: "teeth" and "steed", "flame" and "swayéd".

Seldom, though, do these rhymes follow the requisite pattern of the penultimate syllable rhyming with one in the first part of the line. Full rhyme, in *dróttkvætt* appearing in the even lines, plays little part in Morris's verse, except for "hard" and "thenceward" (again, visual rather than aural rhyme) in the first stanza, "teeth" and "steed" (if we equate the two dentals) in the second, and "there" and "fared" in the third. To summarize, Morris's translation of the second stanza, for example, displays a dependence on alliteration, though less rigidly than *dróttkvætt*, a meter similar to the original, but a much weaker relationship to the original rhyme, either *skothending* or *aðalhending*:

> Thou loath'st not, lord, to redden
> The teeth of the steed of troll-wife;
> I heard that in wide Tunsberg
> Lightly good luck went with thee.
> The townsmen feared to meet there
> The rushing of the bright points;
> Adrad were the stems of steel-din
> Of flame and swayèd elm-bow.

A few stylistic matters still remain to be discussed. *Dróttkvætt* was deliberately obscure, an effect achieved through various means. Its words, often exclusively poetic (known as *heiti*, a literary technique to which Morris adheres in both prose and poetry), added to this obscurity, and the Old Norse kenning, cousin to the much simpler Anglo-Saxon kenning, reached new depths of obscurity. *Gunnlaugs Saga Ormstungu*, for example, presents the following kennings: *runnr Gunnar* ("tree of battle" [*Gunnr* is exclusively poetic] = "warrior", in this case, þorsteinn); and *bauga lands lýsi-Gunnr* ("valkyrie of the light of the land of the rings" = "valkyrie of the light of the arm" = "valkyrie of gold" = "woman").[55] *Magnússaga*'s kennings are less extreme. In the first poem, *Magnússaga*'s skald refers to Hákon's warriors as "hawks" (in this case, ironically — Magnús had just routed Hákon's troops). In the second stanza, the poet refers to "reddening the teeth of the troll-wife's steed", that is, "reddening the teeth of the wolf" (by providing carnage). In both cases, Morris maintains the obscurity by maintaining the kennings. Of course, the encomiastic intent, so typical of skaldic poetry, is here represented as well, and the usual satirical elements are likewise transferred to Morris's version.

The most difficult problem in dealing with skaldic verse is the poet's unlimited syntactic freedom. In many cases, the full meaning of the stanza could not be ascertained until the last word, even the last syllable, was spoken — which often struck like a thunderbolt. Also, simply by position, the first and last syllables of each quatrain played especially important roles; these two quatrains, or half-stanzas, complemented and counterbalanced each other. Morris's versions transfer this balance and emphasis. In all three stanzas, the quatrains begin and end with important elements, and each quatrain is syntactically independent. In addition, within each quatrain, *dróttkvætt* often makes use of parenthetical statements to separate the sentence into two parts. Although *Magnússaga*'s three poems provide few examples of this usually pervasive feature, the one parenthetic clause, *mein fekk margr af Kœnu maðr*, in poem three, Morris prefers to attach to the following phrase, rather than treating it as an interruption of the sentence beginning that quatrain (the prose context suggests that *hann* refers to Erling, the subject of the first clause.

A final word about skaldic poetry in general, and about *dróttkvætt* in particular: more than anything else, it is a challenge to the translator. An inflected language, Old Norse lent itself to endless intricacies of position and separation of words. In the second poem, for example, *gríðar fáks* goes with *tenn at rjóða*, and *í víðu* with *Túnsbergi*, creating a chiasmic effect. To deal with this problem, Magnússon and Morris followed the usual procedure of students of Old Norse ("to be deplored", according to Gordon, and "pernicious", says Frank[56]), rearranging the words into prose order before attempting translation. So Magnússon would turn the Icelandic poetry into prose, then into English, which Morris would finally "metrify". Limited by the strict word-order requirements of modern English, Morris could offer only subject-verb inversion and occasional periodic constructions to produce a similar effect. As a final product, Morris's *dróttkvætt* bears only limited resemblance to the original in poetic technique; yet the translation is certainly accurate, and much of the original spirit shines through.

Morris's attention to the manuscript does not end once his translation is in the hands of the printer. A comparison of the Morris–Magnússon manuscript with the final published form re-emphasizes Morris's devotion to accuracy. First, Morris watches for superficial errors that sneaked past him in his first revision. For example, in Chapter VII Morris revises a sentence by Magnússon but omits the necessary negative; in the printed version the "not" reappears. In the same chapter, Magnússon's "grapnelled" becomes Morris's "grappelled"; Morris, though, catches the misspelling and changes it to "grappeled" for the final version. Similarly, in a chapter dealing mostly with the Danes, the Norwegians in the chapter also become Danes — the reflex of a common medieval confusion about the peoples of early Scandinavia; Morris, however, catches the mistake and returns to the Norwegians their nationality in the final version (XXX). So also, in Chapter XXXI, *Ormr* becomes "Olaf" in a chapter about Olaf's beginnings, but Morris later changes it. At the same time, Morris keeps an eye out for style, and several times revamps his translation to read better. In Chapter X, for instance, Magnússon translates, "The chief cause of which was their fondness", but Morris changes it to read "for the cause most of their friendship"; still dissatisfied, though, Morris finally settles on "mostly for the cause of their friendship". Two chapters later, "by that so doing" becomes "furtherance" and finally "goings on". When a geographical problem arises, Morris tries several versions: "beyond the land", "off the land", "round the land". Morris was, indeed, quite a stickler for perfection.

Beyond this, Morris continued to strive for syntactically parallel constructions. Aiming to maintain the same word order, Morris prefers "go not up" to "not go up" (*gǫngum ekki upp*). Even when perfect parallelism is not altogether possible, Morris gets as close as he can: "It was over with all other flocks", his first revision, gives way to "scattered were all other flocks" for *þá var eytt flokkum ǫllum ǫðrum*. He pays the same close attention to retaining the reflexive: "Against him" becomes "against himself" (*á sik*) (XXXIII); again, four chapters later, "him" must be changed to "himself" for *hann . . . sik*. Carefully following the original, Morris inserts "upon" finally in "come nigh upon them" to preserve *at*. The conditional must also remain, so Morris changes "the odds were great" to "the odds would be great" to accommodate *mundi vera* (XIII). Obviously, Morris considered syntax an important element not to be lost from the Icelandic.

Cognates, of course, were a major preoccupation for Morris; he refused to give up until the translation was in print. "Said" becomes "quoth" to match *kvað* (VI), "years" yields to "winters" for *vetr* (I), and "scow" finally represents *skúta*. Morris follows this course even to the point of consonants: "clad themselves" becomes "clothe themselves" to retain the aspiration of *klæðask* (XXXII); the same holds true for "thee" rather than "you" for *yðr*, though Morris here is aiming for the polite form, as well. Once again, Morris seems to be watching closely: not satisfied with "the banner fared at heel of the earl", he changes it to "the banner of the earl fared a-heel", reflecting *á hæl* in the original (XIV). In addition, Morris inserts his old favourite, "let", in "let blow [the trumpets] ", *láta blasa*. At the same time, though, Morris is able to hold his impulses in check. Magnússon's "Michael's mass" becomes "Micklemass", but then Morris relents and settles on "Michaelmass" (XVIII).

By far the most important result of this final revision is the elimination of several errors in translation and inadvertent additions or deletions. Magnússon, probably trying to retain a cognate, or perhaps confused by the cognate, translates *mjúkliga* as "meekly", but Morris changes it to "tenderly", though it slipped past him in the first revision (XXI). "Do shamefully" more accurately becomes "do dastardly" (*Á engum manni niðumk ek.*), and "peace-speaking" "peace-making" (*sættargørð*) (XXIX). In Chapter XXXV, as well, Morris adds "same" to "mother" for *sammœðri*. *Smyrja*, "anoint", is mistranslated by Magnússon "swearing", but Morris changes it to "smearing", perhaps obscuring the religious connotation of the word but retaining the literal sense and the cognate (XXI). (This correction occurs where the manuscript escaped, for one page, Morris's first revision, which suggests that Morris did not have their manuscript translation before him when checking the printer's proofs – or he would have made more extensive revisions when he noted the little attention this section received.). Magnússon also added certain words, probably hoping to make a particular sentence clearer. Morris, however, prefers to follow the original and finally deletes some of Magnússon's additions, such as "together" (XXVI), and "at that time" (VI). Most important, though, is Morris's addition of translation for lines left out of their manuscript. In Chapter XLII, ... *báru inn í stofuna. Bað konungr menn þa til ganga ok líkit*, through a minor slip by the translators, remains untranslated until the final version. Though Morris still omits the first four words, he adds, "and the king bade men step up and ken the body". This final version, as it turns out, is more important than it first seems.

The point of the foregoing study ought to be clear by now – Morris's translation is amazingly accurate, and faithful to its source. Morris must have followed the Icelandic closely, even though Magnússon offered him an English translation. He was a much more conscientious translator than many have implied. He constantly sought words close to the Icelandic, often emending sentence structures to achieve similar syntax and word order. Even his controversial use of cognates is founded on the principle that the fullest possible representation of every aspect of the Icelandic text is of primary importance. Whether all Morris's translations are this accurate lies beyond the scope of this study, but it is unlikely that the attention Morris paid to his other translations would be any less than to this, his last translation – when he was debilitated by illness and near death.

V

Unfortunately, the controversy does not end here. Morris's theory of translation, in fact his theory of language, will always spur discussion. Often his translations were attacked the way the Ossianic Fragments and Chatterton's work were in the previous century, although Morris, at least, did not pretend his works were rediscovered antiquities. Instead Morris's critics claimed he wrote in a language that never existed. But Morris did not invent language, he imitated it, as Karl Litzenberg pointed out some years ago.[57]

Morris's language, of course, belongs to a long tradition of archaism, but of a very specialized school going back to Sir John Cheke in the sixteenth century and to Sir Thomas Smith and the somewhat fanatical Johannes Goropius Becanus. Like them, Morris saw the importance of the Saxon elements in the language. More specifically, Morris believed the dignity of style inherent in Iceland literature "cannot be reached by the Romance element in English. If it is to be reached at all — and then only approximately — it must be by means of the Teutonic element in our speech — the nearest akin to Icelandic."[58] This sentiment is indeed reminiscent of Cheke's, as stated in a letter to his friend, Thomas Hoby, in 1561: "I am of this opinion that our own tung should be written cleane and pure, unmixt and unmangeled with borrowing of other tunges, wherein if we take not heed bi tiim, ever borowing and never payeng, she shall be fain to keep her house as bankrupt."[59] Cheke practised this theory in his well known translation of St Matthew's Gospel, which includes "crossed" for the usual "crucified", and "hundreder" for "centurion".

The argument, in both cases, takes on political overtones. Goropius argued that German was the original language, and the perfect language for the exchange of ideas. Less fanatical, Sir Thomas Smith often traced English words to their Saxon origins. In the next century, pride in the Germanic origins of the English nation grew. John Hare frequently refers to the Germanic kingship of the English, and calls the English "children of Germany".[60] The Norman invasion, of course, was an unfortunate occurrence the effects of which were played down.

These feelings were certainly not alien to William Morris, three hundred years later. Speaking of the Norman Conquest, Morris laments, the "Teutonic elements" in the language are the few reminders of England before that day in 1066 that rendered "Harald the Hapless the last King of the English". He maintains, "What had happened was serious enough: England had fallen into the hands of a Romanized landlord and from henceforth was a part of the great European Feudal System: its development as a pure branch of the Teutonic family was stopped forever; because the countries to whom it was now to be bound were, whatever their blood was, developed from Roman provincials, and had not even a language of their own, but were compelled to speak a dialect of Latin".[61] But the language was not the only area to suffer, contends Morris; though "there is no room for regret" concerning the development of architecture, "literature also became Frenchified and here to its great misfortune as I think". Morris proceeds to state his case even further: "The great works of the English poets since Chaucer's time have had to be written in what is little more than a dialect of French and I cannot help looking on that as a mishap. If we could only have preserved our language as the Germans have theirs, I think we with our mingled blood would have made the world richer than it is now...."[62] Naturally, when Morris approached the task of translating the Icelandic sagas for his *Saga Library*, he attempted to point out to his English audience the common Germanic roots of Icelandic and English.

Morris, of course, would look scornfully upon this whole discussion. Of critics, he said, "To think of a beggar making a living by selling his opinion about other people!... and fancy any one paying him for it!".[63] Perhaps Magnússon's words to the critics would be more helpful: Morris's style, he says, "is a matter of taste; therefore, not of dispute".[64] Still, though, we face the problem of what saga-translations we are to recommend or, in fact, read ourselves. Laing's translations, of course, are accurate enough, though not translated directly from the Icelandic; but they often lack spark. The same might be said of many other translations. One might argue that the sagas are, after all, straightforward and written in simple language, but the saga-writer's audiences enjoyed a cultural connection we cannot. Morris's translations, in their strangeness, in their vitality, point out this different age, this different spirit — and the difference in Morris's language makes all the difference. One might still say of Morris, as Ben Jonson did of Spenser, "In affecting the ancients, he writ no language";[65] at the same time, though, one would have to continue Jonson's comment and suggest that Morris, too, should be read "for his matter".[66]

NOTES

1   Walpole's *Castle of Otranto* (1764) was inspired, supposedly, by a dream Walpole had in his "little Gothic castle", Strawberry Hill. Lewis's *The Monk* (1797) develops the most macabre elements in the Gothic Revival. Mrs. Radcliffe's *Mysteries of Udolpho* (1794) actually takes place in the sixteenth century and depends on Gothic architecture, as did *Otranto*, for its air of darkness and the supernatural. The same might be said for the poets of the period, as shown for example by Keats's "Eve of St Agnes" (1819), Wordsworth's "Tintern Abbey" (1798), and Coleridge's "Christabel" (*c.* 1800) and "Kubla Khan" (1816). For Shelley, the darkness of Gothic existed in the moral depravity of some of his characters, such as the Count in *The Cenci* (1819), Shelley's unsuccessful attempt at writing for the stage, which Shelley in his Preface says takes place in "a vast and gloomy pile of feudal architecture". His skills of Gothic description reach their height with the horrific decay in "The Sensitive Plant" (1820). *See* Clark 1950; Chandler 1970; Seaton 1935; Mjöberg 1980, 207–238.

2   For example, the great library of Robert Cotton, which included the manuscripts of *Sir Gawain and the Green Knight, Pearl, Beowulf*, as well as The Lindisfarne Gospels, was first placed in the British Museum in 1753, though Cotton collected many of the manuscripts in the late sixteenth century. *Beowulf* was first transcribed, by an Icelander, Grímur Jónsson Thorkelin, in 1787.

3   Kittredge 1902, xli–l; Bartholin 1689; Mallet 1755, translated by Percy 1770. *See also* Mallet 1756 and Percy 1763, which included translations and the Icelandic originals of *Hervararkviða*, *Krákumál*, *Höfuðlausn Egils*, *Hákonarmál Eyvindar*, and *Vísur Haralds harðráða*.

4   Cottle 1797; Herbert 1804–1806; Dasent 1842; Laing 1844; Dasent 1843; Dasent 1861; Dasent 1866; Thorpe 1851–1852.

5   Morris and Magnússon 1870; Morris and Magnússon 1868–1870; Morris and Magnússon 1891–1905.

6   Green 1893; Gosse 1879, 21–39 (a discussion and plot summary rather than a true translation); Cleasby and Vigfússon 1874; Vigfússon and Powell 1879; Sweet 1886; Vigfússon and Powell 1883.

7   Laing 1844, p. v.

8   W. E. Henley, according to M. Morris 1936, I, 455.

9   Vigfússon and Powell 1883, I, cxv.

10   R. H. Stoddard in *Appleton's Journal*, 7 (22 June 1872), 675; quoted in Litzenberg 1936a, 421. For other accounts of critical attitudes towards Morris, *see* Gardner 1975 and Faulkner 1973.

11   Hoare 1973, 76 and 67. Miss Hoare is answered by Ellison 1972, 139-175 (for refutations *see* p. 154). J. N. Swannell agrees with Hoare: *see* Swannell 1961b, 13.

12   Hollander 1959, xx.

13   Litzenberg 1936a, 419, n. 4.

14   Nordby 1901.

15   Ker 1957, 205.

16   Gordon 1957, lxxvi.

17   Eddison 1930, 233, 235.

18   W. H. Lewis 1966, 147-148. For a concordance of Lewis's comments on Morris, *see* Kranz 1974, 154.

19   C. S. Lewis 1939, 38. Swannell seems to misinterpret Lewis's remark and implies that Lewis is criticizing Morris: *see* Swannell 1961a, 375.

20   Litzenberg 1947, 1-27, *see* p. 2. Though I cannot claim to have read all the scholarship in this field, Litzenberg seems to be the only twentieth-century scholar to support wholeheartedly Morris' work. *See* further Litzenberg 1933, 1936b and 1936c.

21   Examples include Swannell and Ellison (*see* notes 11 and 19 above), and Maxwell 1961, 383-393. Swannell, in fact, claims "his translations ... are a hindrance rather than a help, to the modern reader who tries to use them as a substitute for the originals" (Swannell 1961b, 20).

22   Henderson 1950, 4-5.

23   In his Envoi to *The Earthly Paradise*.

24   Mackail 1899, I, 31. Mackail here was paralleling — or perhaps even paraphrasing — Matthew Arnold: "And yet, steeped in sentiment as she lies, spreading her gardens to the moonlight, and whispering from her towers the last enchantments of the Middle Ages, who will deny that Oxford, by her ineffable charm, keeps ever calling us near to the true goal of all of us, to the ideal, to perfection . . .'. (Preface to *Essays in Criticism* [London and Cambridge: Macmillan and Co., 1865], p. xviii). The standard modern biography is Thompson 1977.

25   Burne-Jones 1904, II, 45.

26   Mackail 1899, I, 39.

27   According to Litzenberg's reckoning in Litzenberg 1935, 93. The number varies, of course, depending on how one interprets "Northern influence".

28   Ellison 1972, 152.

29   This closeness is geographical as well as literary: Morris travelled to Iceland twice, first in 1871, and again in 1873. *See* M. Morris 1911, VIII. *Victorian Poetry*, Vol. 13, Nos. 3 and 4 (Autumn-Winter 1975) includes a number of articles that discuss Morris's literary activity, one of which, Harris 1975, 119-130, is particularly relevant to this study.

30   In a letter to Stefán Einarsson, 3 November 1925, quoted in Einarsson 1934, 31-32.

31   Quoted in Einarsson 1934, 32; originally printed in *The Cambridge Review*, 30 January 1913. Einarsson also wrote a biography of Magnússon: Einarsson 1933.

32   Brooke 1964, 281; quoted in McDowell 1923, 152, and in Swannel 1961b, 4.

33   Morris and Magnússon 1891-1905, VI, xv; also in M. Morris 1911, I, 469.

34   M. Morris 1911, VII, xv-xvii.

35   Morris was not the first Englishman with whom Magnússon had worked, though. The son of a minister in eastern Iceland, Magnússon sailed to England in 1862 to supervise the printing of an Icelandic New Testament by the British and Foreign Bible Society. Aboard the same ship was G. E. J. Powell, a wealthy young Welshman returning from a tour of Iceland, so popular among English in the mid-nineteenth century. (Einarsson 1934, 18; lists other prominent Englishmen who visited Iceland about that time and wrote about it including S. Baring-Gould, Lord Dufferin, F. Metcalfe, and C. S. Forbes.) Though their friendship continued, and the two corresponded years later, their association was short-lived; nevertheless, it produced a well received, if unprofitable, edition of *Icelandic Legends*: Powell and Magnússon 1864-1866; and they attempted an Icelandic-English dictionary that never progressed beyond the manuscript stage. In 1863, and again in 1868, Magnússon sent Powell

translations to polish off the *Saga of Hávarðar Ísfirðingr* and *Egils Saga* but neither ever appeared. Powell, frustrated, resolved "to renounce literature for evermore" (in a letter dated 9 July 1869, quoted in Einarsson 1934, 22), and Magnússon went on to do his independent and well regarded translations of *Lilja* and *Thómas Saga Erkibiskups* (Asgrimsson, 1870; Magnússon, 1875–1883). He then met Morris, and the two of them began an 18-year collaboration that was to produce a voluminous stream of Icelandic translations.

36   Morris considered his "Lovers of Gudrun" to be "the best thing I have done", in a letter to Charles Eliot Norton dated 21 December 1869 (Henderson 1950, 32).

37   Morris and Magnússon 1875; W. Morris 1869 and M. Morris 1911, X; *Grettir* appeared in 1869, but was republished in M. Morris 1911, VII; *Viglund* appeared in M. Morris 1911, X. W. Morris confirms this chronology in a letter to H. Buxton Forman, the editor of Keats and Shelley, dated 8 December 1873 (Henderson 1950, 61).

38   *See also* Litzenberg 1936b.

39   Henderson 1950, 324.

40   Mackail 1899, II, 247. Morris's association with Quaritch as a bookseller went back some years. Morris was an inveterate collector of old books and manuscripts; he would at times barter for months to obtain an especially desired book. Even near death, he sent his secretary, Sydney Cockerell, to Stuttgart to negotiate the purchase of a twelfth-century English bestiary (Mackail 1899, II, 339). For a description of just how enthusiastically Morris acquired medieval books, *see* Mackail 1899, II, 323–324.

41   Mackail 1899, II, 316–317. Magnússon translated others, but Morris was never able to revise them for publication. According to an advertisement in *The Athenaeum*, June 1892, *The Saga Library* was also to include the *Eddas*, the *Vǫlsunga Saga, The Orkney Saga, The Sagas of Eric the Red* and *Thorfinn Karlsefne, The Story of Grettir the Strong, Gunnlaug's Saga, Frithiof's Saga, The Saga of Viglund the Fair, Egil's Saga, Njal's Saga, The Saga of the Laxdalers*, "and several others".

42   Morris and Magnússon 1891–1905, VI, vii.

43   Morris and Magnússon 1891–1905, VI, xiii; also in *The Cambridge Review* (26 November 1896), and restated in M. Morris 1911, VII, xvii. Of the first volumes, I have seen manuscripts of *Howard the Halt* (Huntington Manuscript 6426) and *Olaf Tryggvison* (Huntington Manuscript 6437); I am working on a comparative study of the two methods.

44   Einarsson 1934, 27. The entire Morris–Magnússon manuscript is listed in Catalogue 36, 1908, of W. Heffer and Sons, Cambridge, as having 678 pages. The catalogue echoes Magnússon in saying, "Any serious attempt at a sound criticism on William Morris' position towards old Icelandic literature must be based exclusively on the evidence of this unique document".

45   Anderson incorporated his study into his 1942 Ph.D. dissertation for Harvard University, *Scandinavian Elements in the Works of William Morris*. Professor Anderson has written to me that he intends to publish articles based on his dissertation, but declined to discuss his work.

46   Swannell 1961a.

47   Morris and Magnússon 1891–1905, VI, xiii.

48   *The Story of King Magnus, Son of Erling*, Huntington Manuscript 6463. Permission to quote granted by The Huntington Library, San Marino, California.

49   Einarsson 1934.

50   I have used the Icelandic of Aðalbjarnarson. 1951, III, 372–417.

51   One is reminded of C. S. Lewis's "un-man" in *Perelandra*; Lewis acknowledged that Morris exerted a strong influence on his work: *see* Henderson 1950, 205.

52   I would refer the reader to Hellander 1968, and to Frank's indispensable, and eminently readable, guide to *dróttkvætt: see* Frank 1978.

53   A short vowel followed by two or more consonants; and long vowels, diagraphs, or diphthongs followed by at least one consonant.

54   All consonants alliterate with themselves, as do the consonant-clusters *sp, sk* and *st*; all vowels alliterate with each other and with *j*.

55   Nordal and Jónsson 1938, 96.

56   Gordon 1957, xlii; Frank 1978, 11.

57   Litzenberg 1937, 327–363.

58   M. Morris 1911, VII, xviii.

59   Jones 1966, 102.
60   Jones 1966, 222.
61   Lemire 1969, 176, 178.
62   Lemire 1969, 177.
63   Mackail 1899, I, 134.
64   Morris and Magnússon 1891–1905, VI, viii.
65   "Discoveries", in *The Works of Ben Jonson*, 9 vols. (London: Bickers and Sons, 1875), IX, 194.

66   I am grateful to several people for their kind advice in the preparation of this article, including Robert Farrell, Dorothy Mermin, and Vilhjálmur Bjarnar of Cornell University, and Karen Kossuth of Pomona College, who first brought this manuscript to my attention. I would also like to thank The Huntington Library for permission to use this manuscript, and for prompt response to any questions I posed about it over the past five years.

APPENDIX A

Morris's revisions in *Magnússaga*, Chapter I

Snorri	*Magnússon*	*Morris*
Síðan	From the time that	Sithence
varð þess víss	knew what	was ware of this
		Add: what was the rede making of
hver ráðagørð	were brewing	*Delete*
boð	word	bidding
þeim er hann vissi	who he knew	of whom he wolted that
at trúnaðarvinir hǫfðu verit	had been close friends	they had been trusty friends
handgengnum	household	liegemen
	farther	*Delete*
Grégóríí	Gregories	of Gregory
þeim	with all these	*Delete*
áttu tal sitt	the counsel was taken	they took the rede together
halda	keep	hold
flokkinum	band	flock
fastmælum	vows	oaths
milli	between	betwixt
Síðan tǫluðu þeir	Then they had a parley as to	Sithence they talked hereof
til konungs taka	were to make king	should take to king
leitaði	searched	sought
ef þat væri ráð hǫfðingja	if it was the plan of captains	if it were the rede of lords
eða annarra lendra manna	and other mighty men	and other rich men
dóttursonr	who was a daughter's son	the daughter's son
Jón Hallkelsson	Jon son of Hallkell	John Hallkellson
flokkinn	band	flock
Skjaldvararson	son of Skialdvor	Skialdvorson
at þat	that it	that that
ráð	counsel	rede
til konungs	for king	to king
af konungaætt	of kingly race	of kingly kin
til ráða fyrir flokkinn	for captain over the band	for ruling the flock
vits	wisdom	wits
mundu betra verða til liðs	wood speed the gather of a host	would be better for the hosting
Árna konungsmág	Arni King's brother in law	Arni King's Stepfather
ef hann vildi láta taka til konungs nǫkkurn sona sinna	if he wished any of his sons to be declared king	if he would let take to king any of his sons
bezt ættborinn	Best born as to race	best born of kin
harðráðr	hard-counsellor (i.e., bold and firm)	hard-redy *Delete*
landráðamaðr góðr	a good hand at public affairs	land-redy man *Final:* a man good at ruling in the land

Snorri	Magnússon	Morris
eigi skorta til þessa ráðs framkvæmð	not be short of means to further this counsel	lack for furtherance of this rede
Tóku margir vel undir þetta ráð	For this many gave good cheer	Many took well to this rede
Svá heyrisk mér til sem er þessa máls er leitat við	From what I hear it seems that sounded on this matter	So hear I herein as if have been sought to on this matter
heldr færisk undan jafnvist þótt at tígnin fæsk þeim	want rather to go back quite as certain if in any case the honour comes to him	had rather excuse them even as sure though the honour shall be fast to him
er fyrir beitisk flokkinum sem áðr hefir nú mjǫk mǫrgum farit	who taketh the lead of the band as it has gone with many now	who ruleth the flock as it hath now fared with mickle many
þeim er slík stórræði hafa upp tekit	who have taken such great affairs upon themselves	who have taken up such big matters
týnt með lífinu Mun sá þess þurfa, er gengr í þenna vanda, at setja ramligar skorður við, at eigi sæti hann þá mótgangi eða fjándskap af þeim, er nú eru í þessu ráði.	lost yea their own life to boot And he who undertakes this, will have to set up stout stays against being thwarted by and coming in for enmity from those who now are bonded in this fellowship in full good faith	tyned and life withal And he will need this, who goes into this trouble, to set strong stays that he sit not the withstanding and enmity of them who now are bound to this rede.
Allir játtu því at gera þetta samband með fullum trúnaði þat er frá mér at segja næst . . . bana mínum mér þykki háskasamligsta	They all said yea to joining this fellowship in good faith. it is to be said of me next to my very death I deem most exceedingly fraught with peril	Yea all said it to make that fellowship with full troth that is to say of me next to my bane methinketh Most perilous
þá vil ek heldr til þess hætta at láta yðr	yet I will rather take upon me the risk to leave it to you to look to this (to do for you what you request me to do)	yet I will rather risk it to let you to look to it
flokksins ráð ok fýsi Allir játtu því til konungs síðan til handa handgengnir . . . Inga konungi hafði hverr þeira slíkar nafnbœtr	band the will and wish They all said yea thereto for king thereupon into his service in King Ingi's service each one had the same title	flock the rede and desire They all yeasaid it to king sithence under his hand King Ingi's liegemen they had each one the same nameboot
áðr	formerly	erst

APPENDIX B: TRANSLATIONS

Icelandic   *Magnússon*

Chapter III

Ǫnundr kvazk eigi mundu
við orrostu kosta,
fyrr en sunnan sigldi
Sigurðr jarl með húskarla.
Mjǫk fara Magnúss rekkar
mætir upp of stræti,
en Hǫkonar haukar
hart skunduðu undan.

Onund said he would not strive
in battle until earl Sigurd
sailed from the south with his
house-carles. Very worthy warriors
of Magnus fare up into the streets;
       = leading warriors
but the hawks of Hakon hied them
hard away.

Chapter III

Greitt frák, gumna dróttinn,
griðar fáks, í viðu,
trauðr esa tenn at rjóða,
Túnsbergi þér snúna.
Hræddusk bjartra brodda
býjarmenn við rennu.
Uggðu eld ok sveigðan
alm dynviðir malma.

Lord (thou) art not loath to redden
the teeth of troll-queen's steed;
I heard that the men in broad Tunsberg
were easily turned away from thee. The
townsmen feared in face of rush of
bright points; stems of metals' din
                                            bow
took fright at fire and swayed elm

Chapter XX

Urð dró austan fjarðar
Erlingr at víkingum,
mein fekk margr af Kœnu
maðr, es hann fór þaðra.
Fœrðr vas fleinn meðal herða
Fríreks. Ofar nekkvi
skolldi, óþarfr ǫldum,
illgjarn við tré Bjarni.

                                            upon
Erling drew Urd (fate, doom) at the
vikings east-side of the firth; many
man got hurt from Cock-boat, as he
fared thither. A fluke was brought
between the shoulders of Frireck.
Evil yearning Biarni, unprofitable to
men, dangled somewhat higher against
the tree.

OF SKALDIC VERSE

Morris	*Published*

Morris

Quoth Onund never would he
strive in the brunt of battle
Till from the South Earl Sigurd
Should sail with all his house carles
Much folk of worthy warriors
Of Magnus up the street fare
But hard away from thenceward
The Hawks of Hakon hied them.

Published

Quoth Onund never would he
Strive in the brunt of battle
Till from the south Earl Sigurd
Should sail with all his house-carles.
Much folk of worthy warriors
Of Magnus up the street fare,
But hard away from thenceward
The Hawks of Hakon hied them.

Thou loath'st not, Lord
~~Lord thou art loath in nowise~~ to redden
The teeth of the steed of troll-wife
I heard that in wide Tunsberg
Lightly were men turned from thee
The townsmen feared to meet there
The rushing of the bright points
Adrad were the stems of steel-din
Of the flame and the swayéd elm-bow.

Thou loath'st not, lord, to redden
The teeth of the steed of troll-wife;
I heard that in wide Tunsberg
Lightly good luck went with thee.
The townsmen feared to meet there.
The rushing of the bright points;
Adrad were the stems of steel-din
Of flame and swayèd elm-bow.

Erling drew on the Vikings
Fate on the Eastward firths there
Was many a man, of Cock-boat
Gat hurt as he fared thither.
Fared was a fluke twixt shoulders
of Frireck; but the ill-willed
Biarni, to men unhelpful
'Gainst tree hung somewhat higher.

Erling drew on the Vikings
Fate on the Wick-firth's eastside;
Was many a man of Cock-boat
Gat hurt, as there he fared on.
Fared was a fluke twixt shoulders
Of Frirek; but the ill-willed
Biarni, to men unhelpful,
'Gainst tree hung somewhat higher.

[Hann lét bera kaðla tvá á byrðinginn ok tengja við] skútur tvær, lét róa svá, eptir sem byrðinginn rak fyrir. En er eldrinn var mjǫk kominn inn at býnum, þá heldu þeir kǫðlum, er á skútunum váru, svá at eigi mátti býrinn brenna. Reyk lagði, svá þykkt í býinn, at ekki sá af bryggjunum, þar sem fylking konungs stóð. Síðan lagði Erlingr ǫllu liðinu útan eptir á veðrit eldinum ok skutu upp á þá. En er býjarmenn sá, at eldrinn nálgaðisk hús þeira, ok margir urðu sárir af skotum, þá gerðu þeir ráð sitt ok sendu Hróald prest langtǫlu út á fund Erlings at taka sér grið ok býnum af Erlingi ok rufu fylking konungs, þá er Hróaldr sagði þeim, at griðin váru tekin, En er býjarmannalið var brot farit, þá þynntisk ið á bryggjunum. Eggjuðu þá sumir Hákonar menn, at við skyldi taka, en Ǫnundr Símunarson sagði svá, er þá hafði mest ráð fyrir liðinu: „Eigi mun ek berjask til ríkis Sigurði jarli, en hann sé hvergi nær." Síðan flýði Ǫnundr ok þá allt lið með konungi ok fóru upp á land, ok fell þar mjǫk mart manna af Hákonar liði. Svá var þá kveðit:

> Ǫnundr kvazk eigi mundu
> við orrostu kosta,
> fyrr en sunnan sigldi
> Sigurðr jarl með húskarla.
> Mjǫk fara Magnúss rekkar
> mætir upp of stræti,
> en Hǫ́konar haukar
> hart skunduðu undan.

þorbjǫrn Skakkaskáld segir svá:

> Greitt frák, gumna dróttinn,
> gríðar fáks, í víðu,
> trauðr esa tenn at rjóða,
> Túnsbergi þér snúna.
> Hræddusk bjartra brodda
> býjarmenn við rennu.
> Uggðu eld ok sveigðan
> alm dynviðir malma.

Quoth Ormund never would he
Strive in the brunt of battle.
Till from the South Earl Sigurd
Should sail with all his house Carles
Much folk of worthy warriors
Of Magnus up the street fare
But hard away from thence ward
The Hawks of Hakon hied them.
Thou loath'st not, lord
~~Lord the out loath in~~ to redden
The teeth of the steed of troll-wife
I heard that in wide Tunsberg
Lightly were men turned from thee
The townsmen feared to meet thee
The rushing of the bright points
Adrad were the stems of steel - dim
Of the flame and the swayed elm-bow.

THE VIKING MYTH

Kristján Eldjárn

Sometime Director of the National Museum, Iceland

WHEN I WAS INVITED to speak about the Viking Myth to this distinguished audience, I gladly, but somewhat imprudently, accepted. I was brought up on this myth, the myth of the Saga Time — the term which is more often used in my country than is the term Viking Age. I remember the long winter evenings in our home on a farm in northern Iceland when my father read aloud to his household from some old Viking saga. We were proud to know that even our valley had a saga of its own, the *Svartfdaela saga*, telling how brave men came across the sea in the Age of Settlement to establish their homes on the various farms all around us. Of course we admired the ancient heroes, but looking back I find it peculiar how little we were affected by the violence and the relatively frequent killings in these stories. A famous incident from the so-called Sworn Brothers' Saga (*Fóstbrœðra Saga*) will illustrate what I have in mind. One of the two heroes of this saga, a character noted for being rather too quick to reach for his axe, at one point cuts off the head of an entirely innocent and harmless person. When asked why he has done such a grotesque thing, he calmly replies: "It is true enough that the man had done me no harm. But he stuck out his neck in such an inviting manner that the opportunity was simply too good to miss". I would not say that we sided with the Viking fellow in this or similar cases, but we certainly did not have much sympathy for his victim, either. It lies in the nature of the myth to skip lightly over the cruel acts of the Vikings and at the same time to see their valour and gallantry through magnifying lenses.

Now in spite of having been exposed in my young days to the Viking Myth in full vigour through saga reading, I very much fear that it really is a bit too big a subject for me to do it any justice in a single lecture. But I feel it is a worthy subject, and I am proud to have been given an opportunity to take part in this Viking Symposium and Series, held under the auspices of the Metropolitan Museum of Art and Cornell University.

The period in the history of northern Europe, and to a certain extent western Europe as well, that historians have taught us to refer to as the Viking Age is usually thought of as having lasted from about the year 800 to about the year 1050. When greater precision is called for, the years often chosen to mark the beginning and end of this period are 793, when seafaring men from the north, in a lightning raid, descended on the Island of Lindisfarne off the Northumbrian coast and sacked its monastery; and 1066, the year of the fateful battles of Stamford Bridge and Hastings, the first of which put an end to Scandinavian attempts to conquer English territory, and the second of which resulted in the firm establishment on the throne of England of William the Conqueror, who, by the way, was himself of Viking descent. There is no objection to continuing to use these dates, as long as we keep in mind that by the end of the eighth century the

Scandinavians for a long time had undoubtedly been engaging in piracy as a sideline to their farming, and that before 1066 the Viking Age had begun to ebb, bit by bit. By that time the Vikings — or Norsemen — had long since lost control of all the territories in which they had established themselves for longer or shorter periods. Wherever they had occupied settled regions, they had since been driven out and had returned to their northern homelands. Ultimately, their only permanent gains of new territories were a few islands in the Atlantic Ocean which they discovered and settled — rather harsh and inhospitable islands, at that, and certainly very different from the fertile southern lands which they had dreamed of possessing and with which they had enjoyed a more or less brief acquaintance. These islands might seem to be but a small addition to the Norse area, but among them was Iceland, which was to become a sort of storehouse for the lore and legend, as well as the historical tradition, of the Viking Age. Looked at from this point of view, Iceland was an important addition. If this remote island had not been discovered and settled by the Norsemen towards the end of the ninth century, much of what we know about the Viking heritage might now very well be lost for ever.

But even if the Scandinavians proved unable to hold on to the lands they invaded, Viking warfare had important consequences. It opened up the great world to the Norsemen. They had in various ways come into contact with other peoples, with larger and, let us say, more civilized nations, and had adopted elements from those cultures. Above all, they had been converted to Christianity, with all the consequences that was bound to have. And through getting to know and mixing with other peoples, they gained a new understanding of themselves, a clearer sense of their own identity, of their own strengths as well as their weaknesses, of what was within their power and what was beyond it. And the Viking raids initiated a development in the balance of power among nations, traces of which are to be seen to this day. No doubt the civilization of the Vikings lacked the refinement of some of the cultures with which they came in contact, but it contained strong and vital elements which in their own way made themselves felt wherever the Vikings went. The Vikings were not merely receivers of culture but shapers of it.

But my subject is not the Viking heritage in general; rather, it is one aspect of that heritage: the memory it left behind, the memory of the Vikings that survived when there were no longer any Vikings around. Out of this memory grew the Viking Myth, the image of Viking life reflected in the minds of successive generations through the ages — a matter which has proved to hold a singular fascination during bygone centuries, and continues to do so.

Memories of the Vikings and their manner of conducting themselves have been preserved in one way or another in all the countries where their impact was felt. These memories are of many kinds, and certainly not all of them are favourable to the early visitors from Scandinavia. But to cover this subject even superficially would be a hopeless undertaking, and I shall have to confine myself to the homelands of the Vikings, the Norse or Scandinavian region. Quite naturally, memories of the Viking Age have always been most abundant and most alive in these countries, and, strange as it may seem, nowhere more so than in Iceland, which of all the Norse countries was the one farthest removed from the great events around which these memories centred.

Long before the Viking Age came to an end, people throughout the Scandinavian countries had, of course, begun to tell stories about the eventful life of the Vikings —

about their warlike exploits abroad or other contacts with foreign peoples, about adventurous voyages and daring raids, and about quick profits — that is to say, loot and plunder. It is not difficult to imagine those who had stayed at home listening in open-mouthed wonder as the returning Vikings told of their heroic deeds in strange and distant lands. The foundation of the Viking Myth thus must have been laid early, a foundation so solid that it has never since wholly given way; the myth has merely taken on different forms and served different purposes at different times. Let me give a few examples, in chronological order, out of a very great number of similar anecdotes.

The first example comes from Iceland. The date is 1119. In that year a wedding feast was held at the farm of Reykhólar, the home of an important chieftain. A contemporary chronicle, whose accuracy we have no reason to doubt, includes an account of this feast. It lasted for seven days; clearly no one felt pressed for time. There was entertainment of various kinds, including dancing, wrestling, and story-telling. About the story-telling the chronicle (*Sturlinga saga; see* R. K. Gordon) has this to say:

> Hrólfur of Skálmarnes told a story about Hröngriður the Viking and about Ólafur, King of the Sea-raiders, and about þráinn the Berserk breaking into the grave-mound, and about Hrómundur Gripsson. This story Hrólfur himself had put together.
>
> Ingimundur the Priest told a story about Ormur the Poet of Barrey Island, including many verses and at the end a fine poem he himself had composed on the subject. And yet many knowing men consider this story a true one.

Few passages have been quoted more often by scholars in the field of Icelandic and Old Norse literature than this description of a wedding feast in the year 1119. It is a fixed point in the discussion of the origins and development of Old Norse literature and saga writing. It shows us that the Viking Myth is already in full flower in the early twelfth century. By that time people have begun to tell exaggerated and fanciful tales about Vikings and berserks and their heroic deeds, including their favourite sport of breaking into ancient grave-mounds, fighting it out with the mound-dweller, and carrying off his treasure. Some of these stories were composed by the story-tellers themselves, as the passage just quoted makes clear, but still people believe them in some degree or another and can even trace their genealogies to the principal characters. People believe them because they want to believe them, and nothing can shake their belief, not even the fact that no less a man that King Sverrir of Norway — who, to be sure, lived a little later than this — called these stories "lying tales", though admittedly "most entertaining lying tales". What we have here, then, is the Viking Myth fully formed and serving a double function: invigorating the farmer tired from his labours with marvellous tales of the exploits of his illustrious forefathers, and providing entertainment at festive gatherings.

My second example, also from Iceland, dates from about 1650. Around that time there was a great poet, the Reverend Hallgrímur Pétursson, whose supreme achievement is a sequence of hymns on the passion and death of Christ, known as the Passion Hymns (*Passíusálmar*), which were learned and read aloud and sung in every Icelandic household well into this century. Pétursson also set himself a very different task and wrote a poem he called *Aldarháttur* — "A Mirror for the Age" we might call it — a long poem in resounding leonine hexameters, in which he praises the heathen heroes of northern antiquity in glowing terms. He extols their courage and warlike prowess, speaks admiringly of their Viking raids, and even lists among their virtues their observance of the heathen duty to avenge affronts and injuries. Surely nothing could be more contrary to the Christian command of love and forgiveness. How is it possible that one of the greatest religious poets of Scandinavia should thus glorify the conduct and the morality of the heathen Vikings of old? The answer is simply that the pious clergyman is dazzled by the lustre of the Viking Myth as it is embodied in the old literature. Of course he does not write his poem with the intention of exalting heathendom at the expense of Christianity — nothing could be further from him. He writes it to present his readers with an idealized picture of the heroism and manliness of the Viking Age with which they can contrast the miserable and degraded state to which he considers his own age to have sunk. The poem shows us two things: how very much alive the Viking Myth is for this seventeenth-century clergyman, and how it was used to stir people to action.

A third example comes from Copenhagen, the Danish capital. The year is 1808, the occasion a performance of *Hakon Jarl* or any one of the numerous dramas of the great romantic poet Adam Oehlenschläger, all of which deal with northern antiquity and its glorious heroes. On stage the characters appear in a most absurd mixture of costumes from different cultural and historical periods, each anachronism more wonderful than the next. But the play itself is suffused with passionate worship of antiquity — of the incomparable Viking Age. The Viking is represented as valiant and noble, a hero in the best sense of the word, who even in the face of death does not know the meaning of fear. His gods come close to rivalling the great divinities of classical Greece and Rome. Everything is idealized, raised to an almost superhuman plane. The romantic conception of antiquity is seen here in its purest form. The poet wants to demonstrate, to his countrymen and to everyone else, that the ancestors of the Norse peoples, far from being barbarians, were no less beautiful, free and noble than the heroes of classical antiquity. Here we see Viking Myth raised on high in the work of a great poet and made visible on the stage of the Royal Theatre itself.

My fourth example represents an approach to the subject very different from that of the other three. It dates from 1952, the year in which the Nobel Prize winner Halldór Laxness published his novel *Gerpla*, which appeared on English under the title *The Happy Warriors*. This novel is set in the Viking Age and is based largely on *The Sworn Brothers' Saga* and the *Saga of St Olaf* in Snorri Sturluson's *Heimskringla*, though it also draws on many other sources, both Icelandic and foreign. In it the Viking Myth is turned upside down, so to speak. The Viking and the life of the Viking are mercilessly stripped of all idealization. The Vikings are represented as actually inferior to other men in physical stature and vigour. They are uncouth brutes and murderers, cruel and treacherous, little better than mere barbarians. The novel is a masterpiece of irony and sarcasm, but also rich in humour. It is a deliberate reaction against a long-standing and, to the author's mind, extravagant and false Viking-worship and boasting of ancient greatness, both in Iceland and in the other Norse countries, and even elsewhere. The author wants to remove the gloss from the old traditional picture, and he spares no effort to reverse almost every stereotype that up to this time had passed for truth. Undoubtedly the novel also has a larger underlying purpose, in that it is intended to set before our eyes the abomination of war and violence in general.

I shall stop here and not give you any more examples of the different ways in which the Viking Myth has presented itself at different times. Not that there is any shortage of such examples — in scholarly works, in literature, in the theatre, and especially in art. Before going on, perhaps we should now turn our attention to the reality behind the myth. The myth is, of course, a projection of some sort of reality. But what is that reality, as far as the Vikings are concerned?

Let us first look at the word "viking" itself. No one knows for certain what the origin of this word is. The *meaning* of the word is a different matter. It means, simply, "pirate". But why were these ancient northern pirates called Vikings? Many different explanations have been offered, and we are free to choose whichever one we find most convincing. For my part, I can easily conceive that the word is derived from the well-known verb "víkja" in the sense of "departing, going away, leaving home". This interpretation has the advantage of agreeing well with one important matter relating to the causes of the Viking voyages themselves.

What was the reason that Danish and Norwegian country boys left their native soil to try their fortune as pirates or conquerors of territory in distant lands? No doubt several causes combined to produce this effect. But on the whole scholars seem to agree that one of the principal causes was overpopulation in the homelands of the Vikings. One consequence of this was that it became increasingly difficult for young men to obtain land for farming. The eldest son or the elder sons of a farmer would inherit the paternal estate; often it had to be divided up among several sons. The farms thus became smaller, and when they became too small to be further divided, the youngest sons did not have many opportunities to choose from. Perhaps their only choice was to take to the sea, for whatever it was worth. Such men were forced to depart — "víkja" — from the farms of their fathers; they had to leave home while their older brothers settled down as farmers in tolerable circumstances, and this may very well be why they were known as Vikings. This interpretation may, of course, be wrong, but it has at least one thing to recommend it: it throws a bit of light on the opposition between farmer and Viking.

But the etymology of a word is one thing and its meaning in established usage another. There is no doubt at all that in the old language of the north the name "Viking" was given to men who banded together to man ships for the purpose of sailing along the coasts to prey upon merchant vessels or on other pirate vessels that happened to cross their path; they did not disdain, either, to raid ill-defended coastal settlements where they could pick up something of value, whether silver, weapons, cattle or slaves. In other words, the Vikings were men who pursued piracy as an occupation — true professional pirates.

It is quite a different matter that in modern usage the term "Viking" tends to be applied to the entire population of the Norse countries in the so-called Viking Age. I say "the so-called Viking Age" deliberately, because even this term is of relatively recent origin, having come into use only in the last decades of the nineteenth century. It is thus a creation of modern historians, and in itself there is nothing wrong with that. The same thing may be said about the modern use of the word "Viking" to mean all the people living in the Norse countries during the Viking Age. It is a handy use of the word, but it is far from corresponding to the concept it expresses in the language of the Viking Age itself. At that time a Viking was a pirate, but if he abandoned that occupation and returned home, or settled down as a farmer in a hitherto unsettled country, he was no longer a Viking. He was a Viking only as long as he was on board a Viking ship, not at any other time. And it is in this ancient and strictly limited sense that I am here talking about Vikings. It was around these men, who for a longer or shorter time were engaged in piracy and warfare on Viking ships, that the great and long-lived myths were built, not around those who stayed at home.

Piracy is an occupation of great antiquity and has been practised all over the world. It is noteworthy, though perhaps entirely natural, that the behaviour of pirates everywhere seems to be pretty much the same. No doubt many parallels to the Vikings could be found, and I at least am certain that no one who studies the history of Dutch, French and English pirates of the seventeenth century and their conduct towards the Spaniards in the Caribbean Sea can fail to be reminded of the Vikings, of their brutal and ruthless treatment of defenceless populations in western Europe, of their greed for every kind of wealth, but also of their valour and endurance and a certain kind of magnanimity when the occasion seemed to call for it. Between 1668 and 1671 a certain Frenchman, apparently by the name of Exquemelin, served as ship's surgeon on various pirate vessels, including the ships of the fleet of the renowned Henry Morgan. This Exquemelin left a book in which he describes the life and conduct of the pirates, and as far as I know, his accounts are thought to be reliable. Reading them is like meeting our Vikings in person. These seventeenth-century pirates either carried on their plundering activities in single ships or banded together to form fleets. They plundered merchantmen wherever they could find them; made sudden raids on towns, especially those on islands or in isolated places; carried off any valuables they could lay their hands on; and took hostages whom the townspeople were then forced to ransom, on pain of the town's being burned down and the population killed. Pirates frequently massacred defenceless people, or captured them and sold them into slavery. They plundered churches wherever they could, and their conduct was generally characterized by violence and ruthlessness. All these things are also reported of the Vikings in our sources, and there seems to be no reason to doubt their accuracy.

In spite of everything, one must not forget that these pirates had their own code of conduct. Among them there obtained a certain unwritten law, a kind of blood-brotherhood, and this, too, reminds us of the Vikings. They risked their lives for each other and when it came to dividing the spoils, there was generally no question of anyone being cheated out of his share. Some of these men returned to normal civilian occupation once they were satisfied with the proceeds of their piratical ventures, but many continued, turning professional and ceasing to belong to any particular nation, instead giving their allegiance only to the pirate community. All of this recalls the Vikings. Exquemelin says: "They live in no particular country; their home is wherever there is hope of spoils, and their only patrimony is their bravery".

I wonder if this would not serve pretty well as a description of the professional Vikings of the ninth and tenth centuries. And some of Exquemelin's stories of pirate boldness sound as if they had been lifted from a collection of Viking tales. I cannot refrain from giving you one example.

A group of English and French pirates, part of the force assembled by Henry Morgan for the purpose of sacking the city of Panama, is besieging the fort of San Lorenzo, which is held by a strong Spanish garrison. For quite a while the pirates have been making no headway, and they are in a bad mood. And here I quote Exquemelin:

Now as the Frenchmen stood there, lamenting their ill fortune, an arrow came flying through the ear of one of them and pierced his shoulder and stuck there. Among the defenders of the fort were some Indians, and their arrows were more dangerous than the Spaniards' bullets. With marvellous self-command, amid the tumult of battle, the man pulled the arrow from the wound himself and said to those around him: "Pay heed, brothers. With this arrow I shall bring about the the destruction of the Spaniards".

I suspect that among my readers there are some who have already recalled a famous episode from Snorri's *Heimskringla*, which formed part of his account of the Battle of Stiklastaðir , where the former Viking and later royal saint, King Olafur Haraldsson, was killed in the year 1030. The battle is over, and wounded members of the king's defeated army have sought shelter in a barn, where a woman is ministering to their wounds. Among them is the poet and warrior þormóður Kolbrúnarskáld, looking very pale. The saga continues as follows:

> Then the healer woman said: "Let me see your wounds and bandage them". Then he sat down and cast off his clothes. And when she inspected his wounds she looked closely at the wound he had in his side. She noticed that there was an iron in it, but did not know which path it had taken . . . Then she took a pair of pincers and tried to pull out the iron (which in fact was an arrow head), but it was stuck and would not budge. Also it showed but little, the wound having swollen. Then Thormoth said: "You cut in, to reach the iron, so that I can take hold of it with the pincers, then let me have them and let me pluck it out". Then Thormoth took a gold ring off his arm and gave it to the healer woman, telling her to do with it as she pleased: "It comes from a noble hand," he said, "King Olaf gave me the ring this morning". Thereupon he took the pincers and pulled out the arrow. It had barbs on it and there were fibres of his heart in it, some red and some white, and when he saw that he said: "Well has the king fed us. I am still fat about the roots of my heart". Thereupon he leaned back and was dead.

Exquemelin's story bears a remarkably striking resemblance to the story of the Viking poet þormóður . But there is one great difference, and a highly significant one. The former is presumably an eye-witness account and has an air of realism, whereas the latter is enveloped in the splendour of the Viking myth. When þormóður , returning mortally wounded from the battle, is asked by the healing woman why he is so pale, he answers in an elegant scaldic stanza composed on the spur of the moment. His coolly ironic last words show exactly how the myth required a Viking to conduct himself in the face of death: this is its ideal conception of an heroic death.

Yes, the Vikings were unquestionably pirates, very much of the same kind as their colleagues in various parts of the world at various times. There is no reason to doubt the accounts of their atrocities found in the historical records of the countries that bore the brunt of their attacks. But neither is there any reason to apologise on their behalf. Their conduct must be viewed in the light of their own times. And we must not forget, either, that the soldier is often a very different person in combat than in everyday life at home. Many of those who took part in the atrocities committed during Viking raids returned home and took up the peaceful activities of the farming community. It is not only possible but actually highly probable that many a man, after a blood-stained career as a Viking, settled down as a peaceful farmer and became perhaps an artistically gifted worker in wood or metal, perhaps a first-rate poet, perhaps a lawmaker and peacemaker in his native district. Many a man turned Viking in order to win fame and fortune, and perhaps above all, land, as quickly as possible, but with the firm intention of settling down as soon as ever he could starting a family and leading a peaceful life. Active Vikings at any given time were never more than a tiny fraction of the total population, but on the other hand there were many who at one time or another had been on Viking raids. And no doubt such men enjoyed a certain status in the community if they had acquitted themselves well and gained a certain amount of wealth. Very likely these returned veterans were more than willing to entertain those who had stayed at home with stories about Viking life — many a tall tale, one would suppose. We are told of

one such man who in later life worked as a blacksmith. Standing at the forge he would
often be heard to mutter this ditty to himself:

> Alone did I kill
> eleven men
> in the battle.
> Blow harder, boy!

And the poet-Viking Egill Skallagrímsson is said to have composed the following stanza
when he was in his seventh year — undeniably a somewhat precocious child:

> My mother told me
> I must be given
> A swift-oared ship
> To sail out with Vikings.
> I should stand in the prow
> Of a precious vessel,
> Bring it into harbour
> and hew down the foe.

Whether true or not, a story like this one of Egill serves to remind us who it must have
been that prepared the ground for the Viking myth. The mother who tells her young son
that he has the makings of a Viking leader must surely have had at least her full share of
the tales told by returning Vikings about their own exploits and those of their
comrades-in-arms.

We often read in history books that Vikings settled Iceland and Greenland, and, in
fact, discovered America. Of course these countries, uninhabited up to that time, were
never in any proper sense Viking countries. What business would a Viking have had where
there was no one to fight and no spoils to be had? Still, the history books are right in the
sense that among the settlers of Iceland were many former Vikings, and calling Iceland a
Viking country may be justifiable on the grounds that the community established there
by the settlers contained all the cultural elements characteristic of the Norse peoples in
the Viking Age. This community, through being transplanted to an uninhabited country,
was subject to very special conditions of growth, and as I have already mentioned, the
memories of the race were nowhere preserved as well as there. Why this should have
been so could no doubt be debated back and forth for a long time without conclusive
results, and I shall not enlarge on the matter. But the simple fact remains that a relatively isolated new settlement preserved the memories best. I say "relatively isolated",
because although Iceland was isolated geographically, the Icelanders during the first
centuries of settlement kept up a lively intercourse with the Scandinavian countries,
and with other countries as well, for that matter, so that for a long time the contact with
the homelands to their ancestors remained unbroken. They were thus in a position to
keep up with what was happening in the world around them and at the same time observe
events in the great world undisturbed, from their island out in the Atlantic.

As I have already mentioned, we know on reliable authority that as early as 1100 the
Icelanders had begun to tell, and probably also to write, Viking tales. Most likely that
narrative art had been practised in one form or another from time immemorial. But in the
latter half of the Middle Ages, the Icelanders began to produce, on a large scale, books in

which were preserved the lore and legends of the Norse peoples or, if you wish, the heritage of the Viking Age. They recorded a multitude of ancient poems; they wrote the Eddas, which contain the mythology of the heathen religion; and they composed accounts of the kings of the Norse peoples from the earliest times up to, and indeed beyond, the end of the Viking Age. These last deal especially with the kings of Norway, including the celebrated Viking kings Ólafur Tryggvason and Ólafur Haraldsson, who later became the patron saint of Norway. They wrote fantastically exaggerated tales of Viking adventure, the so-called Mythical–Heroic Sagas, the kind of story, by the way, told at the wedding feast at Reykhólar referred to earlier. Some of these tales probably had some basis in dimly-remembered traditions, but others were pure fiction composed in the style the audience demanded of a Viking tale. And, last but not least, they wrote the often-referred-to Sagas of Icelanders, sometimes rather unfortunately called family sagas, which one is probably safe in regarding as representing the culmination of the almost incredible literary activity of the Icelanders in the twelfth and thirteenth centuries. Most of this literature is anonymous; the authors have left no records of themselves. The one exception is the great historian, Snorri Sturluson, killed in 1241, who completed and perfected the great corpus of narratives relating to the kings of Norway in his masterpiece now generally known as *Heimskringla*, one of the greatest literary works of the Scandinavian Middle Ages.

I do not wish to give the impression that only the Icelanders preserved records of the Viking Age. Least of all would I wish to pass over in silence the *Gesta Danorum*, the great history of Denmark by the late twelfth-century Danish historian Saxo, whose learning earned him the epithet of "Grammaticus". But for our present purpose it really matters very little who preserved all these tales and traditions of the Viking Age. The main thing is that they *were* preserved, for otherwise the Scandinavian cultural heritage would be far poorer than in fact it is.

All of these works of literature were written by medieval Christians two or three centuries after the Viking raids were at an end, but they deal overwhelmingly with the ancient heathen times, the heroic age, the glorious days of the forefathers. Everywhere we find this age in the background. No historian today would dream of accepting these narratives as historical records without many reservations. Still, the element of underlying genuine history, and above all the degree of narrative realism, vary greatly from one work to the next. Some of the accounts strike us, rightly or wrongly, as bearing the stamp of credibility, while others more clearly belong to the world of fairy tale and fantasy. However all that may be, it is unquestionably safe to say that in this old literature we have a clear picture of how people in the later Middle Ages conceived of the Vikings and the life they led. In other words, we get a clear impression of what the Viking Myth looked like in those days. Romantic heroism may be said to permeate practically all of this Old Norse literature. In one way or another the Viking ideal provides the keynote in all of these works. Of course the Viking makes war on innocent people, overpowers them and despoils them, but this is regarded as his right, and he has a corresponding duty to go down with honour in case he finds himself on the losing side. Naturally the Viking is valiant and bold and cuts a brilliant figure, and he knows well how to enjoy the pleasures of this world. Certainly he can be ruthless, but he has his own moral standard and is never guilty of deeds which by this standard are base or infamous: this would turn him from a true Viking into a mere villain. Having been on Viking raids is in these stories considered a great distinction, or even an indispensible part of a young man's education, much as many parents today are ambitious to have their son attend a well-known university. This is how the myth requires these things to have been, and in medieval Icelandic literature the myth is the "leaven that leaveneth the whole lump".

The centuries passed, and the Icelanders continued to read their old sagas in the isolation of their remote island. They lived in the tradition of the past, wrote long narrative poems about ancient heroes, and chanted them to each other to shorten the winter evenings. Nothing quite similar can be said about their cousins on the Continent until they suddenly began to stir, around the beginning of the seventeenth century, and before long to burst into feverish historical activity. The humanism of the Renaissance was beginning to take root in Scandinavia, and people hungered and thirsted for knowledge about their historical origins. Just at this time the Danes and the Swedes discovered that in far-off Iceland books containing such knowledge had been preserved. There began a great race between those two nations to get their hands on the Icelandic manuscripts in which was recorded the ancient history of the north. By the hundreds, or even thousands, these manuscripts were carried to Denmark or Sweden, where scholars fell upon them in a frantic search for their nations' past. What they found was the Viking Age, or rather the Myth of the Viking Age. In due course the art of printing appeared on the scene and these sagas began to be published, and were used as bases for coherent surveys of national history. I need hardly mention that in the seventeenth century, or even in the eighteenth, source criticism was practically non-existent, so that these old tales were generally used uncritically as authentic historical records. As a result, seventeenth- and eighteenth-century historiography has its peculiar aspects. Even so, this was where the Norse people found themselves and their identity. The ground had been well prepared when romanticism made its entry into Scandinavia, which is precisely the time when the Viking Myth becomes so firmly established that its effect is felt throughout the nineteenth century, and even to this day.

The romantic poets took to their bosom the Eddas, sagas and poems of antiquity, and drew on them for innumerable literary creations. A universal feature of this enormous production is an unrestrained idealization of the Viking and of ancient times in general. Among the outstanding poets of this movement one might mention Oehlenschläger in Denmark and Esaias Tegnér in Sweden. Tegnér's cycle of poems based on *Friðþjófssaga*, which represents perhaps the high point of this development, became enormously popular, was translated into a number of languages, and has had a far-reaching influence. Many other poets would be worth mentioning, not least in Norway, where, as was to be expected, the people turned primarily to the Kings' Sagas in their search for their own past. It is generally recognized that these sagas, with the idealization of the great royal heroes of antiquity, did more than anything else to preserve among the Norwegians a sense of national identity through centuries of foreign domination, and ultimately played a significant part in the nation's successful struggle to regain full independence. For centuries *Heimskringla* had its place beside the Bible on the bookshelf in most Norwegian homes. Here we have an excellent illustration of the effect that familiarity with the Viking Age, or perhaps rather the Viking Myth, has been able to produce in modern times. But no less worthy of mention is the effect which romanticism and the romantic poets had on every aspect of intellectual life in their day, in spite of their glaring lack of a proper historical sense, their poetic exaggeration, their anachronisms, and their indiscriminate use of such symbolic features as family gravemounds, heathen temples, thinking and speaking weapons, fantastic helmets with horns or wings, magnificent drinking horns, harps, and so on and so forth, which gradually became inescapable stage properties in all romantic works and from there found their way into innumerable works of art. No matter how strange an impression all this makes on a modern observer, we must never forget that what we have here is the Norse expression of a particular international intellectual movement, nor must we forget how tremendously effective it proved in awakening the self-awareness of the Norse peoples and spurring them on to action in every sphere.

In the latter half of the nineteenth century, the radiance of the Viking Myth began to fade little by little, although it was far from dying out. New times were coming and with them came new attitudes. Particularly important in this connection is the fact that after the middle of the last century, historical criticism and archaeology began to make great strides forward as scientific disciplines. The advance of archaeology in the present century has done more than any other single thing to make it possible to arrive at a realistic picture of the life of the people of the so-called Viking Age in the Norse countries. And that picture differs in many respects from the one required by the romantic myth. Scientific investigations in the fields of history, literary history, and archaeology now show, in a sober and sensible fashion, that even if the ancient Scandinavians were, among other things, pirates and warriors, they were nevertheless at a high level of civilization — as artists, housebuilders, shipwrights, lawmakers and poets.

At the same time these disciplines have also made an inestimable contribution to our understanding of the everyday life of the people of the Viking Age, the life of farmers and fishermen who never went on Viking raids but who constituted the majority and the very foundation of each nation, even if they find little room in the myth or in the work of the romantics, who hardly seem to have been aware that any toiling mass — petty farmers, housecarls, slaves — ever existed. To the romantic myth, only the hero is a man among men. But it is worth observing that simply by drawing attention to the life of the common people — in itself a natural and most excellent thing to do — archaeologists have indirectly given an added impetus to the reaction against the romantic view of the Vikings, providing the leaders of the debunking party with additional reasons for indulging their tendency simply to stand the old image on its head and make the Viking into some kind of anti-hero or mock hero. It seems very likely to me that the great Viking novels of such writers as the Swede Frants G. Bengtson and the Icelander Halldór Laxness, which are brilliant examples of the sort of thing I am talking about, derive some of their strength from archaeology. But because they are every bit as exaggerated as the works of the romantics — though in a diametrically opposed direction — and at the same time entertaining and written by great and famous authors, it is highly probable that they, too, have in certain ways served to distort the image of antiquity. Many people are more willing to believe the picture of the past presented by a good novelist than the one a sober and perhaps sometimes rather dull archaeologist is able to offer.

But what about the Viking Myth today? Is it perhaps finally defunct? Far from it, I should say. There is certainly no less interest in the Vikings and their times today than there was in the past. If anything, the interest is probably on the increase, or so one would judge from the multitude of books about Vikings — scholarly, popular, and fictional — which keep appearing in book-stalls in various parts of the world. The study of the Viking Age is now largely in the hands of the archaeologists. And archaeology, of course, wants to be a science, to be independent not only of myth, but its very opposite. Those who put on the magnificent Viking Exhibition which was first shown at the British Museum in 1980 have obviously done so in a scientific spirit. Nevertheless, it would be rather surprising if somewhere in this exhibition there does not lurk a spark or two from the embers of the good old Viking Myth. It is difficult, even for a scientist, to shake off completely the fetters of so long-standing a tradition.

That the romantic view of the Viking still retains some of its former hold on the popular imagination perhaps appears most clearly from the fact that commercialism has found it profitable enough to enlist it. There are Viking Airlines, Viking Hotels, and Viking God-knows-what in unlikely as well as likely places, to say nothing of motion pictures, the mass media, comic strips, and the souvenir industry. All of these things thrive because the Viking Myth — however altered or modified — lives on. No doubt it will be interesting to see what form it takes and to what uses it is put in the twenty-first century.

Before concluding, there is one thing I must make clear. If what I have been saying has in any way tended to give you an unduly negative picture of the idealized Viking, I want to assure you that that has not been my main intention. At his noblest, the idealized hero of the myth is endowed with qualities which at all times have been thought to deserve honour and respect. The characteristic qualities required of a Norse hero are comprehended in the single term "drengskapur", which implies, among other things, truthfulness, helpfulness, loyalty, fortitude, courage, and self-respect. The hero loves life and knows how to enjoy it, but he can still face death with calmness of mind. There is no reason to think that these virtues belong exclusively to the myth. Undoubtedly they held an honoured place in the moral code of the heathen north, whose essential command — to earn a good reputation in life and to meet death with honour — is expressed in the famous concluding stanzas of the Old Norse poem *Hávamál:*

> Cattle die,
> kindred die,
> every man is mortal;
> but the good name
> never dies
> of one who has done well.
>
> Cattle die,
> kindred die,
> every man is mortal;
> but I know one thing
> that never dies,
> the glory of the great deed.
>
> *(Translated by W. H. Auden and Paul B. Taylor).*

BIBLIOGRAPHY

Abbo Passio 1972, *Abbo Passio Sancti Eadmundi, Three Lives of early English Saints*, ed. M. Winterbottom, Toronto.

Adam, Gesta 1917, *Magistri Adam Bremensis Gesta Hammaburgensis Ecclesiae Pontificum*, ed. B. Schmeidler, *Monumenta Germaniae Historica, Scriptores rerum germanicarum in usum scholarum.*

Addyman, P. V. 1972, The work of the York Archaeological Trust, 1972, *Ann. Rept. Yorks Philos. Soc., 1972*, 20-23.

— , *et al.* 1976, Paleoclimate in urban environmental archaeology at York. England problems and potential, *World Archaeology*, vol. 8, No. 2, 220-33.

— 1974, Excavations in York 1972-73, first interim report. *Antiq. J.*, LIV, 200-31.

— 1975, The work of the York Archaeological Trust, 1975, *Ann. Rept. Yorks Philos. Soc. 1975*, 30-37.

— 1976, The work of the York Archaeological Trust, 1976, *Ann. Rept. Yorks Philos. Soc., 1976, 000-00.*

— 1977, The work of the York Archaeological Trust, 1977, *Ann. Rept. Yorks Philos. Soc., 1977*, 000-00.

— 1978, The work of the York Archaeological Trust, 1978, *Ann. Rept. Yorks Philos. Soc., 1978*, 31-48.

— 1979, The work of the York Archaeological Trust, 1979, *Ann. Rept. Yorks Philos. Soc., 1979*, 28-50.

— 1980a, Eburacum, Jorvik, York. *Scientific American*, 242, No. 3, 76-86.

— 1980b, Excavating Viking-Age York. *Archaeology*, vol. 33, No. 3, 14-22.

— 1980c, The work of the York Archaeological Trust in 1980, *Ann. Rept. Yorks Philos. Soc., 1980*, 27-52.

Akerlund, H. 1973, *Nydamskeppen.*

Albani, C. 1969, *l'Istituto Monachicho nell'antica societa Nordica*, Florence.

Alcock, L. and E. 1980, Scandinavian Settlements in the Hebrides: Recent Research on Place-Names and in the Field, in Thomas, L. M. ed. *Settlements in Scotland 1000 B.C.-A.D. 1000, Scottish Archaeological Forum*, 10, 61-73.

Alexander, J. J. G. 1975, Some Aesthetic Principles in the Use of Colour in Anglo-Saxon Art, *ASE* 4, 145-54.

— 1978, *Insular Manuscripts, 6th to the 9th century. A survey of Manuscripts Illuminated in the British Isles*, vol. 1, London.

Allen, Romilly J. 1903, *The Early Christian Monuments of Scotland*, Edinburgh.

Almqvist, B., and Greene, D. (eds). 1976, *Proceedings of the Seventh Viking Congress, Dublin 1973*. London: distributed by the Viking Society for Northern Research.

Ambrosiani, Björn, 1980, Batgravarnas bakgrund; Mälardalen, Vendeltid, ed. Ann Sandwall, Stockholm, 123-33.

Ambrosiani, Bjørn, 1973, Birka in Jankuhn, H., 1973.

Ambrosiani, Kristina, 1981, Viking-Age Combs, Comb-making and Comb-makers in the light of finds from Birka and Ribe. Stockholm.

Amos, Ashley Crandel, 1980, *Linguistic Means of Determining the Dates of Old English Literary Texts*. Medieval Academy Books no. 90, Cambridge, Mass.

Andersen, H. H., Madsen, H. J., Voss, O. 1976, *Danevirke*, København.

Andersen, Hellmuth, Crab, P. J., Madsen, H. J. 1971, Arhus Søndervold, en byarkeologisk undersøgelse, *Jysk arkeologist selskabs skrifter*, vol. IX.

Anderson, J. 1872-74, Notes on the relics of the Viking period of the Northmen in Scotland, illustrated by specimens in the museum, *Proc. Soc. Antiq. Scot.*, X, 536-94.

— 1873, *Orkneyinga Saga*, transl. and intro., Edinburgh.

— 1900-01, Notices of Nine Brochs along the Caithness coast from Keiss Bay to Skirza Head, excavated by Sir Francis Tress Barry, Bart., M.P., of Keiss Castle, Caithness, *Proc. Soc. Antiq. Scot.*, XXXV, 112-48.

Anderson, Karl O. E. 1942, *Scandinavian Elements in the Works of William Morris.* Thesis (Ph.D.), Harvard University.

Anderson, Thorsten and Sandred, Karl Inge (eds) 1978, *The Vikings*, Proceedings of the Symposium of the Faculty of Arts of Uppsala University.

Andersson, Arne, 1970, Figurative Art of the Early Scandinavian and the Viking Ages, in *The Art of Scandinavia*, 1st ed.

Andersson, Theodore M. 1970, *The Legend of Brynhild, Islandica* XLIII. Ithaca and London.

Anker, Peter, 1970, *The Art of Scandinavia*, London.

Anglo-Saxon Chronicle (A/S. Chron.) 1980, trans. D. Whitelock, *English Historical Documents*, Vol. 1 (London), 2nd ed.

Ann. Fuld. Annales Fuldenses, ed. G. H. Pertz, *Monumenta Germaniae Historica, Scriptores*, Vol. 1.

Ann. Reg. Franc. Annales Regni Francorum, ed F. Kurze, *Monumenta Germaniae Historica, Scriptores rerum germanicarum in usum scholarum.*

Ann. S. Bert. Annales sancti Bertiniani, ed. F. Grat, J. Vieillard and Sc. Clemencet, Paris: *Societé de l'histoire de France*, 1964.

Ann. S. Vaast. Annales sancti Vedastini, ed. G. H. Pertz, *Monumenta Germaniae Historica, Scriptores*, vol. 2.

Ann. Ulster,1887, *The Annals of Ulster*, vol. 1, ed. and trans. W. H. Hennessy, Dublin.

Ann. Xant. Annales Xantenses, ed. G. H. Pertz, *Monumenta Germaniae Historica, Scriptores*, vol. 2.

Anon. 1980, Rare Viking Discovery made by York Archaeologists. *Popular Archaeology*, Nov. 1980, 6.

Arbman, Holger, 1961, *The Vikings.* Translated by Alan Binns. London: Thames and Hudson.

Armstrong, A. M. *et al.* 1950, *The Place-Names of Cumberland (English Place-Name Society)* vols. XX, XXI, XXII), 3 vols.

Arrhenius, B. 1961, Vikingatida miniatyren, *Tor*, 139-64, Uppsala.

Arrhenius, Birgit, 1976, Die ältesten Funde von Birka, *Præhistorische Zeitschrift*, 51 Band, Heft 2. Berlin.

Arwidsson, G. 1942, *Vendelstile, Email und Glas*, Uppsala.

Asgrimsson, Eystein, 1879, *Lilja.* Translated by Eiríkr Magnússon. London: William and Nordgate, *Rerum Brit. Medii ævi scriptores*, 65, 1-2.

Ashmore, P. J. 1978-80, Long cairns, long cists and symbol stones, *Proc. Soc. Antiq. Scot.*, 110, 346-55.

Asser, 1904, *Asser, Like of King Alfred*, ed. W. H. Stevenson, Oxford.

Aðalbkarnarson, Bjarni (ed.), 1951, *Heimskringla*, 3 vols. Reykjavik: Hiðískenzka fornritafélag.

Baesecke, Georg. 1940, *Vor- und Frühgeschichte des deutschen Schriftung*, I: Vorgeschichte. Halle: Niemeyer, 358-65.

Bailey, Richard N. 1978, *The Durham Cassiodorus (Jarrow Lecture, 1978)*. Jarrow.

— 1980, *Viking Age Sculpture in the North*, London.

Bakka, E. 1965, Some decorated Anglo-Saxon and Irish metalwork found in Norwegian Viking graves, *Proceedings of the fourth Viking Congress (York, 1961)*, ed. A. Small, Edinburgh, 32-40.

— 1971, Scandinavian trade relations with the Continent and the British Isles in pre-Viking times, *Early Medieval Studies 3, Antiquarist*, 40: Stockholm, 37-51.

Baldwin Brown, G. 1930, *The Arts in Early England*, VI, part 1. London.

Barley, M. W., ed. 1977, *European Towns. Their Archaeology and Early History*. London, Academic Press.

Barry, G. 1805, *History of the Orkney Islands*, Edinburgh. (Reprinted 1975).

Barry, T. 1979, Wood Quay, Dublin, *Current Archaeology*, VI, No. 7 (No. 66).

Bartholin, Thomas, 1689, *Antiquitatum Danicarum de causis contemptae a Danis adhuc gentilibus mortis libri tres ex vetustis codicibus et monumentis hactenus ineditis congesti*. Hafniæ: Joh. Phil. Bockenhoffer.

Bartsch, Karl, ed. 1965, *Das Nibelungenlied*. Revised by Helmut de Boor. 18th ed. Wiesbaden: Brockhaus.

Bass, George F. ed. 1972, *A History of Seafaring Based on Underwater Archaeology*. Lon.

Batey, C. E., Coggins, D. and Fairless, K. 1980, Excavations at Simy Folds, Upper Teesdale, Co. Durham, 1979. *Arch. Reports, Durham & Newcastle Universities* (for 1979), 3, 20-21.

— (forthcoming), The Late Norse site of Freswick, Caithness, in J. Baldwin (ed.) *Caithness: a Cultural Crossroads*, Edinburgh.

—, Jones, A. K. G., Morris, C. D., and Rackham, D. J. 1981, *Freswick, Caithness. Excavations and Survey at Freswick Links and Freswick Castle, 1979-80, Summary Report*, Durham.

—, —, and —. 1982, Freswick Links, Caithness: Progress Report on Survey and Excavations 1981. *Arch. Reports, Durham & Newcastle Universities* (for 1981), 5, 54-8.

Baugh, A. C. and Cable, T. D., 1978, *A History of the English Language*. 3rd ed., N.Y.

Becker, Alfred, 1973, *Franks Casket. Zu den Bildern und Inschriften des Runenkästchens von Auzon (Sprache und Literatur, 5)*. Regensburg.

Beckwith, J. 1972, *Ivory Carvings in Early Medieval England*, London.

Bekker-Nielsen, H., P. Foote and O. Olsen, eds., 1981. *Proceedings of the Eighth Viking Congress*. Odense.

Bencard, Mogens, 1974, Ribe zur Zeit der Wikinger. *Acta Visbyensia*. Visby: Gotlands Fornsal.

— 1978, Wikingerzeitliches Handwerk in Ribe. *Acta Archaeologica*, 49, 113-38.

Benedixen, Kirsten, 1967, *Denmark's Money*. Copenhagen: The National Museum.

Benton, J. B., ed. 1968, *Town Origins: the evidence from medieval England*. Boston.

Bersu, G. 1949, A Promontory fort on the shore of Ramsey Bay, Isle of Man, *Antiq. J.* XXIX, 62-79.

— 1968, The Vikings in the Isle of Man, *J. Manx Museum*, VII, No. 84, 83-8.

Besteman, J. C. 1974, Carolingian Medemblik. *Berichten van Rijkdienst voor het Oudheidkundig Bodemonder Zoek*, 24. 49-106.

Biddle, Martin, 1974, The development of the Anglo-Saxon town. *Topografia Urbana e Vita Cittadina nell'alto medioevo in Occidente*. Settimane di Studio del Centro Italiano di Studi sull'alto medioevo 21: Spoleto. 203-30.

Biddle, M. 1976, Towns, in D. M. Wilson, ed., *The Archaeology of Anglo-Saxon England*, London, 99-150,

Bigelow, G. F. 1978, *Preliminary Report of the 1978 Excavations at Sandwick, Unst, Shetland Islands*, privately distrib. typescript.

— and McGovern, T. H. M. 1980a, *Excavation of Norse-Medieval Settlement at Sandwick, Unst, Shetland, 1978-79: an Interim Report*, privately distrib. typescript.

— and —, 1980b, *Excavations at Sandwick, Unst, Shetland Isles: the 1980 Season*, privately distrib. typescript.

Binchy, D. A. 1943, The Linguistic and historical value of the Irish law-tracts, *Proceedings of the British Academy*, 29, 195-227.

— 1975, Irish History and Irish law, *Studia Hibernica*, 15, 7-36.

Binns, Sean L. 1956, Tenth Century Carvings from Yorkshire and the Jellinge Style. Universitetet i. Bergen Arbok, Historisk-antikvarisk rekke 2.

— 1963, *The Viking Century in East Yorkshire*. East Yorkshire Local History studies No. 15, York.

Bjørnstad, Margaretha, 1966, Spanga's *Forhistoria*, Stockholm.

Biørnstad, Margaretha and Andersson, Hans, 1963, Die Zeit der Stadtgründungen im Ostseeraum. *Acta Visbyensia I*. Visby: Gotlands Fornsal.

— and —, 1972, Häuser und Höfe im Ostseeraum und im Norden Bevor 1500. *Acta Visbyensia V*. Visby: Gotlands Fornsal.

— and —, 1979, Handelsplats-Stad-Omland. Symposion om det medeitida Stadsväsendet i Mellan-Sverige. Sigtuna 7-8 febrari. Medeltidsstaden 18. Stockholm.

Blackburn, M. A. S. and Metcalf, D. M. 1981, *Viking Age Coinage in Northern Lands BAR*, S 122, Oxford.

Blair, Peter Hunter, 1963, *Roman Britain and Early England (55 B.C.-A.D. 871)*. Edinburgh.

Blindheim, Charlotte, 1975, Kaupang by the Viks Fjord, I and II. Archaeological contributions to the early history of urban communities in Norway. (See Lidén, H. E., 1973.

— 1976, *A collection of* Celtic(?) bronze objects found at Kaupang (Skirringsal), Vestfold, Norway, ed. B. Almqvist and D. Green. *Proceedings of the seventh Viking Congress (Dublin, 1973)*, Dublin 9-27.

— 1978, Trade problems of the Viking Age, ed. T. Andersson and K. I. Sandred. *The Vikings*, Uppsala, 166-76.

—, Herteig, A. E., Lidén, H.-E. 1975, Archaeological Contributions to the Early History of Urban Communities in Norway. *The Inst. for Comparative Research in Human Culture*, Series A 27. Oslo.

Bliss, Alan J. 1958, *The Metre of Beowulf*. Oxford.

Blom, Grethe Authén, 1977, Middelaldersteder. Det XVII nordiske historikermøte, Trondheim. Norway. Urbaniseringsprosessen I Norden. 1; Oslo/Bergen/Tromsø: Universitetsforlaget.

Blomqvist, Ragnar, 1963, Die Anfange der Stadt Lund, *Acta Visbyensia I*.

Blöndal, Sigfús, 1978, *The Varangians of Byzantium*. Cambridge.

Bøe, J. 1934, A Hoard from Western Norway. *Antiquaries Journal*, XII, 440-442.

Bolin, S. 1953, Mohammed, Charlemagne and Ruric. *Scandinavian Economic History Review*, I, 5-39.

Bonjour, Adrien, 1950, *The Digressions in Beowulf*. Oxford.

Bowen, E. G. 1969, *Saints, Seaways and Settlements in the Celtic Lands*. Cardiff.

Bowen, E. G. 1972, *Britain and the Western Seaways*. London.

Boyer, Régis, ed., 1978, Les Vikings et leur Civilisation. Problèmes Actuels. *Bibliothèque Arctique et Antartique 5*. Paris.

Breese, L. W. 1977, The persistence of Scandinavian connections in Normandy in the tenth and early-eleventh centuries, *Viator*, 8, 47–61.

Brodeur, Arthur G. 1971, *The Art of Beowulf*. Berkeley: University of California Press.

Brøgger, A. W. 1929, *Ancient Emigrants. A History of the Norse Settlements of Scotland*, Oxford.

—— 1930, *Den Norske Bosetningen pa Shetland–Orknøyene. Studier og Resultater*, Oslo.

—— and Bugge, Anders, 1925, *Bronsefløjene fra Heggin of Tingelstad*. Norske Oldfrenn 5, Oslo.

Brøndsted, J. 1936, Danish inhumation graves of the Viking Age, *Acta Archaeologica*, 7, 81–228.

Brooke, C. W. L. and Hill, R. M. T. 1977, York from 627 until the Early Thirteenth Century, ed. G. E. Almer and Reginald Cant. *A History of York Minster*. Oxford.

—— and Keir, G. 1975, *London, 800–1216*. London.

Brooke, Stopford, 1964, *Four Victorian Poets: A Study of Clough, Arnold, Rossetti [and] Morris*. 1908. Reprinted, New York: Russell and Russell.

Brooks, N. P. 1979, England in the ninth century: the crucible of defeat, *Transactions of the Royal Historical Society*, Series V, 29, 1–20.

Brown, P. R. L. 1972, The rise and function of the Holy Man in late Antiquity, *Journal of Roman Studies*, 61, 80–101.

Bruce-Mitford, R. L. S. 1948, Sutton Hoo and *Beowulf*, tr. of Sune Lindquist, *Antiquity* 23, 131–40.

——, 1960, Decorations and Miniatures in *Codex Lindisfarniensis*, commentary volume, Oltun and Lausanne.

——, 1969, The Art of the Codex Amiatinus (*Jarrow Lecture*, 1967), *Journal of the British Archaeol. Assoc.* XXXII.

——, 1971, Sutton Hoo and the Background to the Poem, in Ritchie Girvan *Beowulf and the Seventh Century*, 85–98.

——, 1972, *The Sutton Hoo Ship-Burial: a Handbook*. London: British Museum Publications.

——, 1974, *Aspects of Anglo-Saxon Archaeology: Sutton Hoo and Other Discoveries*.

——, ed., 1975a, *Recent Archaeological Excavations in Europe*. London.

——, 1975b, *The Sutton Hoo Ship-Burial: Volume I: Excavations, Background, the Ship, Dating and Inventory*. London.

——, 1978, *The Sutton Hoo Ship Burial*, 2: *Arms, Armour and Regalia*, London.

——, 1979. *The Sutton Hoo Ship-Burial. Reflections after Thirty Years*. The second G. N. Garmonsway Memorial Lecture, May 1973. University of York Monograph Series 2. York: Ebor Press.

Buckland, P. C. 1974, Archaeology and Environment in York, *J. Archaeol. Sci.*, 1, 303–16.

——, 1976, The use of insect remains in the interpretation of archaeological environments, in D. A. Davidson & M. L. Shackley, eds. *Geoarchaeology*, London 269–96.

——, Greig, J. R. A. and Kenward, H. K. 1974, York: an Early Medieval site, *Antiquity*, XLVIII, No. 189, 25–33.

Bugge, Anders, 1927, Gyldne flöyge, *Aarsberetning*, Oslo.

——, 1931, The Golden Vanes of Viking Ships, *Acta Archaeologica*, II. Kobenhavn, 159–84.

Bugge, Sophus, ed. 1965, *Norrœn fornkuædi*...Christiania, 1867; rpt Oslo: Universitetsforlaget.

Bull, Edvard, 1912, *Leding*, Kristiania, Köbenhavn.

Bullough, D. 1975, *Imagines Regum* and their significance in the Early Medieval West, ed. G. Robertson and A. Henderson, *Studies in memory of David Talbot Rice*, Edinburgh.

Burne-Jones, Lady Georgiana, 1904, *Memorials of Edward Burne-Jones*, 2 vols. London: Macmillan.

Byrne, F. J. 1963, review of *Proceedings of the International Congress of Celtic Studies (1959)*, *Irish Historical Studies*, 13.

—— , 1973, *Irish Kings and High Kings*, London.

Cable, Thoms, 1974, *The Meter and Melody of Beowulf.* Urbana, Ill.

Caesar, De Bello Gallico, ed. and trans. H. J. Edwards, Loeb series.

Cameron, Angus, 1969, St Gildas and Scyld Scefing, *Neuphilologische Mitteilungen* 79, 240–46.

Cameron, K. 1976, The Significance of English Place-Names, *Proceedings of the British Academy*, 135–56.

—— , 1971, Scandinavian Settlement in the Territory of the Five Boroughs: the Place-Name Evidence. Part III, the Grimston Hybrids in, eds. Peter Clemoes and Kathleen Hughes, *England Before the Conquest*, 147–63.

—— , Dolley, M., *et al.*, 1969, The Two Viking Ages of Britain: A Discussion. *Medieval Scandinavia*, 2, 163–207.

Campbell, Alistair, ed., 1938, *The Battle of Brunanburh.* London.

Campbell, A. 1961, *An Old English Grammar.* Oxford.

Campbell, J., 1975a, *Norwich: Historic Towns*, ed. M. D. Lobel. London.

—— , 1975b, Review of John Morris, *The Age of Arthur, Studia Hibernica*, 15.

—— , 1978, England, France, Flanders and Germany, ed. D. Hill, *Ethelred the Unready*, Oxford, British Archaeological Reports, 59, 255–70.

—— , 1979, *Bede's Kings and Princes*, Jarrow lecture.

—— , 1982, *The Anglo-Saxons*, Oxford.

Chadwick, H. M. 1912, *The Heroic Age.* Cambridge.

Chadwick, Nora, 1970. *The Celts.* Middlesex.

Chambers, Raymond Wilson, 1912, *Widsith: a Study in Old English Heroic Legend.* N. York.

—— , 1958, *Beowulf: an Introduction to the Study of the Poem with a discussion of the stories of Offa and Finn.* (Supplement by C. L. Wrenn). Cambridge.

Chandler, Alice, 1970, *A Dream of Order: The Medieval Ideal in Nineteenth-Century English Literature.* Lincoln, Nebraska: University of Nebraska Press,

Childe, V. G. 1942–43, Another Late Viking House at Freswick, Caithness, *Proc. Soc. Antiq. Scot.*, LXXVII, 5–17.

Christensen, Arne Emil, 1964, Birka–Hedeby myntene sohn Kilde til skipets historie pa 800–tallet. *Saertrykk fra Norsk Sjøfartsmuseum.*

Chron. Aethel., 1962, *The Chronicle of Aethelweard*, ed. and trans. A. Campbell, Edinburgh.

Chron. Font., Chronicon Fontanellense, ed. G. H. Pertz, *Monumenta Germaniae Historica, Scriptores*, Vol. 2. Hanover.

Clark, Howard B. 1977, The Topographical Development of Medieval Dublin, *Jnl Royal Soc. Antiquaries of Ireland*, 109, 29–51.

Clark, Kenneth, 1950, *The Gothic Revival*, rev. London: Constable.

Clark-Hall, J. R. 1957 (rev. C. L. Wrenn), *Beowulf and the Finnesburg Fragment. A Translation into Modern English Prose.* (With Prefatory remarks by J. R. R. Tolkien. London: George Allen & Unwin Ltd.

Cleasby, R. and Vigfusson, G. 1874 (1959). *An Icelandic–English Dictionary,* 2nd edn., Oxford.

Clouston, J. S. 1919-20, The Orkney Townships, *Scottish Hist. Rev.*, XVII, 16-45.
— , 1925-26, An Early Orkney Castle, *Proc. Soc. Antiq. Scot.*, LX, 281-300.
— , 1931, *Early Norse Castles*, Kirkwall.
— , 1932, *A History of Orkney*, Kirkwall.
Coates, R. 1976, Caithness Place-Names in -bster. *Acta Philologica Scandinavica*, 31, 188-190.
Coggins, D. and Fairless, K. 1978, Excavations in Upper Teesdale, 1972-77, *Univ. of Durham Arch. Reports* (for 1977), 1, Durham, 13-15.
Colgrave, Bertram, ed., 1927, *The Life of Bishop Wilfrid by Eddius Stephanus*. Cambridge.
Collingwood, W. G. 1927, *Northumbrian Crosses of the Pre-Norman Age*. London.
— and Myres, J. N. L. 1936, *Roman Britain and the English Settlements*. Oxford: University Press.
Cottle, Amos (tr.), 1797, *Icelandic Poetry, or the Edda of Saemund translated into English verse*. Bristol: Joseph Cottle.
Cook, Albert Stanborough, 1977, *Some Accounts of the Bewcastle Cross Between the Years 1607 and 1861 (with new preface by Robert T. Farrell)* in W. O. Stevens and A. S. Cook, eds., *The Anglo-Saxon Cross*. Yale Studies in English, vols. 22 and 50, Hamden, Connecticut: the Shoe String Press.
Cramp, Rosemary, J. 1957, Beowulf and Archaeology, *Medieval Archaeology*, I.
— , 1967, *Anglian and Viking York*, Borthwick Institute, York. St. Anthony's Hall Publication 33.
— , 1971, The position of the Otley Crosses in English Sculpture of the eight to ninth centuries, *Kolloquium über spätantike und frühmittelalterliche Skulptur*, Mainz.
— , 1977, Schools of Mercian Sculpture, ed. Ann Dornier, *Mercian Studies*, Leicester.
— , 1978, The Anglian Tradition in the Ninth Century, ed. James Lang, *Anglo-Saxon and Viking Age Sculpture, B.A.R.* 49, 1-32.
Craster, E. 1954, The patrimony of St Cuthbert, *English Historical Review*, 69, 177-99.
Crawford, B. E. 1978, A Progress Report on the First Season's Excavation at 'Da Biggins', Papa Stour, Shetland, *Northern Studies*, 11, 25-29.
— , 1979, A Progress Report on Excavations at "Da Biggins', Papa Stour, Shetland 1978, *Northern Studies*, 13, 37-41.
— , 1980, *Third Interim Report of the Excavations at The Biggins, Papa Stour, Shetland, 1979*, privately distrib. typescript.
Crawford, I. A. 1965, Contributions to a history of domestic settlement in North Uist, *Scottish Studies*, 9, pt. I, 34-63.
— , 1971, *Excavations at Coileagan an Udail (The Udal), North Uist 8th Interim report*, privately distrib. typescript.
— , 1972, *Excavations at Coileagan an Udail (The Udal), N. Uist. 9th Interim report*, privately distrib. typescript.
— , 1973, *Excavations at Coileagan an Udail (The Udal), N, Uist, 10th Interim report*, privately distrib. typescript.
— , 1974, Scot, Norsemen & Gael, *Scot. Arch. Forum 6 Glasgow 1974*, Edinburgh, 1-16.
— , 1975, *Excavations at Coileagan an Udail, North Uist, 12th Interim report*, privately distrib. typescript.
— and Switsur, R. 1977, Sandscaping and C14: the Udal, N. Uist, *Antiquity*, LI, 124-136.
Crocker, W. L. 1976, *The Earlier Medieval Sequence: Notker of St Gall (840-912)*.
Cross, James E. 1956, 'Ubi Sunt' Passages in Old English — Sources and Relationships. *Vetenskaps-Societeten i Lund, Arsbok*, 23-44.

Cross, James E., 1959, On the wanderer lines 80-84, a Study of a Figure and a Theme. *Vetenskaps-Societeten i Lund, Arsbok*, 77-110.

— , 1961, On one Genre of *The Wanderer, Neophilologus*, 45, 63-72.

Cruden, S. 1958, Earl Thorfinn The Mighty and the Brough of Birsay, in K. Eldjárn, ed., *The Third Viking Congress, Reykjavik 1956*, Reykjavik.

— , 1960a, Skaill, Deerness, Orkney, in *Discovery and Excavation in Scotland*, 1960, 45.

— , 1960b, *The Scottish Castle*, Edinburgh and London.

— , 1965, Excavations at Birsay, Orkney in A. Small, ed., *The Fourth Viking Congress, York, 1961*, Aberdeen.

Crumlin Pedersen, Ole, 1978, The Ships of the Vikings, ed Thorsten Andersson and Karl Inge Sandred, *The Vikings*, Uppsala, 32-41.

— , 1980, Unpublished lecture. Metropolitan Museum of Art Viking Symposium.

Curle, A. O., 1938-39, The Viking Settlement at Freswick, Caithness. Report on excavations, carried out in 1937, and 1938, *Proc. Soc. Antiq. Scot.*, LXXIII, 71-110.

Curle, C. L. 1972-74, An engraved lead disc from the Brough of Birsay, Orkney, *Proc. Soc. Antiq. Scot.* 105, 301-7.

— (forthcoming). *Early Christian and Norse Finds from the Brough of Birsay, Orkney*, Soc. Antiq. Scot. Monograph.

Curriculum Development Unit, 1978, *Viking Settlement to Medieval Dublin, Daily Life 840-1540*, Dublin.

Cursiter, J. W. 1866, Notice of a wood-carver's tool-box with Celtic ornamentation, recently discovered in a peat-moss in the parish of Birsay, Orkney, *Proc. Soc. Antiq. Scot., XX*, 47-50.

Curwen, E. C. 1938, The Hebrides: a cultural backwater, *Antiquity*, XII, No. 47, 261-289.

Dahlstedt, Karl-Hampus, 1962, Gudruns sorg: Stilstudier över ett Edda motiv. *Scripta Islendica*, 13, 25-47.

Dalton, O. M. 1909, *Catalogue of the Ivory Carvings of the Christian Era in . . . the British Museum.* London.

Danefæ, Copenhagen, 1980 (ed. P. V. Glob).

Dasent, George Webbe (tr.), 1842, *The Prose of Younger Edda commonly ascribed to Snorri Sturluson, translated from the Old Norse.* Stockholm: Norstedt and Sons.

— , 1843, *A Grammar of the Icelandic or Old Norse tongue translated from the Swedish of Erasmus Rask.* London: Williams and Norgate.

— , 1861, *The Story of Burnt Njal or life in Iceland at the end of the tenth century. From the Icelandic of the Njals saga. With an introduction, maps, and plans*, 2 vols. Edinburgh: Edmonton and Douglas.

— , 1866, *The Story of Gisli the Outlaw. From the Icelandic. With illustrations by C. E. St John Mildmay.* Edinburgh: Edmonton and Douglas.

Davey, Peter, ed., 1978, *Man and Environment in the Isle of Man. British Archaeological Reports*, 54.

Davidan, Olga, 1981, Unpublished lecture at Staten Historiska Museum, Stockholm, 26 March.

Davis, R. H. C. 1971, Alfred the Great: Propaganda and Truth, *History*, 56, 169-82.

Delaney, T. G. 1977, The Archaeology of one Irish Town, in M. W. Barley, ed., *European Towns. Their Archaeology and early History.* New York, Academic Press, 47-64.

De Blácam, Audh, 1928, *Gaelic Literature Surveyed.*

Detter, F. and Heinzel, R., eds., 1903, *Saemunder Edda*, II: Anmerkungen. Leipzig: Wigand.

D'Haenens, A. D. 1969, Les invasions Normandes des l'empire franc au ixe siècle *Settimane di Studio del Centro Italiano di studi sull'alto Medioevo*, 16, 233-98.

Dickens, A. G. 1960, York Before the Norman Conquest, and Anglo-Scandinavian Antiquities. *V.C.H. City of York*, London, 2-22 and 332-6.

Dickinson, Tania M. 1978, On the Origin and Chronology of the Early Anglo-Saxon Disc Brooch. *Anglo-Saxon Studies in Archaeology and History*, I, 39-80.

Dietrich, Gerhard, 1966, Ursprünge der Elegischen in der altenglischen Literatur. Literatur–Kultur–Gesellschaft in England und Amerika: Aspecte und Forschungs-beiträge Friedrich Schubel zum 60. Geburtstag (ed. G. Müller-Schefe und K. Tuzinski). Frankfurt: Dieskrueg, 20-22.

Dinkler, Erich, 1979, Abbreviated Representations in Weitzmann, ed., *The Age of Spirituality: late Antique and Early Christian Art, third to seventh century*. New York.

Dolley, R. H. M. 1954, The so-called Piedforts of Alfred the Great. *Numis. Chron.*, 6th Ser., XIV, 76-92.

—, 1955-57, A neglected but vital Yorkshire hoard, *Brit. Numis. J.*, XXVIII, 11-17.

—, 1965, *Viking Coins of the Danelaw and of Dublin*, London.

—, 1966, *The Hiberno–Norse Coins in the British Museum*, London.

—, 1969, New light on the 1894 Douglas Hoard, *J. Manx Mus.*, VII, No. 85, 121-24.

—, 1976a, Two near contemporary findings of Hiberno-Norse coins from Maughold, *J. Manx Mus.*, VII, No. 88, 235-240.

—, 1976b, *Some Irish Dimensions to Manx History*, Inaugural Lecture, Queen's University, Belfast.

—, 1978, The Anglo-Danish & Anglo-Norse coinages of York, in R. A. Hall, ed., *Viking Age York and the North*, C.B.A. Report No. 27, 26-31.

—, and Ingold, J. 1961, Viking age coinhoards from Ireland and their relevance to Anglo-Saxon Studies. In R. H. M. Dolley, ed., *Anglo-Saxon Coins. Studies to F. M. Stenton*, London.

—, and Skåare, K. 1973, To peningar fra Harald Hardrade funnet pa Vesterhaveøyene, *Nordisk Numismatisk Unions Medemsblad*, 1973, No. 8.

Donahue, Charles, 1948, *Beowulf*, Ireland and the Natural Good. *Traditio* 7, 263-77.

—, 1965, *Beowulf* and Christian Tradition: a Reconsideration from a Celtic Stance. *Traditio* 21, 55-116.

Donaldson, A. M., Morris, C. D. and Rackham, D. J. 1981, The Birsay Bay Project. Preliminary investigations into the past exploitation of the coastal environment at Birsay, Mainland Orkney in D. Brothwell & G. Dimbleby, eds., *Environmental Aspects of Coasts and Islands*. (Symposia of the Association for Environmental Archaeology No. 1), *Brit. Arch. Reports International Ser.* 94, 65-85.

Doppelfeld, O. and Pirling, R. 1966, *Fränkische Fürsten im Rheinland: die Gräber aus dem Kölner Dom, von Krefeld-Gellep und Morken. Schriften des Rheinisches Landesmuseum in Bonn*, 2, Dusseldorf.

Douglas, D. C. 1942, Rollo of Normandy, *English Historical Review*, 57, 417-36.

Dronke, Ursula, ed., 1969, *The Poetic Edda, Vol. I: Heroic Poems*. Oxford: Univ. Press.

Dúason, Jón, 1941-1948, *Landkönnum og Landnám íslendinga í Vesturheime.* Reykjavik.

Dumville, D. M. 1976, The Anglian collections of regnal lists and genealogists, *Anglo-Saxon England*, 5, 23-50.

—, 1977, Sub-Roman Britain: History and Legend, *History*, 62, 173-92.

Duncan, A. M. 1975, *Scotland: The Making of the Kingdom*. New York.

—, 1977, W. C. Dickinson, revised, *Scotland from the earliest times to 1603*. Oxford.

Dykes, D. W. 1976, *Anglo-Saxon Coins in the National Museum of Wales*, Nat. Mus. Wales, Cardiff.

Edda, 1962, *Edda, die Lieder des Codex Regius*, ed. G. Neckel, 3rd ed., rev. H. Kuhn, Heidelberg.

Eddison, E. R (tr.), 1939, *Egil's Saga Done Into English out of the Icelandic, with an Essay on Some Principles of translation*. Cambridge: The University Press.

Eddius Stephanus. *Vita Wilfridi* in B. Colgrave, ed., 1927, *The Life of Bishop Wilfrid by Eddius Stephanus*. Cambridge.

Edwards, A. J. H. 1925, Excavation of a chambered cairn at Ham, Caithness, and of a hut circle and two earth houses at Freswick Links, Caithness, *Proc. Soc. Antiq. Scot.* LIX, 85-94.

—, 1927, Excavations of graves at Ackergill and of an earth house at Freswick Links, Caithness and a description of the discovery of a Viking Grave at Reay, Caithness, *Proc. Soc. Antiq. Scot.* LXI, 196-209.

Egils Saga, 1933, ed. S. Nordal, *Islensk Fornrit*, vol. 2.

Ehrismann, Gustav, 1932, Geschichte der deutschen Literatur bis zum Ausgang des Mittelalters. I. Teil: Die Althochdeutsche Literatur, 2nd ed. rev. Munich: Beck., 35-44.

Einarsson, Stefán, 1933, *Saga Eiríks Magnússonar*. Reykjavik: Isafolðarprentsmidja.

—, 1934, Eiríkr Magnússon and his Saga-Translations. *Scandinavian Studies and Notes*, 13, No. 2 (May), 17-32.

Ekwall, E. 1918, *Scandinavians and Celts in the North-West of England*. Universitets Arsskrift N.F. Avd 1, Bd 14, Nr 27. Lund.

Eldjárn, K. 1956, *Kumlog haugfé úr heidnum sid á Íslandi*. Reykjavík: Nordri.

Ellis, S. E. 1969, The petrography and provenance of Anglo-Saxon and medieval English honestones, with notes on some other hones, *Bull. Brit. Mus. (N.H.) Mineralogy*, 2 (3).

Ellis-Davidson, H. R. 1969, The Smith and the Goddess in the Franks Casket. *Frühmittelalterliche Studien 3*, 216-26.

—, 1976, *The Viking Road to Byzantium*.

Ellison, R. C. 1972, The Undying Glory of Dreams: William Morris and the 'Northland of Old'. *Victorian Poetry*. Stratford upon Avon Studies, 15, London: Edward Arnold, 139-175.

Ellmers, D. 1972, *Handelsschriftfart in Mittel- und Nordeuropa*. Neumünster.

Ennen, Edith, 1968, The variety of urban development. *Problems in European Civilisation*, ed. John F. Benton, 11-18.

—, 1972, *Die europäische Stadt des Mittelalters*. Göttingen.

—, 1977, Urbaniseringsprosessen: Norden, in Grethe Authen Blom, ed., Det XVII nordisk historikermøte. Trondheim.

Es, W. A. van 1969, Excavations at Dorestad: a preliminary report 1967-1968, *Berichten van de Rijksdienst voor het Oudheidkundig Bodemonderzoek*, 19, 183-207.

Evison, Vera I., 1965, *The Fifth Century Invasions South of the Thames*, London.

Fairhurst, H. 1967-1968, Rosal: a Deserted Township in Strath Naver, Sutherland. *Proc. Soc. Antiq. Scot.*, 99, 145-169.

Falk, Hjalmar, 1912, *Altnordische Seewesen*. Heidelberg.

Farrell, Robert Thomas, 1967, Unity of Old English Daniel, *Neuphilologische Mitteilungen* 69, 533-39. Oxford.

—, 1972, *Beowulf: Swedes and Geats*. London.

—, ed., 1978, *Bede and Anglo-Saxon England*. British Archaeological Reports 46, 96-117.

— and Salu, Mary, eds., 1978, *J. R. R. Tolkien, Scholar and Storyteller*, Ithaca.

Faulkner, Peter, ed., 1973, *William Morris: The Critical Heritage.* London: Routledge and Kegan Paul.

Fell, C. and Lucas, J. 1975, *Egils Saga,* London.

Fellows-Jensen, G. 1968, *Scandinavian Personal Names in Lincolnshire and Yorkshire,* Copenhagen.

— , 1972, *Scandinavian Settlement names in Yorkshire,* Copenhagen.

— , 1975, The Vikings in England: a review, *Anglo-Saxon England,* 4, 181–206.

— (unpubl.), Viking Settlement in the Northern and Western Isles — the Place-Name Evidence as seen from Denmark and the Danelaw.

Fennell, Kenneth R. 1969, The Loveden Man. *Frümittalalterliche Studien 3,* 211–15.

Fenton, A. 1978, *The Island Blackhouse,* D.o.E. guidebook, Edinburgh.

Fenwick, Valerie, ed., 1978, *The Graveney Boat, B.A.R.* 53. Oxford.

Finch, R. G., ed., trs., 1965, *The Saga of the Volsungs.* London and Edinburgh: Nelson Icelandic Texts.

Fitzhugh, William, 1973, *Bulletin of the Canadian Archaeological Association,* 5.

Fleure, H. J. and Dunlop, M. 1942, Grendarragh Circle and alignments, The Braaid, Isle of Man, *Antiq. J.* XXII, 39–53.

Foote, P. G. and Wilson, D. M. 1970, *The Viking Achievement,* London.

Frank, Roberta, 1978, *Old Norse Court Poetry: The Dróttkvætt Stanza. Islandica,* XLII. Ithaca; Cornell University Press.

— , 1979, review of Smyth, 1977, *American Historical Review,* 84, 145–36.

Fraser, I. 1974, The Place-Names of Lewis — the Norse Evidence, *Northern Studies* 4, 11–21.

Fry, Donald, K., ed., 1974, *Finnsburh. Fragment and Episode.* Methuen's Old English Library. London: Methuen & Co., Ltd.

Fuglesang, Signe Horn, 1980, *Some Aspects of the Ringerike Style.* Odense.

Fundber. aus Schwäben, 1938-51, *Fundberichte aus Schwäben,* N.F. 12.

Gaehde, J. E. 1974, Carolingian Interpretations of an Early Christian Picture Cycle to the Octateuch in the Bible of San Paol Fuori le Mura in Rome. *Frühmittelalterliche Studien.* 351-384.

— , 1975, Pictorial Sources of the Illustrations in the Carolingian Bible. *Frühmittelalterliche Studien,* 9.

Gamillscheg, e. 1935, *Romania–Germanica,* vol. 2, Berlin.

— , 1970, *Romania–Germanica,* vol. 1, Berlin.

Gardner, Delbert, 1975, *An 'Idle Singer' and his Audience: A Study of William Morris's Poetic Reputation in England, 1858–1900.* The Hague: Mouton.

Geipel, John, 1971, *The Viking Legacy: The Scandinavian Influence on the English and Gaelic Languages.* Newton Abbot.

Gelling, Margaret, 1979, *Signposts to the Past.*

Gelling, P. S. 1952, Excavation of a promontory form at Port Grenaugh, Santon, *Proc. I. of M. NHAS,* V (3), 307-15.

— , 1958, Recent excavations of Norse Houses in the Isle of Man, *J. Manx Museum,* VI (75), 54-56.

— , 1964, The Braaid site. A re-excavation of one of the structures, *J. Manx Museum,* VI (80), 201-5.

— , 1970, A Norse homestead near Doarlish Cashen, *Med. Arch.,* XIV, 74-82.

— , 1977, Celtic continuity in the Isle of Man, in L. Laing, ed., *Studies in Celtic Survival, Brit. Archaeol. Rep, BAR,* 37, 77-82.

— (forthcoming), Excavations at Skaill, Deerness, Orkney, in A. Fenton and H. Palsson, eds., *Continuity and Tradition in the Northern and Western Isles.*

Gesta Cnutonis Regis Anglorum et Danorum, or *Encomium Emmae Reginae,* tr. into
   Danish M. Cl. Gerta, 1896. Kon Kunds liv og Gaerninger, Selskabet for historiske
   Kildeskriften Oversættelse. Kobenhavn.

Girvan, Ritchie, 1971, *Beowulf and the Seventh Century,* with an *addendum* by Rupert
   Bruce-Mitford. London.

Gjaerder, P. 1964, The beard as an iconographical feature in the Viking period and
   early Middle Ages, *Acta Archaeologica* 35. Copenhagen.

Glendinning, R. J. (forthcoming), Gudrúnarqvida forma: a Reconstruction and Interpretation.

Gneuss, H., 1976, The Battle of Maldon 89, *Ofermód* Once Again. *Studies in Philology,*
   73, 117-37.

Goffart, W. 1980, *Barbarians and Romans, A.D. 418-584: Techniques of Accommodation,* Princetown.

Göller, Karl Heinz, 1963, Die angelsächsischen Elegien, *Germanisch-romanische Monats-
   schrift* 44, N.F. 13, 225-41.

Gordon, B. 1963, Some Norse Place-Names in Trotternish, Isle of Skye. *Scottish Gaelic
   Studies* 10, 82-112.

Gordon, E. V. 1957, *An Introduction to Old Norse,* 1927. Second edition. Revised by
   A. R. Taylor. Oxford: Clarendon.

G[osse], E[dmund] K., tr., 1879, The Egils Saga. *The Cornhill Magazine,* 40, (July),
   21-39.

Graham, H. D. 1850, *Antiquities of Iona,* London.

Graham-Campbell, J. A. 1973, A fragmentary bronze strap end of the Viking Period from
   the Udal, N. Uist, Inverness-shire. *Med. Arch.* XVII, 128-131.

—— , 1974a, A Viking Age gold hoard from Ireland. *Antiq. J.* 54, 269-72.

—— , 1974b, A preliminary note on certain small finds of Viking Age date from the
   Udal excavations, N. Uist, *Scottish Arch. Forum,* 6, 17-22.

—— , 1975-76, The Viking Age silver and gold hoards or Scandinavian character from
   Scotland, *Proc. Soc. Antiq. Scot.* 107, 114-35.

—— , 1976, The Viking Age silver hoards of Ireland, in D. Greene and B. Almqvist, eds.,
   7th Viking Congress, Dublin, 39-74.

—— , 1978, An Anglo-Scandinavian ornamented knife from Canterbury, Kent. *Med.
   Arch.,* XXII, 130-33.

—— , 1978-9, The initial impact of the Vikings on Irish Art, *Saga-book of the Viking
   Society,* 20, 42-48.

—— and Kidd, D. 1980, *The Vikings,* London.

—— , 1980a, *The Viking World.* London.

—— , 1980b, *Viking Artefacts,* British Museum, London.

—— , 1981, Some Viking Age penannular brooches from Scotland and the origins of the
   'thistle brooch', in D. Clarke and A. Grieve, eds., *From the Stone Age to the Forty-
   Five.*

Green, Charles, 1963, *Sutton Hoo: The Excavation of a Royal Ship-Burial.*

Green, D. H. 1965. *The Carolingian Lord,* Cambridge.

Green, W[illiam] C[harles], tr., 1893, *The Story of Egil Skallagrimsson: being an Icelandic family history of the ninth and tenth centuries, translated from the Icelandic.*
   London: Elliott Stock. New York.

Greenfield, Stanley B. 1962, *Beowulf* and Epic Tragedy. *Comparative Literature* 14,
   91-105.

—— , 1966, The Old English Elegies, in E. G. Stanley, ed., *Continuations and Beginnings.
   Studies in Old English Literature.* London: Nelson. 142-75.

Greenfield, Stanley B. 1972, *The Interpretation of Old English Poems*. London and Boston: Routledge and Kegan Paul.

Grieg, S. 1929, Vikingetidens skattefund. *Universitetets Oldsaksamlings Skrifter*, ii, 177–311.

Grieg, S. 1940, Viking antiquities in Scotland, in H. Shetelig, ed., *Viking Antiquities in Great Britain and Ireland*, 2, Oslo.

Grierson, P. 1959, Commerce in the Dark Ages; a critique of the evidence, *Transactions of the Royal Historical Society*, series V, 9, 123-40.

Hachmann, R. 1970, *Die Goten und Skandinavien*. Berlin.

Hall, R. A. Jr. 1966, *Pidgin and Creole Languages*. Ithaca: Cornell University Press.

Hall, R. A., 1976, *Viking Kingdom of York*, exhibition catalogue, York.

—, ed., 1978, *Viking Age York and the North. CBA Research Report*, 27, London.

—, *1978, The topography of* Anglo-Scandinavian York, ed. R. A. Hall, *Viking Age York and the North*, London.

—, 1980a, *Jorvik. Viking Age York*, York.

—, 1980b, Numismatic finds from the excavation of Viking Age York, *Seaby's Coin and Medal Bulletin*, Dec. 1980 (748), 371-373.

—, Daniels, M. J. and York, R. N. 1978, *2,000 years of York: the Archaeological story*, York.

Hamilton, J. R. C., 1951, Life in a Viking settlement , *Archaeology*, 4, 218-22.

—, 1953, *Jarlshof. Official Guide*, H.M.S.O., Edinburgh.

—, 1956a, *Excavations at Jarlshof, Shetland*, H.M.S.O., Edinburgh.

—, 1956b, Jarlshof, a prehistoric and Viking settlement in Shetland, in R. L. S. Bruce-Mitford, ed., *Recent Archaeological Excavations in Britain*, X, London.

Harden, D. B., ed., 1956, *Dark-Age Britain. Studies Presented to E.T. Leeds, with a bibliography of his works*. London.

Hardh, B. 1973-74, Gewundene und geflochtene Halsringe in Skandinavischen Silber-hortfunden der Wikingerzeit. *Meddelanden fran Lunds universitetets historiska museum 1973-74*, 291-306.

—, 1976, *Wikingerzeitliche Depotfunde aus Südschweden* 2 vols (Acta Archaeologica Ludensia, series in 8° minore, no. 6, and series in 4°, no. 9), Lund/Bonn.

Hardh, B. 1977-78, Trade and Money in Scandinavia in the Viking Age. *Meddelanden fran Lunds universitetets historiska museum 1977-78*, 157-71.

Harmer, F. E., 1914, *Select English historical documents of the ninth and tenth centuries*, Cambridge.

Harris, Richard, 1975, William Morris, Eiríkur Magnusson, and Iceland: A Survey of Unpublished Correspondence. *Victorian Poetry*, vol. 13, nos. 3 and 4 (Fall–Winter), 119-130.

Hawkes, Sonia Chadwick, Hawkes, Christopher and Ellis-Davidson, H. R. 1965, The Finglesham Man, *Antiquity* 39, 17-32.

—, 1978, Eastry in Anglo-Saxon Kent; its importance and a newly-found grave. *Anglo-Saxon Studies in Archaeology and History I*, 81-114.

Hedeager, Lotte, 1980a, A quantitative analysis of Roman imports in northern Europe and the question of Roman-Germanic exchange in Kristiansen, Kristian and Carston Daluden-Müller, eds., *New Directions in Scandinavian Archaeology*, Studies in Scandinavian Prehistory and Early History, vol. 1. Copenhagen: National Museum of Denmark.

—, 1980b, Processes towards State Formations in Early Iron Age Denmark, *New Directions in Scandinavian Archaeology*. (*See* Hedeager, 1980a). 217-223.

Hedges, J. 1974-5, Excavation of two Orcadian burnt mounts at Liddle and Buquoy, *Proc. Soc. Antiq. Scot.*, 106, 39-98.

Heimskringla, I, II, ed. B. Aðalbjarnarson,*Islensk Fornrit*, vols 26-27.

Helgasón, Jón, ed., 1952, *Hávamál. Eddadigte*. København.

—, ed., 1952, *Voluspa. Eddadigte*. København.

Henderson, I. 1967, *The Picts*, London.

Henderson, Philip, ed., 1950, *The Letters of William Morris to his Family and Friends*. London: Longmans.

Henry, F. 1967, *Irish Art* during the *Viking Invasions*. London.

Henry, Patrick, L. 1966, *The Early English and Celtic Lyric*. London: Allen and Unwin.

Herbert, William, tr., 1804-1806, *Select Icelandic Poetry, translated from the originals with notes, parts I-II*. London: T. Reynolds, Longman.

Herrmann, Paul, 1922, Erläuterungen zu den ersten neun Bücher der dänischen Geschichte des Saxo Grammaticus. 2. Teil: Kommentar. Leipzig: Engelmann.

Herteig, Asbjørn E. 1959, The Excavation of 'Bryggen', the old Hanseatic Wharf in Bergen. *Medieval Archaeol 3*, 177-186.

—, 1969, *Kongers havn og handels sete*. Oslo.

—, 1973, Bryggen, the Medieval Wharves of Bergen in Blindheim, C., *et al.*, 1973.

Heusler, Andreas, 1957, *Die altgermanische Dichtung*, 2nd ed. rev. Potsdam: Wildpark. 1941, rpt. 1957.

— and Ranisch, Wilhelm, eds., 1903, *Eddica minora: Dichtungen eddischer Art aus den fornaldarsogur und andern Prosawerken*. Dortmund: Ruhfus.

—, 1969 (1906), Heimat und Alter der eddischen gedichte: das isländische Sondergut. *Archiv für das Studium der neueren Sprachen und Literaturen*, 116, 249-81, rpt. in *Kleine Schrifter*, II, Berlin: de Gruyter, 1969, 165-94.

Higgs, E. S., ed., 1972, *Papers in Economic Prehistory*, Cambridge.

Higham, N. G., ed., 1979, *Northern History* 19, 1-18.

Hill, D. 1981, *An Anglo-Saxon Atlas*, Oxford.

Hills, C. 1979, Anglo-Saxon Chairperson, *Antiquity*, 54 (no. 210), 54.

Historia de Sancto Cuthberto, 1892, in T. Arnold, ed., *Symeonis Monachi Opera*, vol. 1, London, Rolls Series.

Historia Regum, 1882, in T. Arnold, ed., *Symeonis Monachi Opera*, vol. 2, London, Rolls Series.

Hoare, A. D. M., 1937, *The Works of Morris and Yeats in Relation to Early Saga Literature*. Cambridge: The University Press.

Holdsworth, P. 1975, Two new structures from Saxon Southampton, *Archaeol. Atlantica*. 1 (2), 199-206.

—, 1976, Saxon Southampton: a new review, *Med. Arch.* XX, 26-61.

Hollander, Lee (intro.), 1959, *Eyrbyggja Saga*. Translated by Paul Schach. Lincoln, Nebraska: University of Nebraska Press and the American-Scandinavian Foundation.

—, 1968, *The Skalds: A Selection of their Poems with Introduction and Notes*. New York: American-Scandinavian Foundation, 1945. Reprinted, Ann Arbor: University of Michigan Press.

Hoffmann, E. 1975, *Die heiligen Könige bei den Angelsachsen und den skandinavischen Völkern*. Neumünster.

—, 1976, *Königserhebung und Thronfolgeordnung in Dänemark bis zum Ausgang des Mittelalters*. Berlin.

Höfler, O. 1956, Der Sakralcharakter des germanischen Königtums, *Das Königtum, seine geistigen und rechtlichen Grundlagen, Vorträge und Forschungen*, III, Konstanzer Arbeitskreis für mittelalterliche Geschichte, Konstanz.

Holmqvist, W. 1955, *Germanic Art During the First Milennium, A.D.* Stockholm.

—, 1960, The dancing gods, *Acta Archaeologica* 31. Copenhagen, 101-27.

Holmqvist, W., *et al.*, 1981-72, *Excavations at Helgö I-IV*. Kungl Vitterhets Historie och Antikvitets Akademien. Stockholm.

— , 1975, Helgö, an Early Trading Settlement in Central Sweden, in Rupert Bruce-Mitford, ed., *Recent Archaeological Excavations in Europe*, 111-132.

Holzapfel, Otto, McGrew, Julia and Piφ, Iφrn, eds., 1978, *The European Medieval Ballad: a Symposium*. Odense: University Press, 1978.

Homans, G. C. 1957, *The Frisian in East Anglia.*

Hope-Taylor, B. 1962, The 'boat-shaped' house in northern Europe, *Proc. Camb. Ant. Soc.* LV, 16-22.

— , 1971, *Under York Minster: Archaeological Discoveries 1966-1971*, York.

Hubert, J., Porcher, J. and Volbach, W. F. 1969, *Europe in the Dark Ages*, London, 266-67, Fig. 295.

Huggins, P. J. 1976, The excavation of an 11th-century Viking hall and 14th-century rooms at Waltham Abbey, Essex, 1969-71, *Med. Arch.* XX, 75-133.

Hughes, K. 1966, *The Church in early Irish Society*. London.

— , 1972, *Early Christian Ireland: An Introduction to the Sources*. London.

Hunter, J. R. 1980, Brough of Birsay: Early Christian, Late Norse settlement in *Discovery & Excavation in Scotland*, 81.

— and Morris, C. D. 1981, Recent excavations on the Brough of Birsay, Orkney, in H. Bekker-Nielsen, P. Foote and O. Olsen, eds., *The Eighth Viking Congress, Aarhus 1977*, Odense, 245-255.

Hvass, S. 1973, Hodde. En vestjysk jernaldersby med social deling, *Mark og Montre* 10-21.

— , 1976, Udgravningerne i Vorbasse, *Mark og Montre*, 38-52.

— , 1977, Vikingebebyggelsen i Vorbasse, *Mark og Montre*, 18-29.

— , 1979, Fem ars udgravninger i Vorbasse, *Mark og Montre*, 27-39.

Hyenstrand, Ake, 1972, Production of Iron in Outlying districts and the Problem of Jämbäraland, *Early Medieval Studies* 4, *Antikvariskt Arkiv*, 46. Stockholm.

— — , 1974, *Centralbygd-Randbygd. Strukurella, ekonomiska och administrative huvud-linjer i mellansvensk yngre järnalder*. Stockholm.

Imelmann, Rudolf, 1920, *Forschungen zur altenglischen Poesie*. Berlin: Weidmann.

Ingstad, Anne Stine, 1978, *The Discovery of a Norse Settlement in America*. Oslo: Universitetsforlaget.

Isachsen, Fridtjof, 1961, Norden, in Axe Stromme, ed., *A Geography of Norden*. Oslo.

Islendingabok, 1968, ed. J. Benediktsson, *Islensk Fornrit*, vol. 1.

Jakobsen, J. 1946, *The Place-Names of Shetland*. London: D. Nutt.

James, E. 1978, Cemeteries and the problem of Frankish settlement in Gaul, *Names, Words and Graves*, ed. P. H. Sawyer, Leeds.

Jankuhn, Herbert, 1963, *Haithabu. Ein Handelsplatz der Wikingerzeit*. Neumünster: K. Wachholtz.

— , *et al.*, 1973, 1974, *Vor- und Frühformen der europäischen Stadt im Mittelalter*. Phil.-Hist. Series 3, 83 and 84. Akad der W. Göttingen.

— , 1975, Die Anfange des Stadtwesens in Nordeuropa, in Herbert Mitscha-Markheim, ed., *Festscrift für Richard Pittioni II*.

— , 1977, New Beginnings in Northern Europe and Scandinavia, in M. W. Barley, ed., *European Towns. Their Archaeology and Early History*. New York, Academic Press, 355-71.

Jansson, I. 1969, Wikingerschmuck und Münzdatierung. Bemerkungen zu einer Neuer-scheiung. *Tor*, XIII, 26-64.

— , 1980, Review of Hall, R. A. ed., Viking Age York and the North, 1978 in *Medieval Archaeology*, XXIV, 274-5.

Jensen, Gillian Fellows, 1968, Scandinavian Personal Names in Lincolnshire and Yorkshire. Copenhagen.

John, E. 1960, *Land Tenure in early England*. Leicester.

Jones, Gwyn, 1968, *A History of the Vikings*. Oxford.

Jones, Richard Foster, 1966, *The Triumph of the English Language: a survey of opinions concerning the vernacular from the introduction of printing to the Restoration*. 1953. Reprinted, Stanford: Stanford University Press.

Jørganson, L. B. and Skov, T. 1978, Trabjerg. Resultaterne af 5 ars udgravinger af en Vikingetidsboplads i NV-Jylland, *Holstebro Museum Arsskrift*, 7-40.

Kaland, S. H. H. 1973, Westnessutgravningene pa Rousay, Orkneyøyeye, *Viking*, 77-102.

—, 1980, Westness, Rousay. Viking period graveyard, foundations, in *Discovery & Excavation in Scotland*, 25.

Karlsson, G. 1974-77. Godar and Höfdingyar in medieval Iceland, *Saga-book of the of the Viking Society*, 19, 358-70.

Kaske, R. E. 1958, *Sapienta et Fortitudo* as the controlling theme of *Beowulf*. *Studies in Philology*, 55, 423-57.

—, 1967, A Poem of the Cross in the Exeter Book, *Traditio* 23, 41-71.

Kendrick, T. D. 1938, *Anglo-Saxon Art to A.D. 900*. London.

—, 1949, *Late Saxon and Viking Art*. London.

Kenward, H. K. 1976, Reconstructing ancient ecological conditions from insect remains: some problems and an experimental approach, *Ecological Entomology*, 1, 7-17.

— et al., 1978, The environment of Anglo-Scandinavian York, in R. A. Hall, ed., *Viking Age York and the North*, C.B.A. Report No. 27, London, 58-70.

Ker, N. R. 1957, *Catalogue of Manuscripts containing Anglo-Saxon*. Oxford.

Ker, W. P. 1897, *Epic and Romance*. Reprinted New York: Dover, 1957.

Kershaw, Nora, ed., 1922, *Anglo-Saxon and Norse Poems*. Cambridge: Univ. Press.

Kiernan, Kevin S. 1981, *Beowulf* and the *Beowulf* Manuscript. New Jersey.

King, A. 1970, *Early Pennine Settlement*, Clapham via Lancaster.

—, 1978, Gauber high pasture, Ribblehead – an interim report, in R. A. Hall, ed., *Viking Age York and the North*, C.B.A. Report, No. 27, London, 21-25.

Kinvig, R. H., 1975, *The Isle of Man. A Social, cultural and political history*, Liverpool.

Kissling, W. 1943, The character and purpose of the Hebridean Black House, *J. Roy. Anthrop. Inst. G.B.*, LXXIII, 75-100.

K[ittredge], G. L. 1902, Gray's Knowledge of Old Norse, in William Lyon Phelps, ed., *Selections from the Poetry and Prose of Thomas Gray*. Boston: Ginn and Co, xli-l.

Kitzinger, E. 1956, The Coffin Reliquary, in C. F. Battiscombe, ed., *The Relics of St Cuthbert*. Oxford. 202-304.

Klaeber, Fr., ed., 1950, *Beowulf and the Fight at Finnsburg*, 3rd ed. rev. Boston: D. C. Heath and Co.

Klindt-Jensen, O. and Wilson, D. M. 1966, *Viking Art*. London.

—, 1969, cf. Sawyer, 1969.

Klumbach, H., ed., 1973, Spätrömische Gardehelme, in *Münchner Beiträge zur vor- und Frühgeschichte*, 15. Munich.

Kögel, Rudolf, 1894, *Geschichte der deutschen Litteratur bis zum Ausgange des Mittelalters*, I, 1. Teil: Die stabreimende Dichtung und die gotische Prosa. Strassburg: Trübner.

Koht, Haluden, 1921, Upphave til dei gamle norske byane. *Norst Historisk tidsskrift*. Oslo.

Kollwitz, R. 1933, *Die Lipsanothek von Brescia* in *Studien zur Spätantike Kunstgeschichte*, 7. Berlin.

Kranz, Gisbert, 1974, *C. S. Lewis; Studien zu Leben und Werk*. Bonn: Bouvier Verlag Herbert Grundmann.

Kuhn, H. 1966, Die Orsnamen der Kolonien und das Mutterland. *Proceedings of the Eighth International Congress of Onomastic Sciences.* The Hague, 260-265.

Kulturhistorisk leksikon for nordisk middelalder, 1956-78. København, Rosenkilde og Bagger.

La Baume, P, 1967, *Das Fränkische Gräberfeld von Junkersdorf bei Köln, Germanische Denkmäler der Völkerwanderungszeit,* Serie B, 3, Berlin.

Lagerqvist, I. O. 1970, *Svenska Mynt,* Stockholm.

Laing, L. R. 1975, *Settlement in Post-Roman Scotland, BAR* 13, Oxford.

Laing, Samuel, tr., 1844, *The Heimskringla; or, Chronicle of the Kings of Norway, translated from the Icelandic of Snorrø Sturleson,* 3 vols. London: Longman.

Lang, J. T. 1973, Some late pre-Conquest Crosses in Ryedale, Yorkshire: a reappraisal, *J. Brit. Archaeol. Ass.* 36.

— , 1977, The Sculptors of the Nunburnholme Cross, *Archaeol. J.* 133, 75-94.

— , 1978a, Continuity and innovation in Anglo-Scandinavian sculpture, in J. T. Lang, ed., *Anglo-Saxon and Viking Age Sculpture and its context, BAR,* 49, Oxford, 145-172.

— , 1978b, Anglo-Scandinavian sculpture in Yorkshire, in R. A. Hall, ed., *Viking Age York and the North,* C.B.A. Report 27, London, 11-20.

Lapidge, M. 1979, Byrhtferth and the Vita S. Ecgwini, *Medieval Studies,* 41, 331-53.

— (forthcoming), Byrhtferth of Ramsey and the early sections of the *Historia Regum* attributed to Symeon of Durham, *Medievalia et Humanistica.*

Lemire, Eugene D., ed., 1969, Early England. *The Unpublished Lectures of William Morris.* Detroit: Wayne State University Press.

Leslie, R. F., 1961, *Three Old English Elegies.* Manchester: Manchester Univ. Press.

— , ed., 1961, *The Wanderer.* Manchester: Manchester Univ. Press.

Levi-Strauss, Claude, 1969, *The Elementary Structures of Kinship.* Translated by James Harle Bell *et al.* Boston: Beacon Press.

— , 1963, The Structural Study of Myth. Translated by Claire Jacobson and Brooke Grundfest Schoepf. *Structural Anthropology.* New York, London: Basic Books.

Lewis, Archibald R. 1958, *The Northern Seas: Shipping and Commerce in Northern Europe A.D. 300-1100.* Princeton.

Lewis, C. S. 1939, *Rehabilitations and Other Essays.* London: Oxford University Press.

Lewis, W. H., ed., 1966, *Letters of C. S. Lewis.* London: G. Bles.

Leyerle, John, 1967, The Interlace Structure of *Beowulf. University of Toronto Quarterly,* 37, 1-17.

Lidén, Hans Emil, 1973, Oslo I. Development of urban structure in the 12th and 13th centuries. II. The beginnings. Archaeological contributions to the early history of urban communities in Norway. The Institute for Comparative Research in Human Culture. Oslo, Bergen, Tromsø.

— , Herteig, A. E. and Blindheim, C. 1975, *Archaeological contributions to the early history of urban communities in Norway.* Instituttet for sammenlignende kulturforskning. Series A. Forelesninger, 27.

Liebermann, F. 1903, *Die Gesetze der Angelsachsen,* Halle.

Lindow, J. 1976, *Comitatus, Individual and Honour: Studies in north Germanic institutional vocabulary.* Berkeley.

Lindqvist, Sune, 1941, Fartygsbilder fran Gotlands forntid, *Föreningen Sveriges Sjöfartsmuseum i Stockholm arsbok,* 9-24.

— , 1948, Sutton Hoo and *Beowulf. Antiquity* 23, 131-140.

Litzenberg, Karl, 1933, *Contributions of the Old Norse Language and Literature to the Style and Substance of the Writings of William Morris.* Thesis (Ph.D.), University of Michigan, 1933.

Litzenberg, Karl, 1935, William Morris and Scandinavian Literature: A Bibliographical Essay. *Scandinavian Studies and Notes*, 13, No. 7 (August), 93.

— , 1936a, William Morris and the Reviews: A study in the Fame of the Poet. *RES*, 12, 416 ff.

— , 1936b, William Morris and the *Heimskringla. Scandinavian Studies and Notes*, 14, No. 3 (August), 33–39.

— , 1936c, William Morris and *The Burning of Njál. Scandinavian Studies and Notes*, 14, No. 3 (August), 40–41.

— , 1937, The Diction of William Morris. *Arkiv för Nordisk Filologi*, 53, 327–363.

— , 1947, The Victorians and the Vikings: A Bibliographical Essay on Anglo-Norse Literary Relations. *University of Michigan Contributions in Modern Philology*, No. 3. Ann Arbor: University of Michigan Press, 1947, 1–27.

Lönnroth, Lais, 1971, Hjálmar's Death Song and the Delivery of Eddic Poetry. *Speculum*, 46, 1–20.

Lot, F. 1945, Que nous apprennent sur le peuplement germanique de la France les recents travaux de Toponomie?, *Revue de l'Academie des inscriptions*, 289–98.

Lowe, E. A., 1950, *Codices Latini Antiquiores*, V. Oxford.

Loyn, H. R. 1962, *Anglo-Saxon England and the Norman Conquest*, London.

— , 1976, *The Vikings in Wales*, Dorothea Coke Memorial Lecture, London.

— , 1977, *The Vikings in Britain.* New York.

Lucas, A. T. 1966, Irish–Norse relations: time for a reappraisal?, *Journal of the Cork Historical and Archaeological Society*, 71, 62–75.

— , The plundering and burning of churches in Ireland, seventh to sixteenth centuries, in E. Rynne, ed., *North Munster Studies*, Limerick.

Lunde, Øyvind, 1977, *Trondheims fortid, i bygrunnen.* Riksantikvarens Skrifter II. Oslo.

Lundström, L. 1973, *Bitsilvar och betalningsringar. Studier i svenska depafynd fran vikingatiden paträffade mellan 1900 och 1970.* Theses and Papers in North-European Archaeology, 2.

Macaulay, D. 1971–72, Studying the Place-Names of Bemera. *Transactions of the Gaelic Society of Inverness*, 47, 313–337.

MacBain, A. 1893–94, The Norse Element in the Topography of the Highlands and Isles. *Transactions of the Gaelic Society of Inverness* 19, 217–245.

MacGregor, A. 1978, Industry and commerce in Anglo-Scandinavian York, in R. A. Hall, ed., *Viking Age York and the North*, C.B.A. Report No. 27, London, 37–57.

Mack, R. P. 1964, *The Coinage of Ancient Britain.* London.

Macail, J. W. 1899, *The Life of William Morris*, 2 vols. London: Longmans.

Maclaren, A. 1974, A Norse house on Drimore Machair, S. Uist, *Glasgow Arch. J.*, 3, 9–18.

Magnou-Nortier, E. 1976, *Foi et Fidelité.* Toulouse.

Magnússon, Eiríkr, ed., 1875–1883, *Thómas saga erkibiskups. 2 vols.* Translated by Eiríkr Magnússon. London: Longmans. *(Rerum Brit. Medii Æviscriptores, 65).* Rolls Series, 2 vols. In Icelandic with English translation and glossary.

Magnusson, Magnus, 1973, *Viking Expansion Westwards.* London.

— , 1980, Vikings 1. London.

— and Palsson, Hermann, trs., 1966, *The Vinland Sagas: the Norse Discovery of America.* New York.

Magoun, Francis P. 1942–43, Deors Klage und Gudrúnarkvida I. *Englische Studien*, 75, 1–15.

Mallet, Paul Henri de, 1756, *Monumens de la mythologie et de la poésie des Celtes. Et Particulièrement des anciens Scandinaves: pour servir de supplément et de preuves à l'introduction à l'histoire de Dannemarc.* Copenhague: Claude Philbert.

Mallet, Paul Henri, 1755, *Introduction à l'histoire de Dannemarc, où l'on traite de la religion, des loix, des mœurs & des usages des anciens Danois.* Copenhague: s.n. Translated by Thomas Percy (Sep. ref.), revised by I. A. Blackwell.

Malmer, B., 1966, *Nordiska mynt före ar 1000* (Acta Archàeologica Lundensia Series in 8°, No. 4). Lund/Bonn.

— , 1973, *Finska fornminnesföreningens tidsckrift.* LXXV.

Malone, Kemp, 1940, *Ecgðeow. Modern Language Quarterly,* 1, 37–44.

— , 1949, *Deor,* London, Figs. 9–13.

— , ed., 1963, *Widsith.* London.

— , ed., 1966, *Deor.* New York.

Marquandt, H. 1961, *Bibliographie der Runen nach Fundorten: 1, Runeninschriften der Britischen Inseln.* Göttingen.

Marshall, D. N. 1964, Report on excavations at Little Dunagoil, *Trans. Buteshire Nat. Hist. Soc.,* XVI, 1–69.

Martens, Irmelin, 1972, Møsstrand i Telemark, *Viking* 36, 83–114.

Marwick, H., 1947, *The Place-Names of Rousay,* Kirkwall.

— , 1951, *Orkney,* London.

— , 1952, *Orkney Farm-Names,* Kirkwall.

Maryon, Herbert, 1946, The Sutton Hoo Shield, *Antiquity* 20, 21–30.

Mathews, G. 1963, *Byzantine Aesthetics,* London 1.

Maxwell, Ian, 1961, On Translation – I: A Review. *Saga-Book,* 15, 383–393.

McDowell, G. T. 1923, The Treatment of the *Volsunga Saga* by William Morris. *Scandinavian Studies and Notes,* 7, No. 6 (February), 152.

McGrail, S. 1974, The Gokstad Faering, Part I. *Marine Monographs and Reports XI.*

— , 1980, Ships, Shipwrights and Seamen, in J. Graham-Campbell, *The Viking World,* 37–63.

McGregor, R. 1978, Industry and commerce in Anglo-Scandinavian York, in R. A. Hall, ed., *Viking Age York and the North,* London.

McRoberts, D. 1965, The ecclesiastical significance of the St Ninian's Isle treasure, in A. Small, ed., *Fourth Viking Congress, York 1961,* Aberdeen, 224–46.

McTurk, R. 1974–77, Sacral Kingship in ancient Scandinavia: a review of some recent writings, *Saga-book of the Viking Society,* 19, 139–67.

— , 1976, Ragnarr Loðbrok in the Irish Annals in B. Almqvist and D. Greene, eds., *Proceedings of the seventh Viking Congress,* Dublin, 1973, 93–123.

— , 1980, Review of Smyth, 1977, *Saga-book of the Viking Society,* 20, 231–34.

Medeltidstaden Riksantikvarieambetet och Statens Historiska Museer. 1. Projektprogram , 1976; 2. Arboga, 1976; 3. Uppsala, 1977.

Megaw, B. R. S. 1938, The Douglas Treasure Trove, a hoard of the Viking Age, *J. Manx Mus.,* IV (57), 77–80.

— and Megaw, E. M., 1951, The Norse Heritage in the Isle of Man, in *The Early Cultures of N.W. Europe,* H. M. Chadwick Memorial Studies, Cambridge.

Meldgaard, Jørgen, 1961, *Fra Brattahlid til Vinland. Naturens Verden,* 353–84.

Mercer, R. J. 1980, *Archaeological Field Survey in Northern Scotland 1976–79.* Univ. of Edinburgh Dept. of Archaeol. Occasional Paper No. 4.

Metcalf, D. M. 1967, The prosperity of north-western Europe in the eighth and ninth centuries, *Economic History Review,* Series II, 20, 344–357.

Meyvaert, Paul, 1979, Bede and the Church Paintings at Wearmouth-Jarrow. *ASE* 8, 63–77.

Midderhoff, Hanna, 1966, Zur Verbindung des ersten und zweiten Teils des Nibelungenstoffes in der Lieder-Edda. *Zeitschrift für deutsches Alterum,* 95, 243–58.

Midderhoff, Hanna, 1968-69, Übereinstimmungen und Ähnlichkeiten in den lieder-eddischen und epischen Nibelungen. *Zeitschrift für deutsches Alterum*, 97, 241-781.

Mierow, C. C. 1915, *The Gothic history of Jordanes in English version*, Princeton.

Mjöberg, J. 1980, Romanticism and Revival, in D. M. Wilson, ed., *The Northern World*, London, 207-38.

Mohr, Wolfgang, 1938-39, Entstehungsgeschichte und Heimat der jüngeren Eddalieder südgermanischem Stoffes. *Zeitschrift für deutsches Alterum*, 75, 217-80.

— , 1939-40, Wortschatz und Motive der jüngeren Eddalieder mit südgermanischem Stoff. *Zeitschrift für deutsches Alterum*, 76, 149-217.

Morris, Christopher D. 1976, Pre-Conquest Sculpture in the Tees Valley. *Medieval Archaeology 20*, 140-46.

— , 1977, Northumbria and the Viking settlement: the evidence for landholding, *Archaeologia Aeliana*, Series V, 4, 81-103.

— , 1979a, The Vikings and Irish monasteries, *Durham Univ. J.* (June), 175-85.

— , 1979b, Birsay 'small sites' excavations and survey 1978, *Northern Studies*, 13, 3-19, and *Universities of Durham & Newcastle Arch. Repts.* (for 1978), 2, 11-19.

— , 1980, Excavations at Birsay 1979, *Northern Studies 16*, 17-28, and *Universities of Durham & Newcastle upon Tyne Arch. Repts.* (for 1979), 3, 22-31.

— , 1981a, Excavations at Birsay, 1980, *Universities of Durham & Newcastle upon Tyne Arch. Repts.* (for 1980), 4, 35-40.

— , 1981b, Viking and native in northern England: a case-study, in H. Bekker-Nielsen, P. Foote and O. Olsen, eds., *The Eighth Viking Congress*, Arhus 1977, Odense 1981, 223-244.

— , 1982, Excavations and Survey at Birsay, Orkney, *Universities of Durham & Newcastle upon Tyne, Arch. Repts.* (for 1981), 5, 46-53.

— (forthcoming), Excavations around the Bay of Birsay, Orkney, *Fornvännen*.

— , Batey, C. E. and Pearson, N. F. 1980, Freswick Links, Broch, possible Norse settlement, midden, in *Discovery and Excavation in Scotland*, 18.

— , — , and Rackham, D. J., 1979, Freswick Links, midden survey — Freswick Castle, in *Discovery and Excavation in Scotland*, 16.

Morris, May, 1936, *William Morris: Artist, Writer, Socialist*. Oxford: Basil Blackwell.

— , ed., 1911, *The Collected Works of William Morris*. 24 vols. London: Longmans.

Morris, William, 1869, *Gunnlaug. The Fortnightly Review*, XI, January N.S.V.

— and Magnússon, Eiríkr, 1875, *Three Northern Love Stories*. London: Ellis and White.

— and — , trs., 1891-1905, *The Saga Library*, in 6 vols. London: B. Quaritch.

— and — , trs., 1868-1870, The Lovers of Gudrun. *The Earthly Paradise*. London: F. S. Ellis.

— and — , trs., 1870, *The Story of Grettir the Strong*. London: F. S. Ellis.

— and — , *The Story of King Magnus, Son of Erling*. Huntington Manuscript 6463.

— and — , *Howard the Halt*. Huntington Manuscript 6426.

— and — , *Olaf Tryggvison*. Huntington Manuscript 6437.

Munn, William A., 1914, *Wineland Voyages*. St John's, Newfoundland: The Labour Press.

Musset, L. 1965, *Les Invasions, Vol. II, Le Second Assaut contre l'Europe Chrétienne*, Paris.

— , 1975, Pour l'étude comparative de deux fondations politiques des Vikings: le royaume de York, et le duché de Rouen, *Northern History*, 10, 40-54.

Myhre, Bjørne, 1973, The Iron-Age Farm in south-west Norway, *Norwegian Archaeological Review, 6*.

Myres, J. N. L. 1969, *Anglo-Saxon Pottery and the Settlement of England*. Oxford.

Myres, J. N. L. 1970, The Angles, the Saxons and the Jutes. *Proceedings of the British Academy*, 1-32.

—— and Green, Barbara, 1973, *The Anglo-Saxon Cemeteries of Caistor-by-Norwich and Markshall, Norfolk. Reports of the Research Committee of the Society of Antiquaries of London, XXX*. London.

——, 1977, *A Corpus of Anglo-Saxon Pottery of the Pagan Period*, 2 vols. New York.

Nansen, Fridtjof, 1911, *In Northern Mists*, 2 vols. (tr. Arthur G. Chater). New York.

Napier, A. S. 1900, The Franks Casket, in *An English Miscellany presented to Dr. Furnivall*, 362-81, Oxford.

National Museum of Ireland, 1973, *Viking and Medieval Dublin National Museum Excavations 1962-73*, Exhibition Catalogue, Dublin.

Neckel, Gustav, 1908, Anhang: die altgermanische Heldenklage, *Beiträge zur Eddaforschung, mit Exkursen zur Helden sage*. Dortmund: Ruhfus.

——, ed., 1962, Edda: Die Lieder des Codex Regius, nebst verwanden Denkmälern. 4th ed. rev. Hans Kuhn. Heidelberg: Winter.

Needham, Geoffrey I., ed., 1976, *Ælfric. Lives of Three English Saints*. Exeter.

Nerman, B. 1941, *Sveriges Rikes Uppkomst*.

——, 1948, Sutton Hoo, en svensk Kunga-eller Hövdinggrav. *Fornvännen 43*, 65-93.

——, 1958, *Grobin-Seeburg, Ausgrabungen und Funde*. Stockholm.

Nicol, D. M., 1974, Byzantium and England. *Balkan Studies 15*, 179-203.

Nicolaisen, W. F. H. 1960, Norse Place-Names in South-West Scotland. *Scottish Studies 4*, 49-70.

——, 1964, Scottish Place-Names: 22. Old Norse þveit, etc. *Scottish Studies 8*, 96-103.

——, 1964, Scottish Place-Names: 23. The Distribution of Old Norse *býr* and *fjall*. *Scottish Studies 8*, 208-213.

——, 1967, Scottish Place-Names: 29. Scandinavian Personal Names in the Place-Names of South-East Scotland. *Scottish Studies 11*, 223-236.

——, 1969, Norse Settlement in the Northern and Western Isles. *Scottish Historical Review*, 98, 6-17.

——, 1975, Place-Names Evidence in McNeill, P., Bicholson, R., eds., *An Historical Atlas of Scotland, c. 400-c. 1600*. St Andrews: Atlas Committee of the Conference of Scottish Medievalists, 2-7 and Maps 3a-6f.

——, 1976, *Scottish Place-Names: Their Study and Significance*. London.

——, 1976, Scandinavian Place-Names in Scotland as a Source of Knowledge, *Northern Studies*, 7-8, 14-24.

——, 1978, Are There Connotative Names? *Names*, 26, 40-47.

——, 1979-80, Early Scandinavian Naming in the Western and Northern Isles, *Northern Scotland*, 3 (2), 105-121.

——, 1980, Place-Names as Evidence for Linguistic Stratification in Scotland, *Nornarapporter*, 18, 211-231.

Nielsen, L. C. 1977-78, Omgard- en vestjysk landsby fra vikingetid, *Hardsyssels Årbog*, Bind 11-12, 59-84.

Noonan, T. 1981, Ninth-century dirham hoards from European Russia — a preliminary analysis, in Blackburn and Metcalf, *Coinage in the Northern Lands, c. 800-c. 1100*, 1981.

Nordal, Sigurdr and Jónsson, Gudni, 1938, *Gunnlaugssaga ormstunga. Íslenzk Fornrit*, III. Reykjavík: Hid íslenzka fornritafélag.

Nordby, Conrad H. 1901, *The Influence of Old Norse Literature Upon English Literature*. Columbia University Germanic Studies, 1, No. 3. New York: Columbia University Press.

Nordhagen, P. J. 1976, An Italo–Byzantine Painter at the Scriptorium of Ceolfrith, *Studia Romana in honorem P. Krarup*, 138-145.

Notker, *Vita Karoli Imperatoris*, ed. G. H. Pertz, *Monumenta Germaniae Historica, Scriptores*, vol. 2.

Obolensky, D. 1971, *The Byzantine Commonwealth*, London.

O'Corrain, D. 1972, *Ireland before the Normans*, Dublin.

—— , 1980, High Kings, Vikings and other kings, *Irish Historical Studies*, 21, 283-323.

Oftedal, M. 1953, Norse Place-Names in the Hebrides, ed. Kjell Falck, *Annen Viking Kongress*, Bergen. *Universitet i Bergen Arbok 1955*, Historisk-antiquarisk rekke, Nr. 1 (Bergen 1955), 107-112.

—— , The Village Names of Lewis in the Outer Hebrides, *Norsk Tidsskrift for Sprogvidenskap* 17, 363-408.

Okasha, E. 1971, *A Handlist of Anglo-Saxon non-Runic Inscriptions*. Cambridge.

O'Kelly, M. J. 1955-56, An island settlement at Beginish, Co. Kerry, *Proc. Roy. Irish Acad.* C57, 159-94.

—— , 1961, A stone bowl of Viking type from Beginish Island, Co. Kerry, *J. Roy. Soc. Antiq., Ireland*. XCI, pt 2, 64-8.

Oleson, Tryggvi, 1969, *Early Voyages and Northern Approaches, 1000-1632*. The Canadian Centenary Series, vol. I. Toronto: McClelland and Stewart; New York: Oxford University Press.

O'Loughlin, J. N. L. 1964, Sutton Hoo: the Evidence of the Documents. *Medieval Archaeology* 8, 1-19.

Olsen, Olaf, 1975, Nogle tanker i anledning af Ribes uventet høje alder. *Fra Vibe Arnt. Festskrift til H. K. Kristensen*.

Olsen, O. and Schmidt, H. 1977, *Fyrkat. En jysk vikingeborg. I. Borgen og Bebyggelsen*. Nordiske Fortidsminder, Serie B — in quarto Bind 3, Copenhagen.

O'Rahilly, Cecile, ed., 1974, *Tain Bó Cúalinge*. Dublin.

O'Riordain, B. 1971, Excavations at Dublin, *Med. Arch.*, XV, 73-85.

—— , 1976, The High Street Excavations, in D. Greene and B. Almqvist, eds., *7th Viking Congress Dublin, 1973*, Dublin, 135-140.

Oxenstierna, Eric Graf, 1966, *The Norsemen*. Translated by C. Hutter. Greenwich, Ct.

Ozols, Jakob, 1976, Der Bernsteinhandel und die Skandinavischen Kolonien in Kurland, *Bonner Hefte zur Vorgeschichte*, 11, 153-59.

Page, R. 1971, How Long did the Scandinavian Language Survive in England. *England Before the Conquest: Studies in Primary History Presented to D. Whitlock*, 165-186.

—— , 1973, *An Introduction to English Runes*. London.

Palliser, D. M. 1978, The Medieval street-names of York, *York Historian*, 2, 2-16.

Palsson, H. and Edwards, P., trs., *Orkneyinga Saga. The History of the Earls of Orkney*, London.

Pattison, I. R. 1973, Nunburnholme Cross and Anglo-Danish sculpture in York, *Archaeologia*, CIV, 209-34.

Paulsen, P. 1956, *A X und Kreuz in Nord- und Osteuropa* (2nd edition), Bonn.

—— and Schach-Dörges, H. 1972, *Holzhandwerk der Alamannen*. Stuttgart.

Pelteret, D. 1980, Slave-raiding and slave trading in early England, *Anglo-Saxon England*, 9, 99-114.

Percy, Bishop Thomas, 1763, *Five Pieces of Runic Poetry*. London: R. and J. Dodsley.

—— , 1847, *Northern Antiquities: or, a description of the manners, customs, religion and laws of the ancient Danes, and other Northern nations; including those of our own Saxon ancestors. With a translation of the Edda, or system of Runic mythology, and*

Percy, Bishop Thomas, 1847 — *continued:*—
other pieces, from the ancient Islandic tongue . . . With additional notes by the English translator and Goranson's Latin version of the Edda. 2 vols. London: T. Carnan & Co., 1770. Revised by I. A. Blackwell. London: Henry G. Bohn.

Petersen, J. 1940, in H. Shetelig, ed., *British Antiquities of the Viking period found in Norway: Viking Antiquities in Great Britain and Ireland,* vol. 5, Oslo.

Phillpotts, Bertha S. 1931, *Edda and Saga.* New York: H. Holt.

Pilch, Herbert, 1964, One Elegiac Genre in Old English and Early Welsh Poetry. *Zeitschrift für celtische Philologie*, 29, 209-24.

Plumet, Patrick, 1976, Les Vikings en Amerique: la fin d'un Mythe in Boyer, Regis, *Les Vikings et leur civilisation, problemes actuels.* Paris: Mouton.

Plummer, C. and Earle, J. 1892, *Two of the Saxon Chronicles Parallel.* Oxford; Clarendon.

——, ed., 1896, *Venerabilis Bedae Opera Historica,* 2 vols. Oxford.

Poussa, P. M. 1981, The Date of *Beowulf* Reconsidered: The Tenth Century? *Neuphililogische Mitteilungen,* 82, 276-88.

Powell, G. E. J. and Magnússon, Eiríkir [*sic*], 1864-1866. *Icelandic Legends.* Collected by Jón Árnason. 2nd Series. London: Longmans.

Pound, N. J. G. 1973, *An Historical Geography of Europe, 450 B.C.-A.D. 1330.*

Powell, Roger, 1956, The Stonyhurst Gospel, (b) The Binding, in C. F. Battiscombe, ed., *The Relics of St Cuthbert.* Oxford.

Radford, C. A. R. 1959, The Early Christian and Norse Settlements at Birsay, Orkney, H.M.S.O. Official Guide.

——, 1946, A lost inscription of pre-Danish Age from Caistor, *Archaeological Journal,* 103, 95-99.

Radley, J. 1972, Economic Aspects of Anglo-Danish York. *Medieval Archaeology,* 15, 37-57.

Randsborg, K. 1980, *The Viking Age in Denmark.* London.

Rasmussen, N. L. 1961, An Introduction to the Viking-Age Hoards. *Commentationes,* I, 1-16.

Regino Chron. Chronicon Reginonis Prumensis, ed. F. Kurze, *Monumenta Germaniae Historica, Scriptores rerum germanicarum in usum scholarum.*

Reid, R. W. K., David, G. and Aitken, A. 1966-67, Prehistoric Settlement in *Durness, Proc. Soc. Antiq. Scot.,* 99, 21-53.

Reuschel, Helga, 1938, Ovid und die ags. Elegien. *Beiträge zur Geschichte der deutsche Sprache und Literatur,* 62, 132-42.

Reynolds, Susan, 1977, *An Introduction to the History of English Medieval Towns.* Oxford.

Riché, Pierre, 1976, La 'Renaissance' intellectuelle du Xᵉ siècle en l'Occident. *Cahiers d'Histoire,* 21, 27-42.

Rigold, G. F. 1961, The supposed see of Dunwich, *Journal of the British Archaeological Association,* Series III, 24, 55-59.

Ritchie, A. 1974, Pict and Norsemen in Northern Scotland, *Scottish Arch. Forum,* 6, 23-36.

——, 1976-77, Excavation of Pictish and Viking age farmsteads at Buckquoy, Orkney, *Proc. Soc. Antiq. Scot.* 108, 174-227.

Ritchie, J. N. G. and Ritchie, A. 1981, *Scotland, Archaeology and Early history.* London.

Robinson, Fred N. 1978, God, Death and Loyalty in *The Battle of Maldon,* in Farrell, R. T. and Mary Salu, 1978, 76-98.

Roesdahl, E. 1970-73, Review of Sawyer 1971, *Saga-book of the Viking Society,* 18, 402-9.

Roesdahl, Else, 1980, *Danmarks Vikingetid*, København.
— , 1982, *Viking Age Denmark*.
Roosval, Jotring, 1930, Acta angaende Kallungeflöydeln. *Fornvännen*.
Roper, M. 1974, The landholdings of St Wilfred in Northumbria, in D. P. . Kirby, ed., *St Wilfred at Hexham*, Newcastle upon Tyne, 61-79.
Ross, A. S. C., ed., 1940, Alfred's translation of *Orosus*.
Roussell, A. 1934, *Norse Building Customs in the Scottish Isles*, London.
Roussell, Aage, 1972, *Bulletin of the Canadian Archaeological Association*, 4.
Royal Commission on Ancient Monuments of Scotland (RCAMS), 1946, *Orkney & Shetland*, 3 vols. H.M.S.O., Edinburgh.
Rygh, O. 1897-1929, *Norske Gaardnavne*, Kristiania, W. C. Fabritius & sønners bogtrykkeri.
Salin, B. 1921, Forgyld flögel from Soderala kyrka, *Fornvännen*, Stockholm 1923.
Sampson, George, ed., 1924, *The Cambridge Book of English Verse and Prose*. Cambridge.
Sawyer, P. H. 1968, *Anglo-Saxon Charters: an Annotated list and bibliography*, London.
— , 1969. The two Viking Ages; a discussion, *Medieval Scandinavia*, 2, 163-207.
— , 1971 (1st edn. 1962), *The Age of the Vikings*, London
— , 1977, Kings and Merchants, in P. H. Sawyer and I. N. Woods, eds., *Early Medieval Kingship*, Leeds 139-58.
— , 1978b, *From Roman Britain to Norman England*, London.
— , 1978a, Wics, Kings and Vikings, in T. Andersson and K. I. Sandred, eds., *The Vikings*, Uppsala, 23-31.
— , 1978c, Some sources for the history of Viking Northumbria, in R. A. Hall, ed., *Viking Age York and the North*, C.B.A. Report No. 27, London 3-7.
— , 1979, *The Charters of Burton Abbey*, London.
— , 1981, The Vikings in Ireland in D. M. Dumville, R. McKitterick and D. Whitelock, *Ireland and Europe: Studies in memory of Kathleen Hughes*, Cambridge.
— , 1982, *Scandinavia and Europe in the Viking Age*, London.
Saxo Grammaticus, 1886, *Gesta Danorum*, ed. Alfred Holder. Strassburg: Trübner.
Saxo, 1979, *Saxo Grammaticus, The History of the Danes*, tr. P. Fisher and H. Ellis Davidson, Cambridge.
— , 1980. *Saxo Grammaticus, Books X-XVI*, tr. E. Christiansen, (Oxford, *British Archaeological Reports*, international series, 84, 1980), vol. 1 of a three volume series.
Scarfe, N. 1972, *The Suffolk Landscape*, London.
Schledermann, Peter, 1980, Notes on Norse Finds from the East Coast of Ellesmere Island, N.W.T. *Arctic*, 33.
Schlesinger, W. 1956, Über germanisches Heerkönigtum, *Das Königtum, seine geistlichen und rechtlichen Grundlagen, Vorträge und Forschungen,* III Konstanzer Arbeitskreis für mittelalterliche Geschichte, Konstanz.
Schmidt, H. 1973, The Trelleborg House Reconsidered, *Med. Arch.*, XVII, 52-77.
Schneider, Karl, 1978, Zu den Inschriften und Bildern des Franks' Casket. *Festschrift für Walter Fischer*. Heidelberg, 1959.
Schoppa, H. 1953, Ein fränkische Holzkästchen aus Weilbach, *Germania*, 31.
Schück, Adolf, 1926, *Studier rörande det svenska stadsväsendets uppkomst och äldsta utveckling*. Uppsala.
Seaton, Ethel, 1935, *Literary Relations of England and Scandinavia in the Seventeenth century*. Oxford, Clarendon.
Selkirk, A. 1973, York, *Current Archaeology*, No. 37, vol. IV, No. 2, 45-52.

Shepard, Jonathan, 1973, The English and Byzantium: A Study of Their Role in the
    Byzantine Army in the Later Eleventh Century. *Traditio,* 29, 53–92.
Shetelig, H. 1940, *Viking Antiquities in England,* (= *Viking Antiquities in Great Britain
    and Ireland,* part IV, ed. H. Shetelig), Oslo.
Shimmin, D. 1978, *Norse settlement at Jarlshof Sumburgh, Shetland, c. A.D. 800–1400;
    a Reassessment.* Unpubl. B.A. Dissertation. Cambridge.
Shippey, T. A. 1978, *Beowulf. Studies in English Literature,* 70. London.
—, 1979, Wealth and Wisdom in King Alfred's *Preface* to the Old English *Pastoral
    Care, English Historical Review,* 94, 351–54.
Shüking, Levin L. 1908, Das angelsächsische Toten-Klagelied. *Englische Studien,* 39,
    1–13.
Sieper, Ernst, 1915, *Die altenglische Elegie.* Strassburg: Trübner, 70–77.
Simpson, Jacqueline, 1956, 'A Note on the Word Frið-stol', *Saga Book of the Viking
    Society,* 14, 3, 200–210.
Sisam, Kenneth, 1953, Anglo-Saxon Royal Genealogies. *Proceedings of the British
    Academy,* 39, 287–348.
—, 1965, *The Structure of Beowulf.* Oxford: Clarendon.
Skaare, Kolbjørn, 1964, Skipsavbildningar pa Birka-Hedeby mynter, *Seartrykk fra Norsk
    Sjøfartsmuseum.*
—, 1976, *Coins and Coinage in Viking Age Norway,* Oslo.
Skovmand, R. 1942, 'De danske skattefund fra vikingetiden og den ældste middelalder
    indtil omkring 1150'. *Aarbøger for nordisk oldkyndighed og Historie,* 1-275.
Small, A. 1966, Excavations at Underhoull, Unst, Shetland. *Proc. Soc. Antiqs. Scot.,*
    XCVIII, 225–48.
—, 1967–68, The distribution of settlement in Shetland and Faroe in Viking times,
    Saga Book of the Viking Soc., XVII, pt. 2-3.
—, 1968, A Historical Geography of the Norse Viking Colonisation of the Scottish
    Highlands, *Norsk. Geogr. Tidskrift.,* 22, 1-16.
—, 1971, The Viking Highlands, in E. Meldram, ed., *The Dark Ages in the Highlands,*
    Inverness Field Club, 69–90.
—, 1976, Norse Settlement in Skye, in R. Boyer, ed., *Les Vikings et leur Civilisation.
    Problemes Actuels,* Bibliothèque Arctique et Antarctique V, 29–37.
—, Thomas, C. and Wilson, D. M. 1973, *St Ninian's Isle and its Treasure,* Oxford.
    2 vols.
Smith, A. H. 1937, *The Place-Names of the East Riding of Yorkshire and York,* English
    Place-Names Society, vol. XIV, Cambridge.
Smyser, H. M. 1965, Ibn Fadlan's account of the Rus . . . , in J. B. Bessinger and R. P.
    Creed, eds., *Medieval and Linguistic Studies in honour of Francis Peabody Magoun,*
    London.
Smyth, A. P. 1975, *Scandinavian York and Dublin,* Vol. 1. Dublin.
—, 1975–76, The Black Foreigners of York and the White Foreigners of Dublin,
    Saga-book of the Viking Society, 19, 101–17.
—, 1977, *Scandinavian Kings in the British Isles, 850–880.* Oxford: Oxford University
    Press.
—, 1978, The Chronology of Northumbrian History in the ninth and tenth centuries,
    in R. A. Hall, ed., *Viking Age York and the North.* London, 8–10.
—, *Scandinavian York and Dublin,* vol. 2, New Jersey.
Speake, G. 1970, A seventh-century coin pendant from Bacton, Norfolk, and its orna-
    ment. *Medieval Archaeology,* 14, 1–16.
—, 1980, *Anglo-Oxford Animal Art,* Oxford.

Stanley, E. G. 1966, *Continuations and Beginnings: Studies in Old English Literature,*Lon.

Stasser, Karl Theodor, 1928, *Wikinger und Normannen.*

Stenberger, M. 1947-1958, *Die Schatzfunde Gotlands der Wikingerzeit*, I-II. Stockholm: Almqvist and Wiksel, vol. 1.

——, 1958, Traditionsbundenhet i vikingatids gotländsk bracteatkorst. *Tor*, IV, 113-33.

——, 1963, *Sweden*, New York.

——, 1979, *Det forntida Sverige*, 3rd ed. Stockholm.

Stenton, F. M., 1970, *Anglo-Saxon England.* Oxford, 3rd ed. Oxford University Press.

Sterckx, C. 1970, Les jeux de damiers celtiques, *Annales de Bretagne*, 77, 597-609.

——, 1973a, Les trois damiers de Buckquoy, Orcades, *Annales de Bretagne*, 80.

——, 1973b, Les jeux de damiers celtiques, *Études celtiques*, 13, 733-49.

Stevenson, R. B. K. 1968, The brooch from Westness, Orkney in B. Niclasen, ed., *Fifth Viking Congress, Torshaven, 1965*, 25-31.

Stewart, J. 1965, Shetland Farm Names, in A. Small, ed., *The Fouth Viking Congress, York, August, 1961,* Aberdeen University Studies, 149. Edinburgh, 247-66.

——, 1967, The Place-Names of Shetland, in A. T. Cloness, ed., *The Shetland Book*, Lerwick. 136-140.

Stoumann, I. 1977, Vikingetidslandsbyen i Saedding *Mark og Montre* 1977, 30-42.

Straume, Eldrid, 1977, Glas-gefasse mit Reparatur in norwegischen Grabfunden der Völker-wanderungzeit. *Festschrift zum 50 jahrigen Bestehen des Vorgeschichtlichen seminars Marburg, Marburger Studien zur Vor- und fruh- geschichte, eds. Frey, Otto-Herman und Roth, Helmut.*

Sturluson, Snorri, 1961, *Heimskringla: Sagas of the Norse Kings*, trans. Samuel Laing, ed. Peter Foote. London: Dent; New York: Dutton. (Everyman's Library).

Sullivan, Richard E. 1978, *The Walter Prescott Webb Memorial Lectures: XII.*

Sutherland, C. H. V. 1937, *Coinage and Currency in Roman Britain.* London.

Swannell, J. N. 1961a, William Morris as an Interpreter of Old Norse. *Saga Book of the Viking Club*, 15.

——, 1961b, William Morris and Old Norse Literature. *Transactions of the William Morris Society*, 13.

Swarzenski, H., 1967, *Monuments of Romanesque Art.* London.

Sweet, Henry, 1866, *An Icelandic primer with grammar, notes and glossary.* Oxford: Clarendon.

Tallgren, A. M. 1934, Die 'altpermische' Pelzwarenperiode an der Pečora, *Finska Forn-minnesföreningens Tidskrift*, 40, 152-81.

Tanner, Vaïno, 1941, *De gamla nordbornas, Helluland, Markland, och Vinland. Budkavlen* XX, 1-72.

Taylor, A. B. trans., 1938, *The Orkneyinga Saga, A new translation with introduction and notes*, London and Edinburgh.

——, 1967-68, The Norsmen in St Kilda, *Saga-Book*, XVII, 116-144.

Tebbutt, C. F. 1962, An Eleventh-Century Boat Shaped Building at Buckden, Huntingdonshire, *Proc. Camb. Ant. Soc.* LV, 13-15.

Theophilus, 1961, *De Diversi Artibus*, tr. C. R. Dodwell. London.

Thietmar Chron. 1955, Thietmari Merseburgensis Episcopi Chronicon, ed. R. Holtzmann, *Monumenta Germaniae Historica, Scriptores rerum germanicarum in usum scholarum.*

Thompson, E. A. 1965, *The Early Germans.* Oxford.

——, 1966, *The Visigoths in the time of Ulfila.* Oxford.

Thompson, E. P. 1977, *William Morris: Romantic to Revolutionary.* New York: Pantheon.

Thompson, J. D. A. 1956, *Inventory of British Coin Hoards, A.D. 600-1500*, London.

Thorpe, Benjamin, 1851-1852, *Northern Mythology, comprising the principal popular traditions and superstitions of Scandinavia, North Germany, and the Netherlands. Compiled from original and other sources.* In three volumes. London: Edward Lumley.

Thorvildsen, Elise, 1972, Dankirke, *Nationalmuseets Arbejdsmark*, 47-60.

Todd, M. 1975, *The Northern Barbarians*. London.

Tolkien, J. R. R. 1936, *Beowulf:* The Monsters and the Critics. *Proceedings of the British Academy 22*, 245-95.

Trætteberg, Hallvard, 1966, Merke og flöy, *Kulturhistoresk Leksikon for nordisk middelalder*, B, XI, Oslo, 549-55.

Trillmich-Buchner, W. and Buchner, R., eds., 1968, *Fontes saeculorum noni et undecimi Historiae Ecclesiae Hammaburgensis*, in *Quellen zur deutschen Geschichte des Mittelalters*, vol. 11.

Tschan, F. J. [Adam of Bremen.] *History of the Archbishops of Hamburg–Bremen.* New York.

Turville-Petre, E. O. G., 1953, *The Origins of Icelandic Literature*, Oxford: Clarendon Press.

— , 1976, *Scaldic Poetry*. Oxford: Clarendon Press.

Utterström, G. 1955, Climactic Fluctuations and Population Problems in Early Modern History. *The Scandinavian Economic History Review.* III, 3-47.

Vandersall, Amy L. 1972, The Date and Provenance of the Franks' Casket. *Gesta.* XI/2, 9-26.

— , 1975, Homeric myth in early medieval England: The lid of the Franks' Casket, *Studies in Iconography*, 1.

Vercauteren, F. 1936, Comment c'est-on defendu au ixe siècle dans l'empire franc contre les invasions normandes?, *Annales du xxxe congrés de la Fédération Archéologique de Belgique*, 1936, 117-32.

Vierck, Hayo, 1967, Ein Relieffibelpaar aus Nordendorf, *Bayerische Vorgeschichtsblätter*, 32, pt. 1.

Vigfússon, Guðbrandur and Powell, F. York, 1879, *An Icelandic prose reader with notes, grammar and glossary*. Oxford: Clarendon.

— , 1883, *Corpvs poeticvm boreale. The poetry of the Old Northern tongue from the earliest times to the thirteenth century. Edited, classified and translated with introduction, excursus, and notes.* Vol I, *Eddic Poetry.* Vol. II. *Court Poetry.* Oxford: Clarendon.

Vita S. Anskarii, 1829, *Vita Sancti Anskarii*, ed. D. C. F. Dahlmann, *Monumenta Germaniae Historia, Scriptores*, Vol. 2.

Vita S. Oswaldi, 1879, ed. J. Raine, *Historians of the Church of York and its Archbishops*, Vol. 1. London, Rolls Series.

Vita S. Rimberti, ed. G. H. Pertz, *Monumenta Germaniae Historica, Scriptores*, Vol. 2.

Volbach, W. F. 1976, *Elfenbeinarbeiten der Spätantike und des frühen Mittelalters, Katalogue vor- und frügeschichtlichter Altertämer*, 7, 3rd edition, Mainz.

Vries, J. de, 1956, Das Königtum bei den Germanen, *Saeculum*, 7, 289-309.

— , 1958, Das zweite Guðrúnlied. *Zeitschrift für deutsche Philologie*, 77, 176-99.

— , 1963, tr. B. J. Timmer, *Heroic Song and Heroic Legend.* Oxford.

Wade-Martins, P. 1970, North Elmham, *Current Archaeology*, II, No. 8 (No. 19), 226-31.

— , 1980, *Excavations in North Elmham Park, 1967-72. (East Anglian Archaeology*, Report No. 9, Norfolk), 2 vols. Dereham.

Wainwright, F. T. ed., 1962, *The Northern Isles*, London.
— , The Scandinavian Settlement, in *The Northern Isles*, Edinburgh, 117-62.
Wainwright, F. T. and Finley, H. P. R. 1975, *Scandinavian England*, Chichester.
Wallace-Hadrill, J. M. 1971, *Early Germanic Kingship in England and on the continent*, Oxford.
Wallace-Hadrill, J. M. 1975, The Vikings in Francia, *Early Medieval History*, Oxford,
— , 1975, The Vikings in Francia, *Early Medieval History*, Oxford, 217-36.
Warner, R. 1975-76, Scottish silver armrings: an analysis of weights, *Proc. Soc. Antiqs. Scot.*, 107, 136-143.
Waterer, J. W. 1968, Irish Book Satchels or Budgets, *Medieval Archaeology*, 13.
Waterman, D. M. 1959, Late Saxon, Viking and Early Medieval Finds from York, *Archaeologia*, 97, 59-105.
Wattenbach–Levison, Deutschlands Geschichtsquellen im Mittelalter, 1952-73, ed. W. Levison and H. Löwe, 5 vols., Weimar.
Webster, L. E. and Cherry, J. 1972, Medieval Britain in 1971, *Med. Arch.* XVI, 147-212.
Weitzmann, K., ed., 1979, *The Age of Spirituality: Late Antique and Early Christian Art, Third to Seventh Century*, New York.
Wenskus, R. 1961, *Stammesbildung und Verfassung*, Köln.
— , 1964, Bemerkungen zum *Thunginus* der *Lex Salica*, in P. Classen and P. Scheibert, eds., *Festschrift Percy Ernst Schramm*, Wiesbaden, 217-36.
Werkmeister, O. K. 1964, Three Problems of tradition in Pre-Carolingian figure-style from Visigoth to Insular Illumination, *P.R.I.A.* 63, Section C, number 5, 167-89.
Whitelock, D. 1952, *The Beginnings of English Society*, Harmondsworth.
— , ed., 1955, *English Historical Documents*, vol. 1, London.
— , 1959, The Dealings of the Kings of England with Northumbria, in P. Clemoes, ed., *The Anglo-Saxons* (Studies for B. Dickins), Cambridge, 70-88.
— , ed., 1963, *Sermo Lupi ad Anglos*, 3rd edition, London.
— , 1979, *English Historical Documents*, vol. 1, London, 2nd edition.
— , Douglas, D. C. and Tucker, S. I. 1965, *The Anglo-Saxon Chronicle. A Revised Translation*, London.
Wieselgren, Per, 1935-36, *Qvellenstudien zur Volsungasaga*. Acta et Commentationes Universitatensis Tartuensis, B. Humaniora XXXV (1935), 1-154. B. Humaniora XXXVII (1936), 155-238. B. Humaniora XXXVIII, 239-430.
Wilson, D. M. 1957, An unpublished fragment from the Goldsborough hoard, *Antiq. J.* XXXVII, 72-73.
— , 1961, An Anglo-Saxon Bookbinding at Fulda (*Codex Bonifatianus* 1), *Antiquaries Journal*, XLI, 1861.
— , 1968, Archaeological evidence for the Viking settlements and raids in England, *Frümittelalterliche Studien*, 2, 291-304.
— , 1969, The Vikings' Relation with Christianity in the North of England. *Journal of the British Archaeological Association*, 30, 37-46.
— , 1970a, *The Vikings and their Origins*, London.
— , 1970b, *Reflections on the St Ninian's Island Treasure*, Jarrow lecture, Jarrow.
— , 1970, Manx Memorial Stones of the Viking Period. *Saga-Book of the Viking Society*, 18, 1-18.
— , 1971, The Norsemen, in G. Menzies, ed., *Who are the Scots? A search for the Origins of the Scottish Nation*. London, BBC publication, 103-113.
— , 1974, *The Viking Age in the Isle of Man. The archaeological evidence*, Odense.
Wilson, D. M. 1976a, The Scandinavians in England, In D. M. Wilson, ed., *The Archaeology*

of Anglo-Saxon England, 393–403.

— , 1976b, Scandinavian Settlement in the North and West of the British Isles — An Archaeological Point-of-View. *Transactions of the Royal Historical Society 5,* 26, 95–113.

— , 1978a, The Dating of Viking Art in England, In J. T. Lang, ed., 1978, 393–403.

— , 1978b. Civil and Military Engineering in Viking Age Scandinavia. Paul Johnstone Memorial Lecture, Occasional Lecture II, London: National Maritime Museum.

— , 1980, Economic Aspects of the Vikings in the West — the Archaeological Basis. The Felix Neubergh Lecture, Gothenburg University. Göteborg: Rundqvists Boktrycker AB.

— and, Caygill, M. L. 1981, *Economic Aspects of the Viking Age.* British Museum Occasional Papers, No. 30, London.

— and Hurst, D. G. 1961, Medieval Britain in 1960, *Med. Arch.,* V, 309–39.

— and — , 1964, Medieval Britain in 1962 and 1963, *Med. Arch.* VIII, 231–99.

— and — , 1965, Medieval Britain in 1964, *Med. Arch.* IX, 170–220.

— and — , 1966, Medieval Britain in 1965, *Med. Arch.* X, 168–219.

— ' 1978a, The Dating of Viking Art in England, in J. T. Lang, ed., *Anglo-Saxon and Viking-Age Sculpture, B.A.R.* 49. Oxford.

Winkelmann, W. 1954, Eine westfälische Siedlung des 8. Jahrhunderts bei Warendorf, *Germania,* 32, 189–213.

Winterbottom, M. 1967, The style of Aethelweard, *Medium Aevum,* 36, 109–18.

Wormald, C. P. 1977, *Lex Scripta* and *Verbum Regis:* Legislation and Germanic Kingship, from Euric to Cnut, in P. H. Sawyer and I. N. Woods, eds., *Early Medieval Kingship,* Leeds, University of Leeds, 105–38.

— , 1978, Bede, *Beowulf* and the conversion of the Anglo-Saxon aristocracy, in R. T. Farrell, ed., *Bede and Anglo-Saxon England,* Oxford, *British Archaeological Reports,* 46, 34–95.

N.B. — Every effort has been made to make this Bibliography complete and accurate, but a few difficulties remain. Certain items are still in press and are so described, others unpublished lectures or private communications. A few items were not in the Cornell library system, or in any source available to Cornell through interlibrary loan, and thus could not be verified.

INDEX